Reading
BOROUGH COUNCIL

Reading Borough Libraries

Email: info@readinglibraries.org.uk
Website: www.readinglibraries.org.uk

Reading 0118 9015950
Battle 0118 9015100
Caversham 0118 9015103
Palmer Park 0118 9015106
Southcote 0118 9015109
Tilehurst 0118 9015112
Whitley 0118 9015115

Author:

Title:

Class no.

To avoid overdue charges please return this book to a
reading library on or before the last date stamped above.
not required by another reader, it may be renewed by
sonal visit, telephone, post, email, or via our website.

"I
my
we

"[Ro
this
book
by Ro

terms, and the fact that he has so clearly relished the achievements
of these poor sick people."

pectator

"A rollicking good story." ***Washington Post***

"*Orwell's Cough* is riveting medical detective work. John Ross offers a truly unique perspective on the literary giants."
  Alex Boese, author of ***Elephants on Acid*** and ***Electrified Sheep***

"As [Ross] constructs the medical portraits, he delves into family history, romantic melodrama and quirkier aspects of the writers' lives. The result is a fascinating, surprising and at times hilarious compilation." ***New Scientist***

"Infectious and original. You'll have trouble shaking it off."
  Mark Crick, author of ***Kafka's Soup***

"*Orwell's Cough* manages the perfect balance: enough medicalese to interest the biologically-minded, and enough details about writers' lives for the literary-minded. As soon as I finished the book, I turned right back to the start and read it again."
  We Love This Book

"We always long to know writers better: more than just their words, we want to immerse ourselves in their lives, to really feel what they felt. Ross does that, plunging you in the day-to-day pains and struggles of some of the most celebrated names in the canon."
  Sam Kean, author of ***The Disappearing Spoon***

"This lively, occasionally squirm-inducing book sketches the case histories of ten writers whose health influenced their literary work... Into a satisfying series of medical mysteries [Ross] injects notes of wry humour and obvious affection." ***Boston Globe***

"If this irresistibly entertaining collection of medical biographies is anything to go by, its author would make a crackerjack after-dinner speaker. Each section consists of a whirlwind tour through the life of a famous literary figure from a doctor's perspective, some of it imagined, and all of it punctuated by witty and fun-loving asides... what sets Ross apart is his pure storytelling ability. Using a fluid and unpretentious style, much like fellow physician and writer Atul Gawande's, he excels at condensing massive amounts of research into pleasurable reading." ***Winnipeg Free Press***

ORWELL'S COUGH

Diagnosing the Medical Maladies and
Last Gasps of the Great Writers

JOHN ROSS

ONEWORLD

A Oneworld Book

This paperback edition first published by Oneworld Publications in 2013

First published in the United Kingdom and the Commonwealth by Oneworld
Publications in 2012
Originally published in the United States by St. Martin's Press,
175 Fifth Avenue, New York, NY 10011 in 2012

ISBN 978-1-78074-225-0
ebook ISBN 978-1-78074-113-0

Printed in Denmark by Nørhaven A/S

Oneworld Publications
10 Bloomsbury Street
London
WC1B 3SR

Stay up to date with the latest books,
special offers, and exclusive content from
Oneworld with our monthly newsletter

Sign up on our website
www.oneworld-publications.com

For Megan

CONTENTS

Author's Note   ix

1. **THE HARDEST KNIFE ILL-USED:** *Shakespeare's Tremor*   1
2. **EXIL'D FROM LIGHT:** *The Blindness of John Milton*   26
3. **DYING FROM THE TOP DOWN:** *The Dementia of Jonathan Swift*   47
4. **SOME SWEET POISONED BREEZE HAD PASSED INTO HER LUNGS:** *The Brontës and Tuberculosis*   70
5. **DISMAL LABYRINTH OF DOUBT:** *The Strange Death of Nathaniel Hawthorne*   97
6. **PERILOUS OUTPOST OF THE SANE:** *The Many Maladies of Herman Melville*   120
7. **SEX AND THE DEAD:** *Brucellosis, Arsenic, and William Butler Yeats*   147
8. **MEDICAL MISADVENTURES OF AN AMATEUR M.D.:** *Jack London's Death by Hubris*   168
9. **AN INFAMOUS PRIVATE AILMENT:** *The Venereal Afflictions of James Joyce*   182
10. **"THE DISEASE WHICH WAS BOUND TO CLAIM ME SOONER OR LATER":** *Orwell's Cough*   199

Acknowledgements   223
Bibliography and Endnotes   225

AUTHOR'S NOTE

In the year 2000, the youth of America grew weary of inhibition and restraint. Rates of syphilis infection, which had fallen to all-time lows in the United States, began to spike upward. The first generation to reach sexual maturity in an era of effective, if onerous, treatment for HIV infection was blasé about the threat of AIDS, leading to an increase in high-risk sexual activity. This indifference was abetted by the more efficient market for anonymous sex made possible by the Internet, as well as advances in amateur pharmacology that made crystal meth cheap and abundant.

At the Boston teaching hospital where I then worked as an infectious diseases specialist, several patients presenting with secondary syphilis initially went unrecognized. Syphilis, which affected half a million Americans in 1945, had become such a rare disease that many U.S. physicians had never seen a case, and were unfamiliar with its manifestations. I put together a PowerPoint talk on syphilis for medical grand rounds, and thought to tart it up with a few Shakespeare quotations, having a vague recollection from my undergraduate days that the Bard was fond of joking about the great pox. I dusted off my battered copy of the *Riverside Shakespeare* and started leafing through it. Holy crap, I thought, there is a *lot* of stuff here on syphilis. My curiosity was piqued, and I did some more digging. Was there a connection between Shakespeare's syphilitic obsession, contemporary gossip about his sexual misadventures, and the only medical fact known about him with certainty—that his handwriting became tremulous in late middle age? I wrote an article that appeared in *Clinical Infectious Diseases,* supposing it to be of scant interest beyond its immediate specialty audience. To my surprise, it generated a fair amount of Internet buzz, and inspired a segment on Jon Stewart's satirical U.S. television programme, *The Daily Show.* I began to think that there might be interest in a book on the topic of writers and disease, written from a medical perspective.

I have taken the liberty of beginning the chapters on Shakespeare, Milton, Swift, Joyce, and Orwell with vignettes that are intended to convey the experience of illness from the point of view of the patient. Those that concern Milton, Swift, and Orwell are firmly rooted in biography. The Shakespeare vignette is entirely conjectural. Joyce is known to have been diagnosed with "gleet," or gonorrhoea, and he was directed to receive treatment from a Dublin practitioner with expertise in this condition. The imagined and rather graphic gonorrhoea treatment described in this chapter is based on state-of-the-art medical care in 1904. The physicians M'Intosh and Mellor are fictional.

Sweating tubs used in the seventeenth-century treatment of syphilis. (The Royal Society)

1. THE HARDEST KNIFE ILL-USED:
Shakespeare's Tremor

The real mystery of Shakespeare, a thousand times more mysterious than any matter of the will, is: why is it that—unlike Dante, Cervantes, Chaucer, Tolstoy, whomever you wish—he makes what seems a voluntary choice to stop writing?

—Harold Bloom

In Shakespeare's tomb lies infinitely more than Shakespeare ever wrote.
—Herman Melville, "Hawthorne and His Mosses"

Twenty years he lived in London ... Twenty years he dallied there between conjugal love and its chaste delights and scortatory love and its foul pleasures.

—James Joyce, Ulysses

His fitful fever returned. Master Shakespeare pulled the hood of his cloak down low over his eyes and hurried from his lodgings in Bishopsgate, walking as quickly as he could on his hobbled legs. He awkwardly dodged a pair of rambling pigs and picked his way through the dung and muck of the city streets. The stench and filth rarely troubled him now, as they had when he first came here from the country. Nearer the bridge, the clamour of the city increased: the clatter of carts, the cries of street peddlers, the gossip of alewives, the drunken braggadocio of London gallants. A black-clad Puritan surveyed the scene sourly and made brief eye contact with Will. The player hung his head and balled his hands into fists—to hide the telltale rash on his palms.

London Bridge was marvellous and strange, a massive structure built over with splendid houses. With relief he entered the dark, claustrophobic tunnel beneath the dwellings. Inside, a continual roar of noise: the tidal rush of water between the ancient piers; waterwheels creaking; apprentices brawling; carters disputing the right-of-way; a blind fiddler playing; sheep bleating on their way to Eastcheap, bound for slaughter. He left the shelter of the bridge, and emerged into painful sunlight on the other side. His shins throbbed and his muscles ached. In spite of himself, he peered up at the great stone gate at the end of the bridge, adorned with traitors' heads on pikes. Shreds of mouldy flesh clung to the grinning skulls, their tattered hair bleached by sun and rain.

In Southwark, he heard the barking mastiffs and the howling crowd at the Bear Garden. He imagined old Sackerson the bear bellowing, lashing out with his claws, chained to a post, set on by dogs. A glimpse of ragged children playing in an alley filled him with thoughts of home and a pang of loneliness and shame. Before a row of brothels he saw a scabby beggar-woman with sunken nose and ulcerated shins. After years of faithful service in the stews, she has been turned out in the street to die of the pox. A chill of fear ran up his spine, and he looked away.

There was a pounding in his head and he felt dull and stupid. He circled many times through a maze of flyblown houses before he stumbled on the place. A servant showed him down a set of stairs. The bard descended into a hot cellar reeking of sulphur. A vast oven filled the room with flickering orange light. The sweaty heads of groaning men peered out from large wooden tubs. But the tubs were not filled with water. A sallow and emaciated man carrying iron tongs scurried round, feeding hot bricks into the tubs through a trapdoor. He poured vinegar onto the heaps of bricks and acrid steam rose up, making the glistening men within moan and shake.

The doctor suddenly appeared beside Will, startling him. He was sleek and prosperous, with a dainty goatee. Though he smiled reassuringly, the poet noticed that he kept a safe distance. In a soothing, urbane voice, the physician explained the treatment: stewed prunes to evacuate the bowels; succulent meats to ease digestion; cinnabar and the sweating tub to cleanse the disease from the skin. The doctor warned of minor side effects: uncontrolled drooling, fetid breath, bloody gums, shakes and palsies. Yet desperate diseases called for desperate remedies, of course.

Shakespeare extended a handful of silver coins. The physician took them with a gloved hand, scrutinized them carefully, and put them in his purse with the hint of a smirk. He pointed Will toward the skinny, pallid man tending bricks at the great oven. When the poet looked round again, the doctor had vanished.

The gaunt man tending the bricks was not quite right in the head. His hands shook, and he seemed both timorous and irritable. When he saw the poet's rash, he cackled and slobbered, revealing a mouth full of rotten teeth. "Bit by a Winchester goose, eh? Ha-ha! A few good sweats will fix that, my lad. Into the powdering tub with you, then!"

The poet stripped and stood ashamed, his flesh covered in scaly blots. He nervously clambered over the side of a tub, and sat down on a plank nailed to the side. Under the plank, the wooden bottom had been removed, leaving an earthen pit. The queer thin man clumsily secured a heavy lid over the top of the tub, leaving an opening just large enough for the poet's head. Then he popped open the trapdoor at the base of the tub and placed a hot metal plate at the poet's feet. He tossed red powder on the plate. The dust disappeared in a mephitic bloom of hissing fumes. The doctor's man repeated this again and again, until Will began to gag. A fine metallic powder settled on his body. The thin man piled hot bricks into the pit under the seat, and doused them with vinegar. As the acid waves of steam billowed upward, the bard started to tremble and sweat. This week would not be a pleasant one.

Even those who know little about Shakespeare are aware that there is a sort of controversy about the authorship of his plays. A vocal and eccentric minority doubts that a man of Shakespeare's background could possess literary genius, and speculates his plays were really written by an aristocrat who wished for some reason to remain anonymous. This belief rests on two snobbish and mistaken assumptions: first, that a great deal of formal education is essential for great writing; and second, that creativity depends on wealth and comfort. A good case could be made that the exact opposite is true. Many great authors were largely self-taught, and either did not attend university or dropped out. Furthermore, a dose of youthful misery may help a writer by serving as a powerful stimulus to fantasy and imagination. A recurrent biographical pattern in great writers is a happy early childhood, followed by an adolescence made insecure by financial catastrophe, the loss of a parent, or other traumas. Such was the case with William Shakespeare.

Shakespeare was born in April 1564, in the market town of Stratford. We know almost nothing about his mother Mary, but quite a lot about his father. John Shakespeare combined something of Falstaff's wit and rascality, Kent's stubbornness and loyalty, and Lear's feckless ill judgment. He made a lawful fortune from the glove trade, and an illegal one from usury and black market wool dealing. His fellow citizens liked him well enough to elect him the town's bailiff, an office akin to that of mayor today. However, the gossamer prosperity of the Shakespeares unravelled in William's teenage years, as John ran afoul of the law and lost much of his money and his lands. Elizabethan England was something between a modern constitutional monarchy and a police state. Spies and informers enforced religious orthodoxy and an oppressive system of trade regulations and monopolies. John Shakespeare was fined heavily, not only for his shady business practices, but also for his repeated failures to attend Protestant services, one of several signs that the family were probably closet Catholics.

If John Shakespeare once hoped to send his brilliant oldest son to get a gentleman's university education, near bankruptcy now made this impossible. Young Will would have studied Latin and rhetoric in the local grammar school until the age of fifteen or sixteen, probably getting more formal education than Dickens, Yeats, or Herman Melville would receive. He then may have served as a tutor in a noble Catholic household in Lancashire. By age eighteen, he was back in Stratford and hastily wed to Anne Hathaway, twenty-six years old and two months pregnant at the time of the marriage. According to tradition, Will toiled in his father's glove shop, and might also have moonlighted as a scrivener or a law clerk. Anne gave birth to the couple's daughter Susanna in May 1583, followed by the twins, Hamnet and Judith, in February 1585. Shortly thereafter,

Shakespeare went to seek his fortune in London. According to a durable—if somewhat dubious—Stratford legend, Shakespeare was whipped for poaching deer on the lands of one Sir Thomas Lucy, a notorious persecutor of local Catholics. Will made matters worse by posting a lampoon of Lucy on his park gate, and fled town one step ahead of Lucy's thugs.

London was home to a burgeoning and intensely competitive theatre scene. Some playwrights were university graduates; others, such as Shakespeare, Kyd, and Jonson, were not. Shakespeare's quick success, rural origins, and lack of a university degree made him the natural target of jealous attacks from the University Wits. These included Robert Greene, George Peele, and that great spendthrift of language, Thomas Nashe, a trio as noted for their depravity as for their abundant literary talents. All three would soon be dead. Their enemies blamed their passing on the pox, or syphilis, the dread disease that became a Shakespearian obsession.

By the early 1590s, Shakespeare had obtained the patronage of Henry Wriothesley, the Earl of Southampton. Wriothesley was an effete dandy of flexible sexuality, with a penchant for poetry. Both of Shakespeare's racy, best-selling narrative poems, *Venus and Adonis* and *The Rape of Lucrece,* are dedicated to him. The dedication for *Lucrece,* published in 1594, suggests that by then Shakespeare and Southampton were on familiar terms: "The love I dedicate to your Lordship is without end . . . what I have done is yours; what I have to do is yours." According to Shakespeare's earliest biographer, Nicholas Rowe, Southampton once presented Shakespeare with £1000, a staggering (and almost certainly exaggerated) sum of money. Thus, by the time Shakespeare was middle-aged, he had achieved substantial wealth and fame. However, his success was blighted by the death of his only son Hamnet in 1596, and perhaps also by a serious health scare that may have left deep marks on his writing.

D. H. Lawrence was struck by how saturated some of Shakespeare's work is with venereal disease: "I am convinced that *some* of Shakespeare's horror and despair, in his tragedies, arose from the shock of his consciousness of syphilis." Anthony Burgess was probably the first commentator with the effrontery to suggest that Shakespeare himself had syphilis. In his novel *Nothing Like the Sun,* Burgess depicted the poor bard as a pocky cuckold. He later characterized Shakespeare as having a "gratu-itous venereal obsession," an observation subsequently echoed by schol-ars Katherine Duncan-Jones and Harold Bloom.

References to syphilis in Shakespeare are more abundant, intrusive and clinically exact than those of his contemporaries. For example, there are only six lines referring to venereal disease in all seven plays of Chris-topher Marlowe. However, forty-three lines in *Measure for Measure*, fifty-one lines in *Troilus and Cressida*, and sixty-five lines in *Timon of Athens* unequivocally allude to syphilis and other sexually transmitted diseases (STDs).

References to syphilis and STDs are not uniformly distributed throughout Shakespeare's plays. In his first fourteen plays, up to *The Merchant of Venice* in 1596, there is an average of only three lines per play on venereal disease. (Most of these occur in *The Comedy of Errors*, dated from 1592–3, which contains twenty-three lines referring to STDs.) In the next twenty plays, from 1597's *Henry IV Part 1* to *Cymbeline* in 1609, there is an average of fifteen lines per play. The final four plays, *The Winter's Tale*, *The Tempest*, *Henry VIII*, and *Two Noble Kinsmen*, average less than two lines per play referring to syphilis and other STDs. (These last two plays are generally accepted as being roughly equal collabora-tions between Shakespeare and John Fletcher.)

Could Shakespeare's mid-career explosion of syphilitic content be explained by a general increase in bawdry on the Jacobean and late Eliza-bethan stages? Perhaps, but this would not explain why Shakespeare takes up the subject of syphilis in the early play *The Comedy of Errors*, only to drop it and return to it with a vengeance later on. Of course, Shakespeare's interest in syphilis does not mean that he was personally infected. Shake-speare would be well aware of the effects of syphilis on London's literary bohemia of the 1590s, just as an observer of the New York arts scene of the 1980s would be unpleasantly familiar with the ravages of AIDS. But is there evidence that Shakespeare's own lifestyle put him at risk for syphilis?

Shakespeare's marriage to Anne Hathaway was marked by long peri-ods of separation. For most of their life, Will lived and worked in Lon-don, while Anne was home in Stratford. They had no children after 1585, when Anne was only twenty-nine. Perhaps this was related to obstetrical complications from the birth of the twins, but it might also suggest that their sexual congress was infrequent. Infamously, he bequeathed her only the "second-best bed." (Despite the ingeniously benign explanations of Shakespeare's biographers, it is hard to believe that the supreme master of the English language intended this as anything other than a sly, final insult.) Away from home, did Shakespeare expend much energy seeking better beds? In a 1602 diary entry, a law student, John Manningham, recorded this salacious anecdote about the playwright and the actor Richard Burbage:

> Upon a time when Burbage played Richard the Third, there was a citizen grew so far in liking with him that before she went from the play she appointed him to come that night unto her by the name of Richard the Third. Shakespeare, overhearing their conversation, went before, was entertained, and at his game ere Burbage came. Then message being brought that Richard the Third was at the door, Shakespeare caused return to be made that William the Conqueror was before Richard the Third.

Even if this story seems too clever to be true, it suggests Shakespeare enjoyed a popular reputation as something less than a paragon of marital fidelity. Shakespeare's high sexual alertness is also borne out by his robust ribald vocabulary. In *Shakespeare's Bawdy*, Eric Partridge defines 1418 sexual or vulgar expressions in the works of Shakespeare, in a glossary of over 200 pages. Shakespeare's amorous reputation is further reinforced in the *Sonnets*, and especially in a peculiar poem entitled *Willobie His Avisa*, published in 1594.

Willobie His Avisa purports to be an earnest moral tract about a virtuous wife who spurns the advances of her would-be seducers. The book was popular and went through several printings, probably because it was actually a literary hoax and satire of the sexual mores of prominent Elizabethans. Authorities found it subversive, and enhanced its scandalous cachet by confiscating and burning copies of it in 1599.

The origins of *Willobie His Avisa* are obscure. In the book's introduction, one Hadrian Dorrell claims to have found the manuscript of *Avisa* in the bedchamber of his friend and fellow Oxford student Henry Willobie. Willobie is away on military service, and Dorrell is so impressed with the epic poem that he cannot resist preparing it for publication. Needless to say, there is no record of a Hadrian Dorrell having attended Oxford at this time, although there was a real Henry Willobie (or Willoughby) at Oxford, who conveniently died in 1596. It remains unclear whether Willobie was the real author of *Avisa*, whether he was the butt of a sophomoric prank, or whether he was only a handy stalking horse for the actual author.

Various failed suitors of Avisa are mocked in the first half of the poem. For example, "Caveleiro," who may represent an Elizabethan noble with the equestrian moniker of Sir Ralph Horsey, is ridiculed as syphilitic: his "wanny cheeks" and "shaggy locks" make Avisa "fear the piles, or else the pox." The second half of the poem concerns the vain attempts of "H. W." to woo Avisa. H.W. is given cynical romantic advice by a man expert in the arts of seduction, the "old player" "W.S.," his "familiar friend." In this passage, the passion of H.W. for the chaste Avisa is described in vocabulary evocative of venereal disease:

> H.W. being suddenly infected with the contagion of a fantastical fit . . . at length not able any longer to endure the burning heat of so fervent a humour, betrayed the secrecy of his disease unto his familiar friend W.S. who not long before had tried the courtesy of like passion, and was now recovered of the like infection . . . he now would secretly laugh at his friend's folly, that had given occasion not long before unto others to laugh at his own . . . he determined to see whether it would sort to a happier end for this new actor, than it did for the old player. But at length this Comedy was liken to have grown to a Tragedy, by the weak and feeble estate H.W. was brought into . . . until Time and Necessity, being his best physicians brought him a plaster, if not to heal, yet in part to ease his malady. In all which discourse is lively represented the unruly rage of unbridled fancy, having the reins to rove at liberty, with the diverse and sundry changes of affections and temptations, which Will, set loose from Reason, can devise . . .

The pointed references to a "new actor," an "old player," "Comedy," "Tragedy," "Will," and a doggerel parody of Shakespeare that follows, strongly suggest that the "old player" is William Shakespeare. Could H.W., the "new actor," be Shakespeare's pansexual patron, Henry Wriothesley? If Wriothesley, one of the kingdom's most prominent nobles, had been the major target of the book's satire, this would explain why the Elizabethan authorities were compelled to burn it. The overbearing medical metaphor, and the striking word choices, "contagion," "disease," "burning," "infection," and "malady," intimate that the "weak and feeble" Wriothesley and Shakespeare are suffering from a sexually transmitted infection, rather than the pangs of unrequited love. "Having the reins to rove at liberty" suggests "running of the reins [kidneys]," Elizabethan slang for gonorrhoea.

The eminent Shakespearean scholar Samuel Schoenbaum was perplexed by *Willobie His Avisa,* but did allow that "this curious work seems to have something to do with the *Sonnets* . . . one can appreciate the temptation to identify 'W.S.' with William Shakespeare, and 'H.W.' with Henry Wriothesley, the proposed Fair Youth of the *Sonnets.*" The scenario in *Avisa*—Shakespeare and Southampton in love with the same woman, with the innuendo that she has infected them both with venereal disease—is remarkably similar to the love triangle, and the obsession with sexual pollution, of Shakespeare's *Sonnets.*

Four hundred years later, critical and popular opinion is still sharply divided on Shakespeare's dense, knotty *Sonnets.* Are they confessional and autobiographical? Is Shakespeare just flattering a vain and wealthy patron? Is he riffing with emotion and personae in a series of consummate poetic performances? Or do the *Sonnets* contain elements of all these possibilities?

The *Sonnets* can be divided into three parts. In the first seventeen sonnets, the lovely youth is urged to marry and procreate; perhaps the youth's family, who were trying to get him to agree to an arranged marriage, commissioned these poems. Such a circumstance would apply to both of the leading candidates for the lovely youth: Southampton and William Herbert, the Earl of Pembroke. Sonnets 18–126 concern the poet's passionate attachment to the callous and selfish youth. (The homoerotic drift of these poems has inspired many comically defensive assertions of Shakespeare's manliness by critics and biographers.) The final poems, Sonnets 127–154, chronicle the poet's sexual enslavement to his dark mistress, who is cruel, capricious, unfaithful, unbeautiful, and infected with venereal disease.

The *Sonnets* are filled with imagery of sin, infection, and defilement: the word "disgrace" occurs nine times; "shame" appears fourteen times. Sexual transgression lies at the heart of the *Sonnets*. The poet and his mistress are lustful and sexually voracious (Sonnets 129, 135, and 151, the "gross" sonnet); hypocritical enemies accuse the poet of promiscuity (Sonnet 121). The lovely youth is also sexually reckless. In Sonnet 35, the poet forgives the youth for his "sensual fault." In Sonnets 40–42, it is made clear that the youth has been sleeping with the poet's mistress, leading the masochistic poet to respond: "Take all my loves, my love" (Sonnet 40). In Sonnet 94, the fair youth is sternly warned of the dangers of venereal disease: "But if that flower with base infection meet/The basest weed outbraves his dignity . . . lilies that fester smell far worse than weeds." This admonition is repeated in Sonnet 95, where the youth's "sins" and lascivious "sport" are associated with cankers, spots, and blots. The poet closes with a priapic warning: "The hardest knife ill-used doth lose his edge."

In Sonnet 144, the poet frets that his "better angel," or "a man right fair," will be "fired out," or venereally infected, by his "bad angel," or "female evil." The *Sonnets* conclude with two variations on a classical theme: a nymph igniting the waters of love with Cupid's stolen torch. Shakespeare transforms this into an ironic metaphor for venereal disease: Cupid's "fire" is the dysuria, or painful urination, of gonorrhoea, and the hot bath is the tub treatment of syphilis. In Sonnet 153, the poet, "a sad distempered guest," seeks this "seething bath, which yet men prove/Against strange maladies a sovereign cure." Specifically, the poet seeks a remedy for the "new fire" acquired from his "mistress' eye." Here, the "eye" of his mistress is her pudendum. In Sonnet 154, the unfortunate poet laments, "Love's fire heats water," or causes burning urine, leading him to seek "a bath and healthful remedy/For men diseased." This bath—as we have seen—was the treatment of choice for a terrifying new epidemic disease: syphilis.

The source of syphilis, a devastating infection caused by the spiral bacterium *Treponema pallidum,* has long been controversial. Witnesses of the epidemic that swept Europe in 1495 believed it was a "new disease." Most agreed that it had come to Europe with Columbus' crew on their return from Hispaniola in 1493. Recent studies support this tradition. Investigators found no traces of syphilis in several thousand fifteenth-century European skeletons. However, up to 14 percent of skeletons from pre-Columbian sites in the Dominican Republic (in the former Hispaniola) had signs of syphilitic bone damage. If syphilis came from the New World, it was a small revenge on the Europeans, who brought measles, malaria, mumps, typhoid, typhus, influenza, diphtheria, yellow fever, and most fatally, smallpox to American shores. The combined effects of these European plagues nearly wiped out the Native Americans. For a while, it looked like syphilis might do the same for Europe.

In 1494, the daft Charles VIII of France invaded Italy with a motley army of international mercenaries. The French rolled through Italy with little difficulty until they reached Naples. The Spanish defenders of Naples had brought syphilis to Italy with them, and allegedly practised a novel form of germ warfare. According to the eponymous anatomist Gabriel Fallopius, the Spaniards "drove their harlots and women out of the citadel, and especially the most beautiful ones, whom they knew to be suffering from the infectious disease . . . and the French, gripped by compassion and bewitched by their beauty, took them in." The French soon had cause to regret their compassion. When the vastly outnumbered Spanish surrendered Naples without a fight on February 22, 1495, the French lost themselves in drunkenness and debauchery. In a few months, Charles's magnificent army disintegrated into a diseased rabble. The French were defeated at the battle of Fornovo in July 1495, and Charles lost both his looted treasures and his Italian kingdoms. His troops were left with only the pox. On their ignominious return to their native lands, the syphilitic soldiers of fortune set off a global pandemic. The great pox soon spread to every nation in Europe. Syphilis came to India with Vasco da Gama as early as 1498, and by 1512 it had spread as far as Osaka, Japan. (Charles VIII died three years after his retreat from Italy, but not from syphilis. He smashed his head into the stone lintel of a doorway while rushing to a tennis match.)

Despite its globetrotting status, syphilis may be "the most disowned infection in history." The Russians blamed it on the Poles, and the Poles blamed it on the Germans. The Germans, the English, and the Italians blamed it on the French, and called it the French disease. The French called it the Neapolitan disease, and blamed it on the Italians. In Japan and India, they blamed it on the Portuguese, while the Portuguese, the Dutch, the Belgians, and the Moroccans agreed to blame it on the Spanish. The Spanish shrugged and called it the malady of the Indies, or the *bubas*, after the nasty skin sores it produced.

The term "syphilis" was not used in English until the nineteenth century. Shakespeare calls syphilis "the pox," "the malady of France," "the infinite malady," "the incurable bone-ache," "the hoar leprosy," "the good-year" or "the goujere," and "Winchester goose." (London's red-light district in Southwark was once under the jurisdiction of the Bishop of Winchester, an episcopal pimp who profited from licensing its prostitutes. A lady of the evening was known as a Winchester goose, a term that came to refer to the pox as well.)

Because of its protean manifestations, syphilis has been called "the great imitator." William Osler, the godfather of internal medicine, said that he who knew syphilis, knew medicine: "Know syphilis in all its manifestations and relations, and all other things clinical will be added unto you." Syphilis has three phases. In primary syphilis, the patient develops a "hard chancre," a genital ulcer with a firm raised border, about two weeks after infection. (Hard chancres may also appear in the mouth or rectum after oral or anal sex.) Today, chancres are usually painless, although in Shakespeare's time, they could be agonizingly painful and highly aggressive, even leading to penile auto-amputation. Although there are no definite references to genital chancres in Shakespeare, the "embossed sores" of *As You Like It* (2.7.67) and the "cankers" in the *Sonnets* are suggestive.

Once the invading army of spirochaetes makes its beachhead in the chancre, they multiply explosively over subsequent weeks, leading to secondary syphilis. The patient has severe flu-like symptoms: high fever, joint pain, swollen lymph nodes, loss of appetite, headache, and neck pain. But the hallmark of secondary syphilis is a copper-coloured rash over the entire body, including the palms and soles. This rash is usually flat and scaly (squamous), but may be pustular. The hair on the scalp, beard, and eyebrows may become thin and mangy; the inside of the mouth may ulcerate; warty lesions known as condylomata lata may blossom about the anus and genitalia. Condylomata lata resemble haemorrhoids, and were popularly known as the "piles." A catalogue of the secondary manifestations of syphilis in *Troilus and Cressida* (5.1.17–23) includes "raw eyes" (syphilis can attack any of the structures of the eye), "limekilns in the palm" (the scaly palmar rash of secondary syphilis), and "bone-ache" (inflammation of the surface of bone, or periosteum). Bone pain from the pox was common in Shakespeare's time, and could keep sufferers awake all night. The shins were a typical location, as noted in Timon's curse from *Timon of Athens* (4.3.151–3):

> Consumptions sow
> In hollow bones of man; strike their sharp shins,
> And mar men's spurring.

If allowed to progress, syphilis reaches its late or tertiary stage. It may involve any organ in the body, though physicians are probably most aware of its propensity to attack the cardiovascular system—causing aortic aneurysms—and its fondness for the central nervous system. It can cause strokes, dementia and insanity (general paresis of the insane), as well as damage to the spinal cord (tabes dorsalis). Shakespeare refers to another classic manifestation of neurosyphilis in *Measure for Measure* (1.2.101–2). Pompey the pimp notes that Mistress Overdone has "worn [her] eyes almost out in the service" because of syphilitic atrophy of the optic nerve. The syphilitic develops relentless loss of peripheral vision, an effect described as "squinting down the gunbarrel sight."

Another form of tertiary syphilis, gummatous syphilis, attacks skin, connective tissue, and bones. Gummatous syphilis is rare today, but it was the most common, violent, and destructive form of syphilis in Shakespeare's time. Its effects were gruesome: "Large rounded tumours [gummas] start to appear at random in muscles or bones, eating away cavities within them . . . they ulcerate the body extensively, exposing the bones and eating away at the nose, the lips, the palate, the larynx, and the genitals." The gravedigger in *Hamlet* (5.1.159–62) explains how busy he is burying patients with gummatous syphilis that are "rotten before they die":

"We have many pocky corpses now-a-days, that will scarce hold the laying in." Mad Timon calls for syphilis to rot the lawyer's larynx, "that he may never more false title plead," and to flatten the noses and "take the bridge quite away" of speculators that sniff out profits at society's expense (*Timon*, 4.3.153–9).

Gummatous syphilis was so widespread that it spawned a new and lucrative branch of medicine: dermatology. Shakespeare accurately describes many of the great variety of syphilitic skin lesions. In *Comedy of Errors* (3.2.137–8), a woman of dubious beauty and virtue has "her nose all o'er embellished with rubies, carbuncles, sapphires." Shakespeare is referring to the syphilid of late syphilis, a "deep indurated nodule that varies from pinhead to pea size and is brownish red in color," found primarily on the face, upper back, and extremities. Lesions of nodular syphilis may also scale and produce plaques, mimicking psoriasis. This white, frost-like appearance may explain Shakespeare's use of the term "hoar leprosy" for syphilis in *Timon* (4.3.36), with a pun on "whore." Alopecia, or hair loss, is also common in advanced syphilis. Timon calls on syphilis to "make curl'd-pate ruffians bald" (*Timon*, 4.3.160). Shakespeare often jokes about "French crowns," a type of gold coin, but also baldness from the French disease. Perhaps, in all this jesting about hair loss and the pox, the follicularly-challenged Shakespeare was having a nervous laugh at his own expense.

Death from syphilis was common in Elizabethan England. Of course, no antibiotics were available in Shakespeare's time, but it also seems that syphilis was then a more fulminant infection. Older strains of *Treponema pallidum* may have been more virulent than those circulating today. The lack of immunity in the population probably contributed to the disease's rapid spread and worse outcomes. Poor hygiene increased the risk of syphilitic ulcers becoming infected with streptococcal and staphylococcal bacteria, while poor nutrition, and a higher prevalence of scurvy and other vitamin deficiencies, may have aggravated the damage done by spirochaetes.

The Renaissance mind struggled to comprehend this terrifying new epidemic. Although the transmission of syphilis by sex (and less commonly, by nonsexual body contact with infected skin ulcers) was well understood in Shakespeare's time, germ theory didn't really emerge until the nineteenth century. (Some doctors came close to formulating a germ theory, but lacked the practical tools to develop it, such as the microscope.) Theories abounded. The syphilis epidemic was blamed on everything from the inauspicious conjunction of the heavenly bodies (Timon calls upon a "planetary plague" to bring the pox to Athens in *Timon of Athens*, 4.3.117), bad air and evil humours, and that old favourite of fundamentalists ancient and modern, divine punishment of human wickedness.

By the sixteenth century, the French disease was rife in England, especially in the boisterous merchant city of London. As syphilis waxed and leprosy faded away, London's leper houses were converted to care for victims of the great pox. (The decline of leprosy in Europe is something of a historical medical mystery. Did the cruel policy of isolating lepers gradually end disease transmission? Did natural selection reduce the number of susceptible individuals in the population? Did the epidemics of bubonic plague that swept Europe preferentially kill off the weaker lepers? Did the rise of tuberculosis, caused by a related bacterium, confer immunity to leprosy to those who survived exposure?) In 1548, surviving records indicate that 24 percent of the patients of St. Bartholomew's Hospital in London, now known as Bart's, were syphilitic; by 1579, the royal physician William Clowes claimed that up to 75 percent of the patients at Bart's had the French disease.

The low standard of sexual morality in Shakespeare's London abetted the spread of the pox. Times were tough in the final years of Elizabeth's reign. The population surged, wages sank, and poverty drove thousands of women into the world's oldest profession. Brothels abounded in the London suburbs and across the river in Southwark. Illegitimate births spiked between 1590 and 1610. Prostitutes, and even "gentlewomen virgins," sought male attention with dresses that bared their nipples. Conditions were ideal for the rapid spread of an STD that went by many names.

In his work, Shakespeare echoed the conventional wisdom that syphilis was relentless and untreatable. *Troilus and Cressida* (5.1.22) refers to syphilis as the "incurable bone-ache," and *Timon of Athens* (3.7.97) as the "infinite malady." Despite this popular perception, hazardous but reasonably effective treatment for syphilis was available in Shakespeare's England.

In 1539, the Spanish physician Ruy Diaz de Isla observed that high fevers often halted the progression of syphilis and might even cure the disease. The reason why was only recently discovered: not only does *Treponema pallidum* lack a protective feature known as the heat shock response, but at least one key metabolic enzyme is highly heat sensitive. A prolonged high spike in body temperature in a syphilitic patient may cause *Treponema pallidum* to literally blow apart.

Elizabethan physicians treated syphilis with a diet of bland, easily digested foods, with mercury, and most effectively, with the sweating treatment. Shakespeare often associates syphilis with stewed prunes: pocky patients were forbidden to eat raw fruit, but could "broil in . . . broths prunes, raisins of the sun, and currants" to purge the bowels. In *Timon of Athens* (4.3.87–8), Timon urges Alcibiades' harlots to "bring down rose-cheeked youth/To the tub-fast and diet." In the sweating treatment, several methods were used to raise the patient's body temperature for as long as he or she could stand it. These included being swaddled in blankets and surrounded by heated bricks or stones; being immersed in a scalding bath; or the tub treatment with mercury steam, as described in the introduction. In *Measure for Measure,* Mistress Overdone's name derives not only from her innumerable sexual encounters, but also because she is "overdone" from too many sessions in the sweating tub. In *Cymbeline* (1.6.126), prostitutes are "boiled stuff"; in *Timon of Athens* (2.2.68), a madam's clients are "chickens" waiting to be scalded. In *Henry V* (2.1.73), Falstaff's mistress Doll Tearsheet sits in "the powdering tub of infamy." The "powder" is the mercury ore cinnabar (mercuric sulphide, HgS). Thrown onto a hot plate and volatilized to mercury vapour, it was absorbed into the body by the respiratory tract; some mercury vapour also condensed on the skin.

For a long time, mercury treatment was the standard of care for syphilis, despite side effects of nerve damage, diarrhoea, rotten gums, loose teeth, and uncontrolled drooling. Salivation was used as a barometer of effectiveness. Savvy physicians adjusted the mercury dose to produce three pints of saliva a day for two weeks. The toxicity of mercury varies, depending on its chemical form, route of administration, and dose. Organic forms of mercury, such as the industrial waste product methylmercury, are the most hazardous to human health. Inorganic forms of mercury, such as cinnabar and the obsolete medication calomel, are moderately danger-ous. Pure elemental mercury, or liquid quicksilver, is the least poisonous. Whopping doses of quicksilver by mouth were once used as a treatment for severe constipation; it pushed out stool by sheer force of weight. In most patients, quicksilver was excreted in the faeces unchanged, and tox-icity was mild. There are cases on record of patients drinking up to four pounds of liquid mercury, without lasting ill effects.

However, liquid mercury becomes highly toxic when it evaporates, as mercury vapour is readily absorbed by the lungs. During the Napoleonic Wars, the sailors of the HMS *Triumph* salvaged 130 tons of quicksilver from a Spanish man-of-war that had run aground. This plunder proved deadly. The liquid mercury had been poured into leather bags, which were packed into kegs, which were stowed in strongboxes. But the damp leather bladders rotted and burst, the quicksilver seeped out of the the barrels and boxes, and soon several tons of mercury were sloshing about the holds of the *Triumph*. A slimy film of mercury amalgam formed on the ship's copper and brasswork. Quicksilver fouled the biscuits, which had to be thrown overboard. The ship became a floating deathtrap, espe-cially for those on the poorly ventilated lower decks, where the air was full of mercury vapour. Mouths swelled and ulcerated, teeth fell out, jaws rotted, faces became gangrenous. Able-bodied sailors became shambling, trembling, paralytic wrecks. Even the rats and cockroaches died before the ship limped back into port.

Despite its nasty side effects, mercury was used to treat syphilis well into the twentieth century. Whether it did any good is unclear. Leonard Goldwater, a modern toxicologist, called the medicinal use of mercury a colossal hoax. Mercury is probably mildly helpful for the skin lesions of syphilis, but relapse rates are high, and it fails to prevent neurosyphilis. The use of mercury for syphilis finally ended when it was shown to be clearly inferior to the first modern antibiotic, Paul Ehrlich's arsenic compound salvarsan.

Aside from the obvious dangers of injecting people with arsenic, sal-varsan had one major limitation: it also did not reliably prevent neuro-syphilis. However, two doctors in the nineteenth century who treated syphilitic Austrian army officers noted that neurosyphilis did not de-velop in officers who developed a high fever from another infection, such as malaria, erysipelas, typhoid, or pneumonia. Drawing on this observation, an Austrian psychiatrist named Julius Wagner-Jauregg had a creative, risky idea. Why not treat syphilitics by deliberately giving them other infections to cause high fevers? Wagner-Jauregg tried injecting strep bacteria at first, but this seems to have killed off too many patients. In 1917, he hit on using a moderately dangerous strain of malaria (specifically, *Plasmodium vivax*) to produce several weeks of recurrent high fevers, followed by quinine treatment to rid the patient of malaria. This treatment, known as malariotherapy, cured many patients with neurosyphilis, while only dispatching a mere 9 percent of those treated. Wagner-Jauregg became the first (and only) psychiatrist to win the Nobel Prize in Medicine.

By the 1940s, though, doctors had realized that neither malaria nor arsenic was an ideal treatment for syphilis. Incredibly, the Elizabethan treatment of syphilis—external heating—was revived, albeit with a more high-tech spin. Fever cabinets were devised, employing radiant light, electrical diathermy, or shortwave radio as heat sources. However, neurosyphilis was also still successfully treated with hot baths of 110°F (43.3°C) to raise body temperature to 105–106°F (40.5–41.1°C) for one hour daily for two to three weeks. These alternative forms of fever therapy were more controllable than malaria and had a mortality rate of only 1 to 2 percent. Thus, before penicillin, the treatment of syphilis evolved little beyond Shakespeare's "seething bath."

If Shakespeare was a philanderer, in keeping with his reputation, he would have been at high risk of syphilis and other sexually transmitted infections. Moreover, both the *Sonnets* and *Willobie His Avisa* seem to tell the same story: Shakespeare and another man share the same mistress, who infects them both with venereal disease. However, if Shakespeare had developed syphilis, his outcome would likely have been better than that of many of his contemporaries. He was all too aware of the symptoms of syphilis, and had the financial means to get access to treatment. Twentieth-century experience suggests that fever therapy for syphilis was reasonably effective, making it less likely that Shakespeare died of syphilis. Moreover, it seems implausible that Shakespeare could have produced a steady stream of works of genius, or occasionally acted in major productions, such as Ben Jonson's *Sejanus* in 1603, if he was suffering from the disfiguring ravages of syphilis.

Syphilis, gonorrhoea, and herpes simplex were frequently confused in Shakespeare's day, as many people were infected with more than one venereal disease. Syphilis and gonorrhoea were wrongly regarded as different manifestations of the same disease. The Scottish surgeon John Hunter perpetuated this confusion. In a misbegotten experiment in 1767, Hunter inoculated his own member with gonorrhoeal pus. Unfortunately, his source patient had both syphilis and gonorrhoea, and Hunter contracted both conditions. More sensibly, but less ethically, Benjamin Bell, another pugnacious Lowland Scot, subsequently conducted a series of equally awful experiments on his medical students, finally establishing that syphilis and gonorrhoea were different diseases.

However, Shakespeare could not have known this. His repeated references to "fire" and urinary symptoms in the *Sonnets* suggest that perhaps he only had gonorrhoea, which is more likely to cause dysuria than syphilis. If he was not also infected with syphilis, then he might have received. sweating therapy and mercury unnecessarily. Either way, his experience of illness likely had psychological repercussions.

The seventeenth-century writer John Aubrey made contradictory comments on Shakespeare's demeanour, based on interviews with his acquaintances. Aubrey stated that Shakespeare was a "handsome, well-shap't man: very good company," but also scribbled that he "was not a company keeper," and "wouldn't be debauched, and if invited to writ that he was in pain." There are several potential explanations for this discrepancy. Aubrey, or his informants, may have gotten their information wrong. Or perhaps Shakespeare had a mercurial personality, and suffered from mood swings or bipolar disorder. Did he become depressed after Hamnet's death? Did some other momentous event change Shakespeare from the merry seducer of Manningham's diary to the withdrawn loner of Aubrey's jottings? And could that event have been related to the increase in references to venereal disease in his work?

Up to 85 percent of patients with venereal disease suffer psychological symptoms, including anger, anxiety, depression, and sexual dysfunction. Psychological side effects of STDs are especially common when patients feel guilty about promiscuity, homosexuality, or extramarital sex. Today's AIDS patients often shoulder a heavy psychological burden, but depressive symptoms and sexual dysfunction are common today even in patients with less menacing STDs, such as herpes. Perhaps the withdrawal described by Aubrey, and the misogyny that crops up in *Hamlet* and *Lear*, were psychological aftershocks of venereal disease.

Alternatively, Shakespeare's preoccupation with venereal disease could have been due to an overactive imagination, rather than a physical ailment. Infectious diseases physicians occasionally see patients who believe they have a sexually transmitted disease, despite every reassurance to the contrary. Typically, they are sensitive young men with obsessive-compulsive tendencies—sometimes from strict religious upbringings—who become guilt-wracked after an adulterous episode, a gay encounter, or sex with a prostitute. They are convinced they have AIDS, despite having no trace of HIV in their bloodstream; they obsess about nonexistent penile sores; their urine still burns after multiple courses of antibiotics, and multiple negative tests for gonorrhoea and chlamydia. I do not think this is the most likely reason for Shakespeare's obsession with syphilis, but it is worth mentioning, as English physicians did report cases of venereal disease phobia in the seventeenth century, when syphilis was as terrifying and relentless as AIDS was in the 1980s.

If Shakespeare did undergo a personality change, there is one other potential explanation. To understand this more fully, we will need to examine Shakespeare's need for help in completing his last plays, and the problem of his deteriorating handwriting.

Collaboration in playwriting was common in Shakespeare's time. Perhaps Shakespeare got his start this way; the early plays, especially the three parts of *Henry VI*, may show traces of other hands besides Shakespeare's. Yet while the mature Shakespeare was occasionally called in to help salvage other plays—much like a modern Hollywood script doctor—he showed little inclination to seek help with his own. One of the striking features of the *Sonnets* is Shakespeare's confidence in his own poetic ability, no matter what setbacks and humiliations assail him in his personal life. Why, then, does Shakespeare enlist the aid of John Fletcher in his final three plays, *Henry VIII*, *Two Noble Kinsmen*, and the lost *Cardenio*? It cannot be because he had lost his gift. While his late style was increasingly idiosyncratic, he was still capable of writing poetry of startling originality and power. It is unfair to compare the intricate and masterful verse in Shakespeare's share of *Two Noble Kinsmen*, his last play, with Fletcher's featherweight portion. The gap between his writing and Fletcher's in these plays must have been painfully obvious to Shakespeare, and it is hard to believe he would not have completed these works himself, had he been able.

It is also surprising that Shakespeare sought outside help for his final plays, as they held particular importance for him. In *Henry VIII*, Shakespeare examines the squalid roots of the English Reformation, and portrays Henry as heartless and shallow. Even in the reign of King James, this was dangerous territory. There may be payback here: the Protestant reforms of Henry VIII indirectly brought Shakespeare's Catholic father to the brink of bankruptcy, thus ruining young Will's hopes to attend university and advance to the status of a gentleman. *Two Noble Kinsmen*, a tale of cousins who become mortal enemies, is Shakespeare's pessimistic final word on warring humankind. According to his biographer Park Honan, "he looks for what is valid, worthy, or possible in human nature, and comes at last to a darkening . . . yet at the end of *Noble Kinsmen* in Theseus's speeches, Shakespeare perhaps implicitly gives thanks for life itself." It seems unlikely that Shakespeare farmed out work on such personally resonant plays out of indifference.

A better explanation for Shakespeare's reliance on Fletcher is that he was physically unable to finish them without help. Perhaps Shakespeare lacked the stamina for sustained writing because of depression, alcohol, or illness, or perhaps he struggled with a handicap that hampered his ability to write. Surviving samples of Shakespeare's handwriting give us a clue as to what might have gone wrong.

The only medical fact known with certainty about William Shakespeare is that his handwriting deteriorated in his last years. There are six signatures by Shakespeare that are agreed to be authentic. Three of these are found on the will that he signed a month before he died, in March 1616. The signature of the first page of his will has been badly degraded by time, and is almost illegible. The signature on the second page is slow, shaky, and tortuous. The worst of his signatures occurs on the third and final page of the will. It reads "By me William Shakspeare" (Shakespeare, like many Elizabethans, was not particular about the spelling of his name). The "William" of this signature is neat and elegant, and looks unlike those of Shakespeare's other signatures, including the clumsy one on the preceding page. Perhaps some kindly clerk or scrivener, watching the poet struggle with his quill, tried to help him out by writing the first three words, leaving only the "Shakspeare" to be filled in. This final "Shakspeare" starts hesitantly but legibly, before tailing off into an unintelligible scribble.

The other three Shakespeare signatures date from 1612–13, and are better than those of the will. However, they are "somewhat nervous," marred by inkblots, and lack the ease and elegance of the one other sample that we have of Shakespeare's handwriting. This is the so-called "Hand D" from the manuscript of *Sir Thomas More,* written primarily by Anthony Munday in 1592–3. Not surprisingly, this play about the iconic English Catholic and martyr ran afoul of Elizabethan censorship, and four different playwrights were called in to help patch it up. The three pages in Hand D are Shakespearian in style and tone, have the bard's typical spelling quirks, and the handwriting resembles those of the signatures. The Oxford edition of Shakespeare's works dates his contribution to 1603–4, although other scholars, including Ernst Honigmann, believe Hand D dates back to 1593–4. Honigmann has argued that the misreading errors common in the early printed versions of many of the later plays, including *Othello, Hamlet,* and *Lear,* are a direct result of "a general deterioration in Shakespeare's writing." If Honigmann's hypothesis is correct, Shakespeare's handwriting gradually worsened beginning at age thirty-six, when he wrote *Hamlet* in 1600, until his death at age fifty-two in 1616. Perhaps his handwriting difficulties were related to the fall in his writing output after 1603, from averaging two new plays per year to only one.

Why would Shakespeare have had shaky handwriting? Parkinson's disease is intriguing, but seems unlikely. For one thing, it was not described until after the Industrial Revolution (it is sometimes blamed on as-yet unidentified pollutants). Furthermore, patients with Parkinson's disease have tiny handwriting (micrographia), whereas Shakespeare's tremulous writing is normal in size. Writer's cramp has been invoked, but this is also doubtful. Patients with writer's cramp primarily suffer from muscle spasm, although they can have mild tremor as well. True writer's cramp is a disease of professional scribes (it was originally known as scrivener's palsy) who write for long hours on a daily basis. This does not seem to have been Shakespeare's pattern of composition. He seems to have written in short frantic bursts ("he never blotted out a line," as Ben Jonson sourly observed), with more leisurely periods of revision.

Another possible cause of Shakespeare's worsening handwriting is essential tremor, a common condition that affected the late Katharine Hepburn. Its age of onset is often in the mid-thirties, which matches the age when Shakespeare's handwriting began to deteriorate. Essential tremor worsens with stress and exertion, and can impair handwriting. Patients often find that alcohol alleviates essential tremor. They may dabble in alcohol as self-medication, which might fit with the tales of Shakespeare's drinking that circulated in Stratford in the decades after his death.

To complicate matters, alcohol itself can damage the cerebellum and produce an intention tremor—a tremor that worsens while the patient is engaged in a task. There is some evidence for intention tremor in Shakespeare's writing: his signatures are legible at the beginning, but undecipherable at the end. While the cause of Shakespeare's tremulous handwriting cannot be known with certainty, there is one more diagnosis that would be consistent with an intention tremor, social withdrawal, and treatment for venereal disease: mercury poisoning.

Mercury poisoning was common in Shakespeare's time. Sir George Carey, patron of Shakespeare's acting company from 1597 to 1603, developed tremor, mental torpor, and weight loss after mercury therapy for syphilis. John Webster refers to mercury poisoning in his 1612 play *The White Devil* (1.2.27–8), where Camillo is described as "a gilder that hath his brains perished with quicksilver." Mercury poisoning was an occupational hazard of gilders, who used quicksilver in the manufacture of gold leaf; in the context of the play, the insinuation is that the balding and licentious Camillo has mercury poisoning from syphilis treatment.

Chronic poisoning with mercury vapour has three major manifestations: intention tremor, gingivitis (gum disease), and a constellation of personality changes known as erethism. Erethism was first described in hatters, who used mercuric nitrate solution in the making of fine felt,

THE MERCURY POISONING OF SIR ISAAC NEWTON

~⊙~

Isaac Newton, that other great universal genius that England has produced, suffered from a prolonged episode of paranoia, insomnia, and social withdrawal in 1693, when he was fifty years old. Old friends came under attack: the virginal Newton accused the philosopher John Locke of trying to "embroil me with women." In addition to his pioneering work in physics and mathematics, Newton was also an enthusiastic alchemist. His months of derangement coincided with a period of absorption in chemical experiments, during which he would stay up late and even fall asleep in his fume-filled laboratory. Mercury use in alchemy was ubiquitous, and Newton once joked that his prematurely grey hair was due to quicksilver exposure. Testing of surviving samples of Newton's hair have shown poisonously high levels of mercury. One hair showed 197 parts per million (ppm) of mercury, compared to typical modern values of less than 1.4 ppm. Newton set aside alchemy, and recovered to become Master of the Royal Mint and President of the Royal Society, although his eccentricities and occult speculations increased. Reassuringly, he calculated that the end of the world would come no sooner than A.D. 2060.

leading to the expressions "hatter's shakes" and "mad as a hatter." (Felt was once made by treating fur with camel urine, or with more readily available human urine. Supposedly, mercury came to be used when it was realized that exceptionally lustrous felt resulted from the use of urine from a hatter who was being treated for syphilis with mercury, which he was excreting in his urine.) Personality changes in hatters included timidity, social phobia, and irritability. The word erethism is derived from the Greek word for red, from the tendency of the patient to blush in embarrassment. Perhaps erethism explains why Shakespeare was no longer a "company keeper."

The severity of mercury poisoning is directly related to the intensity of exposure. If Shakespeare was treated just once for syphilis, he probably had only a moderate degree of mercury exposure. This may not have had any immediate effects on his nervous system. However, an intention tremor from mercury exposure may only appear years after exposure, as the effects of ageing unmask prior damage to the brain. This is consistent with the gradual worsening in Shakespeare's handwriting as he gets older. Mercury vapour does not usually affect cognition and intelligence unless exposure is particularly severe. It is tempting to speculate that the tangled syntax and "clotted verse" of Shakespeare's last plays was somehow related to mercury exposure, but this may just represent a natural evolution into greater stylistic complexity with age.

Shakespeare's death was probably not directly related to syphilis or mercury. According to Stratford lore, Shakespeare died of a fever contracted after a drinking bout. Perhaps this was typhoid: the death rate was unusually high in Stratford that spring, and the Avon River basin was endemic for typhoid even into modern times. Evidence from the plays suggests that Shakespeare was familiar with typhoid fever. Dr Abraham Verghese has noted that Falstaff's fatal illness is a classic depiction of the characteristic "muttering delirium" of typhoid. (This condition can also be seen with other infections, however, and is not diagnostic of typhoid fever.)

Shakespeare's obsession with syphilis in the plays and *Sonnets*—and the contemporary gossip about his promiscuity—provides circumstantial evidence that he may have had an STD. The Elizabethan sweating treatment for syphilis could be surprisingly effective in curing syphilis, given *Treponema pallidum*'s exquisite sensitivity to heat. However, Shakespeare might have been cured of syphilis only to be poisoned by mercury vapour, eventually leading to a tremor and personality changes. Shakespeare's suppressed rage at this experience may surface in plays such as *Timon of Athens* and *Troilus and Cressida* and certain of the *Sonnets*. However, it appears that Shakespeare's unusually large capacity for empathy enabled him to overcome his bitterness and anger. His final plays, which he may have physically struggled to complete, are characterized by a mood of acceptance and reconciliation, and a lessened preoccupation with sexual pollution. Perhaps Shakespeare's chancre ultimately enlarged his understanding of the moral complexities of character and circumstance, and increased his sympathy and tolerance for the failings and weaknesses of others.

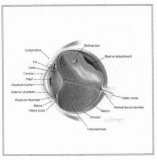

Cross section of the eye, demonstrating retinal detachment. (figure by Jennifer Fairman)

2. EXIL'D FROM LIGHT:
The Blindness of John Milton

Milton was great; but was he good? His brain was right; how was his heart?
—*Charlotte Brontë,* Shirley

Hatred . . . is in some cases a religious duty.
—*Milton,* De Doctrina Christiana

"Master Ellwood, your Latin lesson must wait. I am full with verse to bursting, and wanting to be milked." Milton sat impatiently in the feeble winter sunlight that streamed through the cottage windows. Though his chestnut hair was still thick, his age was betrayed by the shadows that lingered in the deep lines of his face. Motes of dust danced in the air before him, but the poet saw them not.

Thomas Ellwood's plain Quaker attire hung limply about him. The weight he had lost in prison made him look even younger than he was. He took off his gloves, sat at the table, uncorked the ink bottle, and readied a clean sheet of foolscap. He had not been afraid when his religious beliefs landed him in jails full of roarers, thugs, and cutthroats. But Ellwood was wary of Milton's sharp tongue, and unnerved by the clear grey eyes that wandered without ever quite meeting his gaze.

Ellwood took up a swan quill and blackened it in the ink bottle. Milton began to dictate in a high ringing voice:

> O loss of sight, of thee I most complain!
> Blind among enemies, O worse than chains,
> Dungeon, or beggary, or decrepit age!
> Light the prime work of God to me is extinct,
> And all her various objects of delight
> Annull'd, which might in part my grief have eased . . .

In the scullery, the poet's voice was barely audible, a distant oracular drone. Betty the serving girl idly scrubbed a glazed dish with meaty hands. A tower of dirty pots loomed above her. Milton's teenage daughters Mary and Deborah slinked past. Frilly ribbons tumbled from their hair. Books were tucked inside their cloaks in a paltry attempt at concealment. Anne, the oldest, limped behind, dragging a leg along in a tortuous semicircle. One side of her face sagged like melted wax. Betty scowled at the bare shoulders and low necklines of the girls. "You look like a bunch of bloody doxies." Saucy Mary laughed and stuck out her tongue. "How many shillings do you think we can get for a Chaldean grammar at St. Paul's?"

In the sitting room, the poet paused briefly as Ellwood refreshed his quill, and droned on:

> Inferior to the vilest now become
> Of man or worm; the vilest here excel me,
> They creep, yet see, I dark in light expos'd
> To daily fraud, contempt, abuse and wrong,
> Within doors, or without, still as a fool,
> In power of others, never in my own;
> Scarce half I seem to live, dead more than half.
> O dark, dark, dark, amid the blaze of noon,
> Irrecoverably dark, total Eclipse
> Without all hope of day!

Betty sneered. "I have strange news for you, my mistresses. Doctor Paget was here yesterday while you were out. He has a young cousin that your father intends to marry." Deborah shot back on her way out the door: "It would be no news to hear of his wedding, but if we could hear of his death that would be something." The chanting continued from the front room as Ellwood scratched furiously upon the page:

> Then had I not been thus exil'd from light;
> As in the land of darkness yet in light,
> To live a life half dead, a living death,
> And buried; but O yet more miserable!

In middle age, John Milton went blind in relentless, excruciating fashion over a period of several years. Abetted by vast stubbornness and tyrannical ingenuity, he overcame a seemingly insuperable handicap for a professional writer, and realized in old age his youthful dream of becoming a great epic poet. Completing *Paradise Lost* despite his loss of sight was an extraordinary achievement that has deservedly made him an inspiration to the blind. But it is quite possible that *Paradise Lost* might never have been written at all had Milton not been blind. For one thing, his experience of illness and defeat may have provided him with a maturity and emotional depth that he had previously lacked. For another, had he not gone blind, he might otherwise have been dead.

If Milton was stubborn, he came by it honestly enough. His grandfather Richard was a cantankerous old papist who preferred to pay hefty fines rather than attend the mandatory services of the Church of England. When his son John, Milton's father, turned Protestant, grandfather Richard disinherited him. Milton senior moved to London and prospered as a scrivener and moneylender. Despite his talent for making money, his passions lay elsewhere. The elder John Milton had an artistic bent, and was a poet and songwriter of note. This self-made man indulged his brilliant and unusual son John, providing him with opportunities for education, scholarship, and artistic creation that he never had himself.

John Milton was born on Bread Street in the heart of London in 1608. As a boy, young John might have seen Shakespeare on his way to the nearby Mermaid Tavern for a merry meeting with Ben Jonson. Milton's father was a great admirer of Shakespeare, and the two may have been acquainted, as Milton senior was involved with the London theatre scene.

At the death of Richard Burbage, who first acted Hamlet and Lear, Milton's father became a trustee of the Blackfriars Playhouse, of which Shakespeare had once been part-owner. Milton's father wrote a commendatory poem about Shakespeare that appeared in the First Folio, and Milton's own first published poem was a tribute to Shakespeare that appeared in the Second Folio (these poems were the seventeenth-century equivalent of today's dust jacket blurbs). In his maturity, Milton would often attain Shakespeare's majesty of language, if seldom his wit or playfulness.

Young John was fluent in Greek and Latin from childhood, had a private tutor, and read each night until midnight or one o'clock, squinting in the candlelight. We are told that his father ordered the maid to sit up with him night after night. (The maid's opinion of this practice has not been preserved.) At sixteen, after attending a local grammar school, young John went to Christ's College, Cambridge. Milton's teenage years and young adulthood show signs of social maladjustment. His bookishness, long auburn hair, and feminine features earned him the jeering nickname "The Lady of Christ's." In turn, Milton sneered at his fellow students as boors and yokels who mispronounced Latin.

One of several peculiar episodes in Milton's life is his quarrel with his college tutor, which culminated in Milton being whipped. This was apparently an unusual occurrence at Cambridge. Perhaps Milton, who had trouble keeping his mouth shut or his pen still, enraged his tutor by showing up his ignorance. Years later, one of Milton's many enemies implied in a private letter that Milton's offence was graver in nature: "He well deserved to have been both out of the university and out of the society of men. If [Milton's rhetorical opponents] knew as much of him as I, they would make him go near to hang himself." Two of Milton's recent biographers have suggested, on this slender evidence, that the whipping was a punishment for a "homoerotic sexual scandal" or some other sexual transgression. Milton may have been briefly "rusticated," or expelled, and transferred to another tutor on his return. This beating almost certainly contributed to Milton's hatred of intellectual authority.

Many of Milton's college compositions survive, including a speech he gave at a salting, the traditional, moderately abusive initiation dinner for new students at Cambridge. Its contents are as might be expected, such as fart jokes in polished Latin. After receiving his Master of Arts degree from Cambridge in 1632, the graduate rejected a career in the church or in the law. Instead, Milton spent the next five years on his always-indulgent father's country estate, engaged in "uninterrupted leisure . . . entirely devoted to the perusal of the Greek and Latin classics." He also plugged away at his poetry. Milton's literary gifts and grating pomposity are both evident in his early work. In the Latin poem "Ad Patrem," Milton exults that because of his scholarship, he need "no longer mingle unknown with the dull rabble," and his walk "shall be far from the sight of profane eyes." He also wrote religious poems, such as this odd lament about the circumcision of Christ: "He . . . now bleeds to give us ease/Alas, how soon our sin/Sore doth begin/His infancy to seize!"

Milton's major composition during his years in the country was a masque entitled *Comus*. Masques were courtly spectacles, acted by a mix of plebeian professionals and royal amateurs. These could be licentious entertainments; the dresses worn by the ladies of the court often bared their breasts, if the costuming sketches by Inigo Jones, the great Jacobean architect and stage designer, are to be believed. By contrast, Milton's *Comus* is an elaborate and tedious celebration of chastity. (Ironically, Milton became an enthusiastic proponent of polygamy in his old age, as was discovered when his theological treatise *De Doctrina Christiana* came to light in 1823. If polygamy was wrong, he thundered, then Moses and Abraham were mere "whoremongers and adulterers." Milton's polygynous propagandizing was probably influenced by his ensuing domestic miseries.)

As Milton wrote in praise of virgins and divine foreskins, England drifted toward political and religious anarchy. Charles I dissolved the House of Commons, and attempted to govern as an absolute monarch. His unpopular and arrogant Archbishop of Canterbury, William Laud, tried to drag the English church closer to Rome and farther from Calvin and Luther. Both men were badly out of touch with their times. With literacy and wealth came scepticism and independent thinking. A newly assertive middle class clamoured for more power for Parliament, and less for the Church and Crown. Laud responded by fining, jailing, or cropping the ears of the most vociferous dissenters. Thousands of Puritans left England for Massachusetts at this time. (Unluckily for Charles I and for the Irish, an East Anglian gentleman named Oliver Cromwell decided at the last minute to stay home.)

Milton's Puritan convictions hardened. His most famous poem from this period, the pastoral elegy "Lycidas," is interrupted in mid-flow by a jarring polemic against the corruption of the English clergy. At age thirty, he travelled to Italy, where he met the persecuted Galileo, an experience that intensified his hatred of censorship and love of intellectual freedom. On his return, he abandoned the Muses to write tirades against the great wickedness of bishops. Milton's pamphlets (short books, really) are the seventeenth-century equivalent of political smear campaigns. They impress more with their mastery of insult, rather than their command of logic. His enemies are accused of everything from wearing stinky socks to having clandestine sex with servant girls in garden sheds. Milton is obsessed with winning his argument at any cost. In the words of Samuel Johnson, "he loves himself rather than truth."

In 1641, after the death of his sister Anne, Milton adopted her sons Edward and John Phillips. As Edward later wrote, his uncle's household was characterized by "hard study, and spare diet." Milton was inspired by the arrival of his nephews to start a small school. At age thirty-three, it was his first real job. Milton had absurdly unrealistic notions of the scholastic capacity of the average boy. His pupils had to slog through a variety of great and not-so-great authors in Greek, Latin, and Italian. On Sundays, they celebrated the Sabbath by reading the scriptures in the original Hebrew, "whereto it would be no impossibility to add the Chaldee and the Syrian dialect."

This atmosphere of despotic pedantry may have been partly responsible for the collapse of Milton's first marriage in 1642. His teenaged wife Mary Powell, daughter of a merry, prodigal country squire, "found it very solitary: no company came to her, oftentimes [she] heard his nephews beaten, and cry." Perhaps his poor nephews were slow to learn their Chaldean. In any case, three weeks after the wedding, Mary fled for home, having found delight neither in Milton's bed nor his politics. Civil war had finally erupted, and the Powells were staunch royalists who disapproved of Milton's Puritanism.

Milton's pattern of interpersonal difficulties suggests that he had a degree of high-functioning autism, or Asperger syndrome. People with Asperger syndrome struggle in realms of social interaction that are intuitive for most people. They may have remarkable intellectual gifts, but ordinary human behaviour is mysterious to them. They may be deficient in empathy and understanding of others, and have narrow interests and activities that result in them being labelled as nerds. All this may lead to severe problems with social and occupational functioning.

Some facts support a diagnosis of Asperger syndrome in Milton. His scrap with his tutor, his disdain for his schoolmates, his late adoption of gainful employment, his wildly erroneous expectations of what the average boy could digest intellectually, his marital problems, and his later difficulties with his daughters, all display a certain social dysfunction. Milton's twin obsessions with defunct writers of antiquity and bitter theological wrangling also have an Asperger flavour. The venom of his political and religious writings suggests a certain failure of empathy. But in fairness to Milton, he was also capable of warmth and generosity. Milton's friends found him a charming conversationalist, especially on intellectual matters, although they were always wary of his savage wit. His nephews remained fond of their uncle when they were grown, despite the beatings. Milton also helped many of those on the losing side in the English Civil War. He intervened to save the poet Spenser's Catholic grandson from having his lands seized, and also stuck his neck out to help the royalist playwright William Davenant, Shakespeare's syphilitic godson, get out of the Tower of London. (Davenant repaid the favour by helping Milton get out of prison at the Restoration.) Most surprisingly, Milton sheltered his in-laws after Parliamentary troops confiscated their lands.

Persons with Asperger syndrome may thrive in a supportive atmosphere that allows them to pursue their obsessions and exercise their talents. If Milton did have Asperger syndrome, he was fortunate to have a father who appreciated his unique gifts, tolerated his eccentricities, and supported him financially throughout his adult life.

Milton's response to his runaway bride was to pen a diatribe in favour of divorce. *The Doctrine and Discipline of Divorce* earned him more notoriety than any of his other works, as well as a laughably inappropriate reputation as a libertine. Milton took on a daunting theological challenge here, as the Gospel of Matthew is rather unequivocal about marriage: "What therefore God hath joined together, let not man put asunder. . . . whosoever shall put away his wife, except it be for fornication, and shall marry another, committeth adultery." But Milton is up to the task. Apparently, Jesus is just exaggerating: "Christ meant not to be taken word for word, but like a wise physician, administering one excess against another to reduce us to a perfect mean." (Milton refers here to the ancient theory of the four humours that dominated medicine until the nineteenth century. Disease arises from too much of one humour, and is treated by removing the excess or administering its opposite. For example, fever from a surfeit of blood is treated by bloodletting with leeches, or by the ingestion of "cold" foods, such as chicken or fish.)

Milton makes a more intellectually robust argument for divorce on the grounds of incompatibility. However, he undermines this with psychosexual weirdness that brings to mind the seminal obsessions of General Jack D. Ripper in *Dr. Strangelove:* a man trapped in a loveless marriage is forced to waste "the best substance of his body." He places a curious emphasis on the folly of prohibiting divorce simply because the marriage has been consummated once. If a married couple "have tasted in any sort the nuptial bed," and been found "suitably weaponed to the least possibility of sensual enjoyment," then they are doomed till death to "grind in the mill of an undelighted and servile copulation." The peculiar phraseology makes one wonder exactly what awkwardness transpired during the unhappy couple's honeymoon.

Milton's divorce pamphlets provoked an uproar and a call for censorship. His response was to write *Areopagitica,* his best prose work, a passionate and eloquent defence of free speech. Memorably, he likened the effect of bigotry on our judgment to the distorting visual effects of eye disease: the "first appearance" of truth to "eyes bleared and dimmed with prejudice and custom, is more unsightly and implausible than many errors."

Early in the war, Charles's army seemed about to march on London. To the enduring embarrassment of his biographers, Milton stuck a weaselly sonnet on his door addressed to any royalist officer who might pass by, begging him to spare the "muses' bower." In return, the poet offers to "spread thy name o'er land and seas." This would be a bit like George Orwell sending a nice, polite letter to Hermann Goering, offering to write a laudatory essay about the Luftwaffe if they would kindly avoid dropping a bomb on his flat.

In 1645, Mary came back, "making submission and begging pardon on her knees before him," according to Edward Phillips. Her family may have pressured her to reconcile with Milton. The Powell family finances, always precarious, were further ruined by the war, which was going badly for the royalists. Moreover, Milton was one of Richard Powell's major creditors, by virtue of Mary's unpaid dowry. We lack insight into the remainder of the marriage, but it is worth noting that Milton elsewhere urged that men should wield "despotic power" over women. "Servile copulation" apparently took place, as Mary gave birth to four children. Three survived to adulthood, all daughters. Although Milton's personal life took a turn for the better around this time, ominously, the vision in his left eye had already begun to fail.

Later that year, Milton published an edition of his collected poems. When his vanity was wounded by the clumsy likeness that had been engraved for the frontispiece, Milton took revenge in characteristic fashion, displaying both his elitism and sadistic sense of humour. He had the unfortunate artist add this inscription to the portrait in Greek, a language that was unknown to all but the most learned: "Since you do not recognize the man portrayed, my friends, laugh at this rotten picture of a rotten artist."

As the English Civil War dragged on, Milton's political views grew more radical. In 1649, he wrote *The Tenure of Kings and Magistrates*, defending the right of the young English republic to chop off the king's head. For this, Milton was rewarded with the well-paid position of Secretary of Foreign Tongues, officially responsible for diplomatic correspondence, and unofficially responsible for overseas propaganda.

The downfall and death of Charles I opened up the possibility that England might turn into a democracy, but it soon became something between a military dictatorship and a theocracy, largely due to the machinations of Oliver Cromwell. Cromwell was one of those remarkable men thrown up in times of flux and revolution, a cunning and opportunistic alpha male, far more suited by temperament and inclination for kingship than the weak and foolish Charles I. At the outbreak of war, he was an obscure forty-three-year-old member of Parliament. He raised a troop of horse, and after a series of victories quickly became lieutenant-general of cavalry. His manic ferocity made him a natural military commander, and his promotion of men based on merit, rather than social standing, earned him the zealous loyalty of his troops. As David Hume noted, he was a fervent Puritan, "devoted to religion, though he perpetually employed it as the instrument of his ambition." Cromwell adopted the title of Lord Protector in 1653, and became king of England in all but name. (He was later formally offered the crown, but reluctantly declined it, perhaps from fear of assassination as much as any moral scruples.)

With the demolition of the established order, strange sects flourished. Ranters practiced free love; Muggletonians denied the immortality of the soul; Fifth Monarchy Men declared that the end of the world was near. Most dangerous of all were the Levellers. Not only did they reject king and aristocracy, they also rejected rule by the rich, arguing that the right to vote should be extended to the common man, and not restricted to men of means. Cromwell and most of the other high-ranking officers in the New Model Army were gentlemen by birth, and took a dim view of the Levellers, who had strong support amongst the rank and file of the army. Cromwell said of them, "you have no other way to deal with these men but to break them in pieces," and suppressed them with his usual shrewdness and brutality.

Milton's infatuation with Cromwell is another ignominious chapter in his biography. The Secretary for Foreign Tongues was besotted with the Lord Protector. In 1654, Milton gushingly called Cromwell "the author, the guardian, and the preserver of our liberties," despite the fact that he had dissolved Parliament at gunpoint, made himself dictator for life, and was now being addressed as "Your Highness." (Milton was no democrat. He believed elections were a nuisance to be avoided whenever possible. His ideal state consisted of an oligarchy elected for life, a free press, no state church, and especially no bishops.) His fawning and scybalous sonnet to Cromwell is one of the viler works ever written by a major English poet. Milton praises Cromwell for literally making the rivers of Scotland run red with blood, and for bringing a sort of "peace and truth" to the British Isles:

> To peace and truth thy glorious way has ploughed
> And on the neck of crowned Fortune proud
> Hast reared God's trophies and his work pursued
> While Darwent stream with blood of Scots imbrued.

The Orwellian "peace and truth" brought to Ireland by Oliver's army included war crimes, mass starvation, enslavement and deportation of prisoners of war to the West Indies, and ethnic cleansing on a grand scale. Milton himself pushed for a policy of severity against the Irish in one racist propaganda piece, calling them "inhuman rebels and papists," and a "treacherous" race of "savages" and "barbarians." His recent biographers Gordon Campbell and Thomas N. Corns note that "Milton produced a tendentious dossier designed to launch and excuse a dubious war of aggression. He would not be the last public servant to do so; though he may, perhaps, have been the first."

If Milton's defence of colonialism and exultation over dead Scotsmen was a form of moral myopia, he was well on his way to actual physical blindness. Milton began to lose sight in his left eye in 1644, when he was thirty-six. The right eye also became affected five years later. As Milton's eyes slowly failed, he was treated with "issues and setons." These were wounds made, hopefully not in the eye itself, but in the skin nearby. An issue was a skin ulcer made with a lancet or hot iron, and kept open with a pea or other foreign body. A seton was a skin tract created by passing a needle through a skin fold, and leaving a thread or strip of linen embedded in the skin. In theory, this allowed evil humours to escape from the affected body part. In practice, it was useless and conferred a risk of serious skin infection.

In 1652, Milton became totally blind, but continued in his employment, to the befuddlement of foreign diplomats. According to Samuel Johnson, negotiations with Sweden were once delayed due to Milton's ill health, leading the Swedish ambassador to wonder that, "Only one man in England could write Latin, and that man blind."

Why did Milton develop progressive blindness over a period of several years? Some theories are preposterous, and may be quickly dismissed. These include that Milton was actually an albino, despite the fact that his portraits clearly show his reddish-brown hair, or that he had a brain tumour called a craniopharyngioma that spontaneously shrank after causing his blindness.

Milton was vain about his appearance. He insisted that his eyes looked outwardly normal, a fact that was confirmed by one of Milton's early biographers. This would rule out several common eye problems, such as various diseases of the cornea, the surface of the eye. It would also exclude cataracts. These opacities in the lens would be visible as a haziness in the pupil.

The immune system can sometimes attack the optic nerves, leading to blindness. This condition, known as optic neuritis, is often associated with multiple sclerosis. This seems unlikely as a cause of Milton's blindness. Optic neuritis usually presents with sudden loss of vision, which often gets better without treatment in a few weeks. However, Milton's eyes worsened over a period of several years. In optic neuritis and multiple sclerosis, the symptoms get worse with exercise, a sign with the grandiose name of Uhthoff's phenomenon. This is because the damaged nerves work less well at a higher body temperature. Milton actually believed that his vision improved with exercise.

Chronic glaucoma has long been a favoured diagnosis for Milton's blindness. In chronic glaucoma, the aqueous humour, the fluid in the front of the eye, does not drain properly. This causes a slow buildup of pressure inside the eye. Usually, this is painless, and results in a very gradual loss of peripheral vision, until the patient feels like he is squinting down a long tube, so-called "tunnel vision." Glaucoma is a poor fit for Milton. He first lost the vision on his temporal side, or the outer portion of his vision. This is unusual in glaucoma, which tends to affect the vision on the nasal side of the eye first. He had heaviness and pain in the eyes (which is unusual in chronic, although not acute glaucoma); he saw flashes of light (phosphenes); and the objects that he saw appeared to move, and were distorted in shape. All these symptoms would be unusual in glaucoma, but would be typical of a retinal detachment related to severe myopia.

Milton was probably myopic, or nearsighted, from youth. One of his early biographers tells us "his eyes were none of the quickest," and Milton admitted, "my eyes were naturally weak." There may have been a genetic predisposition to myopia, as Milton's mother and his daughter Deborah, who was forced to read to her father in seven languages after he became blind, also had poor eyesight. But Milton's strongest risk factor for myopia was his "voracious . . . appetite for knowledge" as a child: "From twelve years of age, I hardly ever left my studies, or went to bed before midnight."

Myopia is a disease of civilization. It is rare in preliterate societies, but becomes common as schoolgoing and literacy increase. The strongest predictor of myopia is intense "near work" in childhood, especially reading or computer work. In severe myopia, the eye is abnormally long. The eye is mostly filled with vitreous humour, a jellylike substance. In a very myopic eye, this elongated vitreous humour may tug on the retina, the layer of visual cells that is fixed to the back of the eye. Rarely, the retina may weaken, break down, peel away from its blood supply, and die off. Patients typically describe this as a curtain or veil in the outer part of the eye (Milton called it a "mist") that worsens with time. The traction on the retina irritates it, leading to the sparks of light described by Milton. (These phosphenes can be produced in people with normal eyes by pressing gently on the closed eye.) In early retinal detachment, the viable but mobile retina may sway in the vitreous fluid, leading to the distortions in vision that Milton described: "all things that I could discern, though I moved not myself, appeared to fluctuate, now to the right, now to the left." Before Milton became utterly blind, his vision was slowly reduced to "a minute portion of light as through a crevice."

Retinal detachment affects both eyes in 15 percent of patients, as it did with Milton. Half of all retinal detachments are related to severe myopia. Other causes of retinal detachment include diabetes and sickle cell disease. Patients with these conditions can develop scar tissue that tugs on the retina, as well as fragile new retinal blood vessels that are prone to bleed and detach. Neither diabetes nor sickle cell disease is likely in Milton's case. In the modern era, retinal detachment can also be an occasional complication of cataract surgery.

No treatment was available for retinal detachment in Milton's time. Today, sight can be saved in most patients with retinal detachment by draining the fluid under the retina, and then using laser therapy or cryotherapy (freezing) to create scar tissue to hold the retina in place. The eye surgeon also places a belt around the middle of the eye called a scleral buckle, which relieves the traction on the retina and pushes the vitreous humor against it.

Milton developed other problems with his health in middle age. He was prone to headaches from youth, but these worsened, and he was also greatly troubled with painful and embarrassing digestive complaints: "At the same time my intestines [were] afflicted with flatulence and oppression." He also began to suffer from gouty arthritis, which left "his knuckles . . . all callous." In old age, Milton was "pale but not cadaverous, his hands and fingers gouty, and with chalk stones." These "chalk stones" were tophi, the orangey deposits of uric acid in the joints that are seen in severe gout. Milton's gout and abdominal pain may have been unrelated problems. But taken together, they suggest the insidious onset of lead poisoning. Lead damages the kidneys and leads to a buildup of uric acid, causing gout, and it also damages the nerve supply to the intestines, leading to constipation and severe attacks of belly pain (lead colic). Lead poisoning also causes anaemia, perhaps explaining Milton's pallor, and headaches can be a sign of mild lead encephalopathy.

In Western countries, lead poisoning is usually a disease of poor children in run-down houses with crumbling coats of old lead paint. Toddlers like to chew on poison paint chips, which taste sweet, and they may also breathe in household dust laced with lead. Tragically, about one in fifty American children has learning disabilities from lead exposure. Although lead poisoning is now a disease of poverty, for most of human history, it was a disease of affluence.

Lead is abundant in nature, melts at a low temperature, and is easy to work with. Its use was widespread in ancient Rome. It has been argued, not entirely convincingly, that lead poisoning among the Roman aristocracy led to moral decay, the lunacy of Caligula and Nero, and ultimately to the fall of the Roman Empire. The Romans used lead pipes in their aqueducts to carry water (the word plumbing comes from the Latin word for lead, *plumbum*). Rainwater for home use was often collected from lead roofing and stored in lead tanks. Roman cosmetics, hair dye, tableware, cooking pots, and paint all contained lead. It was even added to wine as a preservative and sweetener. Sugar cane was unknown in the Roman world. The only sweeteners in Roman times were honey and *sapa*, a syrup made by boiling grape juice or spoiled wine in lead vats. This turned sour vinegar into sweet lead acetate. *Sapa* was widely used as a seasoning in cooking sauces. A good host in ancient Rome provided his dinner guests with vials of it to sweeten their wine to suit their individual palate. Lead exposure reduces fertility and leads to spontaneous abortions; Roman prostitutes are supposed to have used *sapa* as a contraceptive and abortifacient. Perhaps drinking *sapa* also contributed to the low birth rate among Roman noblewomen.

Modern studies have shown that the amount of lead in ancient Roman skeletons rose to unhealthy levels as Rome's wealth and power grew, peaked in the final two hundred years of the Roman Empire, and fell rapidly thereafter. (Getting pillaged by barbarians does seem to have one bright side: a lower risk of lead poisoning.) It would be silly to blame the fall of Rome on lead poisoning alone. The Roman Empire was under great and continuous strain from foreign invaders, civil wars, civic corruption, deforestation, soil erosion, crop failures, inflation, and epidemics of smallpox and malaria. But it can't have helped matters that some members of the ruling class were stupefied by lead.

How might Milton have been exposed to lead? In prosperous English households like Milton's, lead was found in glazed earthenware and pewter vessels, and was sometimes added to wine, which Milton drank with his meals. An archaeological dig at a colonial Virginia plantation that was farmed during Milton's lifetime confirms the role of affluence as a risk factor for lead poisoning. Skeletons of the plantation owners had five times as much lead in them as the skeletons of slaves and indentured servants. But there is also a good chance that Milton suffered from lead poisoning at the hands of his doctors.

As he slowly went blind, Milton searched frantically for medicine to fix his eyes. One of his early biographers called this his "perpetual tampering with physic." What drugs, or "physic," might Milton have used? Herbal medicines formed the bedrock of English pharmacy in the seventeenth century. Many were worthless, if also harmless. However, some were quite active, if potentially poisonous, and are still around today in one form or another, including foxglove (the source of the heart drug, digitalis) and autumn crocus (the source of colchicine, an excellent medication for gout). These herbal remedies were augmented by many substances of doubtful therapeutic value, including cat-ointment, human sweat, human placenta, human ordure, saliva of a fasting man, oil of spiders, oil of scorpions, oil of puppies boiled with earthworms, and foxes' lungs (for asthma, of course).

A good sense of state of the art medicine in Milton's time can be obtained with a glance at the practices of Théodore Turquet de Mayerne. Mayerne was no quack, but one of the most eminent doctors of his time, the royal physician to James I and his son Charles I. (Mayerne also treated

Cromwell, who seems to have had bipolar disorder, for depression.) Mayerne was an expert on gout, which he treated with a wide variety of horripilating therapies. In addition to the usual herbal concoctions, he also used crabs' eyes (actually stones with antacid properties found in crawfish stomachs), water of frog-spawn, antimony, oil of arsenic, and bloodletting, preferably from haemorrhoidal veins. Another of Mayerne's preferred drugs for gout was powder made from the filings of a human skull. This was one type of "mummy," a fashionable seventeenth-century medicine made from human body parts. Sometimes this came literally from Egyptian mummies, but more often it was prepared from the cadavers of executed criminals. Ideally, the corpse was first exposed to moonlight. Chunks of "muscular flesh" were then cut off, sprinkled with myrrh and aloe, soaked until tender, and hung out to dry. We are reassured that it "comes to resemble smoke-cured meat, without any stench," and it was suitable for eating, or applying as a poultice to wounds.

A favourite form of mummy was usnea, or moss from the skull of a man who died violently. Usnea was plentiful in seventeenth-century England, given the damp and mild British climate, and the abundance of bodies hanging from gibbets at crossroads and severed heads rotting on pikes. Another popular panacea of Milton's time was Goddard's drops. It was used in gout, as well as "faintings, apoplexies, lethargies and other sudden and alarming onsets." Charles II spent a small fortune to get the secret formula for Goddard's drops. As it turned out, the active ingredients were powdered human bones and viper's flesh. One authority, William Salmon, advised "if you want it for gout in any particular limb it is better to make it from the bones of that limb." In other words, ground-up left foot bones were best for gout of the left foot, and so on. History does not record whether Milton used any of these advanced medical therapies.

Where did the dreadful idea come from to use lead, a deadly poison, as a medicine? Lead compounds are actually an ancient remedy for belly complaints in some parts of the world. Mild lead poisoning causes constipation; perhaps this helped those with diarrhoea from bacterial and parasitic infections. Today, lead and other heavy metals may be found in herbal remedies from India and China. One Ayurvedic medicine widely used in India and Pakistan, Kushta surb, has a lead content as high as 73 percent. Western devotees of alternative medicine have sometimes been unwitting victims of lead poisoning. Because traditional medicines are legally considered to be dietary supplements in the United States, monitoring for their safety is minimal. In a study by Robert Saper and colleagues, one out of five herbal medicines for sale in South Asian groceries in Boston in 2003 contained toxic amounts of lead, arsenic, or mercury.

The use of lead in mainstream Western medicine began with the Renaissance physician Paracelsus, the genius, rebel and crackpot who may have originated the popular stereotype of the mad scientist. Perhaps, like Isaac Newton, he inhaled too many toxic heavy metal fumes in the course of his alchemical experiments. Paracelsus mocked the old Galenic dogma that disease resulted from an imbalance of the humours. Although his own theory of disease was an uneasy farrago of astrology, alchemy, and common sense, his core ideas are recognizably modern. He believed that illness resulted from the failure of specific organs, and that it should be possible to find specific remedies for specific diseases. The most promising compounds, according to Paracelsus, were the powerful metals and minerals used in alchemy. Paracelsus was an astute clinical observer for his time. His treatise on diseases of miners is a classic of occupational medicine. He is also regarded as the founder of toxicology. Presumably, some of his expertise in this field came from accidentally poisoning patients with his favourite cures: mercury, arsenic, lead, antimony, and tin.

No matter what medicines Milton used in his "tampering with physic," it is likely that he would have eventually taken some mixture containing lead. Because of the rising influence of Paracelsus on medicine in Milton's time, "salts of lead were gradually added to the witches' brew of plant and animal matter as treatment for virtually all ailments." For example, when he wasn't feeding his gouty patients crushed skulls or bleeding their haemorrhoids, Mayerne used sugar of lead to "sweeten their humors." Unfortunately, while it may have sweetened their humours, it worsened their gout by making their kidneys retain more uric acid. Mayerne also treated urinary tract infections by squirting "ocher of vitriol and sugar of lead" up the urethra. Lead has a weak antibacterial effect, so conceivably this might have helped, although it must have been none too pleasant.

The medical use of lead continued well into the nineteenth century. Analysis of locks of Beethoven's hair taken at his death in 1827 showed that he had high levels of lead in his system for at least the last year of his life. His spasms of abdominal pain, his moodiness and irritability, and even his deafness might have resulted from chronic household lead poisoning from adulterated wines, pewter vessels, and lead-glazed dishes. Unfortunately, Beethoven's doctor probably finished him off by treating him with lead salts for pneumonia, then placing lead poultices on his abdominal wound.

Milton's troubles multiplied. In 1652, he lost not only his sight, but also his wife Mary, who died in childbirth, and his only son John, who was just one year old. He remarried in 1656, to a woman named Katherine Woodcock. She gave birth the following year, but the mother and child soon fell ill and died. Cromwell's sudden death in 1658 ushered in a period of political instability that ended with the restoration of charming and hedonistic Charles II in 1660. This was applauded by a public weary of Cromwell's meddling mullahs, who had outlawed three traditions integral to the English identity: Christmas, the theatre, and picturesque profanity.

The Restoration was a disaster for Milton. Much of his savings were wiped out, and he went from comfortable and respected civil servant to fugitive and prisoner. His books were burned by the public hangman, and he was tossed in the Tower of London. Yet unlike others who had advocated the execution of Charles I, Milton did avoid being hanged, drawn, and quartered. This barbaric punishment consisted of being hung until nearly dead, then cut down and revived, only to be disembowelled and emasculated, made to watch helplessly as your entrails and genitals were burnt, and finally to have your head lopped off and your body chopped up into quarters. He was spared mainly because it was thought that God had already punished him enough by mysteriously striking him blind.

On his release from prison, impoverished and disgraced, but stubborn and resilient as ever, Milton finally realized his childhood dream. Over several years, he completed a massive poem, painstakingly dictated in bits and pieces. This epic of disobedience, rebellion, punishment, and defeat, a poem that seemed at times oddly sympathetic to Satan himself, was *Paradise Lost*. Without the humbling experience of sickness, failure and defeat, Milton never would have felt it necessary to justify the ways of God to men.

When Milton became blind, his young daughters Mary and Deborah were expected to read to him in Greek, Latin, Italian, Spanish, French, Hebrew, and of course the Syrian dialect. (His eldest daughter Anne was disabled. Her cousin Edward Phillips laconically noted, "Whether by ill constitution, or want of care, she grew more and more decrepit.") Milton taught them to pronounce the words, but refused to teach them their meanings, and insisted, "One tongue is enough for a woman." Phillips called this "a trial of patience, almost beyond endurance; yet it was endured by both for a long time; yet the irksomeness of this employment could not always be concealed, but broke more and more into expressions of uneasiness." The bad blood intensified when Milton married a woman named Betty Minshull, barely older than the daughters. Milton did not bother to tell them, and they heard about it from the servant girl. Mary's reaction was "that it was no news to hear of his wedding but if she could hear of his death it was something." The daughters accused Betty of being a shrew; she accused them of petty thievery. Milton took Betty's side, cut the daughters out of his will, aside from the Powell dowry he had never received, and sent them away to master "curious and ingenious sorts of manufacture, that are proper for women to learn." (In fairness to Milton, his obnoxious opinions about women were conventional in his day and long after. Not even the Levellers had anything progressive to say about the rights of women.)

Milton's abdominal pain seems to have abated after he became completely blind; aside from gout, he was fairly healthy in his old age. Perhaps when he lost his sight entirely he stopped using medicines spiked with lead, allowing some of the lead accumulated in his body to slowly leach out. All accounts of Milton's life stress his happiness and serenity in his old age. Despite all his losses and his gout, he was "not ever observed to be impatient," and "he would be cheerful even in his gout-fits, and sing."

Milton needed a lot of help to write *Paradise Lost*. After his daughters departed, Milton dictated ten to thirty lines each morning to one of his many admirers. If they were late, Milton complained that he had been waiting to be "milked." These young men also read to him. In return, he taught them the finer points of Latin and Greek. Milton's early biographers agree that he had writer's block at certain seasons of the year, although they disagree as to whether this was in the winter or the summer.

There is a form of winter depression, seasonal affective disorder, associated with the shorter days in Northern latitudes in winter, and which responds to sunlamps and light therapy. Oddly enough, seasonal affective disorder has been reported even in blind patients, especially those like Milton with a little residual light perception.

Much of the interest in *Paradise Lost* from a modern perspective is in its apparent ambivalence. Satan gets the best lines in *Paradise Lost,* and many readers find him the poem's most compelling figure. Milton's own experience of rebellion and defeat gave him an uncommon amount of sympathy for the devil; William Blake famously believed that Milton was of the Devil's party without knowing it. There is a strain of modern criticism that suggests that Milton was deliberately trying to make God look cruel and arbitrary, and wonders whether he finally had any religious beliefs at all. This is almost certainly mistaken. Milton seems to have been quite sincere in his attempt to justify the ways of God to man. A steadfast libertarian, he thought that the risk of eternal damnation was a small price to pay for the privilege of free will. His attitude toward God, even in the face of blindness, was always one of quiet resignation to the divine will, as in the lovely Sonnet XXII:

> Yet I argue not
> Against heaven's hand or will, nor bate a jot
> Of heart or hope; but still bear up and steer
> Right onward.

Even when Milton's religious notions strike us as strange, as in his wistful defence of polygamy or his beliefs that angels had sex and liked to nosh, they are rooted in his deep reading of scripture, sometimes interpreted in idiosyncratic fashion.

Milton expired peacefully at the age of sixty-five; according to an early biographer, "He died in a fit of the gout, but with so little pain or emotion, that the time of his expiring was not perceived by those in the room." It is impossible to say what killed Milton, but it was probably not gout, which causes excruciating joint pain, but is rarely fatal. Gout infrequently leads to kidney failure, but this would cause a lingering death, with delirium and swelling of the legs and belly. A more plausible cause for Milton's sudden death is a cardiac arrhythmia.

Milton's reputation soared in the centuries following his death. Although he has been battered by twentieth-century critics, notably T. S. Eliot, he continues to surprise us with his relevance. After 9/11, a row broke out in the pages of the *Times Literary Supplement* about whether Milton's *Samson Agonistes* could be taken as a hateful tract in favour of suicide bombing. Even if *Samson Agonistes* is a covert revenge fantasy, with Samson as a blind Puritan fallen on black days, Dalila as a faithless royalist wife, and the Philistines as a stand-in for Charles II and the Cavaliers, there is a great gulf between writing a poem and blowing up Windsor Castle, or urging others to do so. While Milton is not guilty of fomenting terrorism, he was certainly blind to the many paradoxes of his own life and career: a poet who wrote of mercy and forgiveness, but spent years writing mudslinging pamphlets; an apostle of freedom who toiled for a dictator, and was a domestic tyrant himself; and an advocate of religious toleration who acquiesced in violence perpetrated in the name of religion, a practice that has lamentably continued down to our own day.

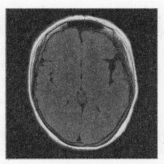

MRI in early frontotemporal dementia, with atrophy of the right frontal and temporal lobes. (Courtesy of Thomas C. Lee, M.D.)

3. DYING FROM THE TOP DOWN:
The Dementia of Jonathan Swift

Swift is a diseased writer. He remains permanently in a depressed mood which in most people is only intermittent, rather as though someone suffering from jaundice or the after-effects of influenza should have the energy to write books . . . Yet curiously enough he is one of the writers I admire with least reserve, and Gulliver's Travels, *in particular, is a book which it seems impossible for me to grow tired of.*
> —*George Orwell, "Politics vs. Literature:*
> *An Examination of* Gulliver's Travels"

The least miserable among them, appear to be those who turn to dotage, and entirely lose their memories.
> —*Jonathan Swift,* Gulliver's Travels

Young . . . found Swift at some distance gazing intently at the top of a lofty elm, whose head had been blasted. Upon Young's approach he pointed to it, saying, "I shall be like that tree; I shall die first at the top".
> —*Thomas Sheridan,* Life of Doctor Swift

He prowled the room like a nervous animal as the rain pelted down outside. An eavesdropper in the muddy streets of Dublin might have mistaken this fretful energy for his furious intensity of old. But the Dean's blue eyes were dull and lustreless, and his silent jowly face hung slack and vacant. Mrs Ridgeway gently took the Dean's arm and led him to the table, the ruddy housekeeper and her ward looking like a parody of society elegance. Mrs Ridgeway was a modest woman, but she took a proprietary pride in her care of the old man, who was, in fact, quite clean, decent, and presentable. She saw herself as something like the curator of a museum, wherein the Dean was a living relic of his own greatness. As they passed a mirror, Swift beheld a sliver of himself in the firelight. His face contorted in a savage spasm, but whether of mirth or rage she could not say. In a moment it had gone, and his face was blank once more.

The housekeeper saw him into his chair. With deft hands she cut his meat in pieces. The Dean watched the shiny knife dip and flutter like a silver wasp. When she had done she withdrew to her chair by the fire, took up her needlework, and avoided his gaze. The Dean hated to be watched as he ate, and could stare an hour at his food before he touched it.

His eyes lingered on the bright blade left carelessly on the table. He sat placid and still for a long time. All of a sudden he grabbed the knife, held it in front of him and stood rocking on his heels as if hesitating before action. Mrs Ridgeway leapt across the room, hollered for Brennan, and cursed her own stupidity. She was no small woman but the Dean was surprisingly sturdy beneath his baggy clothes. They grappled and reeled like drunken bears as Brennan and the other servants burst in. "Take it soft, *a chara,* that's the good man," Brennan spoke soothingly as he held the Dean's arm immobile and prised his fingers open. The knife clattered harmlessly to the floor and Mrs Ridgeway pounced upon it.

Released, the Dean sagged heavily back into his chair, panting and dishevelled. He howled softly, a child whose plaything has been snatched away. Then he spoke for the first time in months, clutching himself and repeating over and over: "I am what I am. I am what I am. I am what I am . . ."

Jonathan Swift was a difficult and unaccountable man: a parson without piety; a chaste adulterer; an Irish patriot who longed to be an English bishop, and lamented that he would die in Dublin like a poisoned rat in a hole; a grave man who rarely laughed but wrote outrageous satires; a misanthrope capable of great kindness to individuals; a social climber who habitually sabotaged himself with his mutinous tongue and pen; a fussy man obsessed with order, notorious for his disorderly relations with two women; an establishment man with the bomb-tossing instincts of an anarchist. If every joke is a tiny revolution, as Orwell said, then Swift is one of our most dangerous and unlikely revolutionaries.

In 1835, repairs to St Patrick's Cathedral in Dublin exposed the grave of Jonathan Swift. Sir William Wilde took advantage of this unique opportunity to examine the Dean's mortal remains. Sir William, father of Oscar, was an eye surgeon and antiquary, famous for his scholarship and patriotism, not to mention his brood of illegitimate children and dismal hygiene. A Dublin riddle asked: Why does Wilde have black fingernails? Answer: because he scratches himself. Wilde was also notorious for his lax operating room technique. According to one improbable tale, he once removed a man's eyeballs, intending to replace them momentarily, but his cat got to them first and gobbled them up.

As he peered into the musty grave, Sir William marvelled at the similarity of Swift's head to "those skulls of the so-called Celtic aborigines." Swift would have been amused to learn of his striking resemblance to a Celtic aborigine, as his forebears were all impeccably English.

In Swift's boyhood, Ireland was an unruly imperial frontier, England's Wild West. There were lush unploughed fields and virgin forests rich in timber. There were hostile, impoverished natives with strange customs who spoke broken English. And there were the newcomers, carpetbaggers and fortune seekers of all stripes, bent on accumulating as much land and loot as possible. Into this anarchy boldly strode that sure sign of civilization, the lawyer. Four Swift brothers, all lawyers, came to Dublin with the Restoration. The eldest, Godwin, was "perhaps a little too dexterous in the subtle parts of the law," as his nephew Jonathan delicately put it, or a bit of a shyster, as we might say today. This dexterity made Godwin a wealthy man.

Little brother Jonathan, the writer's father, was less lucky. He married a woman named Abigail Erick, who "brought her husband little or no fortune," as his disapproving son wrote many years later. One night in 1667, returning from the circuit courts, he "brought home the itch with him, which he had got lying in some foul bed on the road. Somebody advised him to use mercury to cure it, which prescription cost him his life in a very few days after his return."

This fatal "itch" was probably scabies, a mite that chomps its way through the superficial layers of the skin, trailing eggs and faeces as it goes. These leavings are intensely irritating. People that are infected may be kept awake all night, frantically scratching their armpits, waists, and groins. Mercury ointment is an ancient cure. As we have seen, acute exposure to mercury leads to bad breath, rotten gums, and uncontrolled drooling. But in high enough doses, mercury also leads to kidney failure, as it makes the lining of the kidney tubules slough off. Perhaps it was this that led to the rapid demise of Jonathan the elder. (Mercury poisoning from skin ointments still happens today, but not as a result of scabies treatment. Mercury compounds are one of many toxic cosmetics used as skin lighteners by women of colour in Africa, Asia, and Latin America.)

Lawyer Jonathan left behind a daughter Jane and a pregnant wife, who gave birth eight months later. This boy, also named Jonathan, arrived just in "time enough to save his mother's credit." Young Jonathan was alternately coddled and neglected. Soon after his birth, his overly affectionate wet nurse absconded with him to England, where she had pressing family business. Swift stayed there with her for the first three years of his life. This sounds improbable, but seems to have been true. Swift later claimed that under her tutelage, he read the Bible fluently by age three, when the wayward nurse finally returned him home to Dublin. At the age of six, Swift was separated again from his mother when his uncles packed him off to boarding school. Shortly thereafter, his mother and sister went to England to live with relatives in Leicester. He would not see her again for another fifteen years. No one found this negligent or unusual, including Swift, who saved his bile for his uncles. (In *Gulliver's Travels,* Swift described lawyers as "a society of men among us, bred up from their youth in the art of proving, by words multiplied for the purpose, that white is black, and black is white, according as they are paid.")

Swift was sent to a grammar school in Kilkenny that was a bastion of Ireland's ruling Protestant elite. Swift remembered his teachers as brutal pedants who could not quite quash the joys of childhood: "I formerly used to envy my own happiness when I was a schoolboy, the delicious holidays, the Saturday afternoon, and the charming custards in a blind alley; I never considered the confinement ten hours a day to nouns and verbs, the terror of the rod, the bloody noses and broken shins."

Swift, like many other successful people, nursed his grievances and used them to feed his ambition. This began early in childhood: "I remember, when I was a little boy, I felt a great fish at the end of my line which I drew up almost on the ground. But it dropped in and the disappointment vexeth me to this very day, and I believe it was the type of all my future disappointments."

At age fourteen, he went to Trinity College, Dublin. He was often in hot water for cutting classes and skipping chapel, and his grades were indifferent at best. He excelled at Greek and Latin, but in his own words, "too much neglected some parts of his academic studies, for which he had no great relish by nature." Swift only received his BA degree *speciali gratia*, or by special grace of the university. This was a black mark, a sort of Latin asterisk. However, when Swift later took his MA at Oxford, the English authorities supposedly mistook this for a sign of distinction, and expedited his enrolment.

Swift blamed his poor academic performance on depression from "the ill treatment of his nearest relations." This maltreatment was a drastic reduction in the subsidy provided by Uncle Godwin, who had been squandering his fortune in a series of unsound investments. By the time he was sixty, it was clear that Godwin had premature dementia, and had "fallen into a kind of lethargy, or dotage, which deprived him by degrees of his speech and memory."

Swift left Trinity College when Ireland was again engulfed by war. James II, the last and most inept of the Stuarts, was too autocratic and too Catholic for English tastes, and he was overthrown in 1688 by the Dutchman William of Orange. James fled to Ireland, and the Irish unwisely rallied to his cause. After the defeat of the Jacobites, as James's followers were known, Irish Catholics were stripped of many of their civil rights. The Glorious Revolution, as it was called, also led to the birth of political parties in England. Whigs were urban capitalists who favored a limited monarchy and religious liberty (for Protestants, at least). Tories were rural aristocrats who favoured a strong monarchy and a state church. Tories accused Whigs of Puritanism and republicanism; Whigs accused Tories of covert Jacobitism. (Tory comes from Gaelic *tóraidhe*, or outlaw, in reference to the Jacobite desperadoes hiding in the Irish hills.)

Swift went over to England, and was happily reunited with his mother. The uncles pulled some strings and got him an appointment as secretary to an old family friend, Sir William Temple. Temple had once been the most eminent statesman in England. He had grown weary of parroting the lies of his masters, as many diplomats must, and retired to the country to write his memoirs. But his retirement was marred by tragedy. Temple and his wife had nine children. Eight died young, of the usual childhood diseases. Their last surviving child seemed to have a bright future ahead of him. John Temple was only thirty-two when he was appointed Secretary of War. One of his first acts in office was to free an imprisoned Irish general, on the condition that he would work to end the Irish revolt. Instead, the general joined the rebels. John, who seems to have inherited a depressive tendency from his mother, committed suicide by jumping into the roiling waters under London Bridge. His death took place just before Swift's arrival.

Swift worked for Temple on and off for the next ten years. Their relationship was stormy. At its best, Swift was perhaps almost a surrogate son. The two worked closely together. Swift read widely in Temple's library, imbibed his opinions, and was dazzled by the worldly old man's tales. Temple was a man of letters and an elegant prose stylist. Swift learned to write with Temple's polish and balance, to which he added his own rude energy and invention. Much of *A Tale of a Tub*, Swift's surprisingly modern satire of religion, was probably written during this time. Swift also laboured over his first poems. John Dryden, his second cousin, read this stilted stuff and wisecracked, "Cousin Swift, you will never be a poet." Swift never forgave him. In time, he proved Dryden wrong, with poetry that was shockingly different in style and subject from his moralistic early works.

Swift and Temple were too proud and too moody not to fall out eventually. Swift chafed under Temple's peevishness, and perhaps tired of Temple's tedious retelling of his exploits with women. Swift also resented Temple's inability, or unwillingness, to help him get a better-paying post elsewhere. For their part, the Temples found Swift an insolent boor, full of "bitterness, satire, moroseness." Swift's manners did not improve when he was suddenly struck by the strange malady that plagued him with dizzy spells for the rest of his life, and eventually made him nearly deaf.

Swift's illness began not long after he first entered Temple's service in 1689. He blamed it on an astonishing orgy of apple-eating: "I got my giddiness by eating a hundred golden pippins at a time." When his attacks of vertigo came on, Swift was incapacitated for days at a time, and could not walk without tottering. Within a few years, the episodes also included ringing in his ears, a fullness in his head, and hearing loss, and they also grew more frequent. In the beginning, Swift was well for months at a time between attacks, and even as late as 1720, the episodes were quite intermittent. He wrote, "What if I should add, that once in five or six weeks I am deaf for three or four days?" As he aged, his symptoms were more constant, if less severe. In 1731, when he was sixty-four, he wrote: "The giddiness I was subject to, instead of coming seldom and violent, now constantly attends me more or less, though in a more peaceable manner."

Swift was probably suffering from Ménière's disease, or progressive failure of the inner ear. Unfortunately, this disorder is fairly common, affecting up to one person in 500. The inner ear is a network of fluid-filled tubules. Part of this apparatus, the snail-shaped cochlea, is responsible for hearing. The other part, the three semicircular canals, provides our sense of balance. These canals look like a cluster of tiny hoop earrings. When your head moves, endolymphatic fluid swishes around inside the canals, moving microscopic hairs, or cilia. The movement of these hairs leads to nerve impulses that enable the brain to track the body's orientation in space. In Ménière's disease, the cochlea and the semicircular canals are damaged, swollen, and irritable. Patients have fluctuating hearing loss, especially in low frequencies, a spinning sensation (vertigo), tinnitus, or a dull low roaring sound, and a feeling of fullness or pressure in the ears. Symptoms are usually episodic at first, but tend to persist as the disease wears on and the inner ear degenerates.

Ménière's disease probably has different causes in different individuals. These include viral infections, head trauma, and autoimmunity. Food allergies may sometimes be involved, so perhaps Swift was right about the role of fruit in provoking his illness. There may be a genetic predisposition in some individuals. Syphilis was once a common cause, but is now rare. The treatment of Ménière's disease includes avoidance of factors that precipitate attacks, such as emotional stress and sleep deprivation. Sodium loads, caffeine, and alcohol may cause fluid shifts in the inner ear, and should also be avoided. Antihistamines may be helpful in treating allergic symptoms, and may also blunt the sensation of dizziness. Diuretics, which promote fluid and salt loss from the kidneys, may be helpful, probably because they also affect electrolyte balance in the inner ear. Anti-inflammatory therapy with prednisone may be of some benefit. Surgery is sometimes performed to decompress the inner ear, or in extreme cases to sever the nerve connections between the semicircular canals and the brain.

Swift was shrewd enough to recognize provocative factors for his attacks, and became a hypochondriac, fussing about food and exercise. Today we think of fruit as one of the foundations of a healthy diet, but to Swift it was poison: "I have eat mighty little fruit; yet I impute my disorder to that little, and shall henceforth wholly forbear it." He also thought his attacks were provoked by alcohol, snuff, and lack of sleep. Swift tried to drink in moderation. When his companions forced alcohol on him, he furtively watered it down.

Swift took a variety of useless medications for his "giddiness." These included asafoetida, the herb so foul-smelling that it is known as devil's dung, as well as "nasty steel drops" (a crude iron supplement). Swift also took something that he called "a vomit." This vile treatment was based on the ancient Galenic theory of ridding the body of evil humours. It could have been one of many drugs, ranging from the merely unpleasant (ipecac) to the potentially toxic (arsenic or antimony). Had Swift taken arsenic or antimony only rarely, he probably would not have had long-term side effects, as most of the dose would have quickly left the body in the urine and from both ends of the gastrointestinal tract. His doctor pal John Arbuthnot prescribed confection of alkermes (a scarlet syrup in which the active ingredient was crushed parasitic insects), the vigorous laxative castor oil, and cinnabar of antimony (mercuric sulphide). Swift thought the cinnabar helped. This is just possible: some mercury compounds are mild diuretics.

Ménière's disease, like other chronic illnesses, has a big impact on quality of life. Anxiety and depression are common in severe Ménière's disease, and Swift was increasingly subject to both. Some patients with Ménière's describe a state of mental dullness, so-called "brain fog." As he aged, Swift had more trouble with concentration and memory, although much of this may have been due to his supervening dementia. He also became more isolated because of his deafness. This was torture for Swift. He was social by nature, and one of his chief joys was witty conversation. When the attacks were at their worst, he could only make out shrill sounds: "When the deafness comes on, I can hear with neither ear, except it be a woman with a treble [soprano], or a man with a countertenor." This loss of low-pitched hearing is characteristic of Ménière's disease. He was also miserable from tinnitus. He described it as "the noise of seven watermills" or "a hundred oceans rolling in my ears."

Swift's contemporaries thought that his dizziness and deafness were linked to his madness and senility, but these were probably separate disease processes. Not many conditions cause vertigo and hearing loss, with the much later development of dementia. One physician has suggested syphilis. Syphilis can certainly cause vertigo, deafness, and dementia, but this is unlikely in Swift for several reasons. When syphilis does cause hearing loss, it tends to progress quickly to deafness, and the intermittent thirty-year period of symptoms that Swift experienced would be distinctly unusual. Another argument against the diagnosis of syphilis is that there is no evidence that Swift had sex with anyone, ever. Swift's contemporaries did not believe that he was sexually active. Could Swift have acquired syphilis in the womb from maternal infection? This is again unlikely. Most congenital syphilitics have low intelligence, whereas Swift's verbal intelligence was off the charts. Swift also had none of the obvious signs of congenital syphilis, such as a lumpy forehead, curved shins, misshapen teeth, deep creases around the lips, and scarring of the lens of the eye.

In 1694, Swift left Temple, went back to Dublin, and took holy orders in the official Protestant church, the Church of Ireland. This was not motivated by great religious fervour. Swift was frustrated with Temple's inability to advance his prospects, and saw the church as another way of rising in the world. In this, he was disappointed once again. He was sent to the tiny parish of Kilroot, outside Belfast. The Church of Ireland was especially feeble in Northern Ireland, which was dominated by Presbyterians, and Swift found himself preaching to a nearly empty church. While there, he courted an unlucky lady named Jane Waring. His love letters to her, if they can be called that, are vehement, passive-aggressive, and altogether incompetent. They corresponded until about 1700, by which time Swift had another woman in view.

Swift lasted a year in Kilroot, and by 1696 he was back in England as Temple's secretary, again hopeful that Temple could secure a church position for him. When Temple died in 1699, Swift expected King William III to appoint him to a comfortable living on Temple's recommendation, but this fell through. Swift, as so often, made matters worse for himself. Temple had made Swift his literary executor. When Swift published Temple's posthumous memoirs, he left in material that was unflattering to the family of a confidante of Queen Anne, who had by this time succeeded King William. Swift made more enemies in high places with the best-selling *A Tale of a Tub*. This was published anonymously, but was widely known to have been written by Swift, and was viewed by many, rightly or wrongly, as hostile to Christianity.

In 1699 he was given a small parish in Laracor, outside of Dublin. In the next several years, he was often in London, lobbying for the diversion of tax revenue to the Church of Ireland. As the Whigs were then in power, and unsympathetic to the state church, he was unsuccessful. He amused himself in his spare time by writing satires, and became well known in literary circles, eventually becoming friendly with Pope, Gay, Addison, and Steele. When the Tories took over in 1710, Swift made himself invaluable to the new regime as a propagandist and spin doctor. He was on intimate terms with both the First Minister, the Earl of Oxford, and the Secretary of State, Viscount Bolingbroke, and in fact mediated between them in their frequent and increasingly vicious quarrels.

Swift was agonizingly close to his long-cherished bishopric in England, but the Tory ministry collapsed in 1714, and the only post his powerful friends could get for him was the Deanery of St Patrick's Cathedral in Dublin. The Dean was responsible for the day-to-day administration of the cathedral. He was also the master of the Liberty of St Patrick's, a five-acre maze of streets and alleyways outside of the jurisdiction of the city. He was a great favourite of the beggar women of the liberties, giving them money or overpaying for the plums and gingerbread that they sold. "One of these mistresses wanted an eye; another, a nose; a third, an arm;

a fourth, a foot . . . some of these he named thus for distinction's sake, and partly for humour; Cancerina, Stumpa-Nympha, Pullagowna." He lent small tradesmen money during economic downturns, judged their disputes, and gave a third of his income to charity. Although Swift eventually made himself at home in the Deanery, when he first arrived there in 1714 he fell into depression. Some of this may have had to do with Swift's burgeoning female trouble.

Women found Swift strangely attractive. He was not handsome but possessed great wit and force of character. His friend and early biographer, Lord Orrery, noted that Swift had a "seraglio of very virtuous women who attended him from morning till night, with an obedience, and awe, and an assiduity, that are seldom paid to the richest, or the most powerful lovers." More bluntly, James Joyce said of Swift's love life that he "made a mess of two women's lives." These were Esther Johnson, or Stella, and Hester Vanhomrigh, better known as Vanessa. The precise nature of Swift's relationship with them remains controversial to this day. Stella was said to be the illegitimate daughter of Sir William Temple, and received a small inheritance from him on his death. She was Swift's pupil when she was a child and he was a young man in Temple's household. (Swift was most comfortable with women in a teacher-pupil relationship.) In 1701, when she was twenty, Stella moved to Dublin with an older companion named Rebecca Dingley. Ostensibly, this was because the cost of living was cheaper in Ireland than England, but rumour had it that she came in pursuit of Swift.

In Dublin, Swift saw Stella daily, but only when Dingley was present; he was said to have a rule never to be alone with Stella. When Swift lived in London from 1710 to 1714, he wrote silly, affectionate letters to her, sometimes descending to the level of baby talk; these were later published as the *Journal to Stella*. While in London, he also started spending time with the Vanhomrigh family. The widow Vanhomrigh had moved to London after the death of her husband, who had been Lord Mayor of Dublin. Her daughter Hester, nicknamed Vanessa by Swift, was lively, clever, younger than Stella, and oddly infatuated with him. She was also expected to inherit a great deal of money. Swift exchanged bantering letters with her that suggest an unusual degree of intimacy for him: "I long to drink a dish of coffee in the sluttery, and hear you dun me for secrets, and—drink your coffee—why don't you drink your coffee?" (Coffee was some sort of in-joke between them; a "sluttery" is a messy room, probably without the sexual connotation it would have today.)

When Swift returned to Dublin, he was alarmed to learn that Vanessa planned to move there as well; her mother had just died, and she had to settle her inheritance. He begged her to be discreet: "If you are in Ireland while I am there, I shall see you very seldom. It is not a place for any freedom, but where everything is known in a week, and magnified a hundred degrees." He tried to deflect her romantic attentions onto another clergyman, which seems to have enraged her, for the letters suddenly stopped. When they resumed a few years later, she was more in love than ever: "I was born with violent passions, which terminate all in one, that inexpressible passion I have for you. Consider the killing emotions which I feel from your neglect of me, and show some tenderness for me, or I shall lose my senses." Swift's early letters to Vanessa were flirtatious. He even wrote to her in French, in the only missive in the four volumes of his surviving correspondence that could be described as a love letter. But as her ardour grew, he panicked, backpedalled, and switched to damage control mode: "Cad assures me he continues to esteem and love and value you above all things, and so will do to the end of his life; but at the same time entreats that you would not make yourself or him unhappy by imaginations."

"Cad" is a nickname Swift gave himself, from the epic poem he had written for her years before, *Cadenus and Vanessa*. ("Cadenus" is an anagram of "decanus," Latin for "the Dean." This inspired Joyce to put Swift in *Finnegans Wake* as "the Cad.") Cadenus is a scholar, proud of his young pupil Vanessa, who becomes befuddled when Vanessa proclaims her love. Cadenus confesses:

> He could praise, esteem, approve,
> But understood not what was love.

This is reminiscent of a line in a poem of Swift's to Stella, "I ne'er admitted love a guest." Laetitia Pilkington, who knew Swift after Stella died, said, "I really believe that it [love] was a passion he was wholly unacquainted with, and which he would have thought it beneath the dignity of his wisdom to entertain."

The ending of *Cadenus and Vanessa* is coy and ambiguous:

> But what success Vanessa met,
> Is to the world a secret yet . . .
> Must never to mankind be told,
> Nor shall the conscious muse unfold.

But the final act of their relationship would prove to be disastrous. Vanessa got wind of Dublin rumours that there was a more tangible obstacle to her pursuit of Swift: that he was secretly married to Stella. Vanessa wrote Stella a blunt letter asking if this was true. Stella passed Vanessa's letter on to Swift, and stormed out. Swift rode his horse out to Vanessa's country house, threw the letter at her feet without saying a word, and never spoke or wrote to her again. Vanessa died of tuberculosis a few months later, in June 1723. She left the bulk of her estate to the philosopher and churchman George Berkley, whom she barely knew. Perhaps she did this to spite Swift, who had mocked Berkley's project of building a university in Bermuda. She also instructed her executors to publish *Cadenus and Vanessa* and her correspondence with Swift, to the latter's mortification. Swift spent the months after her death wandering alone through the poorest and most degraded parts of Ireland on horseback, an experience which is thought to have inspired the Yahoos of *Gulliver's Travels,* which he was writing at the time. (The unsavoury episode where Gulliver is jumped by a naked Yahoo nymphet probably has a subconscious connection to Vanessa.)

We could easily dismiss the secret marriage as another Irish story, except that most of those who knew Swift believed it. His friend Lord Orrery called Stella "the concealed, but undoubted wife of Dr Swift." His young protégée Laetitia Pilkington wrote: "Stella, whom he has so beautifully praised through his writings, was actually his wife, though they never, I am convinced, tasted even the chaste joys which Hymen allows." That is to say, they never had sex. Swift is supposed to have married Stella in 1716, to mollify her jealousy for his flirting with Vanessa, but with the condition that they live apart and keep the marriage secret.

Stella died in 1728, after a long illness; some said that the publication of *Cadenus and Vanessa* set off her final decline. There is a story that she asked Swift on her deathbed to publicly acknowledge the marriage, but he refused. "Swift made no reply, but turning on his heel, walked silently out of the room, nor ever saw her afterwards during the few days she lived. This behaviour threw Mrs Johnson into unspeakable agonies." When Stella finally died, Swift had a breakdown, with a severe attack of his Ménière's disease and a depressive episode. Years after her death, the mere mention of her name could make him burst into tears. Orrery blamed Swift's appalling behaviour on "the excessive coldness of his nature"; more charitably, we might speculate that he was incapable of dealing with his emotions, except by denying them completely.

There is another factor that may help to explain Swift's strange conduct toward women: his obsessive-compulsive disorder (OCD). Patients with OCD have recurrent thoughts and repetitive behaviours that are not realistic responses to life problems, and are severe enough to impair life functioning. Obsessions and compulsions most often relate to security, for example, prompting a parent to obsessively check on a sleeping infant, or to keep rechecking a locked door; orderliness, leading to a hypersensitivity to objects that are misaligned or misplaced in the physical environment; fears of privation, resulting in hoarding behaviours; and phobias about filth, leading to compulsive cleaning and handwashing. OCD is common, affecting up to 3 percent of the population. This suggests that there may be an evolutionary benefit to OCD, particularly milder degrees of OCD that do not impair everyday functioning. Someone with mild OCD may be better prepared for a famine, bear attack, or barbarian invasion, or less likely to contract an infection from poor hygiene.

Swift was clean to a degree that was extraordinary in the eighteenth century. An early biographer wrote that he "was one of the cleanliest men in his person that ever lived. His hands were not only washed . . . with the utmost care, but his nails were kept constantly pared to the quick, to guard against the least appearance of a speck upon them. And as he walked much, he rarely dressed himself without a basin of water by his side, in which he dipped a towel and cleansed his feet with the utmost exactness." This might not seem terribly fastidious today, but was regarded as highly eccentric in his time, when it was customary to wash clothing, but rarely the body. Perhaps Swift's cleanliness was another reason that women found him attractive. Of note, both Stella and Vanessa were also said to be immaculate. Swift once wrote to poor Jane Waring, whom he had courted in his youth, that her looks and money, or the absence thereof, did not greatly matter to him, as "cleanliness in the first, and competency in the other, is all I look for."

The converse of Swift's cleanliness was an abhorrence of filth. This was severe enough to impede Swift's success at work and love. Swift publicly chastised his church superiors for their dirtiness and body odour, which probably didn't help him get promoted. Sexual disgust is common in OCD; up to 50 percent of patients with OCD have some form of sexual dysfunction, most often low libido. Sex, dirt, and disease are closely linked in Swift's mind; perhaps this nexus inhibited Swift from entering into a physical relationship with Vanessa or Stella. This association grew stronger as Swift got older, and is the subject of some of his most notorious poems. In "Strephon and Chloe," a bridegroom is comically disillusioned on the wedding night by his wife's less angelic nature:

> Strephon who heard the foaming rill
> As from a mossy cliff distill;
> Cried out, "Ye gods, what sound is this?
> Can Chloe, heavenly Chloe piss?" . . .
> But, e'er you sell yourself to laughter,
> Consider well what may come after;
> For fine ideas vanish fast,
> While all the gross and filthy last.

In a related poem, "The Lady's Dressing Room," the swain errs by exploring his lady's chamber in her absence, and blunders into her chamber pot:

> And first, a dirty smock appeared,
> Beneath the armpits well besmeared . . .
> Now listen while he next produces,
> The various combs for various uses,
> Filled up with dirt so closely fixed,
> No brush could force a way betwixt;

A paste of composition rare,
Sweat, dandruff, powder, lead, and hair . . .
But oh! It turned poor Strephon's bowels,
When he beheld and smelt the towels;
Begummed, bemattered, and beslimed;
With dirt, and sweat, and ear-wax grimed . . .
So, Strephon, lifting up the lid,
To view what in the chest was hid,
The vapors flew from out the vent,
But Strephon cautious never meant
The bottom of the pan to grope,
And foul his hands in search of hope . . .
Thus finishing his grand survey,
The swain disgusted slunk away,
Repeating in his amorous fits,
"Oh! Celia, Celia, Celia shits!" . . .
I pity wretched Strephon, blind
To all the charms of womankind;
Should I the queen of love refuse,
Because she rose from stinking ooze?

Another peculiarity of Swift was his reliance on routine. He was punctual and monotonous in his habits. He made lists and counted steps when walking. He disliked the unfamiliar. To settle mind and body, he exercised obsessively: he ran up and down stairs and hills, and walked four to ten miles a day. According to Lord Orrery, "regularity was peculiar to him in all his actions, even in the greatest trifles. His hours of walking, and reading, never varied: his motions were guided by his watch, which was so constantly held in his hand, or placed before him upon his table, that he seldom deviated many minutes, in the daily revolution of his exercises and employments." Swift had a strong belief in social rules and their rigid enforcement. At his dinner table, everyone present, including Swift, was allowed to speak for only a minute at a time without interruption. If they exceeded this, Swift would point to his watch and grumble. He also had precise expectations of his servants. On one occasion, he gave his maid permission to attend a wedding, and even allowed her to take one of the horses, but on discovering that she had left a door open, sent another servant to overtake her and bring her back. On her return, he asked her to close the door, at which point she was free to proceed to the wedding again. His emphasis on routine has a whiff of Asperger syndrome about it; obsessive-compulsive traits are common in those with Asperger syndrome.

Swift hated lies, cant, and hypocrisy. His friend Bolingbroke called him a "hypocrite reversed," meaning that he took pains to exaggerate his vices, and conceal his virtues. He was bad at self-censorship; this got worse as he got older. Orrery said that "in his friendships he was constant and undisguised. He was the same in his enmities. He generally spoke as he thought in all companies and at all times."

In the 1720s, the same decade that saw the deaths of Stella and Vanessa, Swift also reached his peak of productivity as a writer. He became a national hero in Ireland for writing the series of pamphlets known as *The Drapier's Letters*. These began as a response to a British scheme to debase the Irish currency, but expanded into an attack on the injustices of English rule in Ireland, and ultimately questioned the right of the British parliament to govern Ireland at all. In Swift's celebrated essay *A Modest Proposal*, he went further, pushing irony to the brink of nihilism, and perhaps beyond. The anonymous narrator of the *Proposal* suggests a bone-chilling solution to the problems of Irish poverty and the rack-renting of peasants by their landlords: surplus infants should be sold for food. "A young healthy child, well nursed, is at a year old a most delicious, nourishing, and wholesome food, whether stewed, roasted, baked, or broiled, and I make no doubt it will serve equally well in a fricassee, or a ragout."

Gulliver's Travels was a bestseller on its publication in 1726. Even today, it may be the most widely read of English classics, and it remains very funny despite, or perhaps because of, its misanthropy. In bowdlerized form, children enjoy it as a tale of adventure; in unexpurgated form, adults relish its toilet humour and savage satire. Swift may have intended it as a parody of Daniel Defoe's optimistic *Robinson Crusoe*, published a few years before. The plucky Crusoe is marooned after a shipwreck and, with his Anglo-Saxon work ethic, can-do attitude, and faith in divine providence, he vanquishes the local cannibals and sets up a tidy outpost of empire before he is rescued. By contrast, Gulliver's adventures point out the wickedness and injustice of Western civilization, and Gulliver ultimately loses his mind through too close a contemplation of the defects of human nature.

In the 1730s, Swift was famous and miserable. On his birthdays he secluded himself and read the Book of Job. He longed for death. On parting with friends, he would say, "Good night; I hope I shall never see you again." His ears were worse:

> Deaf, giddy, odious to my friends,
> Now all my consolation ends;
> No more I hear my church's bell
> Than if it rang out for my knell . . .

And his mood and self-control deteriorated as well, probably as the first effects of the dementia that would later erode his intellect. Swift once told of seeing "a monkey overthrow all the dishes and plates in a kitchen, merely for the pleasure of seeing them tumble and hearing the clatter they made in their fall." As he got older, Swift was more and more of a monkey in the kitchen, becoming "peevish, fretful, morose, and prone to sudden fits of passion." Orrery said that his "despotic power" over women "gave loose to passions that ought to have been kept under a proper restraint." Some of these unrestrained passions were recorded by Laetitia Pilkington, a young clergyman's wife who became part of the Dean's post-Stella social circle.

Pilkington believed that something was wrong with the Dean well before anyone was really aware, but it went unrecognized because of the preservation of his intellect: "This wrong turn in his brain, I fancy had possessed him a long time before it was taken notice of . . . had he been less witty, it would sooner have been taken notice of." Pilkington became a pupil of the Dean, much as Stella and Vanessa had been, although "he was a very rough sort of a tutor for one of my years and sex, for whenever I made use of an inelegant phrase, I was sure of a deadly pinch . . . however I am convinced, had he found me incorrigibly dull, I should have escaped without correction, and the black and blue favours I received at his hands, were meant for merit."

On other occasions, his actions toward her were frankly bizarre. At a Christmas party, Swift took the pitch that was used to seal the wine bottles, and smeared it on her face. "Instead of being vexed, as he expected I would, I told him he did me great honour in sealing me for his own." Swift tried to rattle her composure by making fun of her short stature: "He asked the company, if they had ever seen such a dwarf? And insisted, that I should pull off my shoes till he measured me . . . he then made me stand up against the wainscot, leaned his hand as heavy as he could upon my head, till I shrunk under the weight . . . then making a mark with his pencil, he affirmed I was but three feet two inches high." On another occasion, he invited her to the Deanery early for breakfast, kept her two hours without food, beat her when she had difficulty opening up a locked drawer, and forced gingerbread and rum on her: "He threw me down, forced the bottle into my mouth, and poured some of the liquor down my throat, which I thought would have set my very stomach on fire. He then gravely went to prayers, and I returned home, not greatly delighted, but, however, glad to come off no worse." She was pregnant at the time. Swift's impulse control problems were manifest outside the Deanery as well. At a civic function, he got the attention of the elaborately dressed Lord Lieutenant of Ireland, the highest-ranking British official in the country, by addressing him as "You, fellow with the blue string!"

Swift had a horror of senility. Gulliver was anxious to meet the immortal race of Struldbrugs, who he expected to be a repository of ancient wisdom. Instead, he finds "the most mortifying sight I ever beheld." The Struldbrugs are aged beyond ghastliness, have neither sense nor memory, and are "dead to all natural affection." Swift was agonizingly aware of his intellectual deterioration, although he concealed it for years. In 1735, he wrote to his old friend Alexander Pope: "My memory is going fast; my spirits are sunk nine parts in ten, you will find in this letter fifty blunders, mistakes not only literal and verbal, but half sentences either omitted or doubled." The following year, he published his last major poem, "The Legion Club," an attack on old enemies in the Irish parliament that he believed had sold out the country. He could only rouse himself to write when goaded by bile. In one of his last letters, Swift complains that "I have entirely lost my memory, except when it is roused by perpetual subjects of vexation." This may be the first version of the rueful old joke about the Irish version of Alzheimer's disease, in which the patient forgets everything but his grudges.

Swift's subsequent course will be painfully familiar to those who have cared for patients with dementia. According to Thomas Sheridan, Swift's godson, "About the year 1736, his memory was greatly impaired and his other faculties of imagination and intellect decayed . . . when the understanding was shaken from its seat, and reason had given up the reins, the irascible passions, which at all times he had found difficult to be kept within due bounds, now raged without control, and made him a torment to himself, and to all who were about him." He deteriorated rapidly. He quarrelled with friends, and was prone to angry outbursts. By 1739, "his friends found his passions so violent and ungovernable, his memory so decayed, and his reason so depraved, that they took the utmost precautions to keep all strangers from approaching him."

Despite these precautions, Swift fell victim to elder abuse. A Reverend Doctor Wilson moved into the Deanery, and was alleged to be stealing Swift's money and selling off his books. One night, he took Swift out on the town, and got him intoxicated, apparently with the aim of convincing Swift to appoint him as sub-Dean. Swift fell into a rage and a drunken brawl ensued, in which Swift was battered and bruised. When the news of the beating spread through the city, Wilson went into hiding, for fear of being torn apart by the Dublin mob. A Commission of Lunacy declared Swift incompetent, and took measures to protect him.

Is it possible to ascertain the cause of Swift's dementia? Vascular dementia, the cumulative effect of a series of small strokes, accounts for about 15 percent of dementia cases. This seems unlikely as the cause of Swift's deterioration. Patients with vascular dementia typically decline in an abrupt, episodic, stepwise fashion, quite different from the gradual, insidious mental decline that occurred in Swift. Most cases of dementia, about 70 percent, are due to Alzheimer's disease. This is actually a poor fit for Swift's illness. Alzheimer patients usually have memory loss as the first symptom. They forget names, they lose their keys, they get lost in familiar neighbourhoods. The earliest symptom of Swift's dementia was personality change. He became "peevish, fretful, morose, and prone to sudden fits of passion." He hit and browbeat women. His poems and writings became grosser and smuttier; the mix of humour and revulsion that we think of as peculiarly Swiftian was actually a fairly late development in his style. Dementia with personality change and loss of inhibitions as the first signs, and preservation of intelligence early in the course of disease, is characteristic of frontotemporal dementia, or Pick's disease. This is highly consistent with Swift's clinical course, as noted by psychiatrist Paul Crichton in 1993.

Frontotemporal dementia causes 5 percent of cases of dementia. As the name suggests, the frontal lobes are involved early and prominently. Our enlarged, hypertrophied frontal lobes are one of the anatomical features that distinguish us from the lesser apes. Their major roles are executive function, such as planning ahead and setting goals, and behaviour inhibition, controlling our emotions and our lower urges. Patients with Pick's disease are irritable and prone to angry, inappropriate outbursts, as was Swift. A family history of dementia is often present, as in Swift's case. Another detail is very suggestive of frontotemporal dementia: at Swift's autopsy, the brain was "loaded with water." At death, brains affected with frontotemporal dementia are markedly shrunken, sometimes to even half the normal brain weight, with the remaining space replaced by spinal fluid.

There are well-documented instances of patients with very early frontotemporal dementia who developed enhanced creativity, especially in art. Presumably, mild damage to the frontal lobes prevents them from inhibiting other regions of the brain that are involved in creativity. This disinhibition is similar to taking your foot off the brakes of a car. The phenomenon wears off as the dementia progresses, and the negative effects of further brain damage outweigh the benefits of disinhibition. Not surprisingly, the temporal lobes are also involved in frontotemporal dementia. Selective damage to the right temporal lobe may result in profuse writing, or hypergraphia, by stimulating the language centres of the left temporal lobe. One of the striking features of Swift's career as a writer was his late creative peak. According to Pat Rogers, a recent editor of Swift's poetry, 74 percent of Swift's total poetic output came after he turned fifty, including most of his scatological poems. Swift's creativity is at its zenith in the years immediately before he developed the first signs of dementia. Perhaps minimal damage to his frontal lobes and right temporal lobe spurred both his creativity and his potty humour. Are *Gulliver's Travels* and Swift's scatological poems both byproducts of subclinical early dementia?

Patients with a positive family history and a genetic predisposition to dementia often develop symptoms at an earlier age than Swift did. Two factors may have protected him against early-onset dementia. He exercised compulsively, which seems to delay the emergence of dementia. His skill with the written word may also have helped to ward off dementia. An elaborate prose style was associated with a lower risk of dementia in a large study of autobiographical essays written by American nuns on joining the convent. Nuns who wrote prose with greater idea density were less likely to have dementia several decades later. It is not clear whether writing ability is just a marker for higher general intelligence, or whether there is something specific to writing that lessens the risk of dementia. This doesn't mean that writers cannot become demented, especially if they have a positive family history of the disease, as Swift did. In 1995, Iris Murdoch developed severe writer's block at age seventy-five while working on her final novel, and died four years later from a progressive dementia that was proven to be Alzheimer's disease at autopsy.

In his last years, Swift lapsed into silence. In 1742, he had a bad bout of cellulitis about his left eye, with boils under his arms and on his trunk, probably from a staphylococcal infection. "The torture he was in, is not to be described. Five persons could scarce hold him for a week, from tearing out his own eyes." It has been suggested that he had a cavernous sinus thrombosis, or an infected blood clot inside the brain, but this seems unlikely, as he never lost consciousness and made a full recovery.

Swift was well cared for until he finally died in 1745. Among his papers was found an envelope containing a lock of hair. On it was written, "Only a woman's hair." Swift had accumulated a small fortune, most of which he left to found a hospital for the mentally ill in Dublin, St Patrick's Hospital. It now has wards named after Stella and Vanessa.

> He gave the little wealth he had,
> To build a house for fools and mad:
> And showed by one satiric touch,
> No nation wanted it so much.

He was buried in St. Patrick's Cathedral at midnight three days after his demise. According to his instruction, a Latin epitaph was inscribed in a slab fixed to the wall nearby, freely translated by Yeats three centuries later:

> Swift has sailed into his rest
> Savage indignation there
> Cannot lacerate his breast.
> Imitate him if you dare,
> World-besotted traveler; he
> Served human liberty.

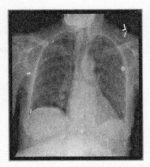

Miliary tuberculosis, often seen in the terminal stages of the disease. The lungs are filled with tiny nodules the size of millet seeds. (author's collection)

4. SOME SWEET POISONED BREEZE HAD PASSED INTO HER LUNGS: *The Brontës and Tuberculosis*

The stronger among the girls ran about and engaged in active games, but sundry pale and thin ones herded together for shelter and warmth in the verandah; and amongst these, as the dense mist penetrated to their shivering frames, I frequently heard the sound of a hollow cough.
—*Charlotte Brontë*, Jane Eyre

It was not immediately obvious that something was dreadfully wrong at the Clergy Daughters' School in the spring of 1825. The girls were always gaunt, dull, and listless, although an attentive observer would have noticed that they were gaunter, duller, and more listless than usual. That they were chronically undernourished was not surprising. Their breakfast was burnt oatmeal porridge, with "offensive fragments of other substances discoverable in it," followed by a dinner of "indifferent potatoes and strange shreds of rusty meat. . . . redolent of rancid fat." At five o'clock, the girls had half a slice of bread and a mug of coffee or sour milk, and at bedtime a piece of oatcake with a glass of greasy water. The food was often so revolting that the girls refused to eat, despite their constant hunger. Appetites were not augmented by the slovenly habits of the cook.

One schoolgirl later recalled, "I perfectly remember having once been sent for a cup of tea for a teacher who was ill in bed, and no teaspoon being at hand the housekeeper stirred the tea with her finger she being engaged in cutting raw meat at the time."

The Clergy Daughters' School was suffocatingly small. All fifty-three girls slept in a single room above the schoolhouse, two to each tiny bed. The students included four members of the Brontë family: Charlotte, who would include a scathing portrait of the school in *Jane Eyre,* her little sister Emily, and their older sisters Maria and Elizabeth. The oppressive brand of Christianity practised at the school added to the girls' miseries. The school had been founded by the Reverend William Carus Wilson, who was well known as a preacher and as a sort of writer for children. His demoralizing moral tales featured naughty little girls struck dead while lying or having temper tantrums, and condemned to an eternity of fiery torment. The curriculum featured heavy doses of sermon reading and scripture memorization. On Sundays, the girls walked across the windswept plain to the dank stone church two miles away for both morning and afternoon services, returning at night cold and hungry to the draughty dormitory. In the winter, they suffered from chilblains from trudging through the snow in their thin shoes, followed by hours of sitting in the frigid church with soaking feet.

Carus Wilson intended the Clergy Daughters' School to be a model institution. The social options for the daughters of poor clergymen were limited. They had no dowries and hence little chance of marrying well, and it was unthinkable that they would marry below their class. Thus they faced a lifetime of lonely spinsterhood. Still, suitably educated, they might at least be moulded into stoic and uncomplaining governesses. Only some of the costs of the school were paid by the parents; the remainder was raised from wealthy patrons.

The school did put an admirable premium on cleanliness. However, the girls were expected to wash up in the mornings with water that might literally be freezing cold; ice sometimes formed in the basins of water that had been left out the night before. Discipline was harsh. Punishments for girls who were academically backward or untidy included public humiliation and flogging.

A low-grade fever began to spread that spring, eventually affecting up to forty girls. Carus Wilson was oblivious to their growing emaciation, their coughing, and their spectral pallor in their white pinafores. However, he was alarmed when the stuporous girls became "too dull and heavy to understand remonstrances, or be roused by texts and spiritual exhortation." The doctor who was summoned inspected the kitchen, sampled a mouthful of food, and promptly spat it out upon the floor.

Of the fifty-three students at the school, one died there, and eleven others left the school in poor health. Six of these girls died shortly after leaving, including Maria and Elizabeth Brontë. Many of the other children, including young Charlotte and Emily, were permanently removed thereafter by their appropriately panicked parents. Carus Wilson had succeeded in making the Clergy Daughters' School a model, but not in the way that he had intended. With its gloom, crowding, and malnutrition, the Clergy Daughters' School was a model breeding ground for tuberculosis. It was the place where the seeds were planted that would destroy England's most famous literary family.

More claptrap has been written about the Brontës than any other group of English writers. This is especially true of their deaths, which have become fodder for the sort of speculation that reveals more about the psyche of the biographer than the afflictions of the subject: Charlotte died as a way of resolving her repressed sexual desire for her father; smothered by the Victorian patriarchy, Charlotte committed passive suicide by starvation; Emily starved herself to death to achieve mystical union with the Absolute; Emily and Charlotte had anorexia nervosa; Charlotte's death in pregnancy was due to hysterical rejection of the foetus. Most egregiously, "noted criminologist" James Tully revealed "a startling vision of the extraordinary truth" in his trashy novel *The Crimes of Charlotte Brontë*: Charlotte's husband, the dour, upright Reverend Arthur Bell Nicholls, was in reality a serial killer and lothario who impregnated Emily, poisoned her and her brother Branwell to shut them up, talked Charlotte into poisoning Anne, and finally bumped off Charlotte himself. Startling indeed! The worst aspect of all this nonsense is that the Brontës were tough-minded women who would have hated being portrayed as victims. Their personalities were most unusual, as were the circumstances that had shaped them.

Despite their exotic name, the Brontës were actually of Celtic extraction. Their father was born Patrick Brunty, or Prunty, as he sometimes spelled it, in County Down, Northern Ireland. His father, Hugh, was a Protestant small farmer with a reputation as a master storyteller; he may have been related to the eighteenth-century Gaelic poet and scholar Pádraig Ó' Prónntaigh. Like W. B. Yeats, young Pat Brunty was immersed from youth in Irish folklore, and his weird tales would later frighten and delight his children.

In the rising of 1798, one of the rebellions against English rule that regularly convulsed Ireland, Patrick's younger brother joined the United Irishmen, and went on the run after the rebels were defeated. The ensuing anarchy strengthened Patrick's innate conservatism and horror of revolution, although his views on poverty and social reform remained surprisingly liberal. (Charlotte, in particular, would inherit his Tory and anti-Catholic biases.) The rebellion may also have sparked Patrick's desire to get out of Ireland.

Patrick was a man of keen intelligence and unusual drive. At sixteen, he established a village school. He somehow managed to become proficient in Greek and Latin, and became a tutor to the children of one of the minor gentry. He used this connection to get accepted at Cambridge University, where he eked his way through with money from tutoring and academic prizes. At twenty-five years old, lanky and awkward, with a broad Northern Irish accent, he must have stood out among his classmates, who were much younger and generally from well-to-do and aristocratic families. In a vain attempt to fit in, he replaced his suspect Irish name with the more impressive-sounding Brontë, Greek for "thunder." The name Brontë also had patriotic overtones: England's greatest national hero, Horatio Nelson, had recently been made "Duke of Bronte" by the King of Naples.

After graduation Patrick was ordained, and worked in a succession of rural parishes. As a young curate, he was known for his two-fisted, physical approach to religion. On one occasion, he threw a drunk into a ditch for blocking a Sunday school procession; on another, he used his shillelagh to break up a church-bell-ringing contest that was disturbing the sanctity of the Sabbath. He also risked his life to rescue a boy from drowning in the River Calder. He was remembered as "clever and good-hearted, but hot-tempered, and in fact a little queer." Another early parishioner described him as "a very earnest man, but a little peculiar in his manner." Patrick later admitted to being "a little eccentric . . . [but] had I been numbered amongst the calm, concentric men of the world . . . I should in all probability never have had such children as mine have been." As a young clergyman in districts convulsed by strife between labour and mill owners, he started bringing loaded guns with him on his daily walks, a habit he would retain into old age. Tales told of him smashing furniture and burning rugs are probably untrue or overblown, but he once cut the sleeves off one of his wife's dresses that he considered too extravagant. (His daughters favoured dowdy attire, probably as a result of his influence.) The caricature of Patrick as a pistol-packing Hibernian misanthrope in the early Brontë biographies neglects his sensitive side: he also published short stories and books of poetry.

In 1812, Patrick married Maria Branwell, the witty and spirited daughter of a merchant from Cornwall. In six years, Maria gave birth to six children. The eldest, also named Maria, was mature and precocious, given to reading stacks of newspapers and conversing learnedly about politics with her father at the age of seven. A servant noted that she was "untidy," a trait that later caused much woe. The second eldest, Elizabeth, was "gentle," and the most ordinary of the Brontë children. Charlotte, like her father, was "excitable and hot-tempered." The long-desired son, Branwell, was impetuous and redheaded. Emily was remembered as having "the eyes of a half-tamed creature"; she "cared for nobody's opinion, only being happy with her animal pets." Anne, the youngest and prettiest, was the most bashful of a reserved and close-knit bunch.

In 1820, Patrick became vicar of the remote Yorkshire town of Haworth. His wife Maria died the following year after an illness of several months. Charlotte's biographer, Mrs Gaskell, blamed this on an "internal cancer." Uterine cancer has been suggested but seems unlikely, given Maria's youth and the protective effects of childbearing against premature endometrial cancer. Stomach cancer, common in that era, is more plausible. The term "cancer" was then used with less precision than today, so other diagnoses, such as a lingering abdominal infection, are also possible.

In her terminal illness, Maria cried out over and over, "O God, my poor children!" Although her spinster sister Elizabeth and a faithful old servant, Tabby, would help to raise the children, Maria's early death compounded the family's oddness and isolation. The Brontë children had little to do with the villagers. Charlotte sniffily blamed this on their residence "in a remote district, where education had made little progress, and where, consequently, there was no inducement to seek social intercourse beyond our own domestic circle." Mrs Gaskell went further, depicting Haworth as a barbarous, godforsaken frontier town. While this portrait was exaggerated, the Brontës' social horizons were limited by the peculiarly English predicament of the shabby genteel: too poor to mingle with the gentry, too proud to mix with common folk.

Quite apart from class considerations, the Brontës showed little inclination to socialize. Patrick took his clerical duties seriously, but was otherwise a man of "very retired habits," often absorbed in reading, who "did not require companionship, therefore he did not seek it, either in his walks, or in his daily life." With the exception of Branwell, who had other issues, the adult Brontë children struggled with crippling shyness.

The Brontës became highly self-sufficient. In Charlotte's words, "we were wholly dependent on ourselves and each other, on books and study, for the enjoyments and occupations of life." Patrick Brontë had a progressive attitude toward the education of women, and devoted time each morning and evening to the teaching of his children. In the afternoons, they were free to wander on the wild moors beyond the parsonage, an activity that was indispensable for Emily.

In 1824, Patrick made a fateful decision. Believing his young daughters needed further educational attainments to improve their prospects for marriage or employment as governesses, he sent them to the Clergy Daughters' School at Cowan Bridge in Lancashire, even though Maria and Elizabeth were in fragile health, having just recovered from measles and whooping cough. Maria and Elizabeth Brontë arrived at Cowan Bridge in July 1824, followed by Charlotte and Emily.

In *Jane Eyre*, the orphaned Jane is sent off to Lowood, a school for "charity-children." Lowood is a place of cold and hunger, loneliness and violence. The girls shiver in scanty clothes and the "Canadian temperature," and their feet blister and peel from being made to walk in the snow in the dead of winter. The paltry food they get is a "nauseous mess," and the girls dwindle into "semi-starvation." The teachers beat and bully them for trivial offences, and the big girls steal the food of the little ones. The director, Mr Brocklehurst, modelled on Carus Wilson, is "a harsh man; at once pompous and meddling," who "starved us . . . and bored us," and terrifies the girls with "evening readings from books of his own inditing, about sudden deaths and judgments, which made us afraid to go to bed."

A kind and stoic older girl, Helen Burns, with an ominous chronic cough, befriends Jane. Helen's untidiness makes her a favourite target for abuse at the hands of her sadistic teacher, Miss Scatcherd, who whips her and makes her wear the "untidy badge." Helen's cough turns to consumption, or what we would now call tuberculosis. As she wastes away, she re-assures Jane that "the illness which is removing me is not painful; it is gentle and gradual." When most of the girls fall ill with consumption or typhus, public outrage ensues and much-needed reforms result, but too late to help Helen Burns.

Charlotte always maintained that Lowood School was an accurate portrayal of Cowan Bridge. The bulk of the evidence does suggest that the Clergy Daughters' School was almost as bad as Lowood School in *Jane Eyre*. The best that can be said of it was that there were worse places of its kind.

By November 1824, Maria Brontë, the real-life model for Helen Burns, had developed a chronic cough and breathing problems. A doctor treated her by blistering her chest. It was wrongly believed that blisters on the skin overlying a diseased organ helped the inflammation escape. These blisters were produced by applying a poultice of melted wax and lard mixed with cantharides, a powder made from the crushed body of the blister beetle. (Cantharides is better known as the putative aphrodisiac Spanish fly. Would-be Lotharios added it to the food and drink of their unsuspecting quarry. The active compound, cantharidin, was excreted in the urine, leading to supposedly sexy bladder spasms and burning urine. Unwitting targets of seduction who ingested large doses could become seriously ill from bloody ulcers and erosions of the lining of the bladder and gut.) One morning when the ever-stoic Maria was in exquisite pain from her blisters and struggling to get dressed, Miss Andrews (Miss Scatcherd in *Jane Eyre*) grabbed her by her affected side, and loudly up-braided her in front of the other girls for her laziness and dirtiness. The memory still had the power to enrage Charlotte twenty-five years later.

By February 1825, Maria was gravely ill. Patrick brought her back to

Haworth, where she died three months later at age eleven. Three weeks after Maria's death, the school was shut down because of the epidemic. The girls who were well enough to travel were sent to Carus Wilson's house on the Lancashire coast. By this time, Elizabeth was also desperately sick, and was sent home. The day after she arrived, Patrick left to bring Charlotte and Emily home. Elizabeth died two weeks after her return. She was ten years old.

Given the insidious onset of illness, the prominent cough and weight loss, and the prolonged disease course, the epidemic at Cowan Bridge was almost certainly due to tuberculosis. Typhus was blamed for some of the deaths, but this seems unlikely. Typhus is spread by body lice. There does not seem to have been a lice problem at Cowan Bridge; one of its few virtues was a fanatic emphasis on bodily hygiene. Typhus is a fulminant disease, with raging fever, headache, muscle aches, a diffuse, sometimes bloody rash, and delirium; the patient dies or recovers within two weeks. Typhoid fever resulting from the unhygienic practices in the kitchen is more plausible. However, in the preantibiotic era, the usual duration of typhoid fever was about four weeks. Maria Brontë's more chronic course of illness over several months is not consistent with either typhus or typhoid, but would be typical of tuberculosis.

Many think of TB as a quaint disease of only historical interest. However, up to one-third of the world's population has latent infection with TB, and is thus at risk for developing active disease. Two million people die of TB yearly, according to the World Health Organization. In Africa, Asia, and parts of Latin America and the Caribbean, TB rages on unabated, and has actually enjoyed a resurgence due to the HIV epidemic. Prospects for control have dwindled with the recent spread of highly antibiotic-resistant TB strains.

It has long been believed that the bacteria that causes TB, *Mycobacterium tuberculosis,* arose from the bacteria which causes TB in cattle, *Mycobacterium bovis,* and that humans acquired TB about 8,000 to 10,000 years ago when cattle were domesticated. However, this view is probably mistaken. The earliest strains of TB likely evolved along with early humans in East Africa some two million years ago. About 70,000 years ago, cattle TB (*M. bovis*) split off from the bacterial ancestor of human TB.

Exactly how *M. bovis* jumped from humans to animals as diverse as cows, seals, and llamas is unknown, and perhaps unknowable. About 35,000 years ago, all modern strains of *M. tuberculosis* arose in East Africa, at a time when modern humans were migrating beyond Africa to Asia and Europe. The DNA of TB has been detected in four-thousand-year-old Egyptian mummies, and evidence for TB has been found in skeletal remains in much of the ancient world. TB was well known in antiquity to Greek, Roman, Hindu, and Chinese physicians. Hippocrates called it "phthisis," or wasting, because of the characteristic weight loss. (This wasting is a side effect of the huge amounts of chemical signals, or cytokines, which white cells pump out to boost the immune response.)

Until modern times, TB was probably present in most human populations worldwide, smouldering along at a low level. However, it spread explosively with the rapid growth of cities during the Industrial Revolution, as crowding and urbanization aided the spread of TB and many other infectious diseases. Population growth may have also favoured the emergence of more aggressive strains of TB at this time. Earlier in human history, when most people lived in small groups and population was relatively static, evolution may have favoured less virulent TB strains that would coexist with their hosts, instead of killing large numbers of them. But the increased agricultural productivity and more secure food supply that accompanied the Industrial Revolution led to soaring birth rates, ensuring that the supply of persons that were susceptible to TB was constantly replenished.

England was the epicentre of a TB epidemic that went global. At its peak in 1800, TB killed off up to 1 percent of the English population yearly, and death rates from TB remained high for most of the nineteenth century. In the United States, the TB epidemic crested in New England in 1800 (with an annual death rate as high as 1.6 percent), in New Orleans in 1840, and in the Western U.S. in the 1880s. The ensuing slow decline of TB in Europe and the Americas was probably due to better living conditions and improved nutrition, not antibiotics, which did not become available until much later.

Death rates were high enough that natural selection may also have played a role of the decline of TB. Genes enhancing resistance to TB may have been selected for in populations with heavy exposure. Unfortunately, genes that enhance the immune response to TB may increase the risk for various autoimmune diseases, such as rheumatoid arthritis, lupus, sarcoidosis, and Crohn's disease, in which the body is damaged by its own hyperactive immune system.

TB spreads from person to person through the air. When a person with active TB coughs, they generate aerosols containing bacteria suspended in sputum. This is especially likely if TB has created cavities in the lungs. Some of these airborne secretions dry out, and turn into tiny "droplet nuclei," which stay aloft and viable for several hours. Droplet nuclei are the ideal size to drift into the deepest recesses of the lungs, the alveoli, without getting filtered out by the airways.

Once TB gains a foothold in the lungs, there are many possible outcomes. Some people have exceptional natural resistance to the disease: their lung macrophages, amoeba-like immune cells, engulf the bacteria and destroy them completely. In those with poor resistance, the bacteria multiply unchecked, leading to death from overwhelming infection in weeks to months. This is particularly common in children—as may have happened to some of the girls at the

TUBERCULOSIS AND CYSTIC FIBROSIS

Rather oddly, cystic fibrosis (CF), which is associated with severe, recurrent lung infections in children and young adults, may be another condition that has become more common because of genetic selection for TB resistance. About one in twenty-five Caucasians carry a defective gene encoding a protein known as CFTR, the cystic fibrosis transmembrane regulator. The child of two carriers has a 25 percent chance of inheriting two bad copies of the gene, and developing CF. The high frequency of defects in the CFTR gene in persons of northern European ancestry has always been perplexing. Although survival in CF has improved dramatically in recent years, before the modern era, it led to early death from lung infections, malnutrition, or diabetes in most affected children. This should have reduced the frequency of the defective gene to very low levels. The explanation seems to be that having a single bad copy of the gene may protect against death from TB by impairing the function of another protein called arylsulphatase, which *Mycobacterium tuberculosis* needs to manufacture part of its cell wall.

Clergy Daughters' School—but in most patients, the outcome of infection is a sort of bacteriological cold war, in which the immune system attempts to contain the bacteria in enclosures called granulomas. Within the granuloma, dormant bacteria are suspended in cheesy material known as caseum, surrounded by a palisade of macrophages. Idle TB bacilli in granulomas may remain viable for up to several decades, a condition known as latent TB infection. These patients appear well, but infection may be detected by a skin test with purified protein derivative (PPD), or through a recently developed blood test called an interferon-gamma release assay. Sometimes, flecks of calcium appear in granulomas, allowing them to be seen on a chest X-ray.

Today, patients with latent infection are treated with nine months of an antibiotic called isoniazid to prevent the development of active infection. In 10 percent of untreated patients with latent TB, the immune system weakens, and the process of containment breaks down. The cheesy caseum liquifies and is coughed up, and the patient develops a lung cavity teeming with enormous numbers of TB bacilli. In the preantibiotic era, some patients might be able to contain the infection again, but at a huge cost. Each relapse of active infection results in healthy lung tissue being replaced by scar tissue.

Many factors enhance the spread and virulence of TB. Crowding increases the likelihood of inhaling another person's TB bacilli. Poor nutrition, stress, and depression weaken the immune response. As Charlotte would note in Shirley, "People never die of love or grief alone; though some die of inherent maladies, which the tortures of those passions prematurely force into destructive action." Exposure to smoke and air pollution reduce the effectiveness of the first line of defence, the ability of lung macrophages to eradicate TB bacilli. (Poor air quality and rampant cigarette smoking may be facilitating the spread of TB in developing countries today.) Certain age groups—infants, the elderly, adolescents, and young adults—are particularly vulnerable to active TB infection. Heavy drinking is probably an independent risk factor, although this is difficult to disentangle from the poverty and stress that usually accompany alcoholism. Married people are less likely to have TB than singles or the divorced, perhaps because of their lower risk of depression.

TB can spread with awful efficiency in confined spaces, such as prisons, schools, and homeless shelters. Patients with lung cavities are notoriously effective at dispersing Mycobacterium tuberculosis in these settings. In 1992, one tuberculous patron of a tavern in Minneapolis was shown to have infected at least forty-one of his fellow drinkers. In an outbreak on a single U.S. Navy vessel in 1998, twenty-one cases of active TB and 712 cases of latent TB developed among the contacts of a single Marine with pulmonary tuberculosis who went untreated for three months.

If Maria and Elizabeth Brontë died of TB, as seems likely, one of the major effects of their illness was to expose all of their remaining siblings to this highly contagious and virulent infection that may linger in the body for decades, silently awaiting its opportunity.

The loss of Maria and Elizabeth was devastating to the younger Brontës. Maria, in particular, had been a mother to the rest, who barely remembered their real mother. Back in the protective cocoon of family and parsonage, the surviving children, Charlotte, Branwell, Emily, and Anne, withdrew into a lush fantasy world of their own making. Emily would never emerge from it.

When Patrick gave Branwell a box of toy soldiers, the children invented a tropical land called Angria, chronicled in elaborate playacting, maps, and miniscule booklets. This was at first a masculine world of warfare and revolution. As Charlotte grew into adolescence, her contribution became less political and more romantic. Eventually, Emily and Anne became dissatisfied with Angria, and spun off their own kingdom of Gondal, a less exotic realm that was more like their native Yorkshire. Perhaps it resembled the milieu of *Wuthering Heights*. We will never know, as someone destroyed almost all the Gondal writings after the deaths of Emily and Anne. This has generally been assumed to be Charlotte, who disapproved of the morbid tendencies of Emily's and Anne's novels, censored Emily's poems, and may also have destroyed Emily's unfinished second novel. This is somewhat ironic, as Victorian critics had similar moral qualms about Charlotte's own novels.

The Angrian and Gondal writings were a distraction from the children's losses, and a welcome escape from the humdrum routine of the parsonage. They were an intense source of emotional experience, especially for Emily and Anne, who seem never to have been involved in a serious romantic relationship. And they were also a literary apprenticeship that led to the writing of two great novels, *Jane Eyre* and *Wuthering Heights*.

Branwell and Charlotte were preoccupied with Angria for over a decade. Although they outgrew the world of the juvenilia, Emily never did. We have a glimpse of her at twenty-six, in a surviving diary paper. She and Anne have taken a train trip to York, a rare excursion away from Haworth. But the breathless highlight of the journey for Emily was acting out the roles of "Ronald Macelgin, Henry Angora, Juliet Augusteena, Rosobelle Esraldan, Ella and Julian Egramont, Catherine Navarre and Cordelia Fitzaphnold escaping from the Palaces of Instruction to join the Royalists who are hard driven at present by the victorious Republicans." One wonders what their fellow passengers thought of these two odd women.

At fourteen, Charlotte went away to Roe Head, a local boarding school. One of the lifelong friends she made there, Mary Taylor, described her first impression of Charlotte, wearing "very old-fashioned clothes" and looking "like a little old woman, so short-sighted that she always appeared to be seeking something." (All the Brontë children were myopic from their early and continual reading and writing.) She was "very shy and nervous, and spoke with a strong Irish accent." Charlotte must have taken pains to lose her father's accent, as it was not remarked on later. Mary informed Charlotte that she was "very ugly," but soon was humbled by the force of Charlotte's intellect and her aptitude for art and poetry. Although Charlotte's time at Roe Head was generally happy, she returned to Haworth the next year, taking over the education of her sisters.

At nineteen, Charlotte returned to Roe Head as a teacher, accompanied by seventeen-year-old Emily. Like some wild creature wrenched from its native habitat and put on show in a zoo, Emily faltered beyond the bounds of the parsonage, becoming homesick with the disruption of her "very noiseless, very secluded" way of life. According to Charlotte, her symptoms were alarmingly similar to those that preceded the demise of Maria and Elizabeth: "In this struggle her health was quickly broken: her white face, attenuated form, and failing strength threatened rapid decline. I felt in my heart she would die if she did not go home, and with this conviction obtained her recall." Emily returned home, and Anne took her place at Roe Head. It is unclear whether Emily's symptoms were wholly psychological, or whether she also was ill with early tuberculosis or some other physical ailment. In any case, she recovered back in Haworth, free once again to wander on the moors and scribble tales of Gondal.

In the following year, 1836, Charlotte had the first of several depressive episodes. The first one was precipitated by a perceived conflict between her teaching duties and the seductive lure of the world of the imagination. Duty lost, and her mood brightened the next year when she rededicated herself to poetry. Unfortunately, as Charlotte recovered, Anne's health began to break down. Anne also had a period of depressed mood, brought on in her case by religious guilt and doubt. Thus weakened, she developed a febrile illness that left her "wretchedly ill" and short of breath: "Neither the pain nor the difficulty of breathing left her." This episode may represent Anne's first signs of TB, or it might have been a self-limited attack of bacterial pneumonia. Like Emily before her, Anne made a gradual recovery on her return to Haworth. Charlotte's mood darkened again in 1838, and she too left Roe Head for good, suffering from "heavy gloom" and "mental and bodily anguish."

Emily took a job as a schoolteacher in 1839, had another mental and physical breakdown, and went home yet again. Meanwhile, Charlotte had recovered enough to take a position as a governess. Unfortunately, as her first biographer Mrs Elizabeth Gaskell noted, "neither she nor her sisters were naturally fond of children." In that same year, she turned down two proposals of marriage, including one from her father's curate, partly on the grounds that he was Irish.

In 1842, Charlotte somehow talked Emily into travelling with her to Brussels to study French and German at a large boarding school, with the idea that a broader education would help them open their own school for girls back in Haworth. They were lucky that the teacher, Monsieur Heger, recognized their abilities and encouraged their writing. Heger, a distinguished scholar in his own right, was especially impressed with Emily, ranking her "genius as something higher even than Charlotte's." She "had a head for logic, and a capability of argument, unusual in a man, and rare indeed in a woman," but "her stubborn tenacity of will . . . rendered her obtuse to all reasoning where her own wishes, or her own sense of right, was concerned." Heger thought it was a pity that Emily was not born a man, and called her "egotistical and exacting compared to Charlotte, who was always unselfish." Emily and Charlotte were soon taken on as teachers, Charlotte for English and Emily, an able pianist, for music. Charlotte was more popular than the introverted, inflexible Emily, with one striking exception. The only friend Emily is ever known to have made was a sixteen-year-old student named Louise de Bassompierre. Emily gave her a fine pencil sketch of a storm-blasted pine tree. Louise thought that Emily was kinder and more approachable than Charlotte; she was perhaps the only person ever to think so.

At the end of 1842, Charlotte and Emily returned to Haworth. Although Emily had suffered less severely from homesickness in Brussels, she was happy to resume her life of cooking, cleaning, scribbling, and rambling on the moors. Charlotte returned to Brussels, and developed an unrequited passion for Heger, who was married and had a large brood of children. Charlotte, a lonely, vulnerable, and naïve young woman, was captivated by his intense teaching style, which alternated between bullying and conciliation. This led to another depressive episode, severe enough to lead her to thoughts of conversion to Catholicism, despite her prejudices. (Charlotte's love letters to Heger were preserved by Heger's wife, who sewed them back together from the torn fragments she found in her husband's trash.)

Charlotte returned to Haworth in early 1844, and continued to write to Heger for the next year, desperately craving the intellectual and emotional stimulation that he had provided. Although Mrs Gaskell carefully suppressed the whole episode, it caused a literary sensation in 1913 when four of Charlotte's letters to Heger finally came to light. Charlotte's passion for Heger informed her first, posthumously published novel, *The Professor*, and inspired her final novel, *Villette*.

Charlotte's scheme to start a school for girls in Haworth came to nothing, to the relief of all the sisters. A modest inheritance from Aunt Branwell removed immediate financial pressures, freeing the sisters to concentrate on writing. In 1845, Charlotte stumbled upon some of Emily's poems, was thrilled at their "peculiar music—wild, melancholy, and elevating." She tried to talk Emily into publishing them together with poems by Charlotte and Anne. Emily, secretive even with family, was outraged at this invasion of her privacy, but eventually relented: "My sister Emily was not a person of demonstrative character, nor one, on the recesses of whose mind and feelings, even those nearest and dearest to her could, with impunity, intrude unlicensed; it took hours to reconcile her to the discovery I had made, and days to persuade her that such poems merited publication." Emily and Anne agreed, but insisted on anonymous publication, so the sisters adopted the gender-neutral pseudonyms of Currer, Ellis, and Acton Bell. Despite respectable reviews, their self-financed publication of *Poems* in 1846 was an epic flop: only two copies were sold. But seeing their work in print spurred them on to more ambitious efforts. Charlotte wrote *The Professor,* only to have it rejected for publication nine times in her lifetime. Anne completed her fine *Agnes Grey,* a scathing account of the travails of a Victorian governess, based on her six miserable years of personal experience. Emily wrote her astonishing *Wuthering Heights,* an intricately plotted tale of love and revenge, featuring the charismatic and monstrous Heathcliff. In a bit of ominous foreshadowing, three of the major characters in *Wuthering Heights,* the sickly brother and sister, Isabella and Edgar Linton, and Isabella's feeble son Linton, die of a prolonged wasting illness consistent with TB, accurately reflecting the high attack rates for TB within households. *Agnes Grey* (by "Acton Bell") and *Wuthering Heights* (by "Ellis Bell") were not published until December 1847. By then, Charlotte's second novel, *Jane Eyre,* had become a publishing sensation.

Much of the excitement over *Jane Eyre* was due to the radical departure of its central character from the meek and submissive women of Victorian literature. Jane is "poor, obscure, plain, and little," but strong and stubborn, like Charlotte herself. *Jane Eyre* succeeds brilliantly as page-turning melodrama and tart social satire, especially in its first two-thirds, which Charlotte wrote quickly and in a heightened state of inspiration. *Jane Eyre,* like much novel writing, is partly wish fulfilment, but Charlotte's style and invention make Jane and Rochester's unlikely romance plausible. (Charlotte would revisit this scenario in *Villette,* but with a more realistic outcome.) A final, key element of the success of *Jane Eyre* was the mystery of the real identity and gender of its pseudonymous author, Currer Bell.

Success leads inevitably to reaction. Critics began to attack *Jane Eyre* and *Wuthering Heights* for their coarseness and presumed immorality. These attacks intensified with the appearance of Anne's second novel, *The*

Tenant of Wildfell Hall, the story of a woman's flight from her drunken, abusive husband, and perhaps the best case in literature for the proposition that men are dogs. Indignation was further stoked by Charlotte's revelation, after the deaths of Emily and Anne, that the Bells were the virginal daughters of a country vicar. How could proper women write such indecent and improper stuff?

After Charlotte's death, her friend and fellow novelist Mrs Gaskell defended her in *The Life of Charlotte Brontë,* which depicted Charlotte as the docile exemplar of conventional Victorian morality. This portrait was partly true, but concealed a fairly obvious fact: the saintly automaton of Mrs Gaskell's *Life* could not have written *Jane Eyre.* Charlotte was equally influenced by the Bible and Lord Byron. The tension between pious Charlotte and passionate, not-so-nice Charlotte is often reflected in her fiction and her life. We have already seen how Mrs Gaskell covered up Charlotte's infatuation with Heger. It is also worthy of note that Mrs Gaskell largely concealed what she called "the slight astringencies in her character," or what one modern commentator, Lucasta Miller, less daintily calls "Charlotte-as-bitch."

Unfortunately, the gathering controversy over the Bell novels was soon overshadowed by tragedy at home. Branwell Brontë once described himself, only too accurately, as a man of "strong passions and weak principles." His family thought of Branwell as the most talented of the Brontës, but his short, erratic life was a series of increasingly squalid misadventures. He had literary gifts, and was a published poet, but lacked the application of his sisters. Limited abilities ended his career as a portrait painter (Charlotte, Emily, and Anne all had more artistic talent than he did). He was fired from a good job as a railway clerk over a missing sum of money, and sacked from one tutoring post after impregnating a servant girl. He suffered from exalted moods and black depressions; it has been suggested that he had bipolar disorder. One friend noted he was "blithe and gay, but at times appeared downcast and sad." Another remembered him as a "morbid man, who couldn't bear to be alone."

Branwell became a tutor to the sons of a rich invalid, and was seduced by the man's wife, a woman fifteen years his senior. Appropriately enough, her name was Mrs Robinson. She must have possessed considerable force of personality, as she was no great beauty. For two and a half years,

Branwell enjoyed "daily troubled pleasure," before the sickly husband found out and threatened to kill him. When the husband died a year later, the grieving widow made it clear to a heartbroken Branwell that marriage was out of the question, as this would terminate her income from the estate.

After this disappointment, Branwell unravelled, to the dismay and disgust of his sisters. Mrs Robinson sent sums of money, presumably to keep him busy and out of the way, money that fuelled a growing dependence on opium and gin. Branwell now fulfilled his childhood fantasies of the drug-addled, self-destructive poet, but the reality was less glamorous than he had imagined. Dead drunk after one spree, he set his bed on fire and would have incinerated both himself and the parsonage, save for Emily's presence of mind in tossing him and the burning bedclothes to the floor and dousing the flames. As he deteriorated, gripped by mania or delirium tremens, he imagined himself tormented by devils. His final poem was an obscene lampoon on his physician. In September 1848, after eight "months of such utter sleeplessness violent cough and frightful agony of mind," he died of tuberculosis, accelerated by his alcoholism and mood problems.

Shortly after Branwell's death, Charlotte grew anxious for the health of her sisters, especially Emily. "Emily's cough and cold are very obstinate; I fear she has pain in the chest—and I sometimes catch a shortness in her breathing when she has moved at all quickly—she looks very, very thin and pale . . . it is useless to question her—you get no answers—it is still more useless to recommend remedies—they are never adopted." In *Wuthering Heights,* Emily wrote scornfully of the "self-absorbed moroseness of a confirmed invalid," perhaps with Branwell's dramatic excesses in mind. In her own terminal illness, she adopted the equally harmful position of steadfast denial.

Emily Brontë was a strange woman. The slubs in her personality were part of the fabric of her genius, but they also helped to hasten her demise. One possible explanation for her peculiarities is Asperger syndrome. The first diagnostic criterion for Asperger syndrome is impairment in social interaction. Some of our ability to respond to other people's nonverbal cues may be hardwired and intuitive, rather than learned, and these functions may be specifically impaired in Asperger syndrome. On social occasions,

"Emily hardly uttered more than a monosyllable." Acquaintances noted that Emily "could not easily associate with others," and had an "extreme reserve with strangers," perhaps suggesting an element of social phobia, also common in Asperger syndrome. According to one of Emily's biographers, she "seems not even to notice human beings, especially males." Emily told her students that she liked animals better than people. Mrs Gaskell wrote that Emily "never showed regard to any human creature; all her love was reserved for animals."

People with Asperger syndrome are inflexible and logical to a fault, which compounds their social difficulties. According to Charlotte, Emily "was not very flexible . . . her spirit altogether unbending." Mrs Gaskell called her "impervious to influence . . . her own decision of what was right and fitting was a law for her conduct and appearance." Heger marvelled at Emily's "head for logic" and "stubborn tenacity of will": "She should have been a man—a great navigator . . . her strong, imperious will would never have been daunted by opposition or difficulty; never have given way but with life."

The second diagnostic criterion for Asperger syndrome is restricted, repetitive patterns of behaviour, interests, and activities. We have seen how Emily's absorption in the fantasy world of Gondal preoccupied her until her death. People with Asperger syndrome have trouble coping with change, and prefer familiar routines; away from the parsonage, Emily became both physically and emotionally unwell.

Finally, people with Asperger syndrome have clinically significant impairment in social, occupational, and other functioning. Emily failed dismally as a teacher, and was unable to function outside the narrow bounds of home. According to Lucasta Miller, Emily "never seems to have made a single significant friend outside her immediate family." (This is not entirely accurate, as Emily apparently made one friend in Belgium.) Perhaps, like many other persons with Asperger syndrome, she wanted to make friends, but lacked the social graces to do so.

Asperger syndrome is four times more common in men than women. There is evidence that high foetal testosterone levels increase the risk for autism and Asperger syndrome, in both boys and girls. The Cambridge psychologist Simon Baron-Cohen has suggested that Asperger syndrome results from an "extreme male brain": strong on logic and organization, weak on emotion and empathy. (Men may be unsettled by Baron-Cohen's vision of testosterone as a foetal toxin that impairs empathy.) Women with Asperger syndrome in one study were more likely to be tomboyish and either asexual or bisexual. Emily was known as "the Major" because of her domineering ways and her "unparalleled intrepidity and firmness." Heger thought her personality masculine and aggressive. Her writings and sketches display a vigorous interest in violence; Mrs Gaskell tells a disturbing anecdote about Emily mercilessly beating her dog for its misbehaviour, and then tenderly nursing its wounds. The coltish Emily was also an able markswoman who enjoyed target practice with her father in the garden, in between her baking in the kitchen.

According to the Irish psychiatrist Michael Fitzgerald, the Asperger personality has several traits favourable to successful writing. Their interests may be narrow, but they pursue them with workaholic zeal; they may have excellent memory retention for detail; their unique perspective and lack of interest in the opinions of others lead them into original subject matter and means of expression; they often have superior verbal skills; and they may find that artistic creation is therapeutic, a means of overcoming their failure to express themselves in more conventional ways. However, the few scientific studies of creativity in Asperger syndrome showed that patients tended to be excessively literal and had reduced creativity.

Is it possible to square this finding with the occurrence of Asperger traits in some writers? The Asperger patients studied at academic centres may be more dysfunctional than the average person with Asperger syndrome. Writers with Asperger traits may only have a mild form, or *forme fruste*, of Asperger syndrome. (This could also be regarded simply as introversion, a healthy variant within the range of normal personalities.) Or creativity in writers with Asperger syndrome may be modified by other factors related to creativity, such as genes predisposing to mood disorder. This last explanation is especially tempting in Emily's case, given her strong family history of mood disorder, and her own episodes of depression.

If Emily had Asperger syndrome, is this reflected in *Wuthering Heights*? A comparison of *Wuthering Heights* to *Jane Eyre*, both novels of turbulent romance, shows that Emily and Charlotte had vastly different attitudes toward passionate love. In *Jane Eyre*, love is an emotion that is intimately experienced and long repressed, but ultimately and happily fulfilled. In *Wuthering Heights*, passion is seen only from the outside; we are doubly distanced from Heathcliff and Cathy by Emily's ingenious use of two narrators, the obtuse Lockwood and the earthy Nelly Dean. People with Asperger syndrome have trouble grasping and processing the emotions of themselves and others; in *Wuthering Heights*, passion is a powerful, mysterious, irrational, and ultimately destructive force.

Emily had two additional features sometimes seen in Asperger syndrome. She wandered on the moors for hours, and may have been physically hyperactive; her refusal to rest and abandon her usual routines and duties probably sped the course of the tuberculosis that killed her. Persons with autism may have an unusually high pain tolerance; after a dog bite, Emily once cauterized her own arm with a red-hot iron to prevent rabies. Charlotte marvelled at Emily's stoicism in her final illness: "Day by day, when I saw with what a front she met suffering, I looked on her with an anguish of wonder and love . . . on herself she had no pity; the spirit was inexorable to the flesh."

How did Emily get TB? Was she infected as a child from her tuberculous sisters Maria and Elizabeth, with reactivation decades later? Or did her infection come from exposure to Branwell, during his many months of hacking bacilli about the parsonage? Either alternative is possible, and there is no definite answer, although the timing of her illness suggests that Branwell was the immediate source. Branwell's own TB might have been reactivation of infection latent in his own lungs since the illnesses of Maria and Elizabeth, or he could have been infected more recently, especially while boozing in the taverns of Haworth.

Fearless, foolish Emily fought until the end, after months of stubborn denial, months of wasting away, months of chest pain that froze her in mid-breath, months of her cough echoing off the damp stone floors. On November 2, 1848, Charlotte wrote of Emily's "slow inflammation of the lungs" and her perverse denial: "She is a real stoic in illness, she neither seeks nor will accept sympathy . . . you must look on, and see her do what she is unfit to do, and not dare say a word." Emily refused all medication as "quackery" and refused to see a doctor. She was right about the uselessness of the medicines then available, but a doctor might have at least persuaded her to rest, conserve her strength, and build up her weight. Later in the month, a desperate Charlotte even tried reverse psychology: "It is usually best to leave her to form her own judgment and *especially* not to advocate the side you wish her to favour; if you do she is sure to lean in the opposite direction, and ten to one will argue herself into non-compliance." Charlotte wrote of Emily's "hollow, wasted, pallid aspect," "pain in the chest and side," "deep tight cough," and "rapid pant" with minimal exertion. "Her pulse, the only time she allowed it to be felt, was found to be at 115 per minute." Emily's rapid pulse suggests both anaemia, common in chronic infections, as well as the failure of her lungs to load her bloodstream with oxygen. Chest pain is common in TB. It can sometimes point to a pleural effusion, or accumulation of fluid between the lung and the chest wall, which would further increase her shortness of breath.

In December, Emily's "emaciation, cough, weakness, shortness of breath" continued, and was now associated with diarrhoea, an ominous complaint that probably indicated the spread of TB to the bowel, causing malabsorption and more wasting away. On December 18, she nearly collapsed feeding the dogs; leaning in the passage, gasping for air, she pushed her panicked sisters away. The next morning she rose, tried to brush her hair, dropped the comb in the fire, and was too weak to save it from the flames that burnt the teeth to nubs. She somehow dressed and teetered down the stairs and took up her sewing as if it were any other day. By noon her breath came in harsh and dissonant rasps that seemed to issue from some subterranean bellows. When her father carried her upstairs she was so thin it was like carrying a child. The doctor came and went and left no hope behind. Emily's unblinking blue eyes, enormous in their cavernous sockets, grew filmy, their lustre fading slowly in the winter light. When she was gone, her poor dog Keeper howled outside her door for days.

Emily's death was especially devastating for Charlotte. Their relationship was forged of complex bonds of love, rivalry, and awe. Yet no relief was in sight. Even as Emily began her terminal decline, Anne fell ill with the familiar, foreboding symptoms of cough, chest pain, and wasting.

The major biographer of the Brontës writes of Emily and Anne that "the known facts of their lives could be written on a single sheet of paper." This is especially true of gentle, patient Anne. She is supposed to have been in love with her father's puckish curate William Weightman, who died young. She had devout if unorthodox religious beliefs. She was uncomfortable with the dogma that a merciful God would bother to create humans, only to damn them to hell for all eternity, and believed instead that all souls would eventually be saved. Like her more famous sisters, Anne was timid in person, but ferocious in print: the combative feminism of *The Tenant of Wildfell Hall* was a century ahead of its time.

A tuberculosis specialist from Leeds named Mr Teale visited Anne at the parsonage. He prescribed cod liver oil, which may have helped. The vitamin D it contains boosts the body's production of cathelicidin, a protein with antibiotic effects that helps immune cells kill off TB. Mr Teale also prescribed iron supplements. Surprisingly, these may have been harmful. One of the body's primitive defences against infection is to temporarily reduce the availability of iron, which is why patients with TB are usually anaemic. This is bad for the patient, but the harm may be outweighed by the benefit of denying iron to the bacteria, which need it for growth and reproduction. Evidence from Africa suggests that higher iron levels raise the risk of TB. Anne did what she was told, and lasted a little longer than Emily had, perhaps simply because she had common sense enough to rest. She died peacefully on a visit to Scarborough in May 1849, with Charlotte at her side.

Charlotte was enveloped by gloom after the death of her last remaining sibling. She fell prey to insomnia. To sleep, she pushed her body to the point of exhaustion. She trod for hours round the table in the garish crimson parlour in the parsonage, now in the flickering cylinder of light from the oil lamp, now in the shadows. She and Emily and Anne had once spent evenings circling around this same table, talking hopefully of the books that they would write and the shape of their lives to come. Memories may have simmered in her mind: her mother with baby Anne on some distant luminous morning; the years before Maria and Elizabeth died, when all six children filled the parlour, playing, reading, scribbling; Emily hauling a besotted Branwell, mawkish and maundering, home from the Black Bull. Frail puny Charlotte and her father had outlived them all.

As so often with Charlotte, she coped with pain by turning to her writing. She finished *Shirley,* a reactionary novel of riot and romance set in Yorkshire during the Napoleonic Wars; it had previously been set aside when Branwell died. The titular character of Shirley Keeldar, a bold, confident, and intellectual young woman, was based on Emily. The emotional climax of the novel is reached when the other female protagonist, Caroline Helstone, develops an illness with which Charlotte was only too familiar: "Some sweet poisoned breeze, redolent of honey-dew and miasma, had passed into her lungs and veins . . . she wasted like any snow-wreath in thaw; she faded like any flower in drought."

Charlotte visited London several times. She began to drop her anonymity and made herself known to a small circle of literary acquaintances, especially the novelist Mrs Gaskell, who became a close friend. Thackeray mortified her by loudly introducing her to his mother as "Jane Eyre." She still struggled in society from her exceeding shyness and awkwardness, and preferred the comforts of home. Her health was tenuous. She suffered periodically from cough, fever, headache, and poor appetite. On one occasion, she was prescribed "blue pills," whose active ingredient was mercury, that worthless if enduring remedy. She correctly diagnosed herself with mercury poisoning when "my mouth became sore, my teeth loose, my tongue swelled, raw, and ulcerated while water welled continually into my mouth." (The doctor blamed Charlotte's "exceptional sensitiveness of constitution," rather than any error on his part in calculating the dosage.) This episode probably increased Charlotte's morbid self-consciousness about her looks, which she wrongly regarded as "almost repulsive."

In 1853, her accomplished, ironic final novel, *Villette,* was published, based on her years in Brussels and her infatuation with Monsieur Heger. Charlotte struggled with depression while trying to finish it, which explains why its end is so much less inspired than its beginning. The character of Dr Bretton, who rejects the narrator Lucy Snowe, was based on Charlotte's charming publisher George Smith, with whom she had conducted a futile epistolary flirtation.

In 1854, at the age of thirty-eight, she married one of her father's succession of Irish curates, Arthur Bell Nicholls. He was a tall, handsome, and sober man, if intellectually dull by Charlotte's standards. Two years before, Patrick, whose understanding of women was slim, did the only thing that could possibly have made Charlotte take him seriously as a suitor: he refused Nicholls permission to propose to her. Patrick thought that Nicholls was beneath her. His contempt was increased by the curate's comically mopey and lovesick behaviour, which Patrick regarded as ignoble and unmanly. Patrick had another concern that he concealed from Charlotte: he worried that her health was not robust enough to stand the strain of pregnancy. Nicholls and Charlotte persisted, and Patrick finally agreed to the match under extreme duress. He did not attend the ceremony. The marriage was a happy one, but it would be tragically brief.

Charlotte and Arthur honeymooned in Ireland with his relatives, where she was worn out with "fatigue and excitement": "my cough has become very bad—but Mrs Bell has nursed me both with kindness and skill." She was thereafter quite well until she became pregnant six months later. In early January 1855, she developed mild nausea, or what she called "continual faint sickness." Her condition worsened over the following weeks. On February 2, 1855, Patrick wrote, "She has been confined to her bed, where she still lies, oppressed with nausea, sickness, irritation, and a slow feverish feeling—and a consequent want of appetite and indigestion."

The first trimester of pregnancy is usually accompanied by at least some degree of queasiness. This is familiarly known as "morning sickness," although it may persist throughout the day. This nausea may be a side effect of pregnancy-related hormones, such as chorionic gonadotropin, which stimulates nausea centres in the brainstem, and progesterone, which interferes with stomach emptying. It has been suggested that nausea in early pregnancy evolved to protect the developing foetus from dietary toxins by forcing the mother to eat the blandest, least harmful foods during the time period in which the foetus is most vulnerable to birth defects.

When nausea and vomiting in pregnancy is severe, it is known as hyperemesis gravidarum. Charlotte was unlucky enough to be one of the 1 percent of pregnant women who develop hyperemesis, but she was suffering from more than just nausea. On February 14, Arthur reported that she had "weakness & sickness & frequent fever." Fever is not a feature of hyperemesis gravidarum. Pregnancy generally does not affect the course of TB either for better or worse. However, in Charlotte's case, progressive malnutrition from incessant vomiting likely tipped the balance of her long fight against tuberculosis away from her immune system, and toward the tubercle bacilli. (A less likely, but still possible, explanation for Charlotte's severe nausea and vomiting is that she was not pregnant at all, but suffering from Addison's disease, or failure of the adrenal glands. The adrenal glands are frequently involved in advanced tuberculosis. Patients with Addison's disease may have severe nausea and vomiting, weight loss, weakness, low blood pressure, and electrolyte disturbances. The disease was invariably fatal before the availability of corticosteroid therapy, such as prednisone.)

On February 17, Charlotte felt it was necessary to write a will. Soon after, she started to retch up blood. She was so weak that she could say no more than a few words at a time. In one brief letter she managed to write, she noted her "skeletal emaciation." By March, she could not hold a pencil at all, and she entered a "low wandering delirium." Patrick said to their servant Martha, "I told you, Martha, that there was no sense in Charlotte marrying at all, for she was not strong enough for marriage." By March 31, she was dead. The doctor who attended her gave the cause of death as "phthisis"—tuberculosis.

The clinical illnesses of Charlotte and her siblings were all consistent with TB, an extremely common disease in the Victorian era. There is no evidence to support the more extravagant diagnoses that have been proposed, such as poisoning, passive suicide, anorexia nervosa, or hysteria. There was also a substantial family burden of psychiatric illness, which included both Asperger syndrome (certainly in Emily, and possibly in Patrick as well) and mood disorder (Branwell likely had bipolar disorder; Charlotte and Emily certainly had depression).

The remarkable creativity of the Brontë family suggests that there may be specific inherited and biographical features that are conducive to literary genius. These include a genetic endowment that predisposes to both mood disorder and Asperger syndrome, thus infusing a rich lode of emotional experience into an intellect with superior verbal skills, highly detailed memories, and an obsessive work ethic. Early life traumas, such as parental loss, also favour literary achievement by increasing the likelihood that a mood disorder becomes manifest. To nurture this potential, individuals must be exposed to a cultural milieu which values literature, and ideally one which encourages creative writing at a young age. (It is probably also helpful if there is a financial incentive to literary creation.) This unusual powderkeg of volatile and potentially incompatible and maladaptive elements would explain why literary genius is both rare, and prone to misfiring in spectacular ways.

Nathaniel Hawthorne, before and after his trip to Europe. While there, Hawthorne was worn down by drink, depression, family illnesses, and the stress of public appearances. (Left: Peabody Essex Museum. Right: Courtesy of the Library of Congress)

5. DISMAL LABYRINTH OF DOUBT:
The Strange Death of Nathaniel Hawthorne

Certain it is, however, that there was a great consultation and dispute of doctors over the dead body.
   —*Nathaniel Hawthorne,* The House of the Seven Gables

Oliver Wendell Holmes Sr was the most celebrated doctor of mid-nineteenth-century America. Along with the doomed Hungarian physician Ignaz Semmelweis, he is recognized as the father of infection control. In his groundbreaking study of childbed fever, Holmes had argued that physicians might wish to avoid performing autopsies immediately before delivering babies, or if this was unavoidable, they should at least try to change their clothes and wash their hands in between. (This mild and seemingly self-evident recommendation generated fierce opposition.) He had been dean of Harvard Medical School, and coined the word *anaesthesia*. He helped introduce American medicine to that newfangled French device, the stethoscope. He was a poet and novelist, an empiricist and sceptic, a scientist and inventor. He was also, in accordance with the highest ethical and professional standards of his time, a most charming and accomplished liar.

Holmes was an old friend of Nathaniel Hawthorne. In May 1864, he was contacted by the publisher James Fields, on behalf of Hawthorne's wife Sophia, who was worried about the failing health of her husband. Fields was concerned about the dwindling productivity of one of his bestselling authors. Would it be possible to contrive a meeting with Hawthorne for the purpose of an informal consultation?

Holmes later recounted the meeting in *The Atlantic* magazine. Calling at Hawthorne's hotel, he was told that the author had just left, and found him on the street outside. Holmes was shocked at his appearance: "He seemed to have shrunken in all his dimensions, and walked with an uncertain, feeble step, as if every movement was an effort." Despite Hawthorne's "obvious depression," his mind was clear, and he retained his most notable personal attribute, his remarkable skittishness. "There was the same backwardness and hesitancy which in his best days it was hard for him to overcome, so that talking with him was almost like lovemaking, and his shy, beautiful soul had to be wooed from its bashful pudency like an unschooled maiden." Hawthorne complained of "persistent local symptoms, referred especially to the stomach,—'boring pain', distention, difficult digestion, with great wasting of flesh and strength." Overall, "his aspect, medically considered, was very unfavorable."

Hawthorne had no illusions about his condition. He "had no hope of recovering his health. He spoke as if his work were done, and he should write no more." Even so, Holmes felt compelled to offer him words of honeyed reassurance. "It was more important that he should go away as hopeful as might be" in "the ignorance that is comparative happiness," rather than in "forlorn self-knowledge." He prescribed "familiar palliatives," probably laudanum or another opiate, treating Hawthorne "to simple medicine as we treat each other to ice cream," and parted with Hawthorne, whom he would not see alive again. That evening, Holmes met with Fields and his wife Annie, and revealed his true opinion: "the shark's tooth is upon him." (Note to physicians-in-training: it is no longer considered kosher to gossip about your celebrity patients and write essays about their illnesses in magazines.)

* * *

Nathaniel Hawthorne had been born fifty-nine years before, on July 4, 1804. His surname was originally spelled "Hathorne." He added the "w" as an ambitious young man, thinking it better befitted a future famous author. He may also have hoped to distance himself from his more ferocious forefathers, who were a source of shame, pride, and artistic inspiration.

His first ancestor in America, William Hathorne, came to Massachusetts aboard the *Arbella* with Governor John Winthrop in 1630. William was a zealous Indian killer, an implacable opponent of royal authority, a tireless accumulator of land and wealth, and a fearsome judge who punished fornicators, Quakers, and other malefactors with typical Puritan industry, cruelty, and ingenuity. Hathorne's judicial duties kept him busy. For such a godly people, the Puritans had brought a surprising amount of vice to the New World with them.

William's son John is notorious for his role as inquisitor in the Salem witch trials. In transcripts of the trials, John seems harsh, fanatical, and more than a little crazy. It has been suggested that John also had a pecuniary motive at work, as the Hathornes later acquired some of the property of the accused. Subsequent generations of Hathornes failed to prosper in Salem. Local legend attributed this to a curse placed on the family by an accused witch on the gallows. Nathaniel's sea captain father would die of yellow fever in Surinam, leaving debts and little else behind. When news of his demise reached Salem, Nathaniel was not quite four years old.

Young Nathaniel, his two sisters, and his widowed mother moved in with his mother's family. The Mannings were on a different social trajectory from the downwardly mobile Hathornes. His maternal grandfather Richard Manning began life as a blacksmith, prospered running a stagecoach line, and finally got rich in land speculation. Nathaniel's Uncle Robert acted as surrogate father to Nathaniel, although the hardheaded bachelor and his woolgathering, pampered nephew often clashed. Because of a critical lack of space in the Manning household, which was packed with fourteen people, Robert and young Nathaniel shared a bed, which probably didn't help matters. Although this arrangement seems creepy and obviously inappropriate to us, it was not seen as unusual at the time.

Hawthorne's enduring animosity towards doctors had its roots in childhood. At age nine, Hawthorne hurt his foot playing ball, and for over a year needed crutches to walk. The primitive treatments of his physicians included pouring cold water on the foot from a second-storey window, in an exceedingly crude attempt to reduce inflammation. Biographers have suggested that his illness was psychosomatic. More likely, he simply suffered a fracture that was slow to knit because the bones were not properly immobilized. His foot finally healed after being placed in a specially fitted boot.

Hawthorne avoided school whenever possible. Like many writers, his formal education was spotty, although he read incessantly on his own. In fair weather, he sneaked onto the roof to read and watch the ships in the harbour, or went out for long solitary walks with book in hand. The teenaged Hawthorne threatened to run off to sea, but Uncle Robert was determined that he receive a proper college education. At seventeen, Nathaniel was sent off to Bowdoin College in Brunswick, Maine. (Bowdoin, which was impeccably Puritan and Congregationalist, was more to Uncle Robert's liking than Harvard, which had already developed a reputation for liberalism and godlessness.)

Bowdoin had only 114 students when Hawthorne arrived in 1821. Hawthorne's friends there included Franklin Pierce, one of the worst and most unlucky of U.S. presidents, the future naval commodore Horatio Bridge, and the poet Longfellow. Unlike Goody Two-shoes Longfellow, who never ran afoul of the school's strict rules, Hawthorne was fined for drinking, gambling, missing religious services, breaking windows, and the crime of "walking unnecessarily on the Sabbath." Hawthorne excelled at English composition, read what he liked, neglected what bored him, and finished in the middle of his class.

At Bowdoin, the peculiarities of Hawthorne's personality first became manifest to the wider world. Hawthorne was handsome. Tall for his time (5'10"), slender, with lively grey eyes, he affected dark theatrical clothes that made him look like a character out of a Gothic romance. However, many observers were struck by the contrast between Hawthorne's manly, athletic appearance, and his timid and reticent demeanour.

He had few close friends, but those he had were devoted to him, even if they understood him poorly. One friend from Bowdoin, Jonathan Cilley, wrote that "I love Hawthorne, I admire him: but I do not know him.

He lives in a mysterious world of thought and imagination which he never permits me to enter." Another called him "a peculiar and rather remarkable young man,—shy, retiring, fond of general reading, busy with his own thoughts, and usually alone or with one or two of his special friends, Pierce . . . and Horatio Bridge . . . he would sit for a whole evening with head gently inclined to one side, hearing every word, seeing every gesture, and yet scarcely a word would pass his lips."

Hawthorne admitted to being "an absurdly shy sort of person." It was not unusual for Hawthorne to run into a field to avoid meeting strangers on a road. Eye contact was especially hard for him: dining with strangers, he stared at his plate; walking in public, he looked down at the road. He was averse to physical contact: even his wife said, "He hates to be touched more than anyone I ever knew." The editor Evert Duyckinck called him "a fine ghost in a case of iron." His publisher Fields observed that he "blushes like a girl." A Bowdoin professor noted his "girlish diffidence." Herman Melville joked that he was "the shyest grape." George Healy, who painted Hawthorne's portrait, said, "I never had a young lady sit to me who was half so timid." Hawthorne got especially flustered around women. He "could not lay a piece of butter upon a lady's plate without a little trembling of the hand." After nine years of marriage, his wife Sophia wrote of his emotional reserve: "He has but just stepped over the threshold of a hermitage." Even in his final years, Hawthorne's shyness was notorious. According to Henry James, "he erected a tower as an adjunct to the house, and it was a jocular tradition among his neighbors . . . that he used to ascend this structure and scan the road for provocations to retreat." (James was a great admirer and imitator of Hawthorne. His convoluted prose style was like Hawthorne on steroids.)

Hawthorne's pathological shyness is consistent with social anxiety disorder, or social phobia. Social phobia is not rare; between 7 and 13 percent of the population is affected to some degree. In most cases, signs become evident in the early teen years. Perhaps social phobia had something to do with Hawthorne's reluctance to attend school.

Fear of public speaking is the mildest and most common form of social phobia. Hawthorne was forbidden to deliver his prizewinning composition at Bowdoin graduation because of his disciplinary problems. Hawthorne was secretly delighted: "I am perfectly satisfied with this arrangement, as it is a sufficient testimonial of my scholarship, while it saves me the mortification of making my appearance in public at commencement." In later years as the American consul at Liverpool, Hawthorne relied heavily on alcohol to get him through public appearances: "I charge myself pretty high with champagne and port before I get upon my legs; and whether the business is to make a speech or to be hanged, I come up to it like a man—and I had as lief it should be one as the other."

Hawthorne once complained of his aloofness in a letter to Longfellow: "I seldom venture abroad till after dark. By some witch-craft or other . . . I have been carried apart from the main current of life, and find it impossible to get back again." Hawthorne's isolation probably had more to do with genes than with bewitchment. Social phobia has a robust genetic component. Hawthorne himself claimed his "natural tendency toward seclusion" came from his father, a reserved and melancholy man. Hawthorne's mother and his sister Elizabeth were also notoriously hermitic; like the bachelor Hawthorne, they often stayed in their rooms and ate meals alone. According to Hawthorne, he once did not see Elizabeth for three months while they lived in the same house.

Patients with social phobia commonly suffer from other psychiatric conditions, including mood disorders and substance abuse. Hawthorne had several episodes of significant depression, and his reliance on alcohol increased in later years.

Hawthorne's writing allowed him to express himself and overcome his social inhibitions. He admitted that he could share intimacies with strangers through his fiction that he could not confide to his best friends. As Louisa May Alcott realized, he was "a beautiful soul in prison trying to reach his fellow beings through the bars." Nowadays, social phobia usually responds well to antidepressant medication. Had Paxil or Zoloft been available in the nineteenth century, would we still have *The Scarlet Letter*?

Hawthorne toyed with medicine as a profession, but objected that "I should not like to live by the diseases and infirmities of my fellow creatures." For twelve years after graduating from Bowdoin, Hawthorne lived a strange solitary existence spent writing in his attic. Because of his seclusion, and the years he spent away in Maine, Hawthorne was a virtual stranger in his home town of Salem: "I doubt whether so much as twenty people in the town were aware of my existence."

Hawthorne and his mother and sisters scraped by on their remnant of the Manning money. His habits in these years "were as regular as possible," according to his sister Ebe: writing every morning, sometimes a walk in the afternoon, but always an hour-long walk in the evening, regardless of the weather. In the remainder of the day, he devoured books. His obsession with colonial Massachusetts supplied him with a rich vein of raw material, which he would transform into nightmarish scenes of moral ambiguity in stories such as "Young Goodman Brown" and "My Kinsman, Major Molineux."

In 1828, Hawthorne's first novel, *Fanshawe*, appeared, a Gothic potboiler mainly notable for the confidence and verve of Hawthorne's style. The setting is a rural college much like Bowdoin. The main character, Fanshawe, is a Byronic version of Hawthorne himself. Fanshawe's foil is the amiable but dull Edward Walcott, who bears a passing resemblance to Franklin Pierce. Fanshawe wins the heart of the maiden Ellen Langton by saving her from ruffians that would ravish her and plunder her inheritance. Tragically, Fanshawe dies from too intense application to his studies, so Ellen has to settle for Walcott. Hawthorne later burned every copy of *Fanshawe* that he could get his hands on.

Hawthorne had a modest success with his first story collection, *Twicetold Tales*, which appeared in 1837. Until this time, he had no noteworthy romantic entanglements. He now became involved with Mary Crowninshield Silsbee, the "Star of Salem." Silsbee was beautiful, rich, and had a bad reputation as a Yankee drama queen. She tried to embroil Hawthorne in a duel with John O'Sullivan, the newspaperman who coined the phrase "manifest destiny." Silsbee claimed that O'Sullivan had wronged her honour, but Hawthorne was satisfied with O'Sullivan's explanations, and the two were reconciled. Silsbee threw Hawthorne over, and married the historian Jared Sparks. Hawthorne's future in-laws, the Peabodys, found Sparks uncouth, but this did not prevent him from eventually becoming president of Harvard College.

During the debacle with Mary Silsbee, Hawthorne became acquainted with the Peabody sisters of Salem. Elizabeth, the eldest, had designs on Hawthorne. She was a kindhearted and eccentric figure, a patroness of progressive and hopeless causes, and a lovelorn hankerer after intellectual men. In garrulous old age, she would be cruelly caricatured in Henry

James's *The Bostonians* as the feminist Miss Birdseye. Gradually and painfully, it dawned on Elizabeth that Hawthorne was really interested in her youngest sister, Sophia.

Sophia was not as learned as Elizabeth, or as pretty as her other sister Mary, but she was more passionate. She filled journals with breathless scribbling, and covered canvases with slavish copies of other paintings. However, her most notable attribute was hypochondria. Her migraines were refractory to the most advanced remedies of the day, including ether, mercury, colchicum, opium, atropine, and arsenic. Not even leeches and blistering helped. Her alarmed parents packed her off to Cuba, where tropical sun, dancing, and horseback riding worked wonders on her mood. However, Sophia's symptoms relapsed when she returned to the Peabody house in gloomy, wintry Salem, next door to an old burial ground.

Sophia once declared that she could never marry because of her sickliness. Happily if mysteriously, her health recovered after meeting Hawthorne. Their mutual attraction blossomed into an engagement, and forced an unpleasant realization on Hawthorne. If he were to marry, he would need a source of income. In January 1839, Hawthorne used his Democratic Party ties to land a position at the Boston Custom House. At thirty-four, he had his first real job.

Hawthorne prospered for two years, but when the Democrats lost the election of 1840, he quit rather than be fired. At loose ends, Hawthorne joined the utopian community of Brook Farm in April 1841. Part commune, part Platonic academy, Brook Farm was the brainchild of the Unitarian minister George Ripley. Unfortunately for Hawthorne, who sank most of his savings into Brook Farm, this New Jerusalem was unwisely set on a hardscrabble tract of rocks and swamp in West Roxbury, Massachusetts.

Hawthorne, the cynical loner obsessed with the howling wilderness of human nature, was strangely out of place amid the enthusiasts of Brook Farm. His first biographer, his son-in-law George Lathrop, puzzled that "the least gregarious of men should have been drawn into a socialistic community." Hawthorne's pastoral fantasy quickly faded into a monotonous routine of milking cows, pitching hay, and shovelling manure. Sceptical about Brook Farm's financial prospects, he left the community in

November 1841. He lost his entire investment. Racked by feuds and law-suits, and forced by impending bankruptcy to take on a more industrial character, Brook Farm finally succumbed to an outbreak of smallpox and a biblical conflagration. When the colony collapsed, Ripley absquatu-lated to New York, turned to journalism, and married a German heiress.

In July 1842, Hawthorne and Sophia married and moved to Concord, Massachusetts. Concord was the Mecca of American transcendentalism, with Ralph Waldo Emerson as its Mohammed. Sophia and Hawthorne spent happy honeymoon years in Emerson's old home, the Old Manse. Hawthorne thought that Emerson's essays were vague, impressive non-sense. He had more respect for Emerson's disciple, Henry David Thoreau, whom he found impossibly stubborn, but likable and down to earth, and he shared Thoreau's love of nature.

Hawthorne's second collection of short stories, *Mosses from an Old Manse,* appeared in 1846. Many of these later stories were critical of sci-ence and medicine, which Hawthorne saw as lacking in empathy and brimming with hubris. In "Rappaccini's Daughter," Doctor Rappaccini, according to his jealous and equally heartless rival, is the epitome of sci-entific enquiry run amok: "But as for Rappaccini, it is said of him—and I, who know the man well, can answer for its truth—that he cares infinitely more for science than for mankind. His patients are interesting to him only as subjects for some new experiment." Thankfully, in modern med-icine, we no longer have such men as Rappaccini, who value their pub-lications, their grant funding, and their opportunities for academic advancement more highly than the welfare of their patients.

The Hawthornes were still pinched financially. When the Democrats regained the White House in 1844, Hawthorne's old friends, Bridge, Pierce, and especially O'Sullivan, lobbied for a suitable sinecure for the writer. (O'Sullivan was apparently still grateful to Hawthorne for not shooting him.) In 1846, Hawthorne was appointed inspector in the Salem Custom House. He made a comfortable salary for the next three years and wrote little.

The Whigs returned to power in 1849. Hawthorne was fired from the Custom House in June, and his mother fell ill and died in July. Haw-thorne did not crumble under these twin blows. In fact, they unleashed a burst of remarkable creativity. Late that year, the publisher James T. Fields visited Hawthorne at his home in Salem, looking for material. Hawthorne rebuffed him, but as Fields trudged off in defeat, Hawthorne ran after him, and shyly handed him a bundle of papers. On the train back to Boston, Fields read it with mounting excitement. It was the manuscript of *The Scarlet Letter*.

The Scarlet Letter is set in Puritan Massachusetts, and features one of the great heroines in American literature, Hester Prynne. Long after the disappearance of her husband, Hester gives birth to an illegitimate daughter, Pearl, a morbid, elfin child, modelled on Hawthorne's own daughter Una. Hester refuses to reveal the child's father, and is forced to wear the red letter *A* for "adultery" on her dress. Hester's secret accomplice in sin, the pseudosaintly Reverend Arthur Dimmesdale, is literally wasting away with guilt, in an eerie foreshadowing of Hawthorne's own terminal illness. Hester's husband, Chillingworth, another of Hawthorne's fiendish physicians, reappears in disguise, and devotes himself to torturing Dimmesdale's guilty conscience, while pretending to minister to his bodily maladies.

The lusty politicians, fallen evangelicals, and paedophile priests that populate the news show the continued relevance of *The Scarlet Letter,* and the persistent gap between public righteousness and private hypocrisy in America. *The Scarlet Letter* has strongly influenced many writers, especially Henry James, who thought it the best of American novels. It also inspired a particularly awful Demi Moore movie, but it would be unfair to hold Hawthorne responsible for this.

In May 1850, the Hawthornes moved to Lenox, Massachusetts, where Hawthorne met Herman Melville. Their friendship fascinates literary scholars, not least for its homoerotic undertones. The intimacy between Hawthorne and Melville is often exaggerated. Both men were exceedingly busy with writing and family during this time. Despite living just a few miles apart from each other from September 1850 to November 1851, they only met on a handful of occasions. Melville may or may not have made some sort of physical advance on Hawthorne, as one of Hawthorne's biographers has suggested. However, it is unnecessary to invoke a failed sexual overture to explain the apparent cooling in their friendship. Melville's needy, manic letters would have spooked an emotionally glacial man like Hawthorne.

There is a peculiar coda to their relationship. In 1883, Hawthorne's brash young son Julian called on Melville in New York, looking for material for a biography of his father. Melville was much reduced by age and nerves, "a melancholy and pale wraith of what he had been in his prime." With agitation, he told Julian that he had destroyed Hawthorne's letters years before. Julian pressed him for memories of Hawthorne, but it was too much for the old man, who shook his head. However, he did startle Julian with an unusual pronouncement:

> He was convinced Hawthorne had all his life concealed some great secret, which would, were it known, explain all the mysteries of his career . . . some secret in my father's life which had never been revealed, and which accounted for the gloomy passages in his books. It was characteristic in him to imagine so; there were many secrets untold in his own career.

This has provoked much fanciful, if evidence-free, conjecture about possible skeletons in Hawthorne's closet.

Genial, vacant Franklin Pierce and the pathologically reclusive Hawthorne shared an improbable bond. Imagine Gerald Ford and J. D. Salinger as soul mates, or George W. Bush and Thomas Pynchon as best friends forever. Their friendship played a fateful role in each other's lives. Pierce was a born politician, handsome and charming, with a remarkable memory for names and faces. At thirty-two, he became a United States senator, but in Washington's heavily lubricated social scene, his fatal weakness for the bottle soon became apparent. Prodded by his devout, tubercular wife Jane, he resigned from the Senate, and strove mightily to stay sober. In 1852, he astonished himself, and everyone else, by becoming the Democratic nominee for president, winning the convention as a compromise candidate on the forty-ninth ballot. Hawthorne penned Pierce's official campaign biography, a slender volume that could be described as flattering, if not frankly misleading. He lauded Pierce's service in the Mexican War, noting that at the battle of Chapultepec, he was "extremely ill, and was unable to leave his bed for the thirty-six hours next ensuing." Hawthorne neglected to mention that Pierce was suffering from the galvanic gastrointestinal effects of Montezuma's revenge. More reprehensibly, Hawthorne praised Pierce's opposition to abolitionism. Hawthorne's own thinking on slavery and race was painfully naïve, when it was not simply offensive.

Pierce won the election of 1852 handily. Immediately afterward, the Pierces were on board a train that derailed. The accident's only fatality was their sole surviving child, Benjamin, who was crushed before their eyes. Pierce fell apart, incapacitated by booze, depression, and post-traumatic stress disorder. After his pro-Southern administration set the country lurching toward civil war, he left office in disgrace, and slowly drank himself to death.

Pierce rewarded Hawthorne with a plum patronage post, the American consulship at Liverpool. This seemed like a stroke of good fortune, but Hawthorne's time in Europe would ruin both his health and his peace of mind. Pierce commissioned a formal portrait of Hawthorne before his departure. At forty-eight, the author was still handsome, slender and youthful. On his return seven years later, Hawthorne was bald, stout, and ravaged by drink and depression.

At first, Hawthorne relished the money. There was no salary, but the consul pocketed all the fees for his services. Liverpool was the world's busiest seaport. Hawthorne made $2 for each signature on invoices for cargo bound for the States. He banked $10,000 in his first year on the job, a fortune at the time. His other consular duties he found dull and irksome. These included helping fellow Americans down on their luck, giving boozy after-dinner speeches, and dealing with Delia Bacon, the woman who was the first to suggest that someone other than Shakespeare wrote Shakespeare's plays. Bacon had a mental breakdown after she was jilted by a Yale divinity student, who caddishly circulated her love letters for the amusement of his friends. She responded to her mortification in New Haven by writing a rambling manuscript asserting that Shakespeare's plays were really written by Francis Bacon, Sir Walter Raleigh, and Edmund Spenser as propaganda for their subversive political theories. Unable to find an American publisher, Bacon moved to England and befriended Hawthorne's wife. Under spousal pressure, Hawthorne loaned Bacon money, subsidized the publication of her unreadable book, and even wrote a preface praising her sincerity and perseverance, while carefully avoiding saying whether he believed her theory to be true. (Privately, he was less diplomatic, calling her a "Bedlamite" full of "delusions.") The critics savaged her book, and she died in an asylum two years later. However, her intellectual legacy of sketchy Shakespeare theories has continued down to the present tome.

Hawthorne was burnt out by the end of his time in England. An observer said of him in 1856 that he was "utterly prostrated by depression . . . I never saw a man more miserable." He would wrestle with black moods for the rest of his life. (Hawthorne had experienced prior depressive episodes in 1836, when his writing career was stalled, in 1842, when Sophia fell ill just before their marriage, and during 1850–51, when the Hawthornes were suffering from money woes.)

When his term as consul was up in 1858, Hawthorne took his family to Italy. In Rome, his favourite daughter Una fell gravely ill for months, first with hectic malarial fevers, and then with tuberculosis. Visitors then avoided Rome for much of the year because of malaria. In *The Marble Faun*, Hawthorne noted that in Rome, "Fever walks arm in arm with you, and Death awaits you at the end of a dim vista." Una was not expected to live. While she slowly rallied, she was never again well in mind or body. She suffered from manic depression, once landing in an asylum after she became "dangerously insane, spent great sums of money, [and] nearly took the lives of three people." When she died suddenly at age thirty-three, her physician blamed exhaustion and pyrosis, or stomach inflammation.

If Sophia had seemed like a weak link when they married, over the long haul of their marriage she proved infinitely stronger than Hawthorne. He unravelled at Una's illness, and her derangements were a source of particular grief in years to come. While mired in depression, Hawthorne benefited from the attentions of Franklin Pierce, who happened to be touring Europe with his own invalid wife. Curious sightseers saw the pair walking the ancient streets of Rome, two damaged men.

When Una was well enough to travel, the family left for London, where Hawthorne finished his final novel. *The Marble Faun* was an atmospheric tale of art, intrigue, and murder set in Rome. Plotting was a weakness for Hawthorne, and *The Marble Faun* makes little sense at several critical junctures. Hawthorne joked that it was "an audacious attempt to impose a tissue of absurdities upon the public by the mere art of style and narrative." It was a popular and critical success anyway.

Hawthorne and his family were back in Concord in 1860. His last years were unhappy and unproductive. Anxiety and depression gnawed at him, foiling his attempts to write another novel. He obsessively reworked one tale over and over again: a young man's quest for the elixir of eternal life. Hawthorne abandoned this manuscript, published posthumously as *Septimius Felton,* in a fairly advanced state. Perhaps he fretted that he was repeating himself, just as immortal life inevitably would: "As dramatists and novelists repeat their plots, so does man's life repeat itself, and at length grow stale."

Hawthorne returned to the immortality story in the autumn of 1863. He not only still suffered from mood problems, he was now also physically ill. His faltering health is reflected in the new version of the story, now called *The Dolliver Romance.* The main character is no longer a conniving young scientist, but an aged and feeble apothecary named Dolliver, clinging to life for the sake of Pansie, his orphaned great-granddaughter. Pansie is the last of the elfin girls in his fiction based on Una, and Dolliver is none other than Hawthorne himself, ironic in his denial of decrepitude and creeping mortality:

> He never grew accustomed to it, but . . . still retained an inward consciousness that these stiffened shoulders, these quailing knees, this cloudiness of sight and brain, this confused forgetfulness of men and affairs, were troublesome accidents that did not really belong to him. He possibly cherished a half-recognized idea that they might pass away. Youth, however eclipsed for a season, is undoubtedly the proper, permanent, and genuine condition of man; and if we look closely into this dreary delusion of growing old, we find it never absolutely succeeds in laying hold of our innermost convictions.

Hawthorne had initially arranged to have *The Dolliver Romance* published as a serial in *The Atlantic,* but he had to abandon the project because of declining health and abdominal pain. Hawthorne was already sick when he started work on *The Dolliver Romance,* and "had been more or less infirm for more than a year" before he died, according to Pierce. The major early feature in Hawthorne's illness was weight loss. His son Julian wrote: "There was no improvement in Hawthorne's condition during the spring and summer of 1863. He seemed to have no definite disease, but he grew thinner, paler, and more languid day by day."

The poet Ellery Channing recalled Hawthorne's "very delicate health the winter and spring preceding his death." On December 19, 1863, Sophia worried that Hawthorne was "thin and pale and weak," as well as "nervous and delicate," and was making excuses to avoid seeing the doctor. She was alarmed at and lack of appetite stomach complaints: "I am amazed that such a fortress as his digestion should give way." Earlier in the month, Hawthorne insisted on travelling to New Hampshire for Jane Pierce's funeral, despite his condition. The grieving ex-president, noticing how frail Hawthorne seemed at the graveside, gently turned up his coat collar.

Although Hawthorne's weight loss got worse in 1864, his mind remained lucid: "His face was pale and wasted, so that his great eyes, with their dark overhanging brows, looked like caverns with a gleam of blue in them; his figure had become much attenuated, and his once firm and strong stride was slow and uncertain. But his mind was awake, composed, and clear." In March 1864, James Fields's wife Annie was also impressed by the clarity of his eyes, despite his overall deterioration: "His limbs are shrunken but his great eyes still burn with their lambent fire." By May, Sophia wished that "Dr Holmes would feel his pulse; I do not know how to judge of it, but it seems to me irregular."

By March 1864, Hawthorne had been wasting away from his mystery illness for over a year. His family and friends desperately hoped that a change of scenery might rejuvenate him. His publisher William Ticknor, Fields's partner in the firm of Ticknor and Fields, who had performed many kindnesses for Hawthorne, volunteered to travel with the invalid. Ticknor was hale and robust, a shrewd Yankee businessman, as pragmatic as Hawthorne was ethereal. Although Ticknor had wonderful intentions, he was terrible in execution.

On March 28, Ticknor and Hawthorne got off the train in New York, and were greeted by torrents of rain. They had hoped to sail to sunny

Havana, but the weather proved too putrid and tempestuous. They moved on to Philadelphia, where the rotten weather continued. Ticknor caught cold and took to bed. When the cold turned into pneumonia, a doctor was summoned. Hawthorne caustically reported that the physician "proceeded to cup, and poultice, and blister, according to that ancient tribe of savages. The consequence is, that poor Ticknor is already very much reduced, while the disease flourishes as luxuriantly as if that were the Doctor's sole object."

Hawthorne never left Ticknor's bedside. On April 9, Ticknor moaned that he would not live another day, and died before dawn. Dazed and stricken, Hawthorne telegraphed Ticknor's family. Ticknor's son arrived the next day to accompany the corpse back to Boston. Unexpectedly back in Concord, Massachusetts, Hawthorne staggered the mile and a half from the train station to his house. Hawthorne's son Julian later wrote: "When, at last, he reached home, his wife was appalled at his aspect. He showed the traces of terrible agitation; his bodily substance seemed to have evaporated. He appeared to feel that there had been a ghastly mistake,— that he, and not Ticknor, should have died." Death had blundered, taken the wrong man. It was a grim cosmic joke worthy of one of Hawthorne's own tales.

As an adult, Hawthorne was rarely ill, not given to hypochondria, and stayed away from doctors whenever possible. However, after the catastrophe in Philadelphia with Ticknor, he finally agreed to see Dr Holmes, whose behaviour was perfectly acceptable by the standards of his time, but would be considered highly unprofessional today. He prescribed for Hawthorne without performing a proper physical examination, deliberately misled Hawthorne about his dismal prognosis, breached patient confidentiality by gossiping with the Fields, and even wrote a magazine article about Hawthorne's illness.

Holmes suspected that Hawthorne had cancer. Years later, he wrote to Hawthorne's son-in-law, George Lathrop: "I feared that there was some internal organic—perhaps malignant—disease; for he looked wasted and as if stricken with a mortal disease."

Unwillingness to disclose a diagnosis of cancer, or any other terminal illness, was widespread among doctors in the nineteenth and twentieth centuries. William Osler, the most eminent of modern physicians, argued that "the careful physician has but one end in view—not to depress his patient in any way whatever." In 1897, he wrote "What is your duty in the matter of telling a patient he is probably the subject of an incurable disease? . . . One thing is certain: it is not for you to don the black cap, and, assuming the judicial function, take hope from any patient."

An authority on gastric cancer argued in 1941 against full disclosure: "The patient with carcinoma . . . should be told enough to ensure the proper treatment. Usually it is sufficient to state simply that an operation is necessary for obstruction or for tumor. A responsible member of the family should always be informed frankly and fully not only of the presence and nature of the disease but also of the prognosis and the therapeutic possibilities. The word 'cancer' should not be used to the patient . . . the fear of cancer is so great that many patients, if told they have cancer, immediately abandon all hope and in utter panic refuse to make any attempt to deal with it intelligently."

Of course, it is now considered unethical not to tell a competent patient that they have cancer. Although patients have the right to refuse information about their condition, and occasionally still do so, modern patients generally want to know as much as possible about their cancer diagnosis. However, oncologists still struggle with how much to disclose to patients, how aggressively to treat them, and when to tell them that their disease is terminal and not to offer further treatment.

Holmes's pessimism, which he concealed from Hawthorne, was right. Hawthorne had one week to live. When the end came, it was sudden. Fittingly, he was with Pierce. They proceeded through New Hampshire slowly, first by rail, then by carriage. Pierce noticed Hawthorne was having more difficulty walking, and that "the use of his hands was impaired." When they reached Plymouth on May 18, Hawthorne had to be helped to the hotel. Pierce checked on Hawthorne during the night, and realized he was dead. "He evidently had passed from that natural sleep to that sleep from which there is no waking, without suffering, and without the slightest movement."

In considering Hawthorne's perplexing illness, his biographers have often wandered, like Hester Prynne, in "a dismal labyrinth of doubt."

Before arriving at a probable diagnosis, we will first debunk some misconceptions about his illness.

When writers fall ill, there is often a tendency to believe they are suffering from psychological disturbances, rather than physical illness. Presumably, this is because they are sensitive, imaginative, often troubled individuals. This perception may prevail even among friends and family. According to Franklin Pierce, "mental causes are at the bottom of his illness." Hawthorne's sister-in-law Mary Mann asserted "He is a victim of dyspepsia. I cannot help thinking that his malady originates in mental trouble." Even Sophia regarded Hawthorne's illness as "partly mental."

Patients with anxiety and depression, such as Hawthorne, are prone to develop psychosomatic illness, or somatization. However, patients with somatization have multiple complaints that are poorly localized and seemingly unrelated. They complain of generalized aches, dizziness, fatigue, shortness of breath, numbness, diarrhoea, and constipation. They look well, despite their many symptoms. They seek out doctors and elude diagnosis, despite extensive and expensive diagnostic testing. Hawthorne, on the other hand, avoided doctors, looked ill, and had specific complaints related to his stomach.

One biographer has raised the possibility of syphilis. This seems improbable. While the manifestations of syphilis are notoriously variable, relentless abdominal pain and wasting would be rare. There is also no indication that the timorous Hawthorne had any lifestyle risks for syphilis.

Ulcerative colitis has been suggested, which also seems unlikely. Patients with ulcerative colitis can certainly become malnourished and have severe abdominal pain, but their major symptom is profuse diarrhoea with an admixture of blood and mucus. Hawthorne does not seem to have suffered from significant diarrhoea.

An overactive thyroid gland could explain his weight loss, jitteriness, and the irregular pulse noted by his wife. However, it wouldn't explain his persistent abdominal pain. Failure of the adrenal glands, or Addison's disease, is consistent with many of his symptoms. When Addison first described it in 1855, most cases were due to tuberculosis, although most now are due to autoimmune disease. Hawthorne had four of the major symptoms noted by Addison: "anaemia, general languor and debility, remarkable feebleness of the heart's action, [and] irritability of the stomach." However, he lacked the most characteristic symptom, "a peculiar change of colour in the skin." To boost the failing adrenal glands, the pituitary gland pumps out enormous amounts of the hormone corticotropin, which incidentally causes the skin to make more melanin pigment. This bronzed, tanned-looking skin was very prominent in the most famous sufferer from Addison's disease, President John F. Kennedy.

Of all Hawthorne's biographers, Nina Baym was most correct when she suggested "The illness was never diagnosed, but the symptoms suggest some sort of gastrointestinal cancer." The best overall fit for his illness is a cancer that was extraordinarily common in Hawthorne's day: carcinoma of the stomach.

Stomach cancer was the most common cancer in men in the late nineteenth-century United States. Even as late as 1930, stomach cancer was the major cause of cancer death in America, but since that time it has steadily dwindled in importance in industrialized nations. Gastric cancer is still common in developing nations, and worldwide it is the second leading cause of cancer death, after lung cancer.

Hawthorne's presentation was typical of stomach cancer. Patients have the insidious onset of vague discomfort in the upper abdomen, with gradual loss of appetite and weight. Severe anaemia might have caused Hawthorne's irregular pulse. In the age before blood transfusions, patients with gastric cancer were often profoundly anaemic from slow blood loss. Osler noted that anaemia often caused palpitations and a "rapid and feeble" pulse in patients with terminal stomach cancer. Almost all accounts of Hawthorne's illness stress his pallor, a finding consistent with severe anaemia.

Hawthorne complained that the pain in his stomach kept him from lying down at night. This is consistent with a gastric cancer invading the space behind the stomach, or the retroperitoneum. According to that venerable classic, *Cope's Early Diagnosis of the Acute Abdomen,* "Patients with pain of pancreatic or retroperitoneal origin very often prefer the sitting to the recumbent position." Pancreatic cancer could also explain these symptoms, but it was less common than stomach cancer in Hawthorne's time. The yearlong duration of his illness also argues against pancreatic cancer: even today, patients with pancreatic cancer typically survive only six months. According to Osler, the survival of patients with gastric cancer in the nineteenth century was usually between six to eighteen months, consistent with the time course of Hawthorne's illness.

Why was stomach cancer so common in Hawthorne's time, and why it is so rare in America today? In 1919, the Danish scientist Johannes Fibiger fed mice meals of cockroaches infected with a tiny parasitic worm called *Spiroptera*. The unfortunate mice became infected with the worm, and then developed stomach cancer. In 1926, Fibiger won the Nobel Prize in medicine for proving that worms caused stomach cancer. Fibiger's research was ground breaking, revolutionary, and utterly mistaken. No one could duplicate his data. It turned out that Fibiger's mice had developed vitamin A deficiency from their unsavoury diet, and Fibiger had confused the effects of vitamin deficiency on the stomach lining with cancer.

Although Fibiger was wrong, there was something to the infection and stomach cancer link after all. Spiral bacteria had been seen in the stomach in patients with peptic ulcers as early as 1889. However, since they were hard to see, and no one could culture them in the laboratory, the scientific mainstream ignored them. Physicians thought, erroneously, that the major causes of peptic ulcers were stress, smoking, and spicy foods. In the early 1980s, two Western Australian physicians, Barry Marshall and Robin Warren, took an obsessive interest in these bacteria. They succeeded in isolating them from large numbers of patients with peptic ulcer disease, and worked out a technique to grow them in the lab. The finishing touch to their research came when Marshall, with antipodean audacity, drank a suspension of the concentrated bacteria, now known as *Helicobacter pylori*. After a few days, he developed nausea, vomiting, horrible bad breath, sweats, and loss of appetite. Marshall's colleagues performed an endoscopy and found his stomach was eroded, bleeding, and teeming with bacteria. Marshall cured himself with antibiotics, and found consolation in the Nobel Prize he shared with Warren in 2005.

Helicobacter pylori thrives in conditions of poverty, crowding, and poor hygiene. It is probably transmitted by contamination of food and water with faecal matter. In the United States and other developed nations, the rate of *H. pylori* infection is 30 percent, whereas in poor countries infection rates range from 80 to 100 percent. As the United States was less sanitary in Hawthorne's time, the prevalence of *H. pylori* was probably similar to that in poor countries today. The fact that Una suffered from "pyrosis" of the stomach might suggest that all the Hawthornes were exposed to *H. pylori* at some point. Chronic stomach inflammation caused by *H. pylori* doubles the risk of gastric cancer. This is significant, but not enough on its own to explain the epidemic proportions of gastric cancer in Hawthorne's time.

Consumption of salted, smoked, and cured meat was high in nineteenth-century America. These meats are rich in carcinogenic compounds called nitrosamines. There is evidence that the cancer-causing potential of these chemicals is enhanced by the inflammatory changes of *H. pylori* infection, as well as by salt intake. The Yankee diet of salt cod of Hawthorne's childhood was probably ideal for causing stomach cancer, just as the high intake of salted fish in Asian nations today seems to be related to the continuing problem with gastric cancer in those countries.

Two technological innovations played a major role in the decline in stomach cancer in the United States: the icebox and the refrigerator. Iceboxes became common in affluent American homes in the second half of the nineteenth century. By 1900 commercial refrigeration began to be used in the meatpacking industry, making it feasible to transport fresh meat long distances. The home refrigerator became widely affordable to American consumers after World War II. As more Americans could safely store fresh meat, consumption of cured, salted, and smoked meat waned. Similarly, there is evidence that the widespread use of home refrigerators in modern urban China has led to a remarkable recent drop in stomach cancer.

Hawthorne had two other lifestyle risk factors for stomach cancer: a fondness for cigars and red meat. Gastric cancers are nearly doubled in smokers; red meat intake also increases the risk of stomach cancer, especially in persons who also have *H. pylori* infection.

Today, Hawthorne's illness would be easily diagnosed by an upper endoscopy. He would be lightly sedated, and swallow a flexible, lighted, fibreoptic tube. The gastroenterologist would examine the stomach and remove small chunks of ulcerated, abnormal tissue, which a pathologist would look at under the microscope to confirm the diagnosis of cancer. A CT scan would help assess whether the cancer had spread to lymph nodes or adjacent organs, such as the liver. Stomach cancer could not be treated in Hawthorne's time. The treatment is better now, but is not optimal. Early tumours can be cured by surgical removal of all or part of the stomach; chemotherapy may reduce the risk of recurrence in some cases. Yet even today, half of patients with gastric cancer have advanced, incurable disease at diagnosis, and usually survive less than a year.

If Hawthorne's underlying illness was stomach cancer, what was the cause of his sudden demise? While Dr Holmes did not expect Hawthorne to recover, he was surprised by the rapidity of his death, as were Hawthorne's neighbours.

One biographer speculates that Hawthorne died from the spread of tumour to the brain. This idea arose with Franklin Pierce, of all people, who wrote, "The seat of the disease from which Hawthorne was suffering was in the brain or spine." This is possible, but not the most likely cause of his terminal deterioration. Hawthorne did not have the most common findings of a patient with brain metastases, such as headaches, difficulty thinking, or seizures. Hawthorne did have more trouble with his walking and with the use of his hands on the day before his death, which could indicate a neurologic problem. However, brain tumours typically cause weakness only on one side of the body. Hawthorne did not have this, or if he did, Pierce failed to notice it.

According to the Institute of Medicine, almost 100,000 patients die annually in the United States from medical errors. If Dr Holmes had given laudanum or opium for pain, could Hawthorne have been prescribed or dispensed too much, or misread the instructions, and died in his sleep from respiratory depression? This is possible, but less likely given Holmes's awareness of the dangers of excessive medication.

Patients with advanced stomach cancer can develop any number of fatal complications. The cancer may spread throughout the abdomen, leading to bowel blockages, dehydration, and death from kidney failure; the stomach may perforate, and peritonitis ensue; the tumour may invade blood vessels, causing fatal haemorrhage; the cancer may spread to bone, leading to a high calcium level, with weakness of the limbs, stupor, coma, and death. Any of these could have contributed to Hawthorne's death, but there is one final possibility that I think more likely.

Several types of cancer put patients at high risk of forming blood clots, or deep venous thrombosis (DVT). Carcinoma of the stomach is one of these. In one study, 32 percent of patients with gastric cancer were found to have pulmonary emboli, or blood clots in the lung, at autopsy. Long-distance travel is also a well-known risk factor for blood clots: in one study, the risk of DVT was increased fourfold in patients with a history of recent travel. Long periods of time spent sitting, such as on trains, planes—or in Hawthorne's time, carriages—favour the formation of blood clots in the legs, which can then break off and lodge in the lungs. Hawthorne's already high risk of a massive, fatal pulmonary embolism would have been multiplied by his prior travel to Philadelphia, and his final journey to New Hampshire. Thus the travel that family and friends hoped so desperately would revive him may actually have led to his demise.

Arrowhead, the house in Pittsfield, Massachusetts, where *Moby-Dick* was written. Melville had the porch built onto the house to protect his sensitive eyes from sunlight. (Courtesy of the Library of Congress)

6. PERILOUS OUTPOST OF THE SANE:
The Many Maladies of Herman Melville

To him seas were deeper and skies vaster than to other men, and similarly beauty was more actual and pain and humiliation more agonizing.
—*George Orwell*

Herman Melville is not well. Do not call him moody, he is ill.
—*Sarah Morewood, Melville neighbour, 1859*

In December 1831, something snapped in Allan Melvill. Not long before, he had flourished in Manhattan as an importer of French luxury goods. In portraits, his wild forelocks and impossibly long sideburns gave him a worldly rakish air, which was somewhat undercut by a look of wide-eyed credulity. But his ever-shifting places of work and residence belied his façade of prosperity. In reality, he was racking up vast amounts of debt, and squandering both his own inheritance and that of his wife Maria.

Much of this money seems to have evaporated by way of dealings with shadowy, and probably crooked, business associates. By October 1830, Allan was bankrupt. He, Maria, and their eight children, including their young son Herman, fled the city and took refuge with Maria's family in remote Albany, where Allan toiled as a lowly clerk.

Hemmed in by creditors and terrified of prison, he went to New York City one last time to try to settle his affairs. Overwhelmed with bills and claims against him, he slipped out of the city again on December 7, 1831, on board the Hudson River steamer *Constellation*. An early, bitter blast of Arctic cold made the way home unexpectedly difficult. The steamboat made it only as far as Poughkeepsie before a sheet of ice forced it to grind to a halt. Allan was jolted about for the next three days in freezing open wagons, underdressed for the −19°C weather in his fancy city clothes. At nightfall of the third day, he arrived at Greenbush, across the river from Albany. Numb with cold, he stumbled home, hauling his baggage over the frozen river in howling wind and total darkness.

Allan's ordeal left him both exhausted and frenetic. His mind reeled with schemes to recover his lost fortunes, and he soon had a full-fledged manic break. According to his brother-in-law, Peter Gansevoort, Allan "persisted in giving attention to his business—he devoted himself so closely and assiduously, as to produce a state of excitement, which in a great measure robbed him of his sleep." As Allan's mental status became more unstable, "he yielded to the wishes of his friends and remained at home. The excitement however could not be allayed and yesterday he occasionally manifested an alienation of mind. Last night he became much worse—and today presents the melancholy spectacle of a deranged man." Allan's brother, Thomas, hurried to Albany on receiving this news, and "found him *very sick*—induced by a variety of causes—under great excitement—at times fierce, even *maniacal*." Four days later, on January 15, 1831, Thomas wrote breathlessly to Allan's best friend, Lemuel Shaw, chief justice of the Massachusetts Supreme Court, that hope "is no longer permitted of his recovery, in the opinion of the attending physicians and indeed,—oh, how hard for a brother to say!—I *ought not* to hope for it.— for,—in all human probability—he would live, *a maniac!*" On January 27, Thomas informed Shaw that Allan's "strength has failed . . . rapidly." He died the next day, aged forty-nine. His disgrace was so complete that his widow changed the family name after his death, adding an extra E, perhaps in a feeble attempt to confuse creditors.

Allan's affliction was likely delirious mania, a severe complication of bipolar disorder. The condition is also known as Bell's mania, after Luther Bell, the superintendent of the McLean Asylum in Somerville, Massachusetts, who first described it in 1849. (The asylum was the precursor of today's McLean Hospital, whose notable inmates have included the poets Sylvia Plath and Robert Lowell.) In 1934, the psychiatrist S. H. Kraines described it as a "syndrome of a sudden onset, with overactivity, great excitement, sleeplessness, apparent delirium, and distorted ideas; without any clear evidence of a definite toxic infectious factor." Before the modern era of sedative and psychotropic medication, and supportive measures such as intravenous fluids, delirious mania was a lethal condition. Three-quarters of Bell's patients died within three to six weeks, probably from dehydration, anorexia, or cardiac arrhythmias from overexcitement. Contrary to Thomas Melvill's fears that his brother would be left a lunatic if he had lived, the outlook for survivors is good, with most regaining normal mental status and function.

In time, it became apparent that along with a certain verbal flair, Herman Melville had also inherited his father's genetic predisposition to mood disorder. Herman's bipolar disorder fuelled his meteoric ascent as a writer, but also led to a catastrophic mid-career meltdown. The Melvillean burden of mental illness would have especially tragic consequences for Herman's own sons.

Although his family had fallen on hard times, by birth Herman belonged to America's new ruling class. Both of his grandfathers were heroes of the Revolutionary War. One prized family heirloom was a vial of tea leaves that Grandfather Thomas had shaken off his clothes after the Boston Tea Party. Thomas Melvill was a friend of Paul Revere and Samuel Adams, and commanded the artillery battery that drove the British out of Boston Harbor. After the war, he made a fortune as collector of customs for the port of Boston. Herman's maternal grandfather Peter Gansevoort conducted a bloody and obstinate defense of Fort Stanwix against a superior British force in 1777. The Gansevoorts were a remnant of New York's founding Dutch aristocracy; even in Herman's time, their land holdings were baronial in scope.

Herman showed no early indications of genius. When he was seven years old, the future author of the Great American Novel was described by his father as "very backward in speech and somewhat slow in comprehension, but you will find him as far as he understands both men and things both solid and profound, and of a docile and amiable disposition." Two years later, Herman surprised his family by winning first prize in oratory in his school, and his father noted that he had made "rapid progress."

After his father's death, the docile and amiable boy was put to work as a bank clerk to support his family. He was twelve years old. His ambitious sixteen-year-old brother Gansevoort was set up by his uncle in the manufacture of fur hats; Herman would join him in this business in a few years. Deprived of formal education, the brothers became voracious readers in their free hours. As a teenager, Herman joined a debating society, and sent prankish letters and stories to the local papers.

What effect did the collapse of the Melville family fortunes have on Herman's writing career? In gifted individuals, youthful periods of stress and unhappiness might foster literary achievement in two ways. They increase the risk for mood disorders, which have been linked to creativity, and they may also help develop the power of fantasy and imagination. Those who claim that Shakespeare did not write his plays often argue that only some wealthy, privileged, and highly educated person would have been capable of writing them. The premise of this argument is fundamentally mistaken. Literary genius more often arises from disappointment and chagrin than comfort and complacency; the rich and content have no need of imagination. Most great writers have experienced at least temporary emotional or financial hardship. A common biographical pattern in literary figures is the premature death of a parent, or a financial disaster leading to a sharp decline in social status. Swift, Defoe, Byron, Keats, Coleridge, Hawthorne, Melville, Thackeray, the Brontës, Virginia Woolf, and Sylvia Plath all lost a parent in childhood. Poe, Tolstoy, and Conrad were orphans. Byron, Melville, Dickens, Joyce, Yeats, and Shakespeare had debt-ridden fathers and brushes with poverty. Nabokov grew up in circumstances of privilege, but his family lost everything in the

Russian Revolution. Other childhood traumas might foster literary inventiveness, such as the miserable years Shelley and Orwell spent in boarding schools.

After stints as a farmer and a country schoolteacher, Melville embarked on his first sea voyage at age nineteen, a passage to Liverpool. On his return, he and a friend spent a few months looking for surveying work in the Mississippi and Ohio River valleys (Melville had taken some night classes in engineering in Albany). In January 1841, Melville went back to sea aboard the New Bedford whaler *Acushnet*.

The nineteenth-century Yankee whaleship was a floating factory devoted to the slaughter and rendering of great whales, especially the sperm whale. The gargantuan head of the sperm whale is principally comprised of the spermaceti organ, which contains several tons of whale oil. This takes on a semen-like consistency on exposure to the air, hence the misnomer spermaceti (whale sperm). A moderate-sized sperm whale yields over a thousand gallons of sperm oil, which was prized as a clean-burning, bright, odourless lamp oil. (Sperm oil was gradually replaced by kerosene, a product of petroleum distillation that was a near-monopoly of John D. Rockefeller's Standard Oil.)

Desertion rates in whaleships were high. Whaling consisted of long periods of tedium, punctuated by bouts of terror, rather like firefighting or watching the films of Lars von Trier. The unavoidable intimacy of whale and harpooneer made sperm whaling a dangerous and frequently deadly occupation. A bull whale could be up to ninety feet long, weighed about a ton for every foot in length, and smashed rowboats with ease. In at least two celebrated instances, sperm whales stove in and sunk whaleships much larger than themselves. (The spermaceti organ seems to have evolved as a battering ram and shock absorber in male-male aggression.) Whaling voyages were also unique in the American merchant marine for their exceedingly long duration and resultant sexual tension. This passage from *Moby-Dick*, about the working of congealed whale oil to liquefy it, might also allude to the sexual expedients of whalers:

> Squeeze! squeeze! squeeze! All the morning long; I squeezed that
> sperm till I myself almost melted into it; I squeezed that sperm till
> a strange sort of insanity came over me; and I found myself unwit-

tingly squeezing my co-laborers' hands in it, mistaking their hands for the gentle globules . . . Come; let us squeeze hands all round; nay, let us squeeze ourselves into each other; let us squeeze ourselves universally into the very milk and sperm of kindness.

So when the *Acushnet* anchored in the Marquesas Islands of the South Seas, Melville did not hesitate to run off, especially after the ship was greeted by an armada of island women, swimming nude with their clothes held over the water. As Melville wrote in *Typee*, "These females are passionately fond of dancing, and in the wild grace and spirit of their style excel everything I have ever seen. The varied dances of the Marquesan girls are beautiful in the extreme, but there is an abandoned voluptuousness in their character which I dare not attempt to describe. Our ship was now wholly given up to every species of riot and debauchery. Not even the feeblest barrier was interposed between the unholy passions of the crew and their unlimited gratification."

Polynesia was known as a sailor's Eden, despite the snakes that lurked in the lush vegetation. Every sailor knew that "at the Marquesas he might freely indulge in sex, feast on tropical fruit, and then be captured and eaten by cannibals." Disease was another hazard, although this was a greater risk for the natives than the sailors. Like many other societies in the golden age of exploration, Polynesia suffered horribly after its first contact with the West. From 1791 to 1864, the population of the Marquesas fell 80 percent from the usual infectious suspects, especially tuberculosis, typhoid fever, influenza, and smallpox. The survivors were left with other unwholesome Western afflictions. By 1884, 4 percent of Marquesans were lepers. Melville was particularly appalled at the widespread sequelae of riot, debauchery, and unholy passions: the disfiguring ravages of a syphilis epidemic. "One of the most dreadful curses under which humanity labors had commenced its havocs, and betrayed, as it ever does among the South Seas Islanders, the most aggravated symptoms." In *Omoo,* he estimated that two-thirds of Tahitians had syphilis.

Melville and his friend Richard Tobias Greene, the "Toby" of *Typee,* sneaked off to hide in the mountainous centre of the island for a few days, until the crew of the *Acushnet* tired of searching for them and went back out to sea. After several days of hiding in the hills and ravines in a torrential downpour, they became disoriented and, to their horror, blundered into the valley of the Typees, who had a reputation as ferocious cannibals. To their surprise, they were received with gentility and hospitality. Melville admired their egalitarian society and physical beauty; in *Typee,* he seems as impressed with the good looks of the men as of the women. Melville was pleasantly detained there for several weeks, with his mobility somewhat limited by a leg infection, until he was bartered off to the *Lucy Ann,* a dingy, villainous Australian whaleship. The *Lucy Ann* had an incompetent captain, an alcoholic first mate, and a crew that was largely bedridden with venereal disease. When she arrived in Tahiti a month later, a mutiny broke out, with Melville among the mutineers. Elsewhere, this could have had lethal consequences, but in Tahiti it led only to a farcical quasi-incarceration, from which Melville was quietly allowed to escape. After two months of rambling in Tahiti, Melville signed on the Nantucket whaler *Charles and Henry,* and later served on the naval frigate *United States,* arriving back in Boston in October 1844.

Melville regaled friends and family with his tales of adventure. In the past two years, he had become an accomplished storyteller; one imagines his shipboard stories were raunchier than what he told his sisters. At the casual suggestion of his sister Augusta, Melville wrote *Typee,* a charming, substantially embellished yarn of his time in the Marquesas. The novel, with its titillating innuendo and bare-bosomed Polynesian damsels, became a surprise bestseller. *Typee* also had a satirical edge. Melville suggests that, compared to the Westerners who undertook to civilize them, the pagan Polynesians actually had a more just and compassionate society, aside from that minor civic flaw of eating people. The notoriety of "the man who lived among cannibals" dogged him for the rest of his days. Many years later, an embittered Melville would realize that though he would write novels far surpassing *Typee* and its sunny sequel *Omoo,* he would never again approach their commercial success.

Herman's well-connected brother Gansevoort had helped get *Typee* published. Gansevoort was a rising star in the Democratic Party, and was serving as secretary to the American Legation in London. In May 1846, he died at age thirty, after a mysterious two-month malady. Gansevoort's fatal illness is obscure. He suffered mood disturbances (leading his boss and at least one physician to think he was malingering), vision loss, headaches, fatigue, and bleeding from the gums (he had recently had multiple tooth extractions). An autopsy, performed by the venerable Sir Benjamin Brodie, revealed disease of the heart, liver, and kidneys, but the full autopsy report seems not to have survived. Possible explanations include infective endocarditis (a blood infection lodged in a heart valve), disseminated tuberculosis, syphilis, or a lupus-like illness. Gansevoort's premature death was a fresh emotional and financial disaster for the family, and placed unwanted pressures on Herman as the oldest Melville male.

In 1847, Melville married Lizzie Shaw, the clever, plain daughter of Lemuel Shaw, chief justice of the Massachusetts Supreme Court. Judge Shaw had been a childhood friend and crony of Allan Melvill. The old judge retained an abiding, if increasingly perplexed, affection for Herman, long after it became clear that he was a poor provider, indifferent husband and father, and social liability.

In Melville's periods of peak productivity, his work habits were suggestive of hypomania, or unusual elevation of vigour and mood. This had uneven effects on his writing. His hypomania made *Moby-Dick* glow at a pitch of incandescent creativity, in a perfect blend of craft and invention. But in the case of his next novel, *Mardi*, his talents and discipline were not yet commensurate with his energy and ambition, and the book spun badly out of control. *Mardi* began as a straightforward sequel to his South Seas idylls, but it turned into an extravagant, overwritten flop with a bizarre psychosexual subtext. The long hours he spent at his desk without pausing for food or drink made Lizzie worried about Herman's health and sanity. The publisher's reader praised the first part of the book, but warned that later chapters were "quite delirious" and seemed "to have been written by a madman." While *Mardi* showed flashes of the pyrotechnics to come in *Moby-Dick*, it also exposed the fragility of Melville's mental health.

Two novels followed, both written at top speed. *Redburn* is a slight tale of youthful disillusionment, loosely based on Melville's first sea voyage to Liverpool as a painfully naïve teenager. The underrated *White Jacket* is a scathing attack on the barbarity of naval discipline, drawing on Melville's time in the navy. It includes a grisly, grimly funny amputation scene much admired by George Orwell.

In August 1850, Melville and Lizzie travelled to Pittsfield, Massachusetts. One fine day, Herman climbed nearby Monument Mountain with some literary friends, including the physician-author Oliver Wendell Holmes Sr, who was once again in the public eye, this time for unsavoury reasons. Holmes's tenure as the dean of Harvard Medical School was enlivened by the murder of one of the school's big donors, Dr Francis Parkman, by Holmes's mild-mannered but spendthrift chemistry professor, John White Webster. Before his sudden disappearance, Parkman had been hounding Webster over a bad debt. Holmes handled this sensational "trial of the century" with his usual aplomb and evenhandedness. For the defence, he testified to Webster's high moral character. For the prosecution, he admitted that the partially incinerated false teeth found in Webster's laboratory looked awfully familiar. He also praised the professional quality of the dismembered body parts found in the sewage tank of the professor's private toilet, which "very evidently showed a knowledge of anatomy on the part of the dissector . . . I should generally say that there was no botching about the business." Webster was convicted, and confessed before his execution on August 30, 1850. The presiding judge was none other than Lemuel Shaw, Melville's father-in-law.

Also present were the publisher James Fields and his prize author, Nathaniel Hawthorne, who had recently moved to the area. Hawthorne had written a glowing review of *Typee* a few months before. The two writers hit it off immediately, with the taciturn and aloof Hawthorne going so far as to invite Melville to stay with his family for a few days. Two months later, Herman bought a house in Pittsfield, which he named Arrowhead, and he and Lizzie left New York and moved to the Berkshires with their infant son Malcolm. Arrowhead was seven miles away from Hawthorne's house in Lenox.

Melville and Hawthorne had strong intellectual and temperamental affinities. Both were patriots with reservations, trying to forge a national literature; both were sceptics in religion; both tended to depression. There were also differences. Melville was more mercurial, and could be vivacious and extroverted, or moody and irascible. At his best, Melville was the better wordsmith, with a generosity of spirit lacking in Hawthorne. And while the happily married Hawthorne had a robust, if repressed, appreciation of feminine sensuality, in Melville's writings one finds a paucity of women, despite a profusion of seamen.

There is an undercurrent of homoeroticism in the Melville–Hawthorne relationship, at least on Melville's end. In an anonymously published essay by Melville, masquerading as the "ardent Virginian," he used a peculiar metaphor of insemination to describe Hawthorne's effect on him: "Hawthorne has dropped germinous seeds into my soul. He expands and deepens down, the more I contemplate him; and further and further shoots his strong New England roots into the hot soil in my Southern soul."

After he finished *Moby-Dick*, Melville wrote Hawthorne an extraordinary metaphysical love letter: "I felt pantheistic then—your heart beat in my ribs and mine in yours, and both in God's. A sense of unspeakable security is in me this moment, on account of your having understood the book. I have written a wicked book, and feel as spotless as the lamb . . . Whence come you, Hawthorne? By what right do you drink from my flagon of life? And when I put it to my lips—lo, they are yours and not mine. I feel that the Godhead is broken up like the bread at the Supper, and we are the pieces. Hence this infinite fraternity of feeling . . . My dear Hawthorne, the atmospheric skepticisms steal into me now, and make me doubtful of my sanity in writing you thus. But believe me, I am not mad, noble Festus! But truth is ever incoherent, and when the big hearts strike together, the concussion is a little stunning." Passages such as these have spawned an academic mini-industry in gay Melville studies, although there is no definite evidence that Melville ever had a gay relationship.

Moby-Dick was completed at Arrowhead, capping a year of frenzied creativity. Melville again seems to have been in a state of near-mania during its creation. While it was being written, he jokingly asked a friend to send "fifty fast-writing youths . . . because since I have been here I have planned about that number of future works & cant find enough time to think about them separately." Many years later, Lizzie recalled that Melville "wrote *White Whale* or *Moby-Dick* under unfavorable circumstances—would sit at his desk all day not eating any thing till four or five o'clock." *Moby-Dick* is a grand word-drunk adventure story, about religion, fate, free will, politics, sex, race, capitalism, nature, and one man's doomed, obsessive, and quintessentially American attempt to impose reason and order on a disorderly, irrational universe. English critics hailed *Moby-Dick* as an astonishing achievement, Americans found it smutty and subversive: perhaps both were right. Melville once expressed a desire to "write those sort of books which are said to fail." However, he was stung by *Moby-Dick*'s poor reviews and disappointing sales, which triggered a period of declining mood.

Melville's early biographer, Lewis Mumford, wrote of the years that followed, "The word insanity is far too loose to be used about Melville's mental illness, even during the limited period we are considering ... [but] there were moments ... between 1852 and 1858 when the outcome of his physical and mental condition may well have been in doubt." Bipolar spectrum disorders include bipolar I disorder, which requires a frank manic episode for diagnosis, with or without episodes of major depression; bipolar II disorder, which requires at least one hypomanic episode for diagnosis, as well as major depression; and subthreshold, or mild, bipolar disease. Melville's hypomanic episodes and the black depressions that overtook him as he aged are diagnostic for bipolar II disorder.

Melville had two powerful risk factors for bipolar affective disorder: the loss of a parent in childhood, and a robust family history of mood disorders. In addition to his probably bipolar father, both his mother and maternal grandmother suffered from severe depression; a maternal aunt died in an asylum; one maternal uncle suffered from depression, and another from alcoholism, a disease that shares a common genetic vulnerability with mood disorder. Three first cousins were alcoholic; Melville's brother Gansevoort may have suffered from a mood disorder; Melville's brother Allan had depressive tendencies and alcohol problems; his sister Kate probably had obsessive-compulsive disorder, another condition that has a genetic overlap with mood disorder.

Based on a recent study performed by Kathleen Merikangas and colleagues, in which 61,392 adults in twelve countries were asked about symptoms of mood disorders, the United States is the world's leading bipolar nation, perhaps accounting for its national outbursts of irrational exuberance. The lifetime prevalence of a bipolar spectrum disorder in the United States is 4.4 percent, compared to the global average of 2.4 percent.

If American mania is a real phenomenon, it might have resulted from genetic self-selection. After the Revolutionary War, the rebels, an excitable lot of optimists and enthusiasts, stayed here, while the dull, stolid Tories fled to Canada. Historical patterns of immigration could also be involved. In the nineteenth century, a touch of mania might have made a person more likely to jump on a boat and leave friends and family behind, probably forever, to seek their fortune in America. Environmental factors also play a role in the causation of bipolar disorder. Perhaps some rootless, stressful quality of life in America contributes to its apparent excess of mood disorders.

Melville's writings abound with references to madness, including the jocular invocation of depression and suicide in the celebrated opening paragraph of *Moby-Dick*. In a revealing digression in that novel, the peaks and valleys of mood disorder are likened to a soaring, diving eagle: "There is a wisdom that is woe; but there is a woe that is madness. And there is a Catskill eagle in some souls that can alike dive down into the blackest gorges, and soar out of them again and become invisible in the sunny spaces." Learning that a friend had been committed to an asylum, Melville exclaimed, "And he who has never felt, momentarily, what madness is has but a mouthful of brains." In *Billy Budd*, Melville remarks again on the fine line between reason and madness: "Who in the rainbow can draw the line where the violet tint ends and the orange tint begins? Distinctly we see the difference of the colors, but where exactly does the one first blendingly enter into the other? So with sanity and insanity."

After *Moby-Dick*, Melville's life is usually portrayed as a long, painful coda of squalor and obscurity. However, Melville remained highly productive for many years, despite the darkening moods and bouts of back pain and eye trouble that eventually ended his career as a professional writer. In a brittle state, having written six large books in six years, Melville launched into the composition of *Pierre; or The Ambiguities*. His original goal was to make money with a gothic potboiler, but his material got away from him again, and the novel's tone shifted first to literary parody, and then to painfully self-flagellating social satire. Family and friends again became concerned for Melville during the writing of *Pierre*. A worried neighbour wrote that Melville "did not leave his room till quite dark in the evening—when he for the first time during the whole day partakes of solid food—he must therefore write under a state of morbid excitement which must injure his health."

Elements of autobiography in *Pierre* must have distressed his family.

Pierre's parents are unflattering caricatures of Melville's own, and one plot thread involves a possibly incestuous relationship with a woman who may be Pierre's half-sister. (There are tantalizing hints in surviving letters that Allan Melvill might have fathered a child out of wedlock.) For all its tonal shifts and haphazard plotting, *Pierre* remains a fascinating, sometimes enthralling mess.

After *Moby-Dick* and *Pierre,* Melville's exalted moods became infrequent, and he became increasingly saturnine and physically unwell. Bipolar disorder is most notorious for episodes of mania. In the grip of mania, patients may be euphoric, insomniac, disorganized, and even psychotic, and they may commit spectacular indiscretions involving money, sex, substance abuse, or all of the above. However, over the long run, bipolar disorder is predominantly a depressive illness, even in those who have mania and hypomania at the onset of the disease. In bipolar I, the ratio of depression to mania is 3:1, and in bipolar II, Melville's more likely diagnosis, the ratio of depressive to hypomanic episodes averages 37:1.

Why is bipolar disorder relatively common? It seems counterintuitive that evolution would produce large numbers of people suffering from a disease whose major long-term outcome is depression. One answer is that mania, or hypomania, might favour short-term reproductive success, even if there is a depressive price to pay in the long term. Manic and hypomanic people can be charming, witty, energetic, and charismatic, not to mention hypersexual. Another possibility is that there might be an evolutionary advantage to bipolar disorder's little brother, subthreshold bipolar disorder. This condition may be more common than full-blown bipolar disease, has a related genetic basis, and at least anecdotally seems to be more prevalent in high-achieving types.

There may also be an evolutionary trade-off between mood disorders and enhanced creativity, which seem to be associated. Most writers and artists do not suffer from manic depression. However, separate studies by Kay Redfield Jamison and Nancy Andreasen have established that rates of mood disorder and suicide among writers and poets are many times higher than among the general population. There is evidence that the flight of ideas and emotional intensity of hypomania may be particularly conducive to creativity. As Jamison writes, "Poetic or artistic genius, when infused with these fitful and inconstant moods, can become a powerful crucible for imagination and experience."

After the failure of *Pierre*, Melville turned his pen to the lucrative short story market, producing some of his best work, including the baffling, masterful "Bartleby the Scrivener," which from a medical perspective can be read as a story about catatonic depression. The novella *The Encantadas*, which depicts the Galápagos Islands as a kind of Darwinian hell, contains passages of astonishing virtuosity, even for Melville. At other times, Melville toys with his readers. "The Tartarus of Maids" describes the harrowing lives of New England women forced to toil with rags and milky fluids in a paper mill on the Blood River, in what seems suspiciously like a grandiose metaphor for the biological imperatives of the female reproductive tract. In "Cock-a-doodle-doo!," which purports to be about a remarkable rooster, Melville may assume that his well-bred Victorian readers lack his sailor's intimacy with Anglo-Saxon vernacular:

"My friend," said I, "do you know of any gentleman hereabouts who owns an extraordinary cock?"

The twinkle glittered quite plain in the wood-sawyer's eye.

"I know of no *gentleman*," he replied, "who has what might well be called an extraordinary cock."

Oh, thought I, this Merrymusk is not the man to enlighten me. I am afraid I shall never discover this extraordinary cock . . .

"Good heavens! do you own the cock? Is that cock yours?"

"It is my cock!" said Merrymusk, looking slyly gleeful out of the corner of his long, solemn face . . .

I stood awhile admiring the cock, and wondering at the man. At last I felt a redoubled admiration of the one, and a redoubled deference for the other.

Another work from this period, the supposedly patriotic novella *Israel Potter*, contains this memorable judgment on his native country: "Intrepid, unprincipled, reckless, predatory, with boundless ambition, civilized in externals but a savage at heart, America is, or may yet be, the Paul Jones of nations."

During the 1850s, in addition to his mood problems, Melville was incapacitated for weeks at a time with back pain that laid him up in bed, and eye pain and light sensitivity that forced him to stay indoors. Lizzie attributed this to the strain of the creative process: "This constant working of the brain, & excitement of the imagination, is wearing Herman out." He was "toiling early & late at his literary labors & hazarding his health." His brother-in-law noted he was "dispirited and ill." Efforts to procure Melville a sinecure as a foreign consul were unsuccessful. In 1856, Judge Shaw, concerned about "how very ill Herman has been" and how overwork had caused "severe nervous affections," and perhaps also looking to grant Lizzie a respite, paid his way for a long excursion to Europe and the Middle East. Melville visited Hawthorne in Liverpool. Hawthorne's son Julian recalled that Herman was "depressed and aimless" when he arrived at the consulate. According to Hawthorne, Melville was "much overshadowed," and ruminating obsessively over the immortality of the soul and the existence of God:

> Melville has not been well, of late; he has been affected with neuralgic complaints in his head and limbs, and no doubt has suffered from too constant literary occupation, pursued without much success, latterly; and his writings, for a long while past, have indicated a morbid state of mind. Melville, as he always does, began to reason of Providence and futurity, and of everything that lies beyond human ken, and informed me that he had "pretty much made up his mind to be annihilated"; but still he does not seem to rest in that anticipation; and, I think, will never rest until he gets hold of a definite belief . . . he can neither believe, nor be comfortable in his unbelief; and he is too honest and courageous not to try to do one or the other.

Melville's physical illness began in March 1851, with a severe attack of eye pain and photophobia (pain on exposure to light) at age thirty-one. He described it as a "twilight of the eyes," which compelled him to steal about "like an owl." These symptoms were persistent and severe enough that Melville had a porch built onto the north side of his house so he could read outside in shade during the day. It is possible that milder symptoms began even before this. In 1849, Melville described his eyes as "tender as young sparrows."

Melville had many recurrences of eye pain. In February 1854, he suffered a "horrid week" of eye pain. Although Melville's family tended to blame his "eye strain" on overwork from writing, he also suffered attacks on vacation. In January 1857, a relapse occurred in Jerusalem, which Melville attributed to riding in the desert sun. Two months later, in Rome, he would suffer another episode of eye pain, associated with "general incapacity" and "singular pain in chest & in back." In October 1858, Melville's eyes were bothering him again, and he was unable to read. He suffered an "acute attack of neuralgia in the eyes" in April 1864.

His last recorded episode of eye difficulties took place in November 1872. His daughter Bessie blamed this on a viral infection: "Papa has been, or rather *is* quite sick with a bad influenza so that he cannot use his eyes at all." His eyes remained sensitive to light in old age. His granddaughter Frances recalled his wearing "dark glasses" when walking, "as the bright sunshine was sometimes too much for his eyes." Melville does not seem to have suffered lasting visual impairment from these episodes, and could read, write, and make his way about New York unassisted until his death at age seventy-two.

In February 1855, according to a memoir written much later by Melville's wife Lizzie, Melville "had his first attack of severe rheumatism in the back—so that he was helpless." Melville had great difficulty sitting at his writing desk or carrying out any work at his farm for months. That summer, Melville was treated by his old friend Oliver Wendell Holmes Sr, who diagnosed "sciatica" and "prescribed for him." Details of Melville's symptoms and treatment are lacking, as Holmes's casebooks for this period seem not to have survived. Holmes was an early advocate of what is today called evidence-based medicine. He correctly believed that most drugs then available were useless. In 1860, he said, "On the whole, more harm than good is done by medication." With the exception of "opium, which the Creator himself seems to prescribe," and a handful of other medications, "I firmly believe that if the whole materia medica, as now used, could be sunk to the bottom of the sea, it would be all the better for mankind—and all the worse for the fishes." Aping the Creator himself, Holmes may have provided Melville with laudanum, a commonly used form of opium dissolved in alcohol.

Melville was bedridden for weeks with low back and hip pain several times over the next few years. After the initial episode in mid-1855, he continued to suffer "ugly attacks" into early 1856. As noted above, disabling eye, chest, and back pain sidelined Melville in Rome in March 1857. He had a "severe . . . crick in the back" in March 1858 after completing a lecture tour but was well by autumn. Melville's back problems were a factor in his decision to sell Arrowhead and move back to New York City in 1861.

There are three explanations for Melville's physical complaints in the 1850s. Biographers have usually assumed that his symptoms were psychogenic or psychosomatic in origin, following the lead of some of Melville's contemporaries, who described him as neuralgic or neurasthenic. However, at least one friend of Melville's, Sarah Morewood, had insisted in 1859 that his ailments were organic in nature: "Herman Melville is not well," she admonished one correspondent. "Do not call him moody, he is ill."

Alternatively, Melville may have had multiple, unrelated medical conditions. His recurrent attacks of painful eye strain, low back pain, or sciatica, and rheumatism may have been separate problems. The long hours that Melville spent at his writing desk in candlelight would predispose him to low back and eye problems. Perhaps his arthritis was gouty, from overfondness for wine.

There is another possibility that has not been previously considered. Melville may have had a constellation of symptoms that would be recognized today as components of a single disease syndrome. An attractive unifying diagnosis for Melville's illness is ankylosing spondylitis (AS). Oddly enough, the first description of AS was probably published in 1850 by Benjamin Brodie, the London doctor who had performed the autopsy on Gansevoort Melville. Brodie had seen a thirty-one-year-old man with an ankylosed (fused) spine, subject to severe episodes of eye inflammation. Despite this early report, AS was not widely appreciated until the twentieth century.

AS is an autoimmune disease, in which the immune system attacks the body, instead of foreign invaders such as bacteria or viruses. AS most often leads to inflammation in the spine, the sacroiliac joints, which join the spine and the pelvis, and the eyes. Severe disability may result from progressive stiffening and fusion of the spine and sacroiliac joints. It is relatively common in the United States, affecting up to 0.1–0.2 percent of the population. AS is associated with several genes, with the most important being that for HLA-B27. Most Caucasians with AS carry the gene for HLA-B27. The HLA-B27 molecule binds to protein fragments from bacteria and viruses. It then presents these fragments to the immune system, and trains white cells to recognize and attack them when it encounters them. Unfortunately, HLA-B27 is prone to presenting normal body proteins to the immune system instead, leading to an aberrant and self-destructive inflammatory response. HLA-B27 is found in about 8 percent of white people, the vast majority of whom do not develop AS; several other genes are required in addition to HLA-B27 in order to get AS.

Men are three times more likely to develop AS than women, for unclear reasons. Most cases develop between the ages of eighteen and forty; Melville was thirty-one when he had his first attack of eye pain. Melville's description of his eyes as "tender as young sparrows" and his severe photophobia suggest an inflammatory process, rather than eye strain or psychosomatic illness. Eye complaints are common in AS, including nonspecific grittiness, dryness, or conjunctivitis. Full-blown anterior uveitis occurs in 25–30 percent of patients with AS. (Anterior uveitis is inflammation of the iris, the pigmented circular muscle that makes your eyes blue, green, or brown. It controls the size of the pupil in response to ambient light. Uveitis may also involve the ciliary body, the structure that supports the iris.) Anterior uveitis is a dreaded complication of rheumatological disease because of the possibility of visual loss. However, most patients of AS and anterior uveitis before the era of modern therapy did not have lasting visual impairment. Melville's photophobia in old age suggests that he may have had posterior synechiae as a complication of his anterior uveitis. These adhesions or scar tissue between the lens and the iris impede the ability of the pupil to contract properly to protect the eyes from light.

The low back pain in AS is typically dull and insidious in onset, although it can also be severe and episodic, as in Melville's case. (Perhaps Melville had milder initial symptoms that went unrecorded, especially given our sparse day-to-day documentation of Melville's life.) Ankylosing spondylitis may be misdiagnosed as sciatica, because sacroiliitis (inflammation in the sacroiliac joint) may cause buttock pain radiating into the upper thighs, mimicking pain from irritation of the sciatic nerve.

AS takes its name from the immobility and ascending spinal fusion commonly seen in the disease. Descriptions of Melville in later life, but not in his youth, stress his rigid, almost military posture. A college student in 1859 wrote that Melville "stands erect and moves with firm and manly grace." On first meeting his future father-in-law in 1877, Melville's son-in-law noticed his "erect bearing and squared shoulders."

Curiously, Melville's passport applications indicate that he lost 1⅜ inches in height between 1849 and 1856. His height is given at 5' 10⅛" in 1849, and only 5' 8¾" in 1856. Such specific measurements seem unlikely to be the product of error. Patients with AS may lose height by several mechanisms. In the most severely affected patients, a stooped, hunchbacked appearance may develop. This seems unlikely in Melville's case, as observers would not have described him as erect. Patients with longstanding AS often develop osteoporosis and lose height from compression fractures of the spine, but this would not explain Melville's rapid height loss at a relatively young age. The most plausible explanation for Melville's height loss is that in early AS, loss of lumbar lordosis, the slight curvature in the base of the spine, is common. This results in a tendency to lean or tip forward when walking or standing. A common compensatory mechanism is to bend the hip, thus righting the spine again. A muscle contracture of the hip may then develop, leading to a permanent loss of height. Hip flexion contractures are common in AS, and may be accelerated by inflammation of the hip joint, which is seen in 38 percent of AS patients.

During one of Melville's episodes of eye pain, he also had severe back and chest pain. Chest pain is fairly common in AS, and may result from thoracic spine involvement or inflammation of the joints around the breastbone, the costosternal and manubriosternal joints.

Melville's peripheral arthritis affected mainly his hands. It was therefore atypical for the peripheral arthritis of AS, which predominantly involves girdle or "root" joints (hips and shoulders). Some forms of spondyloarthropathy may be complicated by impressive swelling of the fingers, known as dactylitis, or sausage digits.

Although some patients with AS become disabled, the prognosis for most "has generally been considered rather favorable. The disease may run a relatively mild or self-limiting course." This seems to have been the case with Melville. Melville's restless and active nature probably resulted in a better outcome: "Of all therapeutic modalities, only exercise has been shown to curtail progression of spinal stiffness and restriction." Perhaps not coincidentally, Melville's musculoskeletal symptoms abated when he started working as a customs inspector, a job that required him to walk several miles a day. Today, Melville would also be treated with a nonsteroidal anti-inflammatory drug (NSAID), or possibly with a TNF-blocker (an antibody that blocks the action of the inflammatory molecule, tumour necrosis factor).

As Melville's depression took hold and he became entangled in the serpents of negation, his works turned gloomier and more mordant. In 1857, *The Confidence Man* appeared. This great, despairing novel about a Mississippi con artist bent on exposing the universal selfishness of human nature was Melville's last to be published during his lifetime. With it, his literary career seemed to lurch to a close, and he would have gone broke save for handouts from the judge, despite some income from lecture tours. Melville was a poor public speaker who "did not take very kindly to the lecture platform." One reporter noted that "it has rarely been our lot to witness a more painful infliction upon an audience." Although he did grant that Melville had a "good physique," this was marred by his "bilious temperament." Like a rock band that insists on playing their new album in concert, rather than their familiar old hits, Melville made matters worse by droning on about aesthetics and Roman statuary, when his audiences really wanted to hear about cannibals and bare-naked Polynesian ladies.

Melville vaguely described himself as "rheumatism-bound" in January 1862, being "laid up for several weeks with a neuralgic attack." He was still ill in March 1862, and unable to attend the funeral of a relative. By summer he had recovered enough to take several long hikes in western Massachusetts. Melville's back problems do not seem to have recurred thereafter, although he was ill in April 1873 with an unspecified "sudden & severe illness."

Although his physical health was somewhat better in the 1860s, his mental state was as bad or worse, although details are frustratingly sparse. In October 1862, Melville, active and venturesome when well, had a freak riding accident in which he shattered his scapula and broke several ribs. Melville's buoyancy and vigour evaporated. The account by one of his neighbours in the Berkshires suggests a diagnosis of post-traumatic stress disorder (PTSD):

> This prolonged agony and the confinement and interruption of work which it entailed, affected him strangely. He had before been on mountain excursions a driver daring to the point of reck-lessness . . . After this accident he not only abandoned the rides of which he had been so fond, but for a time shrank from entering a carriage. It was long before the shock which his system had received was overcome; and it is doubtful whether it ever was completely.

Studies in the aftermath of 9/11 showed that patients with underlying bi-polar disorder are predisposed to PTSD, with risk about double that of the general population. Patients with active mania or hypomania are es-pecially prone to PTSD.

As he slowly healed up, Melville wrote to a well-wisher, "This recovery is flattering to my vanity. I begin to indulge in the pleasing idea that my life must needs be of some value. Probably I consume a certain amount of oxygen, which unconsumed might create some subtle disturbance in na-ture. I once . . . cherished a loose sort of notion that I did not care to live very long. But I will frankly own that I have now no serious, no insuper-able objections to a respectable longevity. I don't like the idea of being left out night after night in a cold churchyard."

In 1865, family connections landed Melville a job as a customs in-spector in New York. Although the income and routine should have pro-vided a boost, two years later Melville apparently hit bottom, and Lizzie was on the verge of leaving him. In May 1867, her position had become so intolerable that her minister suggested to her brother-in-law that the Shaw family should abduct her. Sam Shaw responded that while his "sister's case . . . has been a cause of anxiety to all of us for years past," that Lizzie's "exaggerated dread" of public opinion restrained her from seeking a separation. If the Shaw family kidnapped her, the separation might be blamed on meddlesome family members, and Lizzie's "patience and fortitude will be turned into arguments against her belief in the insanity of her husband." Despite the fact that she was "ill treated," there was "no way in which she can throw off the responsibility for deciding for herself in this matter."

It is impossible today to gauge the extent of Melville's "ill-treatment" of Lizzie. Herman could be critical of Lizzie and verbally abusive. He may have abused her physically as well: a rumour surfaced decades after his death that he had once shoved her down the stairs. Lizzie's reluctance to leave Herman would be sadly familiar to anyone working with battered wives today. Many perpetrators of spousal abuse are themselves trapped in a downward spiral of depression and substance abuse; perhaps this was the case with Melville.

One of Melville's recent biographers, Laurie Robertson-Lorant, has declared: "Although . . . it's difficult to determine how much Melville drank, it seems certain that during the mid-1850s he came to rely on alcohol for his physical pain and emotional distress." This is somewhat overstating the case. Observers noted that Melville was naturally of a "shy temperament" with a "marked unwillingness to speak of himself, his adventures, or his writings in conversation." While he liked a drink to get "warmed-up" in society, the evidence for alcoholism is scanty. Melville certainly did extol the virtues of alcohol in his writings and correspondence. In 1859, a visitor found Melville "a disappointed man, soured by criticism and disgusted with the civilized world and with our Christendom in general and particular . . . his countenance is slightly flushed from whiskey drinking."

It should not be surprising if Melville had a drinking problem. If he had bipolar disease, his risk of alcoholism would have been high; 46 percent of bipolar I patients, and 39 percent of bipolar II patients, are alcoholic, compared to 14 percent of the general population. The America of Melville's youth was a nation of drunks. In 1830, the average American drank a staggering 7.1 gallons of absolute alcohol (ethanol) per year, with more than half of this coming from spirits. This is over triple the current level of per capita alcohol consumption in the United States. Men tippled at meals, starting with breakfast, at work, and at leisure. In some towns, bells rang at 11:00 A.M. and 4:00 P.M. for a boozy version of the modern coffee break. Votes were bought and business deals sealed with alcohol. Men of all classes and professions were known to indulge, with clergymen and physicians being especially notorious offenders. Women didn't guzzle whiskey or rum, but they were steady consumers of patent medicines fortified with alcohol, and often laced with opium and cocaine. Children drank as well. Colicky infants were soothed with cider at bedtime. Boys were encouraged to drink the sweet dregs of dad's brandy, with the idea that habituation to small amounts of alcohol would prevent dipsomania in later life (the opposite is true: early-life alcohol exposure is a risk factor for alcohol abuse). Even John Locke, the philosophical godfather of the American Revolution, advocated for juvenile inebriation, within limits: a boy's "drink should be only small beer [about 1 percent alcohol] . . . take great care that he seldom, if ever, taste any wine or strong drink. There is nothing so ordinarily given children in England, and nothing so destructive to them. They ought never to drink any strong liquor but when they need it as a cordial, and the doctor prescribes it."

There were several reasons for this countrywide intoxication. Booze was abundant. Most Americans farmed, and there were surpluses of food. Grain was diverted to whiskey-making. Apples were used for cider, which was something of a national drink in the young republic. (John Adams, who abhorred spirits, drank a tankard of hard cider every morning.) Alcohol was more practical than alternative beverages. Milk was too perishable, coffee too expensive, tea was too British. Moderate liquor consumption was thought to be salubrious; drinkers paid cheaper life insurance premiums than teetotallers. This was probably not without reason. Water supplies in most cities and towns contained a generous admixture of human faecal matter, making them wonderful sources of contagion. (In Herman's childhood, well-to-do families like his routinely fled Manhattan in the summers to avoid the routine outbreaks of cholera and typhoid fever.) Water scooped up from rivers and lakes was "purified" by letting the sediment settle to the bottom before consumption. This muck might occupy one-quarter of the bucket, in the case of water from the Mississippi at St. Louis, where Melville had visited in 1840.

Although Herman and Lizzie apparently reconciled, worse was in store that September. Their eldest son Malcolm was found dead in his room, shot in the temple, a pistol in his right hand. He was eighteen years old. Their younger son, Stanwix, who was "heartbroken" at Malcolm's death, became a drifter, and died of tuberculosis in San Francisco.

Twentieth-century Freudians had a field day with Melville's work and tormented personality. They accused him of oral-cannibalistic tendencies, passive and narcissistic homosexuality, and lyric phallicism. Cruellest of all, they blamed Malcolm's suicide on Herman's distant and hostile parenting, labeling him "suicidogenic." This grossly unfair judgment fails to take into account the impetuousness of teenage suicide and the surreptitious nature of teen depression. Contemporary psychiatry has a better appreciation of the biological and genetic basis for depression. Viewed in this light, Herman and Malcolm can both be seen as victims of their stressful childhoods and their genetics. Lizzie also seems to have been prone to depression, increasing Malcolm's genetic loading for mood disorder.

Melville started to write poems in secret in 1860. The smaller scale of poetry provided him with a creative outlet that enabled him to husband his faltering energy. When his poems were published, critics were appalled by their metrical irregularity, odd diction, and slant rhymes. (Critical valuation of Melville's verse has risen in recent decades. He is seen by some as a modernist forerunner of Eliot and Pound.) In 1876, Melville completed *Clarel,* an epic poem on the themes of doubt and belief that had long haunted him, containing one especially poignant couplet:

> Go mad I cannot: I maintain
> The perilous outpost of the sane.

An observer in the 1870s was impressed with Melville's timidity: "In the flesh he did not show either strength or determination; on the contrary, he was the quietest, meekest, modestest, retiringest man you can imagine." Lizzie in 1876 described him during the writing of *Clarel* as being in a "frightfully nervous state . . . if ever this dreadful *incubus* of a *book* . . . gets off Herman's shoulders I do hope he may be in better mental health—but at present I have reason to feel the gravest concern & anxiety about it."

Melville was reclusive in old age. In 1882, he declined an invitation to join the prestigious Authors Club, describing himself as a "hermit," and pleading that his "nerves could no longer stand large gatherings." When he returned from work, Herman would "shut himself up in his room, and no one knew or dared inquire as to what busied him there." While he could be irritable and explosive, he doted on his grandchildren, as one recalled many years later: "Many visitors to that household had cause to fear him but to me he was always gentle and I was never the victim of his moods and occasional uncertain tempers."

In May 1878, at the age of fifty-nine, Melville was incapacitated by bilateral hand arthritis. Melville's sister Frances wrote with relief in late May 1878 that "Herman could again use his right hand. His left is improving." A subsequent episode in March 1884 was diagnosed as "rheumatic gout." This was a rather imprecise diagnostic term used in Melville's day, sometimes used in cases of what would now be called rheumatoid arthritis, although it could be used to refer to any form of arthritis affecting multiple joints.

Lizzie's inheritance finally removed financial pressures, and enabled Melville to retire in 1886 at the age of sixty-seven. (Customs inspectors did not usually survive so long in the job. Melville seems to have been one of New York's rare honest customs men.) While avoiding society, Melville was reasonably active in retirement, often taking his granddaughters for long walks in Central Park. In the year of his retirement, a young acquaintance was impressed with Melville's "vigorous body" and "bright and roving eye," and a newspaper account described his "thick-set figure and warm complexion [which] betoken health and vigor."

At Melville's death, the *New York Tribune* noted that "His tall, stalwart figure, until recently, could be seen almost daily tramping through the Fort George district or Central Park, his roving inclination leading him to obtain as much outdoor life as possible." A granddaughter remembered Melville as a restless old man: "Sometimes I could hear him walking back and forth for a long time . . . the days when he paced up and down in his small study were not often the happiest ones for me, and surely not for him. He must have been walking off energy instead of turning to writing as a safety valve for smoldering fires." She also recalled Melville suffering a "severe nosebleed . . . probably caused by high blood pressure."

Melville's last novel, the posthumously published *Billy Budd*, the tale of an inscrutable father figure and a betrayed surrogate son, was written in declining health. In her fragmentary memoir, Lizzie wrote "Herman had two attacks of erysipelas—the last in April 1890—both of which weakened him greatly." Erysipelas is a streptococcal skin infection. It is more common in individuals who have had prior episodes of severe skin infection (cellulitis), because of the damage that these inflict on the lymphatic system, so perhaps this was a late sequel of Melville's leg infection in the Marquesas.

Melville died in 1891 at age seventy-two, apparently from heart failure related to a leaky heart valve. The death certificate blamed "cardiac dilatation, mitral regurgitation, contributory asthenia." His heart problems might bear some relationship to his other medical conditions. Systemic inflammation from rheumatologic conditions can accelerate the course of coronary disease. Streptococcal infections can lead to rheumatic heart disease, which damages the heart valves; however, this is usually a condition of younger patients and is associated with streptococcal infection of the throat, not the skin. The old sailor and pilgrim was laid beside Malcolm in Woodlawn Cemetery in the Bronx. The public was surprised when the obituaries appeared. Wasn't Melville already dead? Notoriously, the *New York Times* published a reminiscence entitled "The Late Hiram Melville."

In his final years, Herman grew closer to Lizzie. He realized that he could not have maintained his precarious equilibrium without her, and paid tribute to her in his final poems. After his death, his niece wrote, "The poor man is out of his suffering . . . poor Aunt Lizzie must be about worn out with her long and constant care of him." When Lizzie died many years later, "To know all is to forgive all" was found carved inside her writing desk. By the side of Melville's writing desk, partly obscured from view, was found a quotation from Schiller: "Stay true to the dreams of thy youth."

Herman Melville suffered through family tragedies as a child and an adult, had his masterworks maligned by critics, was racked by religious doubt, and battled a host of psychiatric illnesses, possibly including bipolar disorder, post-traumatic stress disorder, and alcoholism. He was also subject to years of ill health, which in retrospect may have been due to ankylosing spondylitis. In Melville's final years he wrote *Billy Budd,* proving that his creative mind could still function on the highest level, and he re-gained a measure of personal happiness. That he did so is a tribute to his physical and psychological resilience, but it also demonstrates how the love, support, and infinite patience of spouses, family, and friends can modify the course of chronic illness for the better.

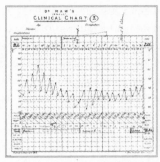

Fever chart from Yeats's attack of brucellosis. Yeats had intermittent fevers for two months, which peaked at 104.9°F on December 27, 1929. (Courtesy of John B. Lyons, M.D.)

7. SEX AND THE DEAD:
Brucellosis, Arsenic, and William Butler Yeats

I pray—for fashion's word is out
And prayer comes round again—
That I may seem, though I die old,
A foolish, passionate man.

—*"A Prayer for Old Age," W. B. Yeats*

I have met you too late. You are too old.
—*James Joyce (age 20) to W. B. Yeats (age 37)*

For weeks, the poet seemed close to death from his mystery illness. Each night, his fevers soared, peaking at 104°F on Christmas Eve, 1929. His mind was a fog, his appetite and energy were long gone, and his bedclothes were continually soaked with sweat. A succession of doctors was stumped. His wife Georgina, better known as George, was panicked and desperate, while his fellow poet Ezra Pound, terrified of contagion, had begun to avoid his sickbed.

Yeats's health had been poor for many years. His blood pressure was at times outrageously high, making him prone to episodes of lung congestion from heart failure. His doctors had advised him to give up his seat in the Irish Senate, and start wintering in a climate less cold and rainy than that of Ireland. At the behest of his increasingly odd buddy Pound, Yeats and his wife had gone to the sleepy seaside resort of Rapallo, in Italy, more than a thousand miles from their Dublin home.

George finally called in a specialist from Genoa, Dr Nicola Pende. He examined Yeats on January 22, 1930, and took blood samples. In a few days, he reported back that Yeats was suffering from Malta fever, or brucellosis. Pende, an opinionated and confident man, recommended treating Yeats with the most advanced medical therapy available: injections of arsenic and horse serum. Yeats would make a tortuous recovery from his illness, but his near-death experience sent his life and poetry veering in a strange new direction.

At the time of his illness, Yeats was sixty-four years old, a Nobel Laureate in Literature, and had been an international celebrity for many decades. By birth, he was a member of the Protestant Ascendancy, Ireland's embattled ruling class. His father, John Butler Yeats, had inherited a modest, heavily mortgaged estate in Kildare, and was studying law when he married Susan Pollexfen, the sister of his schoolfriend George. The practical and the irrational mingled in the Pollexfen bloodlines. William Pollexfen, Susan's father and the poet's grandfather, was a temperamental Victorian millowner who also ran a steamboat line. His children had a heavy burden of mental illness. Susan's sister Agnes had bipolar disorder, as did Agnes's two daughters, and Susan's brother William died in an insane asylum. George Pollexfen, William's favourite uncle, was a gifted storyteller with an obsessive interest in fairies, ghosts, magic, astrology, and the occult. He was also widely regarded as strange, and was committed to an asylum for depression at least once. Another sister suffered badly from depression, as did Susan herself in later years.

The couple was an odd pairing from the beginning. John was loquacious, charming, and irresponsible. Susan was dour and serious, although perhaps she had good reason to be. When she married John in 1863, she expected a comfortable life as the wife of a prosperous Dublin barrister and landowner. Unfortunately for her, John had more bohemian notions.

In 1867, when his eldest son William was two years old, John gave up a promising law practice for a tenuous living as a portrait painter. He was not without talent, but was disorganized and lacked business sense. Worse still, the Pollexfen businesses began to falter. As a result, the Yeats household battled debt, and shuttled between Ireland and London. The instability aggravated Susan's poor health and depression. She had a series of strokes, and died prematurely in 1900.

The couple had six children, four of whom survived into adulthood. The children spent long stretches of time in Sligo with the Pollexfens, where young William was heavily influenced by Uncle George, and absorbed his mysticism and interest in Irish fairy lore. All four children were creative. Little brother Jack became a painter of power and originality. Susan (Lily) and Elizabeth (Lolly) were active in the Arts and Crafts movement: Lily was an embroideress who had trained under William Morris, and Lolly was an artist and printer. The Yeats children inherited the Pollexfen tendency toward mood disorder. As adults, William, Lolly, and Jack all had depressive episodes. Lily had episodes of severe shortness of breath from vocal cord dysfunction, in which the vocal cords inappropriately block the airway during inhalation. This condition, often mistaken for asthma, is poorly understood, but depression and anxiety are triggers in many patients.

Due to money woes and frequent changes of address, William's formal schooling was patchy. He was a mediocre student, and learned to read with difficulty, although he found mathematics much easier. It has been suggested he suffered from dyslexia. His father was at first frustrated with his apparent obtuseness, once throwing a book at his head, but started reading poetry to him every morning. It became apparent that his facility and recall for the spoken word were superb. Many of his poems were composed orally by mumbling in a trancelike state while waving his hands in the air. He often did this in public, attracting unwanted attention from passersby and policemen. His lousy spelling and handwriting deterred him from taking the entrance exams for Trinity College in Dublin, his father's alma mater. His problems with orthography persisted into adulthood. After he became famous, an attempt to land the Chair of English Literature at Trinity College in Dublin was sunk by his misspelling of "professorship" in correspondence.

He attended art school in Dublin as a teenager, but dropped out to write, and became a voracious reader and autodidact. His early work was romantic and mystical in sentiment, Victorian in style, and steeped in Celtic myth. Although he is heavily identified with the Celtic Revival, which drew on the themes and subject matter of traditional Irish literature, his literary career was split between Dublin and London, reflecting his Anglo-Irish ambiguity. Later he helped found the Abbey Theatre in Dublin, and became heavily involved in playwriting and theatrical politics.

Yeats continued to be interested in the occult, which was a rich source of poetic images and ideas. Yeats's credulity has been somewhat overemphasized. He believed that most séances failed to reach the spirit world: "999 mediums out of 1000 never communicate other than subconscious experience." Nonetheless, his mystical interests often entangled him in absurd situations. At one point, he joined something called the Hermetic Order of the Golden Dawn, and helped repel the attempts of a disgruntled former member, Aleister Crowley, to steal some of its magical paraphernalia. Crowley, a self-proclaimed drug fiend, became a posthumous icon to seventies rock gods Jimmy Page and Ozzy Osborne for his Satanism and creative debauchery. Crowley also dabbled in poetry, although his works, as in the collection *White Stains*, were more anatomically oriented than those of Yeats.

As a young man, Yeats was not blessed with savoir faire with women. When he was twenty-three, Yeats met a redheaded Amazon named Maud Gonne, and was instantly smitten. She was a ferociously independent woman of means, having inherited a substantial fortune after her parents died young. Her passion for Irish independence bordered on histrionic. Like many ultra-patriots, her own origins were suspect: she was the daughter of an English army officer. Gonne became Yeats's muse and obsession for the next twenty-eight years. He proposed to her at least four times, and was shot down four times. Maud frequently travelled abroad, ostensibly to serve the rebel cause. However, she was actually leading a double life that she carefully concealed from Yeats: she was the long-term mistress of the right-wing French politician Lucien Millevoye, with whom she had two children. One of these children survived infancy, a girl named Iseult. Maud passed her off as a niece for many years.

While Maud was embroiled with Millevoye in Paris, Yeats lost his virginity at age thirty to a literary woman named Olivia Shakespear. She was unhappily married, wrote novels about unhappy marriages, and had a young daughter named Dorothy. The affair foundered when Yeats began to obsess about Maud again. In 1903, Yeats received a double shock when Maud Gonne married and converted to Catholicism. Yeats once wrote:

> It's certain that fine women eat
> A crazy salad with their meat

Maud Gonne's crazy salad was the soldier and rebel John MacBride. It was a disastrous match. MacBride was a brave, bad man, a vicious and abusive drunk who seduced Maud's half-sister and molested eleven-year-old Iseult. The couple separated in 1906, and MacBride returned to Dublin. (He was executed in the aftermath of the Easter Rising of 1916. This left Maud the honoured and relieved widow of an Irish martyr.) Some steamy letters from Maud suggest that she and Yeats may have physically consummated their relationship in 1908. If so, she quickly moved to restore their relationship to a more spiritual plane. Yeats found solace in the capable arms of Mabel Dickinson, a practitioner of Swedish massage whose father had been the Trinity College Professor of Pastoral Theology.

In 1909, Yeats met an excitable young American who regarded him as the greatest poet alive, and who had come to England expressly to meet him. Ezra Pound had been born in Idaho in 1885 of old Yankee stock. His forebears included whaling captains and a Union cavalry officer in the Civil War, and he was a distant relative of Henry Wadsworth Longfellow. Less reputably, he was also descended from horse thieves and a United States congressman. At the University of Pennsylvania, he was manic and nerdy, a frequent butt of practical jokes, notorious for a flamboyant wardrobe that included lilac socks, gold-headed canes, and floppy, feathered hats. Pound was befriended there by future doctor-poet Williams Carlos Williams, who called him "the livest, most intelligent and unexplainable thing I'd ever seen . . . but not one person in a thousand likes him, and a great many people detest him and why? Because he is so darned full of conceits and affectation." It was said of Pound that his ego could be more equitably distributed among three or four men. He was kicked out of a

Ph.D. programme in English, apparently for being an arrogant nuisance, and landed a job as an instructor of romance languages at Wabash College in Crawfordsville, Indiana. He was soon sacked from there after being found with a woman in his room. The authorities did not buy his explanation that he was only guilty of Christian charity in providing shelter to a stranded chorus girl.

Pound lived with Yeats as his personal secretary for three winters. He toughened Yeats up, helped him shed the last vestiges of Victorianism, and introduced him to modernism and experimental literature. He also taught Yeats fencing, which would have made for a striking spectacle. Pound was a lean bundle of nervous energy, with a vertical mass of russet hair, beady eyes, a foxy Van Dyke, a solitary turquoise earring, and a wardrobe that out-Yeatsed Yeats in foppishness. He was physically graceless, likened to a "galvanized, agile baboon" by one tennis opponent. Yeats was tall and ponderous. His broad forehead was a battering ram covered with a cascade of lank grey hair. A dainty pair of pince-nez perched incongruously on his Roman nose. Yeats had poor sight in his left eye due to keratoconus, a poorly understood degenerative condition of the cornea; this gave him a curious look of "peering into infinity."

William Carlos Williams said that Pound "was possessed of the most acute ear for metrical sequences, to the point of genius, that we have ever known. He is also, it must be confessed, the biggest damn fool and faker in this business." If Pound the poet flirted with greatness, Pound the editor and literary midwife was superb. He helped Yeats, Eliot, Joyce, Williams, Frost, e. e. cummings, and a host of lesser writers. Hemingway said he had learned more about writing from Ezra than anyone else, and praised him in 1925: "Ezra Pound devotes perhaps one fifth of his working time to writing poetry . . . with the rest of his time he tries to advance the fortunes, both material and artistic, of his friends. He defends them when they are attacked, he gets them into magazines and out of jail. He loans them money . . . he writes articles about them. He introduces them to wealthy women. He gets publishers to take their books. He sits up with them all night when they claim to be dying and witnesses their wills. He advances them hospital expenses and dissuades them from suicide. And in the end a few of them refrain from knifing him at the first opportunity." Pound was lucky to have built up this huge reservoir of good will, as he would dearly need it later.

Yeats became anxious to marry and produce an heir. He made a final perfunctory proposal of marriage to Maud in 1916, attaching a condition that made her refusal inevitable: she must no longer meddle in politics. When Maud turned him down, as expected, Yeats shifted his futile romantic attentions to Iseult Gonne, now twenty-two years old. A man with better social radar than Yeats would have realized that this was creepy and inappropriate on many levels, given their thirty-year age difference, his tortuous relationship to Maud, his role as a father figure to Maud's children, the (inaccurate) Dublin rumours that Yeats was Iseult's biological father, and Iseult's alleged history of abuse at the hands of her stepfather.

In 1917, spurned not only by Maud but Iseult as well, a fifty-two-year-old Yeats married the twenty-five-year-old Georgie "George" Hyde Lees. She was the best friend of Dorothy Shakespear, now Dorothy Pound, as she had married Ezra three years before. (Ezra was Yeats's best man.) George had two quintessentially English traits: a thick skin and a stiff upper lip. Both would prove invaluable over the subsequent twenty-one years of marriage to Yeats. Their union was cemented by a mutual interest in the supernatural. They experimented with automatic writing: George would enter a trance, and under the influence of the "Instructors" of the spirit realm, would scribble responses to questions posed by Yeats. He used this to develop the weird fusion of geometry and metaphysics revealed to an indifferent world in his book *A Vision*. While these ideas were utterly barmy, they did inspire several fine poems, including "The Second Coming." The Instructors could also be more down to earth, delivering what Yeats biographer Roy Foster calls "supernatural nagging." They urged Yeats to leave off the occult and get back to writing, to be more attentive to his wife's needs in bed, and to stop asking about Maud and Iseult Gonne and Olivia Shakespear all the time.

Yeats could be astonishingly insensitive. For example, he seems not to have realized the effects of his obsession with Iseult on George's feelings. His oddness, aloofness, and awkwardness were legendary, and suggest that he too may have had a degree of Asperger syndrome. An acquaintance who knew Yeats in his middle age noted that "It is not easy to talk to him in a familiar fashion, and I imagine he has difficulty in talking easily on common topics. I soon discovered that he is not comfortable with individuals: he needs an audience to which he can discourse in a pontifical manner . . . I doubt very much whether he takes any intimate interest in any human being." His wife, George, said that he "had no interest in people as such, only in what they said or did." The writer Vita Sackville-West noted that Yeats was "the sort of person who has no small-talk at all, but who either remains silent or plunges straight into the things that matter to them."

Yeats may have had another trait found in some persons with Asperger syndrome: prosopagnosia, or the inability to recognize faces. A tale is told of Yeats dining at Wellesley College in Massachusetts. Yeats was carrying on a vigorous discussion with his neighbour about the defects of T. S. Eliot's poetry. When Yeats asked the diner on his other side for his opinion, that gentleman held up his place card with "T. S. Eliot" written on it. (Yeats had lunched with Eliot in London on several occasions, and was on friendly terms with him.) On another occasion, Yeats's teenage daughter Anne got on the bus in Dublin to go home from art school. Her father was already aboard, composing poetry in his head in a distracted state, chanting softly and waving a hand in the air. Not wishing to disturb him (and perhaps a bit embarrassed), she did not speak to him, but followed him off the bus. As they approached the gate, he turned to her without recognizing her and said, "Who do you wish to see?"

In November 1918, George became seriously ill with pneumonia during the worldwide flu pandemic that killed at least 50 million people. She was six months pregnant at the time (pregnant women are highly susceptible to influenza and its complications). At the time, she and William had been living in Maud Gonne's house in Dublin, while Maud was under arrest in England for her support of Irish republicanism. Meanwhile, Maud, whose beauty had faded from age, stress, ill health, and constant smoking, had been diagnosed with tuberculosis, and paroled from prison on medical grounds. She was treated with inhalations of wood creosote. Although creosote has antiseptic properties, its medicinal use waned when it was discovered that the amounts needed to kill TB were also fatal to humans, and that it was also carcinogenic. However, one compound derived from wood creosote, guaifenesin, is still commonly used in cough syrup.

Maud snuck into Ireland, violating the terms of her parole, and showed up on the doorstep of her own house. Yeats refused to let her in, citing the dual dangers to George from infection and police. He later questioned her diagnosis of TB, saying that she merely had neurasthenia. This provoked a rupture with Maud, although they would soon reconcile. George recovered, and gave birth to Anne Butler Yeats in February 1919. This was a great surprise, as the Instructors had confidently predicted for months that the couple's first child would be a boy. (The long-awaited male heir, Michael Yeats, came two years later.)

In 1923, after rebellion, independence, and civil war in Ireland inspired some of Yeats's finest poetry, he won the Nobel Prize for Literature. He was one of the few Nobelists whose best work may have been ahead of him. Although his Nobel brought wealth and worldwide fame, Yeats kept an unquiet mind, refusing to accept the indignities of old age:

> What shall I do with this absurdity—
> O heart, O troubled heart—this caricature,
> Decrepit age that has been tied to me
> As to a dog's tail?
>   Never had I more
> Excited, passionate, fantastical
> Imagination . . .

When younger, Yeats had bouts of depression, but no serious medical problems until October 1924, when he became short of breath when delivering a speech. Severe hypertension was diagnosed. The vulgar and brilliant Dublin physician Oliver St John Gogarty, the model for Buck Mulligan in *Ulysses,* gossiped in a letter: "Pain in the region of the heart, when excited with oratory in the Senate—blood pressure 220!!" After two months' avoidance of public life, Yeats's blood pressure was down to 170.

In October 1927, Yeats had influenza. This was followed by "slight congestion in the left lung" and haemoptysis, or coughing up blood, while travelling in Spain in November. In a letter to Gogarty, George vigorously denied it was due to tuberculosis: "the haemorrhage in the lung was due to very high blood pressure (it was *260*) & since the BP has come down to 230 the haemorrhage has practically ceased. There is a small spot on the lung—since the congestion last October I imagine—& the man here thinks it quite unimportant—the blood pressure is what he concentrates on—W. is allowed no reading (but detective stories) no work & no exercise at present. No food after 4:30 pm at all. No wine nothing but toast for tea & breakfast. The diet suits him admirably."

Although blood pressure measurement was routine in medical practice by the 1920s, the seriousness of hypertension as a risk factor for heart disease and stroke was downplayed, and it was seen then and later as the result of "tension and mental strain." Yeats recovered with rest, dieting, and light exercise, and was well for the next two years. Yeats curtailed his public engagements, and in future he and George would winter abroad, in accordance with contemporary recommendations for hypertensive patients to vacation frequently. Systolic blood pressures as high as those of Yeats are almost unheard of today, when the target blood pressure is 140/90 and ideally 130/80, and a wide variety of effective antihypertensive drugs are available.

In 1924, Ezra and Dorothy had moved to Rapallo, followed by the concert violinist Olga Rudge, who happened to be pregnant with Pound's child. Shortly thereafter, Dorothy also became pregnant. Olga's baby daughter Mary was sent off to live with a peasant woman for the next ten years, and Dorothy's son Omar was dispatched to London to be raised by Olivia. The uneasy Pound-Shakespear-Rudge ménage à trois continued in some form for the rest of Pound's life, aside from twelve years that Pound spent locked up in a mental hospital. The Yeatses wintered in Rapallo in 1928. The climate was congenial, but the Pounds were not quite so good company as before, due to their domestic complications and Ezra's growing infatuation with Mussolini and the flaky economic panaceas of social credit. (This pseudoscience was, in essence, a set of feeble pretexts for printing more money.)

The Yeatses returned to Rapallo in 1929, travelling from Dublin to London at the end of October 1929. Shortly after arrival, W. B. had another episode of hemoptysis and congestive heart failure, perhaps precipitated by a viral illness. Tuberculosis again seems unlikely, as his chest

X-ray after recovery was clear. Yeats was prescribed mistletoe extract, a traditional and not terribly effective remedy for hypertension.

George and William left London on November 21, and arrived by train in Rapallo at the end of November 1929. At the beginning of December, Yeats began experiencing fever spikes each afternoon. His fevers remitted in mid-December, but returned on December 20. Yeats dictated his will on December 21. It was witnessed by Ezra, who stayed away thereafter. The first physician involved suspected typhoid fever, but subsequent urine and stool cultures were negative for *Salmonella* (stool cultures were performed twice). Yeats's fever continued unabated over the next three weeks. At the recommendation of physician friends in London, George Yeats asked Nicola Pende to consult. Pende was a distinguished Italian internist who coined the term "endocrinology." He was also, like Pound, an ardent supporter of Il Duce. (In 1938, Pende signed the "Manifesto of Racial Scientists" that was used to justify the persecution of Italy's tiny Jewish minority. Pende originally opposed the document, not because it was pernicious anti-Semitic claptrap, but because it failed to assert the superiority of Romans over Aryans.)

Pende arrived on January 22, 1930, and was "convinced it was 'febbre di Malta'," given the prolonged, undulating fever, and negative tests for typhoid. (Gogarty suspected the same, at long distance.) Pende prescribed injections of *Brucella* antiserum from horses, which Yeats started on January 25, 1930. Antiserum was a major treatment for bacterial infections in the preantibiotic era. Horses, goats, or cows were injected with dead bacteria. The animals' immune systems then made antibodies that stuck to the bacteria. Large amounts of blood were taken from the animals, and the serum, which contained the antibodies, was separated from the clotted blood. Antiserum reduced deaths from pneumonia and meningitis, but it was not as effective as antibiotics later proved to be, and it also caused nasty allergic reactions (serum sickness). The experience with equine, bovine, and caprine antiserum in the treatment of brucellosis was generally favourable, although some patients relapsed after cessation of therapy.

Yeats received antiserum from Milan every other day, and solarson, an arsenic-containing antibiotic, on the alternate days. Solarson, synthesized by Emil Fischer and manufactured by Bayer, was little used outside of Europe. However, according to its inventor, it had one clear advantage over its major competitor, salvarsan: "It does not result in garlic breath, as do other arsenic compounds." The clinical experience with arsenical antibiotics for brucellosis was limited, but favourable. Pende also recommended a "most stimulating," even epicurean diet for Yeats: egg flips with brandy, beef, chicken, and "very dry French champagne in the evening, even if the temperature rises to 105°F." With this cosmopolitan regimen of German arsenic, Italian antiserum, and French champagne, Yeats's sense of well-being improved quickly. (His temperatures stayed high for several days, perhaps as a side effect of antiserum.)

The blood tests ordered by Pende were positive for both "Malta fever" (*Brucella melitensis*, acquired from goats or sheep) and "bacillus of Bang" (*Brucella abortus*, acquired from cattle). Tests at the time were probably unable to distinguish between the two closely related bacteria. If Yeats's infection was acquired from contaminated milk in Dublin or London, *B. abortus* infection was more likely. (*B. abortus* is clinically somewhat milder than *B. melitensis*.)

Brucellosis has been a major human disease since the domestication of sheep, cattle, and especially goats. A two-thousand-year-old carbonized cheese, buried by lava at Herculaneum when Mount Vesuvius erupted in 79 A.D., showed traces of *Brucella* bacteria on a recent analysis. Brucellosis is common in the Mediterranean basin and the Middle East, due to the importance of goats as sources of meat and milk; unpasteurized dairy products are an excellent source of infection. Brucellosis was once so common in Malta that the disease was also known as Malta fever. The high prevalence of the disease there arose from the practice of taking goats from door to door, and delivering fresh milk straight from the goat's body.

Scientific interest in brucellosis picked up during the Crimean War, as the filth and nastiness of siege warfare led to British soldiers coming down with a plethora of unpleasant diseases: cholera and typhoid fever (from consumption of food and water contaminated with faeces), malaria (from mosquitoes), and typhus (from body lice). Army doctors were familiar with all of these diseases, which were common in the colonies and England itself, for that matter. But a new illness puzzled them. They called it remittent fever or Crimean fever. Patients had weeks of high fevers, with inexplicable periods when the fever abated for a few days, then returned with a vengeance, as happened with Yeats. The most striking feature of the disease, which we now know to be brucellosis, was the agonizingly slow convalescence. After the fever resolved, patients had months of depression, irritability, arthritis, and exhaustion. Relapses might occur, involving the nervous system, bones, and joints. The infection could attack the lumbar vertebrae or the sacroiliac joints, which join the spine and the pelvis, leading to excruciating low back pain. Weakness and paralysis could arise from involvement of the nerves and spinal cord. The source of the infection was probably the goats that the army had brought along as a portable food source.

Brucellosis became a scapegoat in one of the great debacles of the British navy, the sinking of the HMS *Victoria* on June 22, 1893. The British Mediterranean Fleet, commanded by the massively bearded and much-feared Vice-Admiral Sir George Tryon, was on manoeuvres off the coast of Lebanon in splendid weather, with thousands of spectators on shore. Tryon was aboard his flagship *Victoria*, the most powerful and certainly the most top-heavy ship in the Royal Navy. The forward deck had a single enormous gun turret, weighing 110 tons, and containing two 16.25 inch guns. The sailors called her "the slipper," because of the ominous way her forecastle fell from view in a rough sea. The fleet was travelling in adjacent columns when Tryon gave the order for the two columns to head toward each other and make a 180° turn. The admiral, a man of fossilized obstinacy, became enraged when his subordinates suggested that this might be physically impossible, as the distance between the columns was the same as the turning radius of the ships. When the ship leading the other column hesitated, Tryon had the yeoman signal "What are you waiting for?" The *Victoria* was promptly rammed, and capsized thirteen minutes later. The engines were unaffected, and the screws continued to turn all the way down, driving her to the bottom like a torpedo. The vortex from the churning propellers sucked hundreds of frantic sailors under. The wreck was discovered in 2004, standing upright, with two-thirds of the ship buried below the muck. It is one of the very few vertical shipwrecks that have been discovered. In the uproar that ensued, it was charitably suggested that late admiral's judgment had been clouded by the lingering effects of Malta fever, which was known to have infected many sailors of the fleet.

George wrote that "Pende . . . was positive that W. had got the original infection in London—based on dates of temps. No goats here (strange, but true) and no case ever known in Rapallo. That's as may be!" As the incubation period of brucellosis is typically two to four weeks, and as Yeats's symptoms began in early December, Pende was probably correct that Yeats's infection had originated in England. The recent introduction of pasteurization and bottling had made scant impact on the quality of the English milk supply in Yeats's time. Today, brucellosis is rare in North America and Western Europe, although it persists in Southern Europe and the Middle East.

Many features of Yeats's illness were typical of brucellosis. According to George, the poet suffered "rheumatic pains and a good deal of sweating at night (to a point of having to change nightclothes)." As noted, joint and low back pain, especially involving the sacroiliac joints, are common and distressing features of brucellosis. Drenching sweats, often malodorous, are also prominent. Constipation is common in brucellosis, but Yeats had "a good deal of diarrhoea," probably as a side effect of arsenic therapy. Yeats had an enlarged spleen, which is found in up to 61 percent of brucellosis patients.

Yeats's fever charts show that his heart rate was low relative to his degree of fever (relative bradycardia). Normally, as body temperature goes up, the heart rate also rises. At Yeats's peak temperature of 104.9°F (40.5°C), his pulse was only ninety-four beats per minute. Yeats's pulse should have been at least 108 beats per minute at this temperature. This phenomenon seems to be most common with infections with bacteria that are able to persist within white cells, such as typhoid fever, Legionnaires' disease, tularaemia, and brucellosis.

George took elaborate measures to prevent Yeats from becoming aware of his temperatures, even enlisting Gogarty in an effort to conceal the gravity of Yeats's illness from him. Although failure to disclose pertinent information to patients is today considered unethical, the practice was widespread in Yeats's day.

Yeats's prolonged illness had one beneficial effect: his blood pressure fell to 150/70, probably as a result of his weight loss. His recovery was slow, compatible with the mean time of three to four months for full return to function after brucellosis in the preantibiotic era. He was anaemic, had lost twenty pounds, and had trouble walking or even standing. His energy and concentration were fitful, and he was nervous, irritable, and restless for months. Brucellosis is associated with reversible neuropsychiatric disturbances, including "depression of spirits . . . loss of memory, irritability of temper, a proneness to shed tears without any adequate occasion, and an unsteady, timorous, childish manner." There is a confusing relationship between chronic fatigue syndrome, or "neurasthenia" in the older literature, and brucellosis. Patients with chronic brucellosis and vague symptoms have sometimes been misdiagnosed with neurasthenia; other patients with post-infectious chronic fatigue symptoms have been misdiagnosed with active brucellosis. The pioneering nurse Florence Nightingale is thought by some to have acquired chronic brucellosis during the Crimean War, although others have argued that her litany of physical complaints was due to bipolar disorder, hypochondria, or post-traumatic stress disorder.

Yeats seems not to have suffered from serious side effects from his arsenic therapy. Arsenic is a classic example of a medication with a narrow therapeutic index, meaning that the effective dose is very close to the amount needed to cause harm. The toxic and therapeutic effects of arsenic both relate to its ability to generate free radicals, resulting in widespread cellular damage. While arsenic has a long and chequered history in medicine, it is more familiar as a poison. Social climbers from Nero to the Borgias have long favoured arsenic trioxide, a colourless, tasteless, and highly lethal poison. In France, it was sardonically known as *poudre de succession:* "inheritance powder." Acute arsenic poisoning may result in gastrointestinal distress, nerve damage, pulmonary oedema (fluid in the lungs), low blood pressure, kidney failure, and cardiac sudden death.

Arsenic as medication dates back to Hippocrates, who used it for skin ulcers, but the modern use of arsenic as an antibiotic dates to Thomas Fowler, who in 1786 reported his favourable experience treating over two hundred patients in the "fenny" regions of England with ague (malaria). Fowler had discovered that a popular patent medicine, "Tasteless Ague and Fever Drops," was composed primarily of arsenic. He decided to produce his own version from arsenic, alkali, distilled water, and spirits of

HEALTH BENEFITS
OF ARSENIC?

~⊸℘~

The human diet contains tiny amounts of arsenic. This may not be a bad thing. Arsenic, in minute amounts, may be an essential trace nutrient in mammals. Chickens, hamsters, goats, and rats that are fed artificial diets that are extremely low in arsenic develop a variety of health problems, including growth retardation, infertility, and heart failure. The addition of arsenic to animal feeds in agriculture stimulates growth. Until recently, the organic arsenic compound roxarsone was added to the feed of 70 percent of broiler chickens in the United States to inhibit the growth of intestinal parasites. This practice, banned in the European Union in 1999, may expose Americans to unhealthy amounts of arsenic in poultry, as well as creating a unique biohazard: toxic chicken manure. Roxarsone was taken off the market in the United States in 2011, but other arsenic compounds are still used in poultry farming. (The organic form of arsenic, which is bound to carbon atoms, is less poisonous than inorganic arsenic.)

In the mountainous Styrian region of Austria in the nineteenth century, peasants fed their horses arsenic and ate huge amounts of arsenic themselves, claiming improved energy, stamina, digestion, and resistance to infection. Women

(continued)

lavender, this last added "merely for the sake of giving it a medicinal appearance, lest, from its being colourless and tasteless, those patients . . . should be tempted to use it with too great freedom; the consequences of which might frequently prove troublesome, if not sometimes dangerous." Fowler's solution was also used with some success in inflammatory conditions such as asthma, eczema, and psoriasis.

In eighteenth-century America, Nathaniel Potter found that Fowler's solution worked as well against malaria as quinine, the modern standard of care, but compiled a daunting catalogue of side effects, including nausea, vomiting, diarrhoea, stomach pain, convulsions, twitching, drooling, bloody urine, gnashing of the teeth, fainting, and death. Potter also noted that his mentor, Benjamin Rush, had used arsenic successfully for syphilis of the skin, a century before Ehrlich's salvarsan.

Arsenic trioxide was used as an early treatment for leukaemia and lymphoma. More recently, arsenic has been shown to be highly effective in a specific type of leukaemia, acute promyelocytic leukaemia, in which it induces cancer cells to self-destruct (technically this is known as apoptosis). Paradoxically, arsenic is also carcinogenic; exposure increases the risk of lung, bladder, kidney, and especially skin cancer.

With arsenic and horse serum, Yeats slowly recovered from his attack of brucellosis, but he was a changed man. Repeated brushes with mortality had affected him profoundly. His poems were wiser and sadder, his personal life more squalid and disorderly. Yeats once wrote, "I am still of opinion that only two topics can be of the least interest to a serious and studious mood—sex and the dead." In his final years, sex and death would dominate his thoughts. He became depressed after the death of his longtime patroness, Lady Gregory, and preoccupied with his loss of sexual function. Yeats, like Hemingway and other ageing writers, equated this with waning creativity. Hoping to reinvigorate his sex life, he underwent a Steinach procedure in 1934 by a fashionable Harley Street "sexologist," a gay Australian Jew named Norman Haire.

The Steinach procedure was simply a vasectomy. Supposedly, termi-

consumed arsenic to develop a rosy-cheeked complexion. (The red cheeks might have been the result of damaged blood vessels in the skin.) The Styrians took arsenic intermittently, and in gradually escalating doses, to minimize toxicity. In the nineteenth century, those accused of arsenic poisoning sometimes invoked the "Styrian defence," claiming that the arsenic in the victim's corpse was the misguided result of self-medication with arsenic for its supposed tonic or cosmetic properties. The liver may be able to develop a tolerance to arsenic by speeding up its elimination from the body. King Mithridates of Pontus is supposed to have developed such a tolerance to foil would-be poisoners:

They put arsenic in his meat
And stared aghast to watch him eat

This stratagem backfired. After Mithridates was defeated by the Romans, his suicide attempt by poison failed, and he was clumsily stabbed to death by a servant.

nating the reproductive function of the ageing testis allowed it to fully devote its flagging energies to the production of testosterone, allowing the return of vigour, youth, and potency. Steinach also claimed that his procedure could cure homosexuality. Steinach did not forget the ladies: they too could be rejuvenated, by liberally dosing the ovaries with radiation. While these assertions have long since been debunked, the Steinach procedure was once part of the scientific and medical mainstream. Freud, like Yeats, was also "Steinached." Although Steinach never won the Nobel Prize in Medicine, he was nominated six times.

Others went further in the quest for the hormonal fountain of youth. In 1889, the distinguished neurologist Charles-Édouard Brown-Séquard reported the results of a sensational self-experiment in the *Lancet*. By injecting himself with crushed testicles from puppies and guinea pigs, he claimed to have augmented his physical, mental, and sexual stamina, and turned the ageing process back thirty years. Brown-Séquard's testicular wonder juice was unleashed on the public as Spermine. It is doubtful that it was able to substantially elevate testosterone levels, as not much testosterone is actually stored in the testis.

In 1920s, the Russian Serge Voronoff made a fortune by implanting slices of vigorous young chimpanzee testicles into aged, well-to-do human scrotums, at a price tag of $5000 per operation. Voronoff also claimed to cure female menopause with implants of monkey ovaries. An international fad ensued, and French authorities had to ban monkey hunting in their African colonies because of the plummeting primate population. Voronoff's celebrity and success spawned creative if unscrupulous imitators. The American charlatan John R. Brinkley made a million dollars a year in the 1920s peddling patent medicines and implanting goat testicles into the credulous, with only occasional fatalities among his patients.

Yeats's Steinach procedure had a remarkable placebo effect on the poet. He had what he called a "strange second puberty," and indulged in a series of amorous adventures with young female admirers. These were probably more important to Yeats as a source of poetic inspiration, rather than sexual gratification. Meanwhile, ribald gossip sped round Dublin. Yeats was mocked as "a Cadillac engine in a Ford car" and "the gland old man." George Yeats simply stayed at home with the children. For the ageing Yeats, she had become less a wife than a secretary and nursemaid. If all this broke her heart she never showed it.

The Yeats—Pound relationship petered out after Yeats's brucellosis attack. In fact, Ezra was alienating many old friends with his bizarre behaviour and Fascist rantings. In 1934, Hemingway and Joyce had dinner with Pound in Paris and feared he had gone mad. That same year, Ezra scrawled the single word "putrid" on a manuscript that Yeats had given to him in Rapallo for editorial comment. From then on, Yeats wintered elsewhere.

Ezra Pound would outlive his old friend by several decades, although this at one time did not seem likely. During World War II, he was indicted for treason for spewing hateful Fascist propaganda over the Italian airwaves. Hemingway read the radio transcripts, and suggested that the only way for the "obviously crazy" Pound to escape the gallows would be to plead insanity: "He deserves punishment and disgrace but what he deserves most is ridicule." At war's end, Pound was caught in Rapallo, locked in a reinforced steel cage, and shipped back to America to stand trial. With the help of Hemingway and other influential literary friends, Pound was, rather dubiously, declared psychotic, and committed to St. Elizabeths Hospital in Washington, D.C. The psychiatrist E. Fuller Torrey, who worked at St. Elizabeths, attributed Pound's mix of "chutzpah and hubris" to narcissistic personality disorder and cyclothymia, a variant of bipolar disorder. When he was released in 1958, Pound was at first unrepentant, flashing a Fascist salute on his return to Italy. But age, ill health, isolation, and depression wore down his braggadocio. He told friends that he started with a swollen head and ended up with swollen feet. In 1963, he admitted to an Italian reporter, "I have lived all my life believing that I knew something. And then a strange day came and I realized that I knew nothing, that I knew nothing at all . . . I was as stupid as if I had been a telescope used the wrong way. Knowledge came too late. Too late I arrived at the certainty that I knew nothing."

Yeats's health took another turn for the worse. In January 1936 in Palma, he was seriously ill with heart failure and atrial fibrillation. His kidneys started to fail, and he was briefly delirious. Gogarty quoted the "quaintly translated" report from Yeats's Spanish physician:

"We have here an antique cardio-renal sclerotic of advanced years."

Why! It sounds like a lord of Upper Egypt. But any touch of bronchitis this winter is likely to carry him off. His heart is enlarged and his kidneys throw back pressure on it.

By August 1936, he had recovered mentally, although he was still physically debilitated: "It is a curious experience to have an infirm body and an intellect more alive than it has ever been."

In addition to being more preoccupied with sex, Yeats was more prone to anger. It has been suggested that the function of his frontal lobe, that brake on our more outrageous impulses, may have been damaged from the effects of chronic hypertension on the small blood vessels of the brain. After one outburst, Yeats wrote a famous quatrain by way of apology:

> You think it horrible that Lust and Rage
> Should dance attendance upon my old age;
> They were not such a plague when I was young.
> What else have I to spur me into song?

Despite worsening dyspnoea and "dropsy," or leg swelling, Yeats was highly productive, and worked at the highest intellectual and creative level. Some of his best poetry was written in his last years, although it was increasingly bleak, ironic, and harshly self-critical. In "The Circus Animals' Desertion," Yeats took a long, pitiless look back at his poetic career, and the illusions that had sustained him—romantic, nationalistic, and otherwise. Old and ill, he must start all over again:

> Now that my ladder's gone,
> I must lie down where all the ladders start
> In the foul rag and bone shop of the heart.

Yeats died of heart failure in France in January 1939, his wife and two mistresses in attendance. He was given temporary burial there, but the outbreak of war made it impossible to repatriate his remains for many years. After the war, it was found that his bones had been misplaced. After confusion and distress, his presumed remains were located and sent back to Ireland in 1948 for burial. Maud Gonne's son Seán MacBride, who had flown kites with Yeats as a boy, represented the Irish government at the funeral. (MacBride was an IRA gunman turned politician and humanitarian; he helped found Amnesty International, and won the Nobel Peace Prize in 1974 for his advocacy of disarmament.) The bones were interred in the shadow of Ben Bulben, on whose slopes, according to the legends, heroes had clashed and lovers sought refuge. As per Yeats's instructions, these lines were inscribed on his headstone:

> Cast a cold eye
> On life, on death.
> Horseman, pass by!

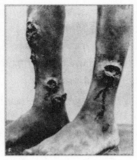

Tropical ulcers due to yaws. Yaws is caused by a subspecies of *Treponema pallidum*, the same bacterium that causes syphilis. Unlike syphilis, yaws is not usually sexually transmitted. (Courtesy of Maurice Reeder, M.D., and Philip Palmer, M.D.)

8. MEDICAL MISADVENTURES OF AN AMATEUR M.D.:
Jack London's Death by Hubris

In the meantime, in my amateur M.D. way, I did my best . . . Here were malignant and excessively active ulcers that were eating me up. There was an organic and corroding poison at work . . . I decided to fight the poison with corrosive sublimate. The very name of it struck me as vicious. Talk of fighting fire with fire! I was being consumed by a corrosive poison, and it appealed to my fancy to fight it with another corrosive poison.

—*Jack London*, The Cruise of the Snark

Jack has finally worn down as perfect a human machine as the world seldom sees.

—*George Sterling, poet and friend*

He hit the road before Kerouac. He was down and out before Orwell. Jack London was the all-American macho man of letters when Hemingway's mother was still dressing little Ernest in girl's clothing. By age twenty-one, when Jack became a full-time writer, he had already been a sailor, seal hunter, tramp, fish warden, oyster pirate, cannery worker, street punk, jailbird, boxer, and gold digger. *The Call of the Wild* catapulted Jack to sudden riches and worldwide fame. His improbable success as a writer was fuelled by manic energy and a faith in self that bordered on delusional. These traits made Jack the first writer to make a million dollars in his career, but they also led directly to his premature demise.

Jack was a man of contradictions. Nietzsche and Darwin clash with Victorian treacle on his pages. He preached socialism, but had a Korean manservant and practised conspicuous consumption. He believed in the brotherhood of man, but nearly everything he wrote is tinged with racism. He praised hardworking, clean-living Anglo-Saxons, but was himself the bastard offspring of a dwarfish spiritualist named Flora Wellman and a con man named William Henry Chaney.

Chaney was born on a farm in the back woods of Maine, deserted the navy in Boston, dabbled in law and journalism in Virginia, disappeared for nine years, became an astrologer in New York, and fled for California after getting out of jail, leaving at least three wives behind in the course of his peregrinations. He met up with Flora in San Francisco. She had grown up in a respectable home in Ohio, but wandered westward after a bout of typhoid fever stunted her growth and left her balding, myopic, and a little unhinged. The two set up an "astrology parlour," but their salad days ended when Flora got pregnant. Chaney demanded that she get an abortion, and tossed her out when she refused. She responded with histrionic suicide attempts with laudanum and a misfiring pistol. The scandal made the local papers, and Chaney slipped away to Oregon. (Years later, when he was a struggling young writer, Jack discovered the sordid circumstances of his nativity, and tracked Chaney down in Chicago. The devious old rogue, perhaps afraid that Jack would cadge money from him, claimed that he was impotent during his relationship with Flora. Moreover, Chaney insinuated that it was impossible to know who Jack's real father was, given Flora's promiscuity.)

After Jack's birth on January 12, 1876, Flora became listless and lost her appetite, possibly suffering from post-partum depression. A doctor recommended an African-American wet nurse, Virginia Prentiss. She became a surrogate mother to Jack, and later lent him the money to buy the boat that he used to raid the oyster beds of the hated Southern Pacific Railroad. After he got rich, he gave her the same pension every month as he gave his mother.

When Jack was eight months old, Flora married a debilitated Civil War veteran named John London. Flora called her son her "badge of shame," which Jack was only to fully understand when he got older. He grew up believing that John was his biological father, and later maintained this fiction for the public after learning of Chaney. Tiny Flora was a domineering mother, resorting to tantrums and fake heart attacks to get her way when necessary. She was also an unrepentant racist who clung to her middle-class, Anglo-Saxon origins, and filled Jack's brain with nonsense about their superiority to their Irish, Italian, Portuguese, and Asian neighbours in the Oakland slums. The family lived on the verge of poverty because of Flora's addiction to sketchy investments and Chinese lottery tickets. The money from John London's odd jobs and Flora's piano lessons and séances was never quite enough. (The neighbourhood children called Jack's home "the spook house" because of the strange yelps his mother made under the influence of the spirit realm.) Young Jack became a "work beast," delivering papers before and after school, working on an ice wagon on Saturdays, and setting up pins in a bowling alley on Sundays.

Reading was his escape. The most fateful event of his childhood may have been finding a battered copy of *Signa* in a ditch when he was eight. This now-forgotten melodrama was the first book he ever owned, and was his most treasured possession. He read and re-read it obsessively, even though it was missing its last forty pages. He did not find out how it ended until he was a teenager. When he discovered the Oakland Free Library at age ten, he started to read two books a week, even with all his other work. The head librarian, Ina Coolbrith, was a poet of note, a friend of Bret Harte and Mark Twain, and an estranged granddaughter of the founder of Mormonism, Joseph Smith. She took an interest in the intellectual urchin, and gently steered his reading in a more literary direction.

When Flora squandered their savings in property speculation, she took Jack out of school at thirteen, and put him to work in a cannery fourteen hours a day for ten cents an hour. He did this for a year until he rebelled and quit. He spent the rest of his teenage years working in a jute mill, sailing San Francisco bay, riding the rails as a tramp, indulging in hooliganism, and occasionally attending school. At seventeen, he sailed to Japan and the Bering Sea on the seven-month sealing voyage that inspired *The Sea Wolf*, reading *Moby-Dick* and *Anna Karenina* along the way.

By the time Jack had turned twenty, most of his buddies from the San Francisco waterfront had died young by drink, violence, or both. This inspired him to cram feverishly to pass the entrance exams for the University of California at Berkeley. Although he was accepted, he ran out of money and lost interest, and dropped out after a term to become a part-time socialist agitator and a full-time writer. After amassing a thick stack of rejection letters, he set off for the Klondike gold rush in the following year. To deter the unprepared, the Royal Canadian Mounted Police turned back miners unless they had a year's worth of food and equipment. Jack had to haul 600 pounds of gear over the thirty-three murderous miles of the Chilkoot trail. This required several trips back and forth over each mountainous section. This was followed by 600 miles of rafting and portaging lakes, rivers, and rapids to get to Dawson City before freeze-up. After months of fruitless prospecting and a bland diet of bread, beans, and bacon, Jack's gums were bleeding, his teeth were falling out, his hair a mat of tangled corkscrews, his joints swollen, his skin saggy and bruised, and his limbs doubled up in pain. He had contracted a classic malady of the Arctic, scurvy.

In a quirk of evolution, humans, guinea pigs, and fruit bats are the only mammals that have lost the ability to make their own vitamin C. This vitamin is needed for the repair of collagen, the major structural protein of the body. Without it, the body slowly turns to a pulpy soup of blood and unravelling tissue. As vitamin C is found in many fresh fruits and vegetables, scurvy is rare in the modern era, except in those with schizophrenia, alcoholism, faddish diets, or gut diseases that affect vitamin C absorption. However, scurvy was once common, especially in winter, when dietary sources are limited, and vitamin C stores in the body begin to give out. Extreme physical exertion, as in polar exploration and long sailing voyages, accelerates its onset.

Jack staggered back to Dawson City, where the primitive hospital was packed with scorbutic tenderfeet. Raw potatoes and a single lemon got him well enough to walk again. He and his companions tore down their cabin and built a raft with the timber, which they floated with additional logs down to Dawson. They sold the wood for $600, and bought a leaky boat for the 1,500-mile descent of the Yukon River to the Bering Sea. They ate goose eggs and raw duck along the way, and were in turn devoured by mosquitoes, gnats, and monstrous mooseflies. His scurvy relapsed after they got under way. He could only walk on tiptoe, and could not straighten his right leg. Halfway down the river, some good Samaritans fixed him up with some precious fresh potatoes and a can of tomatoes. These contained enough vitamin C to get him through the rest of the trip. When they reached the coast, he worked as a coal stoker on a steamship to earn his passage back to California.

He brought back only $4.50 of gold dust, but had something better than gold: a vein of literary ore that he mined until it was exhausted. In the next few years, he produced *The Call of the Wild*, *White Fang*, and most of his Klondike tales, including "To Build a Fire," which is as good as a short story can be. His genius for storytelling was equalled by his talent for self-promotion. He became America's most famous socialist and, in a series of dispatches from the Russo-Japanese War, its most notorious racist. A scandalous divorce from his first wife only added to his dangerous charisma. (The divorce petition alluded to a bout of gonorrhoea in 1902.)

Although Jack is mainly remembered today for his Klondike stories, his literary output was voluminous. In a career spanning nineteen years, he produced forty-nine books written at top speed, driven by his always urgent need for money. Despite its wildly uneven quality, his work is supremely readable, occasionally great, and frequently innovative. Jack wrote the first dystopian novel, *The Iron Heel*, a preposterous vision of a nightmarish America ruled by a militaristic oligarchy that engages in domestic spying, and has crushed labour and the middle class, abetted by a docile press. *The Road*, about his tramping life, *The People of the Abyss*, his moving, first-hand account of poverty in the East End of London, and *The Iron Heel* were major influences on George Orwell. *John Barleycorn* was one of the first memoirs of addiction and (sort of) recovery. *The Scarlet Plague* might be the first postapocalyptic novel. *The Star Rover* was a science-fiction tale of reincarnation, as well as an exposé of the appalling conditions in California prisons. Jack also wrote strange novels that could be described as Darwinian romances, such as *Adventure* and *The Mutiny of the Elsinore.*

Jack was almost certainly bipolar. He had phenomenal reserves of energy, and rarely slept more than five hours a night. To get into Berkeley, he crammed nineteen hours a day for three months. As a struggling young writer, he spent fifteen hours a day at his typewriter, sometimes forgetting to eat, like his hero Herman Melville. Even in the months before his death, his speech was characterized by a manic flight of ideas: "It was something inside of him, his brain just ran sixty miles a minute, you couldn't follow him. He talked better than he wrote."

In *John Barleycorn*, Jack wrote with startling candour about his boozing, depressions, and suicidality. At about sixteen, in the grip of an epic drunk, he had a sudden fancy to end things by jumping off his sloop and going out with the night tide in San Francisco Bay. He swam out into the darkness of the channel and by daybreak was sober, frightened, cold, and losing strength. A Greek fisherman chanced upon him as he was starting to go under and hauled him to safety. (Suicides were frequent in his stories. The burned-out writer in *Martin Eden,* the best of his mature novels, commits suicide by throwing himself off a boat, just as Jack had done.) After his first flush of success and subsequent disillusionment, he had a severe depression, which he called his "long sickness." He was helped in his recovery by his twin passions for socialism (which he later called his "one remaining illusion—the PEOPLE") and his vivacious second wife, Charmian. He blamed later episodes of depression on his heavy drinking. During these bouts, he was infected with a spirit of nihilism, which he called the "White Logic." Like a great many problem drinkers, Jack denied that he was an alcoholic, citing as evidence his occasional bouts of moderation and sobriety: "But mine is no tale of a reformed drunkard. I was never a drunkard, and I have not reformed."

In 1906, Jack London was thirty years old, and at the peak of his career. He commanded unheard-of sums for his writing, and was still in good health, aside from the knees and ankles he had dinged up in various escapades. Possibly in the grip of a manic episode, Jack decided that he and Charmian would circumnavigate the globe, financing the trip with Jack's travel writings along the way. He had a yacht custom-built at enormous expense. Originally budgeted at $7,000, it cost over $30,000. Jack had to deal with workers from forty-seven different unions, an experience which somewhat dampened the ardour of his socialism. One disaster followed another. The luckless *Snark* was impounded for debt, stuck in the mud, and crushed in her mooring between two barges, bending her into the shape of a lima bean.

Once at sea, the watertight bulkheads, the decks, the lifeboats, and the tank containing a thousand gallons of petrol leaked, filling the cabins with fumes and creating a terror of fire. The engine and the windlass were ruined. The electric lights never went on. The wrought iron in the rigging snapped. Seawater and kerosene fouled the stores. Worst of all, the boat was a deathtrap. It refused to heave to in heavy weather, instead lolling helplessly in the troughs. The passage from San Francisco to Hawaii was interminable. Martin Johnson, the young cook from Kansas, told Jack one day that he longed for a sight of land. Jack said that land was less than two miles away. Startled, Martin asked in which direction. "Straight down, Martin, straight down," replied Jack with equanimity.

Jack discovered that his navigator, Charmian's uncle, Roscoe Eames, was ignorant of navigation, and had no idea where they were. Roscoe also believed that the earth was a hollow sphere, with the oceans and the continents on the inside. Jack took over and got them to Hawaii, where he learned to surf, and they patched up the boat as best they could. They crossed a desolate and windless two-thousand-mile stretch of the Pacific to the Marquesas. To pass the time, they fished in politically incorrect fashion: "I can recommend no finer sport than catching dolphin." In the Marquesas, he found that Melville's paradise was sadly lost: "And now all this strength and beauty is departed, and the Valley of the Typee is the abode of some dozen wretched creatures, afflicted by leprosy, elephantiasis, and tuberculosis."

They made it as far as the Solomon Islands, a brutal place that fascinated Jack. Giant cockroaches and centipedes flourished there, and infested the *Snark*. Cannibalism was rife. The Solomons were the centre of a latter-

day slave trade called blackbirding, in which chiefs sold off surplus tribesmen as indentured labour to Australian plantations. Unsanitary
conditions on shipboard and in the plantations led to many deaths among
the workers. Blackbirding was understandably unpopular among the
bartered tribesmen, and traders and other whites in the Solomons were
often murdered in retaliation. The annual mortality from disease, accidents, and homicide among whites in the Solomon Islands was 18 percent.

In the Solomon Islands, the whole crew came down with yaws, and
the *Snark* became a hospital ship. Yaws is a forgotten disease, but it once
infected between 50 and 100 million people worldwide. It still affects
about two million people in remote areas of central Africa, Indonesia,
and Polynesia. It is an heirloom disease of humans, having evolved along
with us; our cousins, the great apes, also suffer from it. Yaws and syphilis
are subspecies of the same bacterium, *Treponema pallidum,* and syphilis
likely evolved from yaws in the Americas.

Unlike syphilis, yaws is transmitted by casual contact or perhaps
insect bites, rather than sex. In the primary stage, patients develop a
small skin sore that heals quickly. Spirochaetes then spread throughout
the body, leading to the secondary stage, in which patients develop
massive, destructive skin ulcers. In a minority of patients, there is a third
or tertiary stage in which yaws attacks bone and cartilage. Yaws was
once endemic in Haiti, until the Duvalier government, in a rare spasm of
benevolence, eradicated it in the 1950s with the help of the World Health
Organization. In the 1990s, one could still see patients there with old
deformities from tertiary yaws, such as curved shinbones and missing
noses.

Jack was the first to get sick. His ankles were badly bitten by mosquitoes in Samoa. He scratched the bites, which may have allowed infection
to creep in. The skin over the bites broke down. Five large ulcers blossomed on his ankles and the soles of the feet. Walking was an ordeal, and
the pain kept him from sleeping. He treated himself with dressings of
corrosive sublimate, or mercuric chloride, alternating with hydrogen peroxide. His first set of sores healed, but another crop broke out on his
hands and shins, on which he dutifully slathered more mercury.

Jack became, in his own words, a "monomaniac on the question of
sores and sublimate." He treated himself, and the other crewmembers

when they let him, with everything in the ship's medicine chest: arsenic, blue vitriol, iodoform, lime juice, hydrogen peroxide, boric acid, and especially whopping doses of corrosive sublimate. Jack believed he cured himself, although he developed a horrific skin reaction that made his hands and feet bloat and slough: "My hands were twice their natural size, with seven dead and dying skins peeling off at the same time. There were times when my toe-nails, in twenty-four hours, grew as thick as they were long." Charmian tried to help with massage, which "caused them to break into a wringing perspiration." Jack worried that he had leprosy, or poisoning from ultraviolet light, but he probably had acrodynia. This is a form of mercury poisoning which causes pink, puffy, painful, perspiring, and peeling hands. It is more common in children than adults. Perhaps Jack was predisposed because of an old episode of frostbite. (It has been suggested that his rash was due to pellagra, or niacin deficiency; this is unlikely, as the fishy diet on board the *Snark* was rich in tryptophan, a precursor of niacin.) Jack wound up in hospital in Australia. He was given arsenic for yaws, which was almost certainly adequate treatment, and also had surgery for a rectal fistula. The voyage of the *Snark* was abandoned, and Jack's beautiful, useless boat was sold off for a fraction of its cost.

The *Snark* was not the last of Jack's financial indiscretions. His manic excess meant that he was perpetually on the verge of bankruptcy, despite a yearly income of $70,000, or about two million dollars today. He was swindled in a Mexican land deal, and lost another fortune investing in a lithography technique. He was enmeshed in lawsuits with the angry stockholders of the bankrupt Jack London Grape Juice Company, and tangled with filmmakers over the movie rights to his novels. He lost $4000 betting against Jack Johnson in a boxing match. He and Charmian often travelled with a retinue of servants. Jack fancied himself a gentleman farmer, and sunk vast amounts of money into his ranch in Sonoma County, California. Beauty Ranch was a hybrid of Versailles and a model farm, sprawled out over 1400 acres. He bought two hundred pedigree hogs and housed them in an elaborate piggery known to his neighbours as the Pig Palace. He bought a Shire stallion and a herd of shorthorn cattle. He converted an old winery for use as stables for his thirty horses.

He built the first concrete silos in California. To fight soil erosion, he adopted the terraced farming techniques he had seen in Korea, and planted 60,000 eucalyptus trees. An artificial lake was created. He squandered untold sums building a grand lodge, Wolf House, of redwood logs, concrete, and volcanic rock. It was earthquake-proof, but not fireproof; a disgruntled employee torched it. Jack paid wages to thirty or forty people on the ranch at any given time, and supported various other hangers-on. His stint in jail as a young tramp made him sympathetic to released prisoners, who were always welcome on the ranch. He entertained lavishly, and hosted a motley assortment of guests, including the anarchist Emma Goldman and the magician Harry Houdini, who became Charmian's lover after Jack's death.

Soon after their return to America, Charmian became pregnant. Her labour was difficult, and their baby daughter died after a botched Caesarean section on July 19, 1910. Jack was devastated. His moodiness and hypochondria got worse. He assembled a small library on venereal disease, and subscribed to the *American Journal of Urology and Sexology,* as well as the less provocative *Uric Acid Monthly.* He obsessed about syphilis, and

WOUNDS FROM MAGIC BULLETS:
ARSENIC IN THE TREATMENT OF SYPHILIS

In 1907, Paul Ehrlich synthesized arsphenamine, or salvarsan. This was also known as "606," as it was the 606th compound Ehrlich synthesized in his dogged quest for a "magic bullet" to combat syphilis. Arsenicals revolutionized the treatment of syphilis. The chancres and other skin lesions of syphilis healed up much more quickly in patients treated with arsenic, compared to patients treated with mercury or bismuth. According to British army data, relapse rates in syphilis were 83 percent with mercury alone, but fell to just 4 percent with the combination of mercury and salvarsan. This suggested not only that salvarsan was much better than mercury, but that mercury alone was probably not effective at all. Arsenic was also superior to mercury in making the blood test for syphilis, the Wasserman reaction, become negative.

Patients treated with arsenic compounds usually had at least minor side effects, such as vomiting, diarrhoea, flushing, rashes, and jaundice. Less common but more severe side effects included nerve damage, bleeding in the brain, and gangrene of the fingers and toes. Some patients developed fever and shaking chills after the first dose of

(continued)

arsenic due to a Jarisch-Herxheimer reaction. This reaction is actually a sign of antibiotic effectiveness. The fever is caused by the sudden death of syphilis bacteria, or spirochaetes, with the release of bacterial components that stimulate the immune system and lead to a brisk inflammatory response. Unfortunately, violent Jarisch-Herxheimer reactions could have catastrophic results. Patients with gummas of the larynx could asphyxiate; patients with syphilis in the brain or spinal cord could have strokes; and patients with syphilis in the coronary arteries could have a heart attack.

The gold standard for cure was return of the Wasserman reaction to negative. In patients with long-standing syphilis, the Wasserman reaction and its modern descendants take a relatively long time to turn negative after successful therapy. An imperfect understanding of this phenomenon may have led to overtreatment with arsenicals. Some syphilologists argued that "the fetish of treatment [is] carried to undesirable lengths." The abdominal pain and loss of sensation in the legs suffered by Isak Dinesen, author of *Out of Africa,* may have been the result of arsenic poisoning from excessive syphilis treatment, rather than tabes dorsalis (syphilis affecting the spinal cord), as traditionally thought.

An arsenical antibiotic, melarsoprol, is still used to treat African sleeping sickness, but a major

(continued)

seems to have blamed himself for his daughter's death. In 1911, he had another course of arsenic therapy, apparently because he was worried about syphilis or residual infection with yaws. That same year, he failed a medical exam for a life insurance policy, for unclear reasons. He gained thirty pounds in weight and had swollen ankles. In 1913, he was operated on for appendicitis, and told that he had diseased kidneys. This was probably based on the finding of protein in the urine, which was one of the few tests of kidney function that was then available. The combination of swollen legs and kidneys that spilled large amounts of protein into the urine suggests that he had a specific form of kidney damage called nephrotic syndrome. This has many causes, but given his known heavy use of mercury, it is very tempting to blame this on mercury exposure.

In the next year, he travelled to Mexico to report on the Mexican Revolution, and came down with dysentery. His joint pains worsened, perhaps as a result of gout, to which he was predisposed because of his drinking and kidney problems. His opium use escalated. Then as now, being rich and famous is no guarantee of good health care. In fact, many sick celebrities succumb to the "VIP syndrome." Doctors, fearful of making a high-profile blunder, tend to overtest and overtreat VIPs, leading to diagnostic confusion and needless complications. Starstruck physicians may also indulge the whims of their celebrity patients, especially their idiosyncratic notions and their cravings for pills. The latter seems to have been the case with Jack. His doctor not only did not discourage Jack from self-medicating, but in fact enabled

> problem with arsenic resistance now exists. Arsenic resistance is widespread among bacteria, and may be evolutionarily ancient, as substantial amounts of arsenic may have been present in primordial ooze. Many common bacteria, such as *E. coli* and *Staphylococcus aureus,* can convert toxic arsenic to less harmful forms and pump it out of their cells.

him to load up his medicine chest with deadly drugs: strychnine, aconite, belladonna, hyoscyamine, heroin, opium, and the cocktail of morphine and atropine that would kill him. Jack learned to inject himself with a silver hypodermic needle, and acted as his own primary care doctor. If he could teach himself to be a great writer, how much harder could medicine be?

Fit, charismatic, and handsome in youth, Jack was a physical wreck at forty. He was in chronic pain from gouty joints, kidney stones, and rotten teeth. As his kidneys gave out, he retained fluid. His ankles, legs, and belly swelled. Walking across a room left him breathless. His self-destructive behaviour didn't help, either. He smoked sixty filterless Russian Imperiales a day. Patients with kidney failure should limit their protein intake, as meat is the major source of the poisonous urea that builds up in the system; Jack stuck to his carnivore diet of raw bonito, undercooked duck, and "cannibal sandwiches" of red meat and chopped onions. Yet even as his drinking and drug taking escalated and his health deteriorated, Jack produced many of his finest stories.

In the last weeks of his life, Jack was irritable and insomniac, and full of plans. His brain was teeming, and he contemplated writing more novels, including one entitled *How We Die*. He worked through the night and dozed at daybreak. He slept two hours in one sixty-hour stretch. On the morning of November 22, 1916, his valet found him unresponsive and blue, a syringe and two empty vials of morphine on the floor. A local doctor, Allan Thompson, was called, and Jack's usual doctors Porter and

Shiels followed after, shoving aside Thompson. Twelve hours of frantic efforts to revive him were unsuccessful. Porter certified the cause of death as "uremia [kidney failure] following renal colic [kidney stone]" and "chronic interstitial nephritis." There was no mention of morphine.

Rumours of suicide soon leaked out, ironically for a writer whose major theme was the struggle for survival. Thompson later claimed there was a cover-up. He had found papers which he believed were calculations of a lethal dose, indicating that Jack had committed suicide. Thompson is correct in that the death certificate is misleading. Patients with uraemia, or untreated end-stage kidney disease, may develop coma, but this is very gradual in onset, and would not progress over to death over a period of hours. The proximate cause of Jack's death was certainly a morphine overdose, something easily treated today with a shot of the opioid-blocker naloxone. The precise dose he gave himself is unknown. Had both vials been full, Jack's dose would have been on the order of 800 mg, but he could also have injected a much lesser amount.

On the other hand, Thompson's assertion that he saw a paper with a lethal-dose calculation is also unconvincing. Jack would have no particular way to determine this, and even today, calculating a lethal dose is an imprecise undertaking. It is also possible, as Jack's biographer Andrew Sinclair has suggested, that Thompson just found scribbled computations related to Jack's royalties.

There is no way to know what Jack was thinking as he injected himself, but his death was more likely inadvertent than intentional. He seems to have been having a manic episode, and was ill and exhausted. He wanted to sleep, but probably not to die. Renal failure and morphine addiction are a bad combination. Ninety percent of an injected dose of morphine is excreted through the kidneys in normal patients. But in patients with kidney disease, morphine accumulates, and the risk of an accidental overdose is high.

Jack's reckless death was of a piece with his life. He had lived fully and to excess, in accordance with his credo:

> I would rather be ashes than dust!
> I would rather that my spark should burn out in a brilliant
>   blaze than it should be stifled by dry-rot.

I would rather be a superb meteor, every atom of me in
    magnificent glow, than a sleepy and permanent planet.
The function of man is to live, not to exist.
I shall not waste my days trying to prolong them.
I shall use my time.

Irrigation treatment for gonorrhoea in 1900. (Ferdinand Charles Valentine, *The Irrigation Treatment of Gonorrhea*. New York: William Wood Co., 1900)

9. AN INFAMOUS PRIVATE AILMENT:
The Venereal Afflictions of James Joyce

I called upon the bard Kinch at his summer residence in upper Mecklenburgh street and found him deep in the study of the Summa contra Gentiles *in the company of two gonorrheal ladies, Fresh Nelly and Rosalie, the coalquay whore.*

—Ulysses

It has been blurtingly bruited by certain wisecrackers . . . that he suffered from a vile disease.

—Finnegans Wake

The doctor's office was perched on the perilous edge of respectability over an apothecary's shop that bordered Nighttown. As James Joyce climbed the rickety stairs, he was passed by a man hurrying down to the street, felt hat pulled low over his head and face buried in the lapels of his overcoat. At the end of the hall, letters of faded gold upon an oaken door proclaimed the presence of John M'Intosh, M.D. Joyce adjusted his spectacles and knocked without conviction. After some clinking of glass and shutting of drawers within, the door opened to reveal a red-faced man of middle age in a good tweed suit with worn elbows. His jauntiness was excessive for the earliness of the hour.

"Come in, young man," cried M'Intosh. He gestured Joyce toward an examination table covered with cracked leather cushions. The office occupied a single cramped room. There was a desk of ponderous mahogany littered with papers and a cabinet filled with bottles bearing Latin inscriptions and narrow rods with curved ends in jars of alcohol. A coatrack was in one corner and a tarnished spittoon in the other. Yellowed lithographs of sporting scenes hung on the wall. A quizzical skull looked down from a bookcase filled with dusty volumes.

"Now what can I do for you?" M'Intosh asked.

"In the course of a nocturnal encounter with the reality of experience," Joyce said, "I appear to have acquired the malady described by Galen. I have been urinating fish hooks for weeks."

"Ah, wayward youth!" said M'Intosh. "Let us look at the affected part."

Joyce dropped his trousers and extricated his pus-encrusted member from his adherent drawers. M'Intosh took it daintily between his thumb and fore finger and inspected it minutely while Joyce sat in quiet sufferance of his gaze. The doctor squeezed the glans beneath the sulcus and prised apart the lips of the swollen meatus. A purulent pearl formed at the tip.

"Yes, gonorrhoea indeed. But I see no chancre, and I do not believe you have been poxed. It should respond nicely to repeated daily irrigation with potassium permanganate. We'll start today with one quart. You will stand up, holding this bedpan under your gear. I'll hold the urethra closed for two minutes after each injection, then you will void into the pan, and we'll repeat until the fluid is used up."

As Joyce watched with anxious eyes, M'Intosh went to the cabinet and produced a jar of indigo crystals. He measured some off and placed them in a huge flask of distilled water, which he warmed over a burner. A bloom of startling lavender spread throughout the flask. He drew some of this fluid up into a glass syringe of prodigious size, with a tapering nozzle on the end. Joyce stood up, feeling woozy. M'Intosh grasped his glans again, inserted the nozzle into the urinary meatus, and slowly depressed the plunger. No, thought Joyce, no please no. His eyes burned with anguish and anger. A dark mutinous wave descended upon his end, his soul swooned slowly, and he fell faintly, softly falling upon the table.

James Augustine Aloysius Joyce was born on Groundhog Day, February 2, 1882—appropriately enough for a man who spent seventeen years writing a circular book, *Finnegans Wake*. Both of his parents came from well-off middle class backgrounds, and his early childhood was comfortable enough, though it later conformed to clichés of downwardly mobile Irish Catholic squalor. The life of his father, John Stanislaus Joyce, has something of a manic-depressive flavour. He was a brilliant raconteur and a charming and witty man-about-town, but as his debts and children accumulated, he succumbed to black moods, drunken rages, and maudlin self-pity. In *A Portrait of the Artist as a Young Man*, James's alter ego Stephen Dedalus recites a litany of his father's failed occupations: "A medical student, an oarsman, a tenor, an amateur actor, a shouting politician, a small landlord, a small investor, a drinker, a good fellow, a storyteller, somebody's secretary, something in a distillery, a tax-gatherer, a bankrupt and at present a praiser of his own past."

James's mother, Mary Jane, was the sort of woman for whom the phrase "long-suffering" seems to have been invented. She bore John Stanislaus ten children, and somehow kept the family together and food on the table, despite a dwindling household income and frequent, debt-driven changes of address. She was the recipient of her husband's verbal abuse, and on at least one occasion, of his physical abuse as well: when James was twelve, he had to jump on his father's back to keep him from strangling his mother.

As a child, James was known in his family as "Sunny Jim" for his cheerful disposition. He was taught to read at an early age by a family retainer named Mrs Conway, the Dante of *A Portrait*. According to James's dour brother Stanislaus (Stannie), she also inculcated the "religion of terrorism" that left permanent scars in his psyche.

Before the calamities of his adolescence, James was the beneficiary of his father's determination to provide him with the best education available in Ireland. For a Catholic, this meant attending Jesuit-run schools. Joyce's career may be seen as either the most spectacular success of the Jesuit educational system, or its most egregious failure. He went to Clongowes Wood

College at age six, and was there for four years until his father's financial difficulties forced him to withdraw James. At age eleven, he continued his education with the Jesuits at Belvedere College in Dublin, where he was accepted for free as a scholar of unusual promise. (It was also thought erroneously, that he might be destined for a career as a prince of the Church.) In the next five years, he became fluent in Latin, French, and Italian, and went through the phases of Catholic enthusiasm, sexual awakening, and religious scepticism described in *A Portrait*. He studied frantically, as the academic prizes he won in national examinations were a major source of income to his family. Although his alter ego Stephen Dedalus was a feeble aesthete, Joyce was actually fit and athletic, a fast runner and hurdler and an avid cricketer. In later years, he regularly beat his frenemy Oliver St John Gogarty, a champion swimmer, in short swimming races.

He took a Bachelors of Arts degree from University College Dublin, graduating in 1902. As an undergraduate, he shocked friends with his freethinking, absorbed European literature, and crashed Dublin's literary circles, where he astonished Yeats and others with his confidence and arrogance. He studied medicine in Dublin for a time, thinking that a medical career would provide him with income to subsidize his writing, but had to quit after another awful financial blunder of his father left him without funds. Had his father been solvent, Joyce may have pursued his medical degree, settled into a life as a Dublin physician and occasional writer, and never written *Ulysses*. He took up a harebrained scheme to study medicine in Paris, which he planned to pay for by teaching English. He did not learn much medicine, but did become proficient at cadging money. He returned home in April 1903 when is mother became seriously ill with what turned out to be liver cancer, and abandoned medicine thereafter without regrets. Many years later, he joked, "I would have been even more disastrous to society at large than I am in my present state had I continued."

Joyce returned to a household that was more chaotic than ever. His father was drunk precisely 3.97 days a week, according to Joyce's brother Stannie, who had a rigid mind-set and perhaps a touch of Asperger syndrome. Stannie idolized his brother and was somewhat in awe of him. In return, Joyce called him his "whetstone," and made fun of his sanctimonious atheism. Stannie appears in *Finnegans Wake* as "Stainusless" and as Shaun the Postman, the sober brother of the manic, creative, and reckless Shem the Penman.

Joyce created a scene by refusing to pray at his mother's deathbed, but did play piano and sing to her. (Joyce had a fine Irish tenor voice. A voice teacher offered to make him a second John McCormack, but he declared he would rather be a first James Joyce.) He worked on an early version of *A Portrait* called *Stephen Hero,* began to write the stories that appeared in *Dubliners,* and dabbled in money-making schemes. These included a ploy to get an Irish-American millionaire to invest in him in return for the American copyrights of his books, a plan to start a Dublin newspaper, and a stint as the assistant editor of the *Irish Beekeeper.*

He took up with Oliver Gogarty, then a carousing medical student. Gogarty wrote limpid lyric poetry, but his muse was better suited to smutty and blasphemous doggerel, some of which Joyce happily preserved for posterity in *Ulysses.* Gogarty called Joyce "Kinch," the sound of a cutting knife. Their friendship was coloured by rivalry and malice. Gogarty cajoled him into hard drinking, allegedly to break his spirit; Joyce had previously avoided inebriation because of the dismal example of his father. His drinking became a lifelong problem. Joyce described himself to Jung as "a man of small virtue, inclined to extravagance and alcoholism."

Gogarty mocked Joyce for his penchant for wenching in Dublin's red-light district, Nighttown:

> There is a young fellow named Joyce
> Who possesseth a sweet tenor voice.
> He goes down to the kips
> With a psalm on his lips
> And biddeth the harlots rejoice.

Joyce was not left unscathed by his evenings in the "kips." In March 1904, Joyce wrote to Gogarty, then at Oxford, apparently complaining of urinary symptoms of some duration (Joyce's letters to Gogarty were lost in a house fire, so we only have Gogarty's side of the correspondence). Gogarty replied that it a sounded like a "slight gleet," or subacute gonorrhoea. He referred Joyce to a Dublin colleague, to whom he sent a separate letter, asking if he "could re-convert his urethra to periodic and voluntary function . . . Mr Joyce is the name of the tissues surrounding the infected part. He may have waited too long and got gleet."

Gonorrhoea, Latin for "the flow of seed," known colloquially as the clap, is an ancient disease of humanity caused by the bacterium *Neisseria gonorrhoeae*. It was named by the Roman physician Galen, who mistook the profuse penile production of pus for a riotous excess of semen. In the United States alone, there are about 700,000 cases a year. Men may first notice swelling of the lips of the urinary meatus, which are often glued together in the morning, with burning during urination that soon becomes excruciating. Penile discharge is creamy and yellow, and may become greenish or bloodstained. The urinary stream may be forked or twisted. Painful nocturnal erections may occur. The corpus spongiosum, the central portion of the penis that contains the urethra, may become inflamed and inelastic, and fail to properly elongate during erections. It may then act like a bowstring, bending the unaffected portions of the penis, the two corpora cavernosa, leading to an agonizing chordee, or crooked erection. Attempts to straighten the erect penis may cause penile fracture. Other torturous complications include infection of the testicles (orchitis) and prostate. Chronic infection may lead to urinary strictures, areas of scarring in the urethra that block the outward flow of urine; the modern surgical specialty of urology began with the development of a variety of alarming devices to correct these blockages. In women, urinary symptoms may be milder or wholly absent, but there is a high risk of complications such as pelvic abscesses and infertility.

It is not known for certain whether Joyce pursued the gleet treatment recommended by Gogarty, but as the matter does not come up again in Gogarty's letters, it presumably got better. Today, uncomplicated gonorrhoea responds to single doses of antibiotics—because of increasing problems with antibiotic resistance, two antibiotics are used in combination, azithromycin by mouth and ceftriaxone given as an injection into the buttock. In Joyce's time, antibiotics were not yet available, and it was treated by repeated irrigations of the urethra with large quantities of antiseptics. In acute cases, the broad-spectrum germicide potassium permanganate was used. This was less irritating, could be performed daily, and would not worsen the already severe inflammation. For more chronic cases, silver nitrate was used. As it is caustic and erodes the lining of the urethra, it could only be given every few days. Silver has proven antibiotic effects, and it is still used in medicine today. Silver ions interfere with DNA transcription and energy generation in bacteria. In ancient times, silver vessels were prized as they prevented spoilage, and in the United States in the nineteenth century, silver dollars were added to milk to keep it fresh. Silver sulphadiazine cream is still used in burn wards to prevent skin infection, and until recently, silver nitrate eye ointment was used routinely in newborns to prevent gonorrhoea infection of the eye from passage through the birth canal. Silver-coated catheters have been developed as an effective, if costly, means of preventing urinary and bloodstream infections in hospitals. Silver is active against gonorrhoea, but not against another common cause of urethritis, *Chlamydia trachomatis*.

A few months after his bout of gleet, Joyce met Nora Barnacle, an auburn-haired, earthy young woman from Galway who worked as a chambermaid in one of the city hotels. Their first date was on June 16, 1904, which Joyce immortalized as Bloomsday, the date on which *Ulysses* is set. This occasion was especially memorable for Joyce, as Nora surprised him by performing a manual labour of love.

When John Joyce heard his son was stepping out with a woman named Barnacle, he quipped that she'd never leave him. Nora was a perfect partner for Joyce, equally adroit at propping him up or cutting him down to size as needed. She was also an excellent source of material, serving as the model for Molly Bloom, and she kept limits on his drinking as well as anyone could have. (She once got him to stop boozing for a time by threatening to get their children baptized.)

In September 1904, Joyce lived in the Martello Tower in Sandycove that Gogarty shared with a mad Englishman named Trench, but fled after the confused episode of nocturnal gunfire that figures in *Ulysses*. Trench awoke from a nightmare, and fired wildly at an imaginary panther. Gogarty, for good measure, squeezed off a few more rounds over Joyce's head as a kind of joke. With this encouragement, Joyce and Nora eloped to Europe the following month, and he landed a job teaching English in Trieste, where he was to spend most of the next eleven years. Nora became pregnant, and gave birth to a son, Giorgio, the following year. Stannie was prevailed upon to join them in Italy for several years. He later wrote a memoir accurately entitled *My Brother's Keeper*. Stannie saved the couple from starvation, bailed Jim out of financial scrapes, and literally dragged him home from bars. (Joyce was thin, with stork-like legs, making it easier when he had to be carried up the stairs.) If his household was often impecunious and chaotic, like that of his father, Joyce himself was the most disciplined and ruthless of writers, subordinating everything to his work. He wrote steadily, completing *Dubliners* in 1907 and *A Portrait* in 1914, despite the onset of the ocular trouble that would make him, in his own words, "an international eyesore."

In July 1907, Joyce was hospitalized for an attack of polyarthritis and iritis, or inflammation of the iris, the part of the eye that gives it its colour. This was attributed to rheumatic fever, but this is almost certainly wrong, as rheumatic fever does not affect the eye. While he was still in hospital with painful red eyes and exquisite sensitivity to light, Nora was admitted, and gave birth to a daughter that they named Lucia. As Joyce well knew, St Lucia, whose name derives from the Latin word for light, was the patron saint of the blind. (In later years, he would burn a candle on December 13, St Lucia's Day.) A recurrence of iritis in May 1908 was bad enough that leeches were applied to his eyes to reduce the swelling. He was scared enough to stop drinking entirely for several months, although his drinking was probably not related to his eye condition. His arthritis and back pain lingered, but slowly improved. By December, he wrote to a sister that he looked "more like a capital S than a capital Z."

As suggested by Dr Alex Paton in 1975, the best explanation of Joyce's complex illness is reactive arthritis. Reactive arthritis is a form of spondyloarthropathy, and is related to ankylosing spondylitis, which may have affected Herman Melville. It is an autoimmune disease, triggered either by a genital infection with *Chlamydia*, or a diarrhoeal illness with *Salmonella*, *Shigella*, or *Campylobacter* bacteria. In a minority of patients, these infections disturb the equilibrium of the immune system, leading it to attack the joints, eyes, and spine. However, there is usually no evidence of ongoing infection, and no clear role for antibiotic therapy. Joyce probably had urethritis with *Chlamydia* either instead of gonorrhoea, or in addition to it; it is common for patients to have more than one sexually transmitted infection. (Reactive arthritis was formerly known as Reiter's syndrome, after Hans Reiter. However, this syndrome had already been described one hundred years before by Benjamin Brodie, and Reiter was also a Nazi war criminal who authorized criminal experiments on concentration camp prisoners.)

The main feature of reactive arthritis is recurrent attacks of joint pain, most often involving the knees, ankles, and feet. About half the patients have low back pain, as did Joyce. Eye involvement is common, and may be the most troublesome aspect for some patients. Conjunctivitis, or inflammation of the superficial covering of the eye, is the most common eye manifestation. About 25 percent of patients have anterior uveitis, the inflammation of the iris that may have led to Herman Melville's eye pain and avoidance of light. Reactive arthritis may be associated with persistent pain with urination. In most cases, there is no evidence of residual infection, and the burning urine is thought to be related to the autoimmune disturbance.

Current outcomes with reactive arthritis are generally good. It is now treated with nonsteroidal anti-inflammatory drugs (such as high-dose ibuprofen), prednisone and other corticosteroids, and in refractory cases with antibodies against tumour necrosis factor, an inflammatory signalling molecule. None of these drugs were available in Joyce's time. He had relapses of iritis and arthritis for years, and would eventually lose nearly all of his sight due to inflammation, operations, and complications.

Joyce made two trips back to Dublin in 1909, trying to get *Dubliners* published and lobbying for a professorship at his alma mater. He also became involved in a venture to bring cinema to his native city that would likely have been profitable had he stuck with it. While in Dublin, Joyce wrote several letters to Nora that are infamous for their creative use of the Anglo-Saxon vernacular, as well as what one psychologist calls their "ubiquitous anal eroticism." (Joyce was once told of an African chieftain who chose his brides by inspecting the backsides of the women of the village, and picking the ones with the grandest posteriors. He replied with a solemn face, "I sincerely hope that when Bolshevism finally sweeps the world, it will spare that enlightened potentate.")

Joyce's sense of well-being was better that year, which he attributed to his use of lithia water—mineral water containing lithium salts. Lithium was used at the time as a mild sedative, and is used today for its mood-stabilizing effects in mania, depression, and bipolar disorder; Joyce had a marked depressive tendency toward the end of his life. However, lithia water did not prevent him from having another disabling attack of back pain and iritis while in Dublin.

In 1914, Joyce embarked on the composition of *Ulysses*. The following year, he moved to Zurich. He had a "nervous collapse" in October 1916, probably an episode of depression, although money from patrons soon removed financial pressures and enabled him to write full-time. In 1917, however, his eye problems entered a new and ominous phase. He had several attacks of glaucoma, including one so sudden and severe that he was overwhelmed with pain in the street, forcing his ophthalmologist to remove part of the iris to relieve the pressure. He was so traumatized after the operation that Nora was not allowed to see him for days, and he developed a new terror of surgery, to add to his phobias of dogs and thunderstorms.

Severe uveitis is a fire that scorches everything around it, leading to "innocent bystander" damage to the delicate nearby structures of the eye. The angry, inflamed iris may stick to the cornea in front of it or the lens behind it, with the formation of adhesions (anterior and posterior synechiae). These adhesions may block the normal flow of fluid inside the eye, leading to glaucoma, or a buildup of pressure in the eye that may damage the optic nerve and lead to blindness. Inflammation next to the normally transparent lens may lead to cataracts, making the lens opaque and preventing light from reaching the retina. Joyce suffered from all these complications.

Joyce made steady progress on *Ulysses*, despite more attacks of iritis. In 1920, he moved to Paris at the instigation of Ezra Pound, who had helped to get *A Portrait* published and steered patronage his way. He finished *Ulysses* the following year, despite spending five weeks in a dark room with iritis again, getting cocaine eyedrops to relieve the pain. Cocaine was then commonly used as an ocular anaesthetic. However, it may have made his glaucoma worse (his later use of atropine and scopolamine might also have aggravated his glaucoma).

Ulysses, the novel that turned the familiar into the heroic, and the particular into the universal, was published in 1922 on Joyce's fortieth birthday. Told that *Ulysses* wasn't fit to read, Joyce replied that if it wasn't fit to read, then life wasn't fit to live. The scandalous content of *Ulysses* includes a minor fixation on venereal disease. Leopold Bloom muses about "a quack doctor for the clap," and frets that his wife's lover may have infected her with "a dose." In the hallucinatory Circe episode, set in a brothel, a prostitute is alarmed that Bloom has a syphilitic "hard chancre," but finds that he merely has a potato in his pants. The Fenian bigot of the Cyclops chapter condemns English "syphilisation" and castigates the libidinous Edward VII as spreading "more pox than pax." Prostitutes are "pox and gleet vendors." In a parody of Bunyan, medical students ward off "that foul plague Allpox" with "a stout shield of oxengut" (a pre-latex condom).

The technical virtuosity of *Ulysses,* its sexual frankness, and the attendant legal battles over obscenity and censorship, conspired to make the book and its shy, formal, and somewhat old-fashioned author notorious. Joyce was uneasy with fame and its absurdities. A young fan once asked to kiss the hand that wrote *Ulysses.* Joyce demurred: "No, it did lots of other things too." F. Scott Fitzgerald offered to jump out a window to prove his devotion to Joyce and Nora. Joyce had another awkward encounter with Marcel Proust. Proust had just risen, Joyce was ready for bed. Joyce complained about his eyes, Proust about his stomach. Each admitted that they were completely ignorant of each other's work. Uneasy small talk about truffles ensued. Joyce claimed afterward that Proust was only interested in duchesses, while he would rather talk about their chambermaids.

Between September 1922 and June 1926, Joyce had nine eye operations, as well as extractions of all his decayed teeth (he had long been in pain from his shambolic Irish dentition). Multiple iridectomies were performed to relieve his glaucoma. A cataract that was a complication of iritis was removed from the left eye. Unfortunately, this complication had a not-so-little complication. The remnants of the lens formed a secondary membrane, or a posterior capsular opacity. Today, this could be burned away with a laser, but this was of course not available in Joyce's time. Several procedures were done to clear the secondary membrane. These did little to improve his sight, and in fact may have made it worse. The worst agonies came from the pain and swelling in the eyes immediately after his operations. Leeches were applied to suck up the blood in the anterior chamber and relieve the pressure in his eyes. Nora once had to hold the leeches in place until they latched on. When this round of surgeries was over, the sight in his left eye was nearly gone. He had to wear thick spectacles to compensate for his mangled lenses, leaving him "nice and bespectacle." What was left of the pale blue of his irises, magnified by his Coke-bottle glasses, was surrounded by a halo of red in the whites of his eyes.

In 1923, while these major surgeries were ongoing, he started *Work in Progress,* as *Finnegans Wake* was first called (he kept the title secret right up until publication). Errors crept into both *Ulysses* and *Finnegans Wake* due to their novelty, complexity, and Joyce's inability to see well enough to correct the proofs. To proofread one section of *Work in Progress,* he required ten assistants. As his eyesight got worse, Joyce scribbled in giant letters, and used a magnifying glass to read. Deprived of sight, his hearing became more acute, and the music of language became an obsession. He almost abandoned *Work in Progress* entirely in 1927, depressed by his loss of vision and the poor reception of the portions that had been published so far. The next year, his weight fell to a paltry 112 pounds (Joyce was six feet tall). He was treated with arsenic, apparently for its tonic effects, and put some weight back on.

In what might have been a joke, Joyce once said that the only "demand that I make of my reader is that he should devote his whole life to reading my works." It is literally possible to spend one's whole life reading *Finnegans Wake,* a work with possibly the greatest idea density of any book ever written. Its eccentricity has been taken by some as evidence for neurosyphilis. *Wake* is certainly self-indulgent and often infuriating, a "crossmess parzel" (Christmas parcel/crossword puzzle), but it is also deliberately and painstakingly constructed: Joyce estimated that it took him 1,200 hours to write the seventeen pages of "Anna Livia Plurabelle." *Wake* is also the funniest and the most Joycean of Joyce's works, the culmination of a lifelong obsession with words, puns, and pushing the boundaries of meaning. The craftsmanship on display in *Wake* is not compatible with neurosyphilis, a disease that causes a brisk and relentless deterioration of the intellect once it becomes manifest.

Finnegans Wake is the dream of the slumbering Humphrey Chimpden Earwicker, or Here Comes Everybody, a Dublin publican who is also identified with Humpty Dumpty, the presumably dead bricklayer Tim Finnegan of the song "Finnegan's Wake," and Finn MacCool, the legendary giant who sleeps below the city of Dublin to someday waken. It is written in English modified with neologisms, puns, and portmanteau words that draw on Joyce's knowledge of over sixty languages. Some of these make sport of his own health problems. "One eyegonblack" refers to Joyce's blind and banjaxed eye, but also puns on the German *ein Augenblick,* meaning an instant or eyeblink. Joyce also appears as a "punsil shapner" with "an infamous private ailment (vulgovariovenereal)." In other venereal wordplay, the Russian general, a recurring character in *Wake*, becomes the "ructions gunorrhal."

Critical opinion is sharply divided on *Wake*. Some see it as surpassing Shakespeare and Dante; others see it as cruel and unusual punnishment. In a development that Joyce would have loved, the reading of *Wake* has become a cult activity. Small groups, ideally with members from many backgrounds and fluent in different languages, meet weekly in an Irish pub to pour over *Wake,* a page at a session, reading it aloud as Joyce intended. In the many years it takes to complete this, some drop out and others join, and when the end is reached, the group starts over again at the beginning.

By 1930, his left eye was functionally blind, and with his right eye he could only read large print held an inch away from the eye. He had one more operation, his eleventh, in May 1930, by a renowned Swiss surgeon, Alfred Vogt. He made a small opening in the secondary membrane, but could do no more because he was afraid the eye might collapse completely; the vitreous body, the viscous jelly that fills most of the eyeball, had been badly damaged by Joyce's prior surgeon. Leeches were again necessary to drain the blood in the eye. The vision in Joyce's left eye made a minor recovery, to about the same small degree as his right eye, but the right eye got worse over the next few years because of worsening glaucoma and another cataract. Another operation was recommended, but Joyce could not bear to go under the knife again.

As Milton had done, Joyce began to use promising young men as his scribes. One of these was a morose Irishman named Samuel Beckett.

Beckett became involved with Joyce's daughter Lucia, but she developed signs of mental illness soon after they broke up. Joyce blamed himself for Lucia's illness. "Whatever spark of a gift I possess has been transmitted to Lucia, and has kindled a fire in her brain." Her illness put him in agonies of depression, and he often tried to deny that she was ill, finding lucid meanings in her cryptic utterances that may or may not have been intended.

Joyce spared no expense in trying to make her well. She had analysis with Jung, injections of seawater, and a form of quackery called protoformotherapy, consisting of intramuscular shots of embryonic tissue. In 1935, Joyce estimated that Lucia's care had cost him £4000 in the past three years, and had involved twenty-four doctors, twelve nurses, eight companions, and three institutions. Out of all the Joyce family, he tried the hardest to keep her from being institutionalized, until it was only too clear that she was a danger to herself and others.

The surviving evidence (much of it was destroyed by the Joyce family) suggests that Lucia's disorder was schizophrenia, perhaps with some admixture of mood disorder, or what is now known as schizoaffective disorder. Schizophrenia is a disease with symptoms both positive and negative. Psychosis, or positive symptoms, is a loss of contact with reality, which may include delusions, hallucinations, and bizarre behaviours. Joyce showed a keen appreciation of this aspect of Lucia's disease: "The patient . . . prefers to live wholly in his or her inner world, losing more and more contact with the outer world." On a visit to uptight 1930s Ireland, Lucia lit a turf fire on the floor, went fishing with a safety pin, put oatmeal in the stew, slept in the fields, went skinny-dipping in the ocean, wore no underwear, unbuttoned the trousers of her friend's boyfriends, and wandered the streets of Dublin ragged and filthy.

Negative symptoms of schizophrenia include blunting of emotion (flat affect) and pleasure (anhedonia), apathy, and poverty of speech (alogia). Lucia suffered from apathy and catatonia. Once a talented dancer and artist, she had a relentless downhill course in terms of her social functioning and ability to work. This is unlike patients with bipolar disorder, who usually have remissions during which they approximate normalcy.

In Kathleen Ferris's *James Joyce and the Burden of Disease*, she suggested that Joyce acquired syphilis in Nighttown, which progressed to tabes dorsalis, explaining his chronic abdominal pain. Joyce is also supposed to have infected Nora, who passed syphilis on to Lucia in the womb, which led to her mental breakdown as an adult. None of this is likely to be true. While tabes dorsalis, a form of syphilis that attacks the spinal cord, may present with attacks of abdominal pain, Joyce did not have the major manifestation of the disease, which is an irregular, reeling, uncoordinated gait. He was an active walker up until his death, and even was known to dance jigs on occasion. His abdominal pain was more likely due to the peptic ulcer disease that ultimately killed him. Lucia had negative blood tests for syphilis, and did not have the disfiguring features of congenital syphilis. (She did have strabismus, or misalignment, of the left eye. Strabismus is one of several minor physical anomalies that are more common in schizophrenics, compared to non-schizophrenics.) Joyce was told by his ophthalmologists that his eye disease was not consistent with syphilis, and that he lacked the abnormally reactive pupils (Argyll Robertson pupils) that are typical in syphilis.

The cause of schizophrenia is unknown. Maternal infections during pregnancy, genetics, and substance abuse play a role in some patients. Urban living may make it more common, or at least result in a worse outcome. Schizophrenia occurs in 1 percent of persons worldwide across countries and ethnic groups, and it leads to decreased reproductive fitness, making its sufferers less likely to have children and pass along their genes. The fact that it is so common, despite impairing reproduction, suggests that schizophrenia may reflect a fundamental vulnerability of the human brain. Schizophrenia preferentially affects recently evolved parts of the brain involved in social thinking and language. These regions are complex and late-maturing, and may be more susceptible to a range of developmental insults. Thus Lucia's schizophrenia may simply have been the result of bad luck, instead of congenital syphilis or some supposed curse of genius.

Joyce had a long history of abdominal pain which got worse with fasting and better with eating, a typical symptom of peptic ulcers. In 1933, he had severe abdominal pain, with fits of weeping, irritability, rage, and weight loss of fifteen pounds. His Parisian physician, Debray, blamed this on "nerves," but Joyce's friends and family insisted that he had peptic ulcers.

Debray sniffed that this was *"une interpretation trop facile"* (an overly simple explanation). While Joyce probably did suffer from depression in his last decade, with Lucia's illness as a major precipitant, Joyce's friends and family were right about his peptic ulcers.

Joyce finished *Wake* in November 1938. In 1939, he was photographed for his second appearance on the cover of *Time* magazine. The photographer was shocked at his pale appearance, perhaps from the slow blood loss that is common in peptic ulcer disease. He had recurrent cramps and abdominal pain, and was mentally spent: *"Finnegans Wake* will be my last book. There is nothing left for me to do but die."

When war broke out, the Joyces left Paris for the small town of Saint-Gérand-le-Puy in the south of France. He drank more and lost his appetite. Nora struggled to create a routine for him, give structure to his days. When the Nazis invaded, Lucia was stuck in an asylum in occupied France, while the Joyces were on the Vichy side. She was now in grave danger, as the Nazi policy toward the mentally ill was forced sterilization or euthanasia. The official in charge of this program was Dr Hans Reiter.

Joyce planned to move Lucia to Switzerland with the rest of his family, but this proved impossible due to the logistical labyrinth created by the German, Vichy, and Swiss bureaucracies. In December 1940, Joyce, Nora, Giorgio, and Giorgio's son Stephen left for Switzerland and settled in Zurich, Joyce having been convinced it would be easier to arrange Lucia's transfer from there. He ate little but was still active, walking every afternoon in the snow with his grandson Stephen. On the early morning of January 10, 1941, he started vomiting, and had another severe attack of abdominal pain. A doctor came to the house and gave him a shot of morphine. Although this helped get Joyce back to sleep, it was a bad idea, as it delayed the care he urgently needed. Matters were worse when the doctor returned later in the day. A surgeon was summoned, who had Joyce taken to hospital by ambulance. Fluid sucked out of a stomach tube was positive for blood. An X-ray of the abdomen revealed free air below the diaphragm, consistent with a bowel perforation (air is normal inside the bowel, but free air in the peritoneal cavity usually indicates a breakdown of the wall of the gut). He was taken to the operating room. Gas and fluid rushed from the incision. A ruptured peptic ulcer in his duodenum was patched up with his omentum, a convenient, free-hanging flap of peritoneum, the lining of the inside of the abdominal cavity. This operation was once commonplace, but has become rare, due to the efficacy of modern medicines for peptic ulcer disease.

The outcome of peritonitis depends on the time lapse between the perforation of the gut and its correction in the operating room—the longer the delay, the higher the mortality. This was especially true in the preantibiotic era, when the only treatment for peritonitis was prompt surgical drainage. The long delay in Joyce's case proved fatal. He developed septic shock, his lungs filled with fluid, and he lapsed into a coma. He bled internally and was transfused. Seventy-two hours after his attack began, he was dead. An autopsy showed bleeding from a second ulcer in his duodenum that had not perforated. The bowel was enormously swollen and congested with fluid, and his aorta was damaged from atherosclerosis. In addition to his ulcer disease, Joyce's autopsy showed yet another explanation of his chronic abdominal pain and weight loss: a scarred, chronically inflamed, "raglike" pancreas, likely a consequence of his bouts of drinking.

A Catholic priest offered to bury Joyce in the rites of the Church, but Nora said, "I couldn't do that to him." When a scholar contacted her years later to ask about Joyce's friendship with André Gide, she replied, "Sure, if you've been married to the greatest writer in the world, you don't remember all the little fellows."

Lucia spent the war safe in her asylum, under the protection of her psychiatrist, Dr François Achille-Delmas, but cut off from communication with her family. When by chance she found out about her father's death by reading of it in the newspapers, she asked, "What is he doing there under the ground, that idiot? When will he decide to come out?"

Orwell during his wartime stint at the BBC. The digits of his left hand demonstrate clubbing, with froglike, spatulate enlargement of the ends of the fingers. Clubbing may be seen in several diseases. In Orwell's case, it was likely the consequence of chronic lung infection. (Courtesy of the BBC Photo Library)

10. "THE DISEASE WHICH WAS BOUND TO CLAIM ME SOONER OR LATER": *Orwell's Cough*

As I warned you I might do, I intend getting married again [to Sonia] when I am once again in the land of the living, if I ever am. I suppose everyone will be horrified, but apart from other considerations I really think I should stay alive longer if I were married.
    —George Orwell, letter to Fred Warburg, August 22, 1949

However great the kindness and the efficiency, in every hospital death there will be some cruel, squalid detail, something perhaps too small to be told but leaving terribly painful memories behind, arising out of the haste, the crowding, the impersonality of a place where every day people are dying among strangers.
    —George Orwell, "How the Poor Die," 1946

Mellor was savouring the last few puffs from his Lucky Strike in the doctors' lounge when Dick, his senior, popped in. "Mellor, have you done an air refill in the abdomen before?" Although the surgeon had a gentle manner, Mellor was intimidated by his burly physique. Mellor stubbed out his cigarette and stammered, "Er, no, I haven't, sir."

"D'ye know that patient Blair on Ward 3? Writer, odd duck. Famous for some sort of animal story. Bit of a bolshie, but a decent chap for all that."

"I heard the nurses talking about him," said Mellor. Or rather, he had heard one particular probationer nurse talking about him, a lively Belfast girl he had been trying to seduce for weeks, thus far with little success. "He scribbles all day in his notebooks, smoking hand-rolled cigarettes with horrid black shag tobacco in his bed."

"Well, the cigarettes won't hurt him," Dick shrugged. "But if he doesn't put on more weight, we might have to take away his newfangled ballpoint pens, just like we did his typewriter."

They walked down the corridor over the worn linoleum. Mellor greeted the ward sister in his most charming manner, but she merely scowled and walked on. Dick said, "Blair has a big cavity in the left lung base. Full of TB, but too large and too far down to collapse with a thoracoplasty. So we did a phrenic nerve block to paralyze the left diaphragm, followed by a P. P.— pneumoperitoneum, I mean. He's been getting weekly refills, no more than 700 cc at a time. So, you'll put the needle smooth and steady into his left upper quadrant. Not too fast—you don't want to puncture his gut. You should feel a sudden give when the needle is through the abdominal wall. Be sure the needle is actually *in* the peritoneal cavity—I don't want him getting subcutaneous emphysema and coming out looking like the Michelin Man. I'll instil the air, you hold the needle in place. The air has to go in slow, to keep him from vomiting or passing out."

"Do you numb the skin with Novocain first?" asked Mellor.

"The first time, yes, because you have to advance the needle so slowly. For refills, you can go faster, and it hurts less to just stick it in without fussing around with local anaesthetic."

The procedure room was bright and windowless, and smelled of damp plaster and carbolic acid. Blair lay waiting on the gleaming metal table, attended by a nurse. He looked ancient. His face was a grinning death's-head with a trim moustache. His limbs were tense and emaciated. Mellor noticed the spatulate quality of his fingers, from the clubbing of chronic lung infection.

"How are you today, Mr Blair?" asked Dick.

Blair smiled. "Not bad, Mr Dick, for a fellow with one working lung." His voice was a high-pitched croak, with a hint of a public school accent.

"Mr Blair, this is Dr Mellor. He will be assisting me with the refill today. We will examine you first." They helped him off with his pyjama top. There was a fresh red scar above his left collarbone, and two old stellate scars on the neck that did not appear to be surgical in origin. His chest with its protuberant ribs was an undulating field of ridges and furrows. When Mellor managed to get a proper air seal with his stethoscope, he heard a cacophonous symphony of crackles and wheezes.

Dick percussed Blair's abdomen. Bruises of various ages from prior refills were visible. "Here, Dr Mellor, in the left upper quadrant," Dick indicated. Mellor gloved up and swabbed the area with acetone and alcohol. Dick handed Mellor an elongated needle linked by red rubber tubing to an elaborate apparatus. There were two large graduated cylinders partly filled with water, a manometer, and an inflation bulb, interconnected with valves and hoses.

Next came the part that Blair hated. His body tensed. With one hand, Mellor pushed the needle hub forward, putting his other hand near the tip of the needle to steady it. The needle passed easily at first, but stalled when it hit the tough, stringy meat of the abdominal wall. Mellor pushed harder and the needle resisted, indenting the skin. It was like trying to burst an unwilling balloon. Blair blanched and gritted his teeth. Mellor leaned forward to put his weight over the needle. There was a give and the needle slid inward. Dick looked at the manometer attentively. "You're in, Dr Mellor."

Dick fiddled with the chrome-plated valves and started pumping, watching the manometer and the water levels in the cylinders. A wave of pain and nausea flooded Blair's belly and radiated outward. His abdomen bulged as it filled with air. Sweat trickled down his forehead. His back ached and his breath grew short. Through a vague mist, he saw the mercury rise in the manometer. The pain went on and on. Dick stopped pumping and closed a stopcock.

"That should do, Dr Mellor," said Dick. Mellor pulled out the needle. A single drop of blood trickled down Blair's flank. "Well done, Mr Blair. That will keep you for another week. Remember, sit partly upright—that will get the air up under the diaphragm and help force the cavity closed." They left the room as the nurse tended to Blair.

As they walked away, Mellor spoke. "Blair never said a word. He's a tough old bird, isn't he?"

"He's not that old. He just looks it," said Dick.

George Orwell, creator of Big Brother and doublethink, was born as Eric Blair in 1903 in India, where his father was busily engaged in what his son would call "the dirty work of Empire." As an adult, Orwell was vague about his father's work, probably deliberately so. Richard Blair was, in essence, an imperial dope peddler. He was a bureaucrat in the Opium Department, ensuring that only the finest narcotics were exported from the fields of Bengal to the slums of China. The opium trade was immensely lucrative, accounting for one-sixth of the Indian government's income. Over thirty-seven years, Richard Blair slowly rose from Assistant Sub-Deputy Opium Agent, Fifth Grade, to the lofty rank of Sub-Deputy Opium Agent, First Grade.

Orwell's parents were ill-matched. His mother Ida had French ancestry, and was raised in Burma, where her father was at one time a prosperous timber merchant. She was seventeen years younger than Richard Blair, and had bohemian, socialist, and literary inclinations. It is generally assumed that Orwell took mainly after his mother, but he probably inherited a certain doggedness and tenacity from his father, as well as a conservative and patriotic streak. When Eric was a few months old, his mother brought him and his sister to England, while his father stayed in India, an arrangement that was not unusual among Anglo-Indian families. The family settled in the pastoral town of Henley-on-Thames, in a time and place that an adult Orwell romanticized as a lost Eden.

Eric had several episodes of bronchitis in infancy, including an episode at eighteen months severe enough to confine him to bed for a week. He was described as "chesty" and "bronchial." He also had measles and whooping cough. Despite this, he looks hearty and chubby in childhood photographs.

At age eight, he was sent to St Cyprian's, an elite preparatory school. Although St Cyprian's was a place of only average snobbery and brutality for its time, it was hellish for Eric. He was a sheltered, somewhat pampered child thrown into a spartan environment of bullying, cramming, and rote learning. Discipline was harsh: his bedwetting led to several beatings. The expectations for him were higher than for wealthier boys. A middle-class student accepted at reduced tuition because of his academic promise, he was under enormous pressure to bring lustre to the institution by winning a scholarship to one of the great English public schools. Given his family's modest means, he could not expect to attend public school, and subsequently Oxford or Cambridge, without scholarship money. Congestion of his airways became a regular event, likely due to influenza and other winter viruses, aggravated by stress and crowding. Years later, Orwell recalled, "In winter, after about the age of ten, I was seldom in good health . . . I had defective bronchial tubes and . . . a chronic cough." When he was fourteen, a neighbour noted: "Eric has a bit of a cough. He says it is chronic."

Despite or because of his miseries, he excelled, and won a scholarship to Eton, the most prestigious of the English public schools; nineteen British Prime Ministers have been Old Etonians. Aldous Huxley, author of *Brave New World*, an influence on *Nineteen Eighty-Four*, was among his teachers. Eric was one of the minority of students who were King's Scholars, or Collegers, who lived in the college, as opposed to the aristocratic Oppidans, who paid full fees, lived in town, and looked down on the more plebian Collegers. Fellow students remembered him as contrarian, aloof, and proudly atheistic. He read extensively, especially H. G. Wells, Shaw, Samuel Butler, and Jack London, and wrote satiric verse. Students at Eton enjoyed considerable freedoms. Eric took advantage of this to slack off academically. His marks were good enough to graduate, but not good enough to get a scholarship to Oxford or Cambridge. Without a scholarship, continuing his studies at university was out of the question.

Although he professed to believe that the Empire was a swindle, he joined the Burma Imperial Police as a round-faced nineteen-year-old, perhaps the only Old Etonian ever to do so. Like his father, he seemed destined for a career in the bleak obscurity of a series of colonial outposts. He had heavy responsibilities at a young age. At one posting, he was chief of police for a city of 200,000 people. At another, he was head of security for an oil refinery, where constant exposure to petrochemical fumes probably further damaged his lungs. He performed his duties with scrupulous fairness, had a knack for the Burmese language, and enjoyed liaisons with Burmese women. Yet as the servant of an Empire he no longer believed in, he was in an impossible position. He came to despise both the pious hypocrisy of British rule and the petty insolence of the Burmese youths who jeered at him.

As described in the essay "Shooting an Elephant," he was once called to deal with an elephant that had run amok and trampled a villager. Although the animal had become placid by the time he arrived, under pressure from the crowd he felt compelled to shoot it anyway. This incident landed him in trouble with his superiors, as the elephant was a valuable beast used to move teak logs by the Steel Brothers conglomerate. As punishment, he was exiled to the far reaches of Burma, where he came down with dengue fever. Happily, this gave him an excuse to take sick leave in England for several months (the normal recovery period for dengue fever is several weeks). His family was shocked at his gaunt and aged appearance, attributable to illness and heavy smoking.

He resigned as soon as he was eligible, and set about in earnest to become a writer. The clarity, concreteness, and seeming offhandedness of his mature style were actually the product of years of toil. (One of his exercises was to copy passages from memory out of Swift and Somerset Maugham, to practise the avoidance of adjectives.) Driven by guilt and a quest for subject matter, he immersed himself in wretchedness. Inspired by Jack London's *People of the Abyss*, he attired himself in shabby clothes and lived with English tramps. After a girlfriend robbed him in Paris, he was forced to work as a *plongeur*, or dishwasher, in several vile restaurants. These experiences provided the raw material for his first book, *Down and Out in Paris and London*, which should not be read by lovers of French cuisine. (This book was the first that appeared under the pseudonym George Orwell.) If he had not been infected with tuberculosis previously, either in childhood or in Burma, it is almost certain that he was exposed during these years of tramping, poverty, and vagabondage.

Orwell's adult health was poor. Although he stood 6'3" tall, his highest recorded weight was 170 pounds. As an adult, he was "chesty" and had "a cough every winter." On his return from Burma, he had episodes of coughing up blood, and claimed to have been tested for TB, with negative results; it is not clear whether this was a skin test or a sputum test. He had four bouts of pneumonia between the ages of fifteen and thirty-four, with the first two occurring while he was still at Eton. In 1929, he came down with pneumonia and was admitted to a particularly nasty Parisian hospital, where the medieval treatments included cupping: Orwell was forced to sit up, and a half-dozen glasses in which a match had been burned to create a partial vacuum were stuck to his back. The resulting blisters were lanced to release "a dessert-spoonful of dark-coloured blood." A corrosive mustard poultice was strapped onto his fresh wounds. "I later learned that watching a patient have a mustard poultice was a favourite pastime in the ward. These things are normally applied for a quarter of an hour and certainly they are funny enough if you don't happen to be the person inside." The patients were ignored by the doctors and medical students, unless—as described in "How the Poor Die"—they happened to have some interesting finding:

> . . . if you had some disease with which the students wanted to familiarize themselves you got plenty of attention of a kind. I myself, with an exceptionally fine specimen of a bronchial rattle, sometimes had as many as a dozen students queuing up to listen to my chest. It was a very queer feeling—queer, I mean, because of their intense interest in learning their jobs, together with a seeming lack of perception that the patients were human beings.

He almost died from another attack of pneumonia in 1933, during which he became delirious and thought he was being robbed by tramps. Orwell was told that sputum smears for tuberculosis were negative during this hospitalization.

When his savings were gone, Orwell supported his writing by teaching and working in a bookshop. For most of his life, his income from writing was a fraction of what he had made as a Burmese policeman, and his father remained appalled at his decision to throw a safe and steady job away. He wrote at a pace of a book a year, experimenting with style and subject matter. His fine first novel, *Burmese Days,* reads like a meaner and funnier Conrad tale. In *A Clergyman's Daughter,* he imitates Joyce, with mixed results. *Keep the Aspidistra Flying,* about an aspiring poet who abandons lucrative if demeaning work in advertising, has been seen as a forerunner of the writing of the Angry Young Men of the 1950s. *The Road to Wigan Pier,* an account of his travels in Lancashire in the depths of the Depression and erratic journey toward socialism, is the first of his books that is primarily political, rather than literary. (Although Orwell's talents were best suited for political writing, he viewed this as a moral duty, and would have preferred to be a purely literary writer.)

In 1935, Orwell met and fell in love with Eileen O'Shaughnessy, an attractive and intelligent young woman who was Oxford-educated and studying for a master's degree in child psychology. The following year, Eileen quit her degree programme and the couple married, despite the doubts of Eileen's friends and a warning from Orwell's mother Ida to Eileen that she was "taking on something!" In accordance with Orwell's masochistic fondness for hardship, they moved into a seventeenth-century cottage in the Hertfordshire countryside with no hot water, no electricity, a chimney that leaked smoke, and an outdoor toilet with a temperamental cesspool. However, the rent was minimal, Orwell had already planted vegetables, roses, and fruit trees, and they made money keeping a small shop.

Shortly after their marriage, the Spanish Civil War broke out between the Nationalists—led by General Franco and supported by Fascist Italy and Nazi Germany—and the Republicans, a motley coalition of liberal democrats, anarchists, Basques, and assorted Communist factions, supported by the Soviet Union. With the support of Eileen, who came along, Orwell went to Spain to fight on the Republican side. They pawned the family silver for travel money. Naïve about the nuances of Spanish politics, Orwell joined the tiny contingent of the POUM, an anti-Stalinist communist militia. This casual decision proved almost fatal.

His comrades remembered Orwell as a recklessly brave if eccentric soldier, scribbling by candlelight, spouting poetry, and addicted to vile tobacco. He led one assault on the Fascist lines, and was the first one into the opposing trenches. Tired of the monotonous diet, he ventured into no-man's-land at night to pick potatoes from an abandoned field. Meticulous about his moustache, he kept up appearances by shaving with wine, which was more readily available than water. Unfazed by cold, mud, lice, and Fascists, he was petrified of another hazard of the trenches: rats. He once provoked a chaotic nighttime exchange of rifle fire by shooting at a monstrous rat that was gnawing at his precious size-twelve boots. (Footwear was an Orwell mini-obsession. During World War II and after, shoes that fit him were simply unavailable in England, and he tried to obtain them through friends with contacts in America. On a sight-seeing trip to Haworth parsonage, he was amazed at Charlotte Brontë's impossibly tiny boots.)

Orwell was quickly promoted to lieutenant, but his commanding officer worried because "He was so tall and always standing up." These concerns were justified. On the morning of May 20, 1937, Orwell looked over the sandbags, his head silhouetted against the rising sun, and was struck by a high-velocity Mauser bullet in the neck. His knees gave out and he fell to the ground. His right arm was paralyzed, he lost his voice, and his mouth filled with blood. He expected to die: "My first thought, conventionally enough, was for my wife. My second was a violent resentment at having to leave this world which, when all is said and done, suits me so well."

It is not easy to plot a trajectory through the neck that does not lead to death from bleeding, loss of the airway, or spinal cord injury, but the bullet managed to find one. It entered his neck below the larynx, just left of the midline, passed to the right of the trachea, paralyzing his right recurrent laryngeal nerve, and came out of the right base of the neck. It just missed the carotid artery, and did not hit any other major blood vessels. The shock wave, or temporary cavity, created by the bullet stunned his right brachial plexus, the nerve supply to the right arm. Over time, he regained nearly all the strength and feeling in his arm, although he was left with numbness in the fingers. The recurrent laryngeal nerve injury left him with a paralyzed vocal cord and a permanently weak voice. His commandant, George Kopp, a charismatic, slippery character, likened the sound of Orwell's speech to the grating brakes of an antiquated Model T Ford.

Nothing needed to be done with Orwell's wound, as the bullet cauterized both entrance and exit wounds. Orwell was again a medical marvel. "The wound was a curiosity in a small way and various doctors examined it with much clicking of tongues and '¡Que suerte! ¡Que suerte!' [What luck!] . . . I could not help thinking it would be even luckier not to have been hit at all."

Orwell's troubles were not over. The Stalinists, who had come to dominate the Republican side, were purging their putative allies, the POUM and the anarchists. POUM men with whom Orwell had fought were being arrested, and some had already died under suspicious circumstances. Orwell and Eileen were being spied on by at least two English communists, David Wickes and David Crook, who had already urged that they be arrested. The Spanish secret police ransacked their room, but failed to arrest them, perhaps out of simple inefficiency. Despite being in grave danger himself, Orwell spent two fruitless days trying to get Kopp out of jail, before he and Eileen fled the country. (Orwell might not have been so keen to help Kopp had he known that Crook reported being 90 percent certain that Kopp and Eileen were having an affair, in a document recently unearthed in Crook's KGB file in Moscow.)

Pushing his endurance to its limits, Orwell wrote a draft of his first great book over a period of four months. *Homage to Catalonia* was an account of his Spanish adventures, and an elegy for a revolution betrayed. The purges, and the subsequent cover-up from Stalin's media apologists, had given Orwell his great theme, the enmity of truth and power. "In Spain, for the first time, I saw newspaper reports which did not bear any relation to the facts, not even the relationship which is implied in an ordinary lie . . . this kind of thing is frightening to me, because it often gives me the feeling that the very concept of objective truth is fading out of the world."

Orwell's health collapsed immediately after finishing *Homage to Catalonia,* in what became a recurrent pattern of overwork and burnout. He had written six books in six years, lived by choice in Victorian discomfort, was still recovering from a bullet wound, chain-smoking, and suffering from his usual winter bronchitis. In March 1938, he began coughing up prodigious amounts of blood. This was difficult to ignore, even for someone as indifferent to his own welfare as Orwell. An alarmed Eileen called her brother Laurence O'Shaughnessy, who conveniently happened to be a chest surgeon and a coauthor of a contemporary textbook on tuberculosis. He arranged for an ambulance to take Orwell to Preston Hall Sanatorium in Kent, under the care of its medical director, Dr J. B. McDougall.

Orwell was in rough shape. His weight had fallen to 159 pounds, and he was hacking up four tablespoons of mucoid sputum daily. His chest X-ray showed scarring and a small cavity in the right upper lobe of the lung. Another X-ray, performed by an early tomography technique, also showed a second small cavity in the hilar, or central, aspect of the right lung. The left side had infiltrates in the lower lung zones, thought to be the result of bleeding into the lung. These infiltrates cleared up eventually, and later chest X-rays revealed underlying chronic bronchiectasis of the left lung. Extensive tests for tuberculosis, including sputum smears, sputum cultures, and a Meinicke test (a now-obsolete blood test), were negative. Orwell also had a negative syphilis test, presumably done as a matter of routine medical care, or perhaps because McDougall saw literary types as suspect. In one place in Orwell's record, it says, "TB confirmed," but this is probably an error, as the summary compiled two months after Orwell's discharge by the assistant director, Dr J. H. Crawford, specifically states that tuberculosis was excluded. The final diagnosis was chronic bronchiectasis of the left lung, with nonspecific scarring of the right lung, possible related to old TB.

Normally, the airways of the lung are slender tubules of cartilage and muscle, lined within by cells with microscopic hairs, or cilia, sticking out from them. These cilia sweep mucus and bacteria upward and outward. In bronchiectasis, the airways, or bronchi, are damaged. The ciliated cells are lost, the muscle and cartilage are thinned, and the bronchial walls weaken and expand. Bacteria and mucus build up, creating a vicious cycle in which infection and inflammation lead to more airway damage, and further bouts of infection. Patients with bronchiectasis have a chronic cough, as Orwell did, and are prone to worsen in the winter, when respiratory viruses abound. Recurrent pneumonia may be a problem, as with Orwell. Coughing up of blood, or haemoptysis, is common. The bronchial arteries are fragile and engorged in bronchiectasis, and may break down in response to inflammation. Major haemoptysis may be fatal, not from loss of blood, but because the patient literally drowns in their own blood.

Bronchiectasis was common in the era before antibiotics. It was often a legacy of bouts of childhood pneumonia or bronchitis that dragged on long enough to cause permanent airway damage. In Orwell's case, the bronchitis he had in infancy might have begun the process, which was probably accelerated when he started smoking as a teenager at Eton. (No physician ever seems to have suggested to Orwell that he quit smoking, perhaps because 87 percent of British doctors smoked at the time.) At present, bronchiectasis is treated with intermittent antibiotics, along with the use of devices to loosen sputum stuck in the airways.

For most of Orwell's six-month stay, he was treated under the presumption that he had tuberculosis. Before antibiotics were available, the treatment of TB in sanatoriums consisted of a strict regime of bed rest and maximum nutrition. Patients who gained weight were more likely to ramp up their immune response, tipping the balance of the long battle against TB in favour of the patient. As patients gained weight and showed improvement on chest X-rays, they were slowly allowed to increase their activity. Restrictions could be extreme. At the famed Trudeau Sanatorium in upstate New York, newly admitted patients were wrapped like mummies, or perhaps swaddled like infants.

A therapeutic effect was sometimes attributed to a sanatorium's supposedly salubrious location. This was probably not true of sanatoriums in the damp lowlands of England and Scotland, but it may well have been true of sanatoriums at high altitude, such as those in Switzerland. TB is less prevalent in the mountains, where the air is thinner, probably because *Mycobacterium tuberculosis* requires much oxygen for optimal growth. The granuloma, or the cage in which the immune system contains TB, is effective partly because it denies TB bacilli access to oxygen, and drives them into a hibernatory state. Conversely, when TB bacilli erode the lung and create an air-filled cavity, this is a disaster for the patient, as the bacteria gain direct access to oxygen and reproduce to enormous levels. Patients whose TB became dormant in the mountains were sent to sanatoriums at lower elevations, and subsequently went home if they remained stable. However, patients who relapsed had to return to high altitude indefinitely.

Orwell was treated by rest, close attention to his weight, vitamin D, and calcium injections. Vitamin D is an immune stimulant, and probably has modest antituberculous effects. (Sunlight, which turns a form of cholesterol into vitamin D in the skin, was also often used as TB therapy.)

Calcium therapy was inspired by the spurious claim that workers with lime and plaster had low rates of tuberculosis. It was harmless, but ineffective. At least Orwell was not treated with gold injections, then in vogue for TB despite their expense, lack of supportive evidence, and sometimes lethal side effects.

Orwell improved significantly, and was discharged. His weight had risen to 168 pounds. He was advised to travel to a warm, dry climate to recuperate, and he and Eileen duly travelled to Morocco. He was also cautioned to abstain from literary work, which he ignored, immediately starting another novel, *Coming Up for Air,* a nostalgic look at the pre-1914 England of his boyhood. Orwell surprised Eileen by expressing a desire to stay in Morocco. As she drily noted, "this seems too reasonable and even comfortable to be in character." After six months, they returned to England and the primitive cottage in Hertfordshire.

When war broke out, Eileen got a job in London working in the Censorship Department. The couple lived apart for several months, with Eileen only travelling to the cottage on alternate weekends, perhaps an indication of her fatigue with his austere lifestyle. In May 1940, he capitulated and moved to London. Orwell was anxious to fight the Nazis. Not surprisingly, he failed three separate medical examinations during World War II—one for military service, and two others for work as a war correspondent. In June 1940, when French resistance to the Nazis crumbled and an invasion of Britain seemed imminent, he joined the Home Guard. To Eileen's dismay, he stashed a Sten gun under the bed and homemade bombs on the mantel. One of Sergeant Blair's raw recruits was his new publisher, Fred Warburg, who praised his "Cromwellian" intensity and democratic spirit.

Orwell worked for the BBC's Indian Section during the war. His work could be described as mild wartime propaganda, aimed at creating a favourable impression of British politics and literature for listeners in India. Orwell was an innovative writer and producer, whose scripts included an imaginary interview with Jonathan Swift. However, his thin, "drizzly" voice made him an indifferent radio presenter, at best. Orwell eventually tired of the mammoth bureaucracy of the BBC, which he described as "halfway between a girls' school and a lunatic asylum." In September

1943, he quit to write for the left-wing *Observer* and *Tribune* newspapers, where he no longer had to deal with the BBC and its censors. (Fittingly, his column for the *Tribune* was called "As I Please.")

Orwell's precarious health stabilized during the war because of his use of the early antibiotic sulphapyridine. This was also known as M & B, after its manufacturer, May and Baker. It was famous for saving Winston Churchill's life in 1942 when he developed pneumonia. M & B quelled Orwell's chronic bronchiectasis for several years, until the bacteria in his lungs became resistant. In 1945, Orwell summarized his medical history as follows: "I have a disease called bronchiectasis which is always liable to develop into pneumonia, and also an old 'non-progressive' tuberculous lesion in one lung, and several times in the past I have been supposed to be about to die, but I always lived on just to spite them."

His improved health coincided with a period of high productivity, and the writing of *Animal Farm*. The manuscript of this book was almost lost when a German V-1 bomb demolished George and Eileen's flat in June 1944. Once again, Orwell cheated death: he and Eileen happened to be visiting her family. Luckily, he was able to salvage the battered typescript from the ruins. It was rejected by two left-leaning publishers for its anti-Soviet slant, as well as the right-leaning T. S. Eliot at Faber & Faber, who objected that the pigs were the smartest animals, and of course best qualified to run the farm. The book was finally brought out by Fred Warburg in August 1945. This book, and its successor *Nineteen Eighty-Four*, brought Orwell wealth and fame, but only when he was no longer able to enjoy either.

Orwell and Eileen had a childless marriage for eight years before they adopted a baby boy in 1944, whom they named Richard. Orwell was convinced he was responsible for their failure to conceive, despite definitive proof. Writing to a female friend in 1945, he stated, "I am also sterile I think—at any rate I have never had a child, though I have never undergone the examination because it is so disgusting." Although the extent and duration of Orwell's early sexual relationships are unclear, Orwell suspected he was infertile prior to his marriage to Eileen. In 1934, he told one girlfriend that he "was incapable of having children," because "I've never had any." Orwell also confided his doubts about his fertility to Pamela Warburg, the wife of his publisher, and his friend Rayner Heppen-stall.

Several medical conditions are associated with both bronchiectasis and infertility. Men with cystic fibrosis (CF) are almost always infertile due to absence of the vas deferens, the tubules that carry sperm away from the testes. However, survival from CF was brief in the preantibiotic era, and it is unlikely that Orwell would have lived until the age of forty-six with CF.

In Young's syndrome, bronchiectasis is associated with blockages in the epididymis, which links the testicles and the vas deferens. It was once common from childhood exposure to calomel (mercurous chloride) in teething powders and worm medication, but has become rare since calomel-containing medications were taken off the market in the United Kingdom in the 1950s. In some patients, there is also a history of painful red fingers and toes from childhood mercury exposure, the acrodynia or pink disease that may have affected Jack London in the Solomon Islands. However, Orwell is not known to have had pink disease or calomel exposure in childhood. As well, the notion of a pandemic of mercury poisoning among the great writers in English might strain the credulity of the reader.

In primary ciliary dyskinesia, or immotile cilia syndrome, the cilia or hairlike projections on the cells that line the airways do not work properly, and recurrent upper respiratory tract infections and bronchiectasis develop. Most men with the condition have immobile sperm, and are thus infertile. Orwell does not seem to have suffered from sinusitis, as do most patients with immotile cilia syndrome. Intriguingly, tuberculosis may infect the epididymis, and TB is a common cause of male infertility in developing nations. This can occur even in the absence of overt pulmonary TB. But in the absence of proof that Orwell was infertile, no definite link can be drawn between his bronchiectasis and possible infertility, especially as Eileen had uterine disease that may have impaired her fertility.

In February 1945, Orwell somehow passed a medical and went to France as a war correspondent for the *Observer*. Either he had found an utterly incompetent physician, or strings were pulled by the *Observer*'s rich socialist publisher, his friend David Astor. Travel to a war zone was an awful idea for a man as fragile as Orwell. Soon after arriving in Paris, he showed signs of strain and paranoia. A haggard Orwell met Hemingway there, and confided in him that he feared assassination as a leading anti-Stalinist. Papa lent him a revolver, and was worried enough that he had someone follow Orwell for the rest of the evening to make sure that he was not out of his mind.

Orwell soon suffered a terrible blow, but not at the hands of the KGB. The war had been rough on Eileen. Her beloved brother Laurence had joined the Royal Army Medical Corps and was killed during the British evacuation from Dunkirk, plunging her into major depression. There had been mutual infidelities and fearsome arguments. Their adoption of Richard was perhaps an act of desperation. To Eileen's surprise, she was delighted at being a mother, and she and Orwell grew close again. However, she had started to have dizzy spells and weakness, which she concealed from Orwell. After his departure, she was found to be anaemic from blood loss from multiple uterine tumours, and told she needed an immediate hysterectomy. It is unknown whether these were benign fibroids or malignant tumours. On March 29, 1945, she went under anaesthesia. Within minutes, her heart stopped and she died on the table. This was probably the result of an unlucky reaction to chloroform, which is no longer used because it causes fatal cardiac arrhythmias in 1 out of 3000 patients.

When Orwell got the telegram notifying him of her death, he was in hospital in Cologne with yet another episode of pneumonia. He left the hospital, downed eight M & B tablets, which may have lost their effectiveness for him, and came back to England on a military transport plane. Orwell was devastated. He later tried to explain the complexities of their marriage: "What matters is being faithful in an emotional and intellectual sense. I was sometimes unfaithful to Eileen, and I also treated her very badly, and I think she treated me badly too at times, but it was a real marriage in the sense that we had been through awful struggles together, and she understood all about my work."

Orwell hired a young woman, Susan Watson, to help him with Richard. (Eventually, his sister Avril would take over Richard's care.) Orwell dealt with his grief by immersing himself in work. In the year after Eileen's death, he produced 130 articles and reviews, and started the book that became *Nineteen Eighty-Four*. Desperately lonely, he made at least four abrupt proposals of marriage to women that he barely knew. He had a brief sexual relationship with one of these women, the witty, voluptuous, brittle beauty, Sonia Brownell, assistant editor of the literary magazine *Horizon*. She would inspire the character of Julia in *Nineteen Eighty-Four*, the lusty girl from the Fiction Department who fixes the great novel-writing machines.

In May 1946, still miserable over Eileen's death, sick of the urban squalor of London, and doubtful of the survival of Western civilization in the nuclear era, Orwell—frail and wheezing, with his shattered throat, palsied arm, and ravaged lungs—set out for the sodden and remote Scottish Isle of Jura, sister and adopted son in tow. He spent most of the next eighteen months there. His biographer Gordon Bowker calls this "one of the many ill-judged decisions in a life littered with misjudgements."

Jura was exactly as Orwell wished, beautiful but arduous. There was no electricity or hot water. His diaries record a monotonous litany of foul weather, especially in the winter: "good deal of rain," "rain and drizzle all afternoon and evening," "dreadful weather," "thunder and heavy rain," "pelting rain," "rain almost continuous," "dense mists," "overcast most of the time," "extremely heavy rain," "violent rain," "filthy day." In many respects, conditions were better than in London, which was suffering from severe postwar shortages. Fish and game were plentiful, peat could be cut for fuel, and there was ample land to farm and garden. Orwell became a familiar apparition to the few inhabitants of the island, a scarecrow in oilskins emerging from the fog armed with shotgun and scythe.

This daily physical effort, a near-drowning when his boat capsized in the whirlpool of Corryvreckan, and his urgent efforts to finish the first draft of *Nineteen Eighty-Four* wore him down, and his body gave out again. In the essay "Why I Write," Orwell stated, "Writing a book is a horrible, exhausting struggle, like a long bout of some painful illness." This was intended as metaphor, but it was literally true of the writing of *Nineteen Eighty-Four*. He coughed up blood, had fever and night sweats, and lost twenty-eight pounds in weight. The last two months of writing were done in bed. A few days before Christmas 1947, he was admitted to Hairmyres Hospital near Glasgow. His attending physician was Mr Bruce Dick (since in Britain, senior surgeons are referred to as Mister, not Doctor). Orwell's chest X-ray showed a new cavity in the left lower lobe. This time, his sputum stains were positive for the thin red bacilli of tuberculosis. As he wrote to a friend, "It is TB, the disease which was bound to claim me sooner or later." Because the positive smears indicated that his TB was contagious, he was no longer allowed to see his son Richard.

Orwell's complex medical history can be summarized as follows: he developed bronchiectasis after a severe respiratory infection in infancy, explaining his annual winter viral and bacterial exacerbations thereafter. Tuberculosis sometimes causes bronchiectasis, but childhood tuberculosis is unlikely given Orwell's chubby appearance in youth and impressive adult stature. At some point, in Burma, during the down-and-out years, or in the trenches and hospitals of Spain, he was infected with tuberculosis, which remained latent for years, but reactivated when he was weakened by overwork, smoking, and repeated flares of chronic bronchiectasis. Several conditions could explain both bronchiectasis and possible infertility, but no firm conclusion can be drawn regarding these.

Orwell was treated with the usual bed rest and aggressive feedings. He had been having pain in his right arm, and it was placed in a cast for three months. His physicians probably thought he had TB of the elbow or shoulder, although his arm pain may just have been a flare-up of the nerve damage from his bullet wound. It was customary in the United Kingdom to immobilize joints that were infected with TB, although this was not the practice everywhere. Alternatively, the cast on his arm may have been intended to keep him from writing.

Orwell was treated with collapse therapy to try to force the cavity shut, and deny oxygen to the TB bacilli. A minor operation was done to paralyze the left diaphragm, the muscle that inflates the left lung. A small incision was made above the left collarbone, a muscle was shoved aside, and the phrenic nerve was tweaked with a pair of forceps, stunning it for several months. Then air was pumped into the belly to force the now-flabby diaphragm up, and hopefully force the walls of the cavity together to collapse it. Refills of air were performed weekly thereafter. If collapse therapy was completely successful, the cavity would close up altogether at the end of six months or so, and be replaced by a fibrous cleft of scar tissue. Unfortunately, it worked less than 50 percent of the time.

James Williamson, another of Orwell's doctors, was impressed by his uncomplaining stoicism. Williamson explained why anaesthetics were avoided: "The first time you did it, you used a local anaesthetic because you had to go very cautiously . . . but after that you just stuck it in, because patients agreed if it was done expertly, one sharp jab was better than fiddling about with anaesthetics and things." Orwell may have disagreed. He later wrote to David Astor, "It seems there's a regular tradition of withholding anaesthetics and analgesics and that it is particularly bad in England. I know Americans are often astonished by the tortures people are made to go through here." Perhaps Orwell's collapse therapy inspired the tortures of the Ministry of Love, where men in white coats prod poor Winston Smith with needles and adjust the dials of a terrible device to produce excruciating pain.

Orwell had the profound weight loss of advanced TB. This may be reflected in the wasting of Winston Smith, which mirrored that of Orwell himself:

> But the truly frightening thing was the emaciation of his body. The barrel of the ribs was as narrow as that of a skeleton: the legs had shrunk so that the knees were thicker than the thighs . . . the curvature of the spine was astonishing. The thin shoulders were hunched forward so as to make a cavity of the chest, the scraggy neck seemed to be bending double under the weight of the skull. At a guess he would have said that it was the body of a man of sixty, suffering from some malignant disease.

Even with modern treatment, it is difficult to get TB patients to gain weight, in spite of early and aggressive nutritional supplementation.

Bruce Dick made an inspired suggestion that Orwell might be treated with streptomycin, a recently discovered antibiotic that was produced by a soil bacterium. Streptomycin was the first drug that was proven to be effective against tuberculosis. A landmark study published in October 1948 showed that four months of treatment with streptomycin reduced the short-term mortality of tuberculosis from 22 percent to 7 percent. This was the first-ever randomized, controlled clinical trial: patients were randomly assigned to receive either the study drug or conventional therapy (bed rest). It was the beginning of the end for prescribing based on bias, habit, or anecdotal experience that had allowed physicians to poison

COLLAPSE THERAPY FOR TUBERCULOSIS

~♥~

Orwell's TB was somewhat unusual in that he had a cavity in the lower lobe of the lung. Most patients with TB have cavities in the upper lobe of the lung, specifically in the apex, or topmost portion of the lung. The apical part of the lung has a higher oxygen tension than the other lung regions, and thus is more favourable to the growth of TB. Most forms of collapse therapy were designed to collapse these upper portions of the lung. In artificial pneumothorax, a needle was stuck into the chest cavity and air pumped in directly, similar to the pneumoperitoneum that Orwell had. This was reasonably effective, but had many limitations. The lung might not collapse properly because of scar tissue between the chest wall and the lung. Even if it worked, the air eventually was reabsorbed, and the lung would re-expand. Regular refills were required. These might have dangerous complications. When "gassing" a patient, it was possible to mistakenly pump air directly into an artery, which could then travel to the brain or heart and cause a stroke, seizure, heart attack, or death. The patient had to stay supine in bed to give the lung the best opportunity to stay collapsed. In some sanatoriums, this was enforced by putting weights on the patient's chest.

(continued)

patients with mercury and other worthless and dangerous nostrums for four hundred years.

Streptomycin was not yet available in Britain, so Orwell asked David Astor to help get some from the United States. Astor paid for it, and obtained approval for importation from the Minister of Health. Orwell improved on the new wonder drug. His sputum smears became negative for TB, and his appetite and energy perked up. Unluckily, he developed a rare side effect, toxic epidermal necrolysis. His skin turned blotchy red all over, and began to peel. He developed blood blisters in his throat and mouth, and could no longer swallow solid foods. When he awoke each morning, he had trouble opening his mouth because his lips were encrusted with blood. His nails and hair fell out. Orwell called it "rather like sinking the ship to get rid of the rats."

Orwell could only tolerate fifty days of streptomycin, rather than the four months that were recommended. His rash resolved after stopping the drug. With Orwell's approval, the leftover streptomycin was given to two very ill doctors' wives with TB, who were subsequently cured. Although the amount of streptomycin that Orwell received was enough to knock back his TB, it was far from adequate to cure him. In fact, single drugs are no longer used to treat TB, because antibiotic resistance and treatment failure are common. Cure of active TB generally requires therapy with three drugs for two months, followed by treatment with two drugs for another four months.

Orwell left Hairmyres in July 1948. His overall state was precarious. His breathing was better, but he had not gained much weight. He was told that he needed to rest, and lead a sedentary lifestyle. At this point, he made perhaps his most dreadful miscalculation. Instead of going to somewhere quiet and comfortable, he returned to Jura, and continued to potter about the farm and fields, finding himself incapable of the crepuscular existence of a valetudinarian. To make things worse, his publisher Fred Warburg, aware that Orwell was sitting on a great, strange, and possibly very lucrative manuscript, urged him to complete *Nineteen Eighty-Four* with all possible speed. By the end of October, the revisions were complete, but even minimal exertion left him breathless and febrile. The manuscript was in a confused state, with many scribbled insertions and deletions, and a clean copy needed to be typed under Orwell's direct supervision. However, no typists could be found

Because of the problems associated with artificial pneumothorax, operations were devised to collapse the tuberculous lung permanently. In thoracoplasty, the posterior ribs were stripped away, leaving behind only their opalescent outer surface, the periosteum. Then the chest wall was pushed in by the surgeon to collapse it. New ribs would regrow from the periosteum, maintaining the lung in the collapsed position, but leading to a severely deformed chest.

In a variation on this procedure, plombage thoracoplasty, the periosteum was stripped off the ribs, and an inert foreign body, or *plombe*, such as paraffin or Lucite (methylmethacrylate) balls, was used as a spacer to keep the lung collapsed. This resulted in a chest X-ray on which it appeared that part of the lung had been replaced with innumerable ping-pong balls. Less satisfactory materials were also used as the *plombe*, including fibreglass, olive oil, gauze, rubber, bone grafts, pectoral muscle flaps, and abdominal wall fat from the same patient or from another patient. Ideally, the *plombe* was removed after the periosteum had regenerated a stable bony plate in the collapsed position, decreasing the risks of infection or shifting of the *plombe*. Collapse therapy was made obsolete in the 1950s by the development of highly effective antituberculous drug therapy.

that wanted to go to Jura, and Orwell undertook to produce the typescript on his own decrepit machine, even though he was now bedbound.

By the time he was done, it was obvious he needed to go back to a sanatorium.

In January 1949, he was admitted to Cotswold Sanitorium near Cranham in Gloucestershire, having had enough of Scotland for the time being. He received another new drug, para-aminosalicylic acid (PAS) as monotherapy. Orwell was sceptical, suspecting it to be "a high-sounding name for aspirins," but it was a legitimate antituberculous drug, albeit much less powerful than streptomycin. Rest and PAS helped for a while. His fever subsided and his appetite picked up. By March, though, he was spitting up copious amounts of blood again. Haemoptysis is always worrisome in cavitary TB, as the cavity, if large enough, may erode into a pulmonary artery, leading to death from rapid exsanguination. An ill-advised rechallenge with streptomycin almost killed him after the first dose.

Nineteen Eighty-Four appeared that summer. It was an immediate commercial and critical success. Orwell admitted to friends that its gloom had much to do with his illness. He called his royalty money "fairy gold," knowing he would never be able to spend it. Another development that summer was a source of titillation for the nurses at Cranham. The cadaverous Orwell was entertaining regular visits from "a well-built blonde lady." Sonia Brownell was back in the picture, and reconsidering his proposal.

By September 1949, he had moved to University College Hospital, London, under the care of Dr Andrew Morland, who had once attended D. H. Lawrence. Morland professed vague optimism, although Dr Howard Nicholson, his junior consultant, later said, "When I first saw him, I had no serious doubt that he was dying." Not much could be done for him. Streptomycin was out of the question, and PAS no longer worked. Today's workhorse drugs for tuberculosis would not appear for a few more years: isoniazid in 1951, and rifampicin in 1959. He received painful injections of penicillin into his wasted muscles. Presumably this was intended to treat his bronchiectasis, as it was already known that penicillin was not active against TB. In what is always an ominous sign, the doctors stopped rounding on him regularly, hoping to avoid terminal awkwardness.

On October 13, 1949, he married Sonia in his hospital room. Many were cynical about her motivations in marrying a suddenly wealthy, desperately ill man, but at least she would prove to be a formidable literary widow, ferociously protective of Orwell's posthumous reputation. Obstinate to the last, Orwell shocked everyone by rallying once more. It seemed he might confound them all and live. A plane was chartered to fly him and Sonia to the Swiss Alps. If he could survive the flight, there was a chance that his TB might stabilize in the thin air of the mountains. However, he died suddenly and alone in his hospital bed from massive haemoptysis in the early morning of January 21, 1950, four days before the plane was to depart. A fishing rod in a corner stood mute testimony to his forlorn hope of escape to the alpine lakes of Switzerland.

Orwell, driven by guilt and obsessed with failure, once observed, "Any life when viewed from the inside is simply a series of defeats." In the end, he lost his battle against tuberculosis. Yet Orwell's masterworks, completed at such a terrible physical cost, represent a triumph of the human spirit over tyranny and lies. Orwell could be foolish, quixotic, and hypocritical, but he was also generous, heroic, loyal, persevering, and above all ruthlessly honest. His central concerns—the debasement of language by politics, the demise of privacy, the despoliation of nature—are even more relevant in the present day. Take Orwell's measure now, and you will find him more indispensable than ever.

ACKNOWLEDGEMENTS

The chapters on Shakespeare and Orwell first appeared in the pages of *Clinical Infectious Diseases*, and the Melville material was originally published in the *Journal of Medical Biography*. I wish to thank the editors and peer reviewers of these journals for their suggestions and support, especially Sherwood Gorbach, the editor-in-chief of *Clinical Infectious Diseases*. I also thank the Oxford University Press and the Royal Society of Medicine Press for graciously consenting to republication of this material in modified form.

I am grateful to Kristen Marangoni and Professor Laura M. Stevens of the Department of English of the University of Tulsa, and to Marc Carlson of the McFarlin Library, for making it possible for me to review materials from the Richard Ellmann papers relating to the illness of Lucia Joyce. Mandy Wise of the University College London Special Collections was extremely helpful in tracking down records from Orwell's stay in Preston Hall Sanatorium. The late Dr John B. Lyons provided copies of Yeats's fever charts and consented to their reproduction; his elegant study of the illnesses of James Joyce served as one inspiration for this project. I am also indebted to Jack Eckert of the Countway Library at Harvard Medical School for reviewing the casebooks of Oliver Wendell Holmes Sr, Dennis Marnon of the Houghton Library at Harvard University for his review of the Melville chapter, and Dr Katharina Busl for her translations from the German. I am also grateful to Dr Nassir Ghaemi for his kind words and critical eye.

I owe a particular debt of gratitude to my editor, Daniela Rapp of St. Martin's Press, for her infinite patience and wisdom, and to my agent Mary Beth Chappell for shaping and championing this work. This book would not have been possible without their efforts. I also thank Esmond Harmsworth for seeing a glimmer of potential in this project. Finally, I am very grateful to my wife Megan and our children for their tolerance, love, and support during the writing of this book.

BIBLIOGRAPHY AND ENDNOTES

1. The Hardest Knife Ill-Used: Shakespeare's Tremor

BOOKS

Amussen, Susan Dwyer. *An Ordered Society: Gender and Class in Early Modern England*. New York: Columbia University Press, 1993.

Bloom, Harold. *Shakespeare: The Invention of the Human*. New York: Riverhead Books, 1998.

Burgess, Anthony. *Shakespeare*. New York: Alfred A. Knopf, 1970.

Crosby, Alfred. *The Columbian Exchange: Biological and Cultural Consequences of 1492*. Westport, CN: Greenwood Press, 1972.

Duncan-Jones, Katherine. *Ungentle Shakespeare*. London: Arden Shakespeare, 2001.

Fabricius, Johannes. *Syphilis in Shakespeare's England*. London: Jessica Kingsley Publishers, 1994.

Greenblatt, Stephen. *Will in the World: How Shakespeare Became Shakespeare*. New York: W. W. Norton, 2004.

Harrison, G. B. ed., *Willobie His Avisa*. Edinburgh: Edinburgh University Press, 1966.

Honan, Park. *Shakespeare: A Life*. Oxford: Oxford University Press, 1998.

Moore, Joseph E. *The Modern Treatment of Syphilis,* 2nd ed. Springfield, IL: C. C. Thomas, 1947.

Moore, Wendy. *The Knife Man: The Extraordinary Life and Times of John Hunter, Father of Modern Surgery.* New York: Broadway Books, 2005.

Nicholl, Charles. *A Cup of News: The Life of Thomas Nashe.* London: Routledge & Kegan Paul, 1984.

Osler, William. *The Principles and Practice of Medicine.* New York: Appleton & Co, 1892.

Partridge, Eric. *Shakespeare's Bawdy.* London: Routledge Classics, 2001.

Picard, Liza. *Elizabeth's London.* New York: St. Martin's Press, 2003.

Pierce, Patricia. *Old London Bridge.* London: Headline Book Publishing, 2001.

Pusey, William. *The History and Epidemiology of Syphilis.* Springfield, IL: C. C. Thomas, 1933.

Quétel, Claude. *History of Syphilis.* Baltimore: Johns Hopkins University Press, 1992.

Schoenbaum, Samuel. *William Shakespeare: A Compact Documentary Life.* New York: Oxford University Press, 1977.

Siena, Kevin P. *Venereal Disease, Hospitals, and the Urban Poor: London's "Foul Wards," 1600–1800.* Rochester, NY: University of Rochester Press, 2004.

Wood, Michael. *Shakespeare.* New York: Basic Books, 2003.

Wells, Stanley, and Taylor, Gary, eds. *William Shakespeare: The Complete Works,* 2nd ed. New York: Oxford University Press, 2005.

ARTICLES

Albers, J. W., Kallenbach, L. R., Fine, L. J., et al., "Neurological Abnormalities Associated with Remote Occupational Elemental Mercury Exposure," *Annals of Neurology* 1988; 24:651–9.

Austin S. C., Stolley P. D., Lasky T., "The History of Malariotherapy for Neurosyphilis: Modern Parallels," *JAMA* 1992; 268:516–9.

Benoit, S., Posey, J. E., Chenoweth, M. R., Gherardini, F. C., "*Treponema pallidum* 3-Phosphoglycerate Mutase Is a Heat-Labile Enzyme that May Limit the Maximum Growth Temperature for the Spirochete," *Journal of Bacteriology* 2001; 183:4702–8.

Brewster, P. G., "A Note on the Winchester Goose and Kindred Topics,"

Journal of the History of Medicine and Allied Sciences, October 1958 (4):483–91.

Broad, W. T., "Sir Isaac Newton: Mad as a Hatter," *Science,* 18 September 1981, pp. 1341–4.

Carney, O., Ross, E., Bunker, C., Ikkos, G., Mindel, A., "A Prospective Study of the Psychological Impact on Patients with a First Episode of Genital Herpes," *Genitourinary Medicine* 1994; 70:40–5.

Clarkson, T. W., Magos, L., Myers, G. J., "The Toxicology of Mercury—Current Exposures and Clinical Manifestations," *New England Journal of Medicine* 2003; 349:1731–7.

Doherty, M. J., "The Quicksilver Prize: Mercury Vapor Poisoning Aboard HMS *Triumph* and HMS *Phipps,*" *Neurology* 2004; 62:963–6.

Feldman, R. G., "Neurological Manifestations of Mercury Intoxication," *Acta Neurologica Scandinavica* Suppl 1982; 92:201–9.

Fessler, A., "Venereal Disease Phobia in the Seventeenth Century," *British Journal of Venereal Disease* 1955; 31(3):190–1.

Jacobowsky, B., "General Paresis and Civilization," *Acta Psychiatrica Scandinavica* 1965; 41:267–73.

Kail, A., "The Bard and the Body. 3. Venereal Disease—'The Pox,'" *Medical Journal of Australia* 1983; 2:445–9.

Keynes, M., "Sir Isaac Newton and His Madness of 1692–93," *Lancet,* 8 March 1980, pp. 529–30.

MacAlpine, I., "Syphilophobia: A Psychiatric Study," *British Journal of Venereal Disease* 1957; 33:92–9.

Mindel, A., "Psychological and Psychosexual Implications of Herpes Simplex Virus Infections," *Scandinavian Journal of Infectious Diseases* Suppl 1996; 100:27–32.

Neal, P. A., Jones, R. R., "Chronic Mercurialism in the Hatters' Fur-Cutting Industry," *JAMA* 1938; 110:337–43.

O'Shea, J. G., "Two Minutes with Venus, Two Years with Mercury: Mercury as an Antisyphilitic Chemotherapeutic Agent," *Journal of the Royal Society of Medicine* 1990; 83:392–5.

Pedder, J. R., "Psychiatric Referral of Patients in a Venereal Diseases Clinic," *British Journal of Venereal Disease* 1970; 46:54–7.

Ross, M. W., "AIDS Phobia: Report of 4 Cases," *Psychopathology* 1988; 21:26–30.

Rothschild, B. M., Calderon, F., Coppa, A., Rothschild, C., "First European Exposure to Syphilis: The Dominican Republic at the Time of Columbian Contact," *Clinical Infectious Diseases* 2000; 31:936–41.

Rubinstein, F., "They Were Not Such Good Years," *Shakespeare Quarterly,* Vol. 40, No. 1 (Spring 1989):70–74.

Stamm, L. V., Gherardini, F. C., Parrish, E. A., Moomaw, C. R., "Heat Shock Response of Spirochetes," *Infection and Immunity* 1991; 59:1572–5.

Verghese, A., "The Typhoid State Revisited," *American Journal of Medicine* 1985; 79(3):370–2.

Vroom, F. Q., Greer, M., "Mercury Vapour Intoxication," *Brain* 1972; 95:305–18.

1 "The real mystery of Shakespeare": Harold Bloom, quoted in "Last Will: How to read between the lines of the Bard's bequests," the *Yale Alumni Magazine,* July/August 2006, p. 35.

5 "I am convinced that *some* of Shakespeare's horror and despair": D. H. Lawrence, *Selected Critical Writings.* Oxford: Oxford University Press, 1998, p. 252.

5 "gratuitous venereal obsession": Burgess, p. 221.

6 "only six lines referring to venereal disease in . . . Marlowe": References to syphilis and STDs in Marlowe are fleeting. In *The Jew of Malta* 2.3.54–5, Barabas threatens Lodowick with "the poison of the city" and "the white leprosy"; in *Jew of Malta* 4.4.34–5, Ithamore exclaims "Pox on this drunken hiccough!" There is a joke on "French crowns" (syphilitic alopecia) in *Doctor Faustus,* Scene 4.35–6. See Frank Romany and Robert Lindsey, eds. *Christopher Marlowe: The Complete Plays.* London: Penguin Books, 2003.

6 "References to syphilis and STDs are not uniformly distributed throughout Shakespeare's plays": In determining whether or not a passage in the plays refers to venereal disease, I have generally sought support from the editorial readings of the Oxford, Arden, or Pelican

editions. I have not included equivocal passages, such as Lear's misogynist rants, some notoriously obscure passages in *Love's Labour's Lost*, the rashes in *Coriolanus*, Lucio's final speech in *Measure for Measure*, and lines in *Troilus and Cressida* and *Timon of Athens* that probably refer to venereal disease, but could be construed as referring to other maladies. My tallies of the number of lines referring to venereal disease in Shakespeare are as follows: one line each in *Part I* and *Part II* of *Henry VI*, *Henry VIII*, and *Two Noble Kinsmen*; two lines each in *Henry VI, Part III* and *A Midsummer Night's Dream*; three lines in *Love's Labour's Lost* and *King Lear*; four lines in *Two Gentlemen of Verona*, *Romeo and Juliet*, *Hamlet*, and *Othello*; five lines in *Much Ado About Nothing*, *Coriolanus*, and *The Tempest*; six lines in *Henry IV, Part I* and *The Merry Wives of Windsor*; eight lines in *Henry V*, *As You Like It*, and *Cymbeline*; nine lines in *Twelfth Night*; thirteen lines in *All's Well That Ends Well*; twenty-three lines in *The Comedy of Errors*; twenty-four lines in *Pericles* (notably, the references to venereal disease occur in Shakespeare's part of this collaborative play); thirty lines in *Henry IV, Part II*; forty-three lines in *Measure for Measure*; fifty-one lines in *Troilus and Cressida*; and sixty-five lines in *Timon of Athens*. I have been unable to find references to STDs in *Richard III*, *Titus Andronicus*, *The Taming of the Shrew*, *Richard II*, *King John*, *The Merchant of Venice*, *Julius Caesar*, *Macbeth*, *Antony and Cleopatra*, and *The Winter's Tale*.

7 "the ingeniously benign explanations of Shakespeare's biographers": Michael Wood, *Shakespeare*. New York: Basic Books, 2003, pp. 338–9.

7 "Upon a time when Burbage played Richard the Third": Duncan-Jones, *Ungentle Shakespeare*, p. 121.

8 "wanny cheeks" and "shaggy locks": *Avisa*, p. 61.

8 "H.W. being suddenly infected": *Avisa*, pp. 115–6. For the venereal implications of this passage, I am indebted to Fabricius, pp. 177–8.

9 "this curious work seems to have something to do with the *Sonnets*": Schoenbaum, pp. 180–1.

10 "Here, the 'eye' of his mistress is her pudendum": The interpretation of the *Sonnets,* for example, the reading of "my mistress' eye" as her pudendum, follows Katherine Duncan-Jones's Arden edition of *Shakespeare's Sonnets,* London: Thomas Nelson, 1997.

11 "drove their harlots and women out of the citadel": Harold L. Klawans, *Newton's Madness.* New York: Harper & Row, 1990, p. 109.

11–12 "the most disowned infection in history": Arno Karlen, *Man and Microbes.* New York: G. P. Putnam's Sons, 1995, p. 124.

12 "Know syphilis in all its manifestations and relations": Mark E. Silverman, T. Jock Murray, Charles S. Bryan, eds., *The Quotable Osler.* Philadelphia: American College of Physicians, 2003, p. 145.

13 "Large rounded tumours start to appear at random": Quétel, pp. 26–7.

14 "deep indurated nodule": M. N. Swartz, B. P. Healy, D. M. Musher. Late syphilis. In: K. K. Holmes, P. A. Mårdh, P. F. Sparling et al. eds., *Sexually Transmitted Diseases,* 3rd ed. New York: McGraw-Hill, 1999, p. 501.

15 "gentlewomen virgins": Fabricius, p. 166.

16 "broil in . . . broths prunes": William Clowes, *A Profitable and Necessarie Booke of Observations.* London: Edmund Bollifant, 1596, p. 161. Available online at: http://www.st-mike.org/medicine/images/clowes_book3.pdf, accessed 21 December 2011.

19 "handsome, well-shap't man: very good company": Oliver L. Dick, ed., *Aubrey's Brief Lives.* London: Secker & Warburg, 1950, p. 275.

19 "not a company keeper . . . wouldn't be debauched": Honan, p. 122.

21 "valid, worthy, or possible in human nature": Honan, p. 409.

22 "somewhat nervous": Samuel Tannenbaum, *Problems in Shakespeare's Penmanship*. New York: The Century Co., 1927, p. 29.

22 "a general deterioration in Shakespeare's writing": E. A. J. Honigmann, *The Texts of "Othello" and Shakespearian Revision*. London: Routledge, 1996, p. 88.

23 "he never blotted out a line": Schoenbaum, pp. 258–9.

23 "a gilder that hath his brains perished with quicksilver": John Webster, *The White Devil*. New York: W. W. Norton, 1966, p. 11–12.

2. Exil'd from Light: The Blindness of John Milton

BOOKS

Ball, Philip. *The Devil's Doctor*. New York: Farrar, Straus and Giroux, 2006.

Beer, Anna. *Milton: Poet, Pamphleteer and Patriot*. New York: Bloomsbury Press, 2008.

Brown, Eleanor. *Milton's Blindness*. New York: Columbia University Press, 1934.

Campbell, Gordon & Corns, Thomas N. *John Milton: Life, Work and Thought*. Oxford: Oxford University Press, 2010.

Darbishire, Helen. *The Early Lives of Milton*. London: Constable & Co Ltd, 1932.

Emsley, John. *The Elements of Murder: A History of Poison*. Oxford: Oxford University Press, 2005.

Garrison, Fielding H. *An Introduction to the History of Medicine*. Philadelphia: W.B. Saunders, 1913.

Hill, Christopher. *God's Englishman*. New York: Dial Press, 1970.

Hill, Christopher. *Milton in the English Revolution*. New York: Viking Press, 1978.

Lewalski, Barbara Kiefer. *The Life of John Milton: A Critical Biography*. Oxford: Blackwell Publishing, 2000.

Martin, Russell. *Beethoven's Hair*. New York: Broadway Books, 2000.

de Mayerne, Théodore Turquet. *A Treatise of the Gout: Written Originally in the French Tongue*. London: D. Newman, 1676.

Parker, William Riley. *Milton: A Biography*. Oxford: Clarendon Press, 1968.

Weeden, Richard P. *Poison in the Pot: The Legacy of Lead*. Carbondale, IL: Southern Illinois University Press, 1984.

Wilson, A. N. *The Life of John Milton*. Oxford: Oxford University Press, 1983.

ARTICLES

Bartley, G. B., "The Blindness of John Milton," *Documenta Ophthalmologica* 1995; 89:15–28.

Carey, J., "A Work in Praise of Terrorism? September 11 and *Samson Agonistes*," *TLS Times Literary Supplement*, 6 September 2002.

Copeman, W. S. C., "Dr. Jonathan Goddard, F.R.S. (1617–1675)," *Notes and Records of the Royal Society of London* 1960; 15(1):69–77.

Dufour, M., "A Note on Milton's Blindness," *Ophthalmoscope* 1909; 7:599–600.

Lessler, M. A., "Lead and Lead Poisoning from Antiquity to Modern Times," *Ohio Journal of Science* 1988; 88(3):78–84.

Markel, H., "Getting the Lead Out: The Rhode Island Lead Paint Trials and Their Impact on Children's Health," *JAMA* 2007; 297:2773–5.

Rosenthal, N. E., DellaBella, P., Hahn, L., Skwerer, R. G., "Seasonal Affective Disorder and Visual Impairment: Two Case Studies," *Journal of Clinical Psychiatry* 1989; 50:469–72.

Saper, R. B., Kales, S. N., Paquin, J., et al., "Heavy Metal Content of Ayurvedic Herbal Medicine Products," *JAMA* 2004; 292:2868–73.

Stroup, T. B., "Implications of the Theory of Climatic Influence in Milton," *Modern Language Quarterly* 1943; 4:185–9.

Sugg, R., " 'Good Physic But Bad Food': Early Modern Attitudes to Medicinal Cannibalism and Its Suppliers," *Social History of Medicine* 2006; 19:225–40.

Wittmers Jr., L., Aufderheide, A., Rapp, G., Alich, A., "Archaeological Contributions of Skeletal Lead Analysis," *Accounts of Chemical Research* 2002; 35:669–75.

27 "O loss of sight," "Inferior to the vilest": Milton, *Samson Agonistes,* lines 67–82.

28 "Then had I not": Milton, *Samson Agonistes,* lines 98–101.

29 "He well deserved . . . homoerotic sexual scandal": Campbell and Corns, pp. 38–9.

30 "uninterrupted leisure . . . entirely devoted to the perusal of the Greek and Latin classics": John Milton, *Second Defence of the People of England,* in Merritt Y. Hughes, *John Milton: Complete Poems and Major Prose.* New York: MacMillan, 1957, p. 828.

30 "no longer mingle unknown with the dull rabble and my walk shall be far from the sight of profane eyes": Milton, "Ad Patrem," in Hughes, p. 85.

30 "He . . . now bleeds to give us ease": Milton, "Upon the Circumcision," in Hughes, p. 81.

30 "whoremongers and adulterers": John Milton, *A Treatise of Christian Doctrine,* trans. Charles Sumner. Cambridge: Cambridge University Press, 1825, p. 241.

31 "he loves himself rather than truth": Samuel Johnson, *Milton,* in *The Works of Samuel Johnson, Vol. 9,* ed. Arthur Murphy. New York: William Durell, 1811, p. 96.

31 "hard study, and spare diet": Campbell and Corns, p. 134.

31 "whereto it would be no impossibility to add the Chaldee and the Syrian dialect": Milton, "Of Education," in Hughes, p. 636.

31 "found it very solitary: no company came to her, oftentimes [she] heard his nephews beaten, and cry": Darbishire, p. 14.

33 "Christ meant not," "have tasted in any sort the nuptial bed," "suitably weaponed to the least possibility of sensual enjoyment," "grind in the mill of an undelighted and servile copulation": Milton, *The Doctrine and Discipline of Divorce*, in Hughes, pp. 703, 712–3.

33 "first appearance to our eyes bleared and dimmed with prejudice and custom, is more unsightly and implausible than many errors": Milton, *Areopagitica*, in Hughes, p. 748.

33 "muses' bower," "spread thy name o'er land and seas": Sonnet VIII, "When the Assault Was Intended to the City," in Hughes, p. 140.

33 "making submission and begging pardon": Campbell and Corns, p. 174.

34 "despotic power": Milton, *Samson Agonistes,* in Hughes, p. 577.

34 "Since you do not recognize": Campbell and Corns, p. 182.

35 "devoted to religion, though he perpetually employed it as the instrument of his ambition": David Hume, *History of England, Vol. 5.* Indianapolis: Liberty Fund, 1983, p. 450.

35 "you have no other way to deal with these men but to break them in pieces": Lewalski, p. 240.

35 "the author, the guardian, and the preserver of our liberties": Milton, *Second Defence of the People of England,* in Hughes, p. 834.

35 "To peace and truth": Milton, "To the Lord General Cromwell," in Hughes, pp. 160–1.

36 "inhuman rebels and papists . . . treacherous . . . savages . . . barbarians": John Milton, *Observations on the Articles of Peace with the Irish Rebels.* In: *Prose Works of John Milton, Vol. 2,* James Augustus St. John, ed. London: George Bell, 1890, pp. 179–99.

36 "Milton produced a tendentious dossier": Campbell and Corns, p. 218.

36 "issues and setons": Brown, p. 19.

36 "Only one man in England could write Latin, and that man blind": Johnson, *Milton*, p. 105.

37 "his eyes were none of the quickest": Darbishire, p. 47.

37 "my eyes were naturally weak," "voracious . . . appetite for knowledge": Milton, *Second Defence of the People of England,* in Hughes, p. 828.

38 "all things that I could discern," "a minute portion of light as through a crevice": Brown, p. 17.

38 "At the same time my intestines [were] afflicted with flatulence and oppression": Brown, p. 16.

39 "his knuckles . . . all callous": Darbishire, p. 33.

39 "pale but not cadaverous, his hands and fingers gouty, and with chalk stones": Wilson, p. 256.

40 "perpetual tampering with physic": Brown, p. 20.

42 "salts of lead," "sweeten their humors": Weeden, p. 55.

42 "ocher of vitriol and sugar of lead": Susan Fitzmaurice, "Margaret Cavendish, the Doctors of Physick and Advice to the Sick". In: Stephen Clucas, ed. *A Princely Brave Woman: Essays on Margaret Cavendish, Duchess of Newcastle.* Burlington, VT: Ashgate Publishing, 2003, p. 227.

44 "Whether by ill constitution, or want of care, she grew more and more decrepit": Darbishire, p. 67.

44 "One tongue is enough for a woman": Parker, *Milton, Vol. I*, p. 586.

44 "a trial of patience, almost beyond endurance": Darbyshire, p. 77.

44 "that it was no news to hear of his wedding": Wilson, p. 220.

44 "curious and ingenious sorts of manufacture": Darbishire, p. 78.

44 "not ever observed to be impatient": Darbishire, p. 33.

44 "he would be cheerful even in his gout-fits, and sing": Darbishire, p. 5.

45 "Yet I argue not": Milton, Sonnet XXII, in Hughes, p. 170.

45 "He died in a fit of the gout": Darbishire, p. 33.

3. Dying from the Top Down: The Dementia of Jonathan Swift

BOOKS

Aitken, George A. *The Life and Works of John Arbuthnot, M.D.* Oxford: Clarendon Press, 1892.

Boyle, John, Earl of Orrery. *Remarks on the Life and Writings of Dr. Jonathan Swift*, 3rd ed. London: A. Millar, 1752.

Delany, Patrick. *Observations Upon Lord Orrery's Remarks on the Life and Writings of Dr. Jonathan Swift.* London: W. Reeve, 1754.

Ehrenpreis, Irvin. *Swift: The Man, His Works, and the Age. Vol. 1. Mr. Swift and His Contemporaries.* Cambridge: Harvard University Press, 1962.

Ehrenpreis, Irvin. *Swift: The Man, His Works, and the Age. Vol. 2. Dr. Swift.* Cambridge: Harvard University Press, 1967.

Ehrenpreis, Irvin. *Swift: The Man, His Works, and the Age. Vol. 3. Dean Swift.* Cambridge: Harvard University Press, 1983.

Pilkington, Laetitia. *Memoirs of Laetitia Pilkington*, Vol. 1. A. C. Elias, Jr., ed. Athens, GA: University of Georgia Press, 1997.

Ellmann, Richard. *Oscar Wilde*. New York: Random House, 1987.

Fitzgerald, Michael. *The Genesis of Artistic Creativity: Asperger's Syndrome and the Arts*. London: Jessica Kingsley, 2005.

Glendinning, Victoria. *Jonathan Swift*. London: Hutchinson, 1998.

Nokes, David. *Jonathan Swift, A Hypocrite Reversed*. Oxford: Oxford University Press, 1985.

Sheridan, Thomas. *The Life of Rev. Dr. Jonathan Swift*, 2nd ed. London: J. F. and C. Rivington, 1787.

Swift, Jonathan. *The Correspondence of Jonathan Swift, D. D.*, Vol. 1, David Woolley, ed. Frankfurt: Peter Lang, 1999.

Swift, Jonathan. *The Correspondence of Jonathan Swift, D. D.*, Vol. 2, David Woolley, ed. Frankfurt: Peter Lang, 2001.

Swift, Jonathan. *The Correspondence of Jonathan Swift, D. D.*, Vol. 3, David Woolley, ed. Frankfurt: Peter Lang, 2003.

Swift, Jonathan. *The Correspondence of Jonathan Swift, D. D.*, Vol. 4, David Woolley, ed. Frankfurt: Peter Lang, 2007.

ARTICLES

Anderson, J. P., Harris, J. P., "Impact of Ménière's Disease on Quality of Life," *Otology & Neurotology* 2001; 22:888–94.

Counter, S. A., "Whitening Skin Can Be Deadly," *Boston Globe*, 16 December 2003.

Crichton, P., "Jonathan Swift and Alzheimer's Disease," *Lancet* 1993; 342:874.

Feygin, D. L., Swain, J. E., Leckman, J. F., "The Normalcy of Neurosis: Evolutionary Origins of Obsessive-Compulsive Disorder and Related Behaviors," *Progress in Neuropsychopharmacology and Biological Psychiatry* 2006; 30:854–64.

Flaherty, A. W., "Frontotemporal and Dopaminergic Control of Idea Generation and Creative Drive," *Journal of Comparative Neurology* 2005; 493:147–53.

Garrard, P., Maloney, L. M., Hodges, J. R., Patterson, K., "The Effects of Very Early Alzheimer Disease on the Characteristics of Writing by a Renowned Author," *Brain* 2005; 128:250–60.

Kendurkar, A., Kaur, B., "Major Depressive Disorder, Obsessive-Compulsive Disorder, and Generalized Anxiety Disorder: Do the

Sexual Dysfunctions Differ?," *Primary Care Companion to the Journal of Clinical Psychiatry* 2008; 10:299–305.

Miller, B. L., Cummings, J., Mishkin, F. et al., "Emergence of Artistic Talent in Frontotemporal Dementia," *Neurology* 1998; 51:978–82.

Miller, B. L., Hou, C. E., "Portraits of Artists: Emergence of Visual Creativity in Dementia," *Archives of Neurology* 2004; 61:842–4.

Pollak, T. A. et al., "De Novo Artistic Behavior Following Brain Injury," *Frontiers in Neurology and Neurosciences* 2007; 22:75–88.

Rauch, S. D., "Clinical Hints and Precipitating Factors in Patients Suffering from Ménière's Disease," *Otolaryngology Clinics of North America* 2010; 43:1011–7.

Sofi, F., Valecchi, D., Bacci, D. et al., "Physical Activity and Risk of Cognitive Decline: A Meta-analysis of Prospective Studies," *Journal of Internal Medicine* 2011; 269:107–17.

Snowdon, D. A., Kemper, S. J., Mortimer, J. A. et al., "Linguistic Ability in Early Life and Cognitive Function and Alzheimer's Disease in Later Life," *JAMA* 1996; 275:528–32.

Söderman, A. C., Möller, J., Bagger-Sjöbäck, D. et al., "Stress as a Trigger of Attacks in Ménière's Disease: A Case-crossover Study," *Laryngoscope* 2004; 114:1843–8.

Van Cruijsen, N., Jaspers, J. P., Van de Wiel, H. B. et al., "Psychological Assessment of Patients with Ménière's Disease," *International Journal of Audiology* 2006; 45:496–502.

Vulink, N., Denys, D., Bus, L., Westenberg, H., "Sexual Pleasure in Women with Obsessive-Compulsive Disorder," *Journal of Affective Disorders* 2006; 91:19–25.

Yimtae, K., Srirompotong, S., Lertsukprasert, K., "Otosyphilis: A Review of 85 Cases," *Otolaryngology—Head and Neck Surgery* 2007; 136:67–71.

Young, F. M., Pitts, V. A., "Performance of Congenital Syphilitics on the Wechsler Intelligence Scale for Children," *Journal of Consulting Psychology* 1951; 15:239–42.

47 "Swift is a diseased writer": George Orwell, *Collected Essays, Journalism and Letters of George Orwell*, Vol. 4. Harmondsworth: Penguin Books, 1970, pp. 257–9.

47 "The least miserable among them": Jonathan Swift, *Gulliver's Travels*. London: T. Allman, 1837, p. 244.

47 "Young . . . found Swift": Sheridan, p. 242.

48 "His eyes lingered on the bright blade": The incident of Swift and the knife is related in Deane Swift's letter to Orrery, Woolley, Vol. 4, pp. 669–70.

48–49 "like a poisoned rat in a hole": Woolley, Vol. 3, p. 295.

49 "those skulls of the so-called Celtic aborigines": William Wilde, *The Closing Years of Dean Swift's Life*. Dublin: Hodges and Smith, 1849, p. 59.

49 "perhaps a little too dexterous," "brought her husband little or no fortune": Jonathan Swift, "Fragment of Autobiography," *The Prose Works of Jonathan Swift, Vol. XI*. London: George Bell and Sons, 1907, pp. 374–5.

49–50 "brought home the itch with him," "time enough to save his mother's credit": Pilkington, p. 31.

50 "a society of men among us": Swift, *Gulliver's Travels,* p. 286.

50 "I formerly used to envy": Wholley, Vol. 1, p. 217.

51 "I remember, when I was a little boy": Wholley, Vol. 3, p. 230.

51 "too much neglected some parts": Ehrenpreis, Vol. 1, p. 60.

51 "the ill treatment of his nearest relations": Swift, "Fragment of Autobiography," p. 376.

51 "fallen into a kind of lethargy": Boyle, p. 14.

52 " 'Cousin Swift, you will never be a poet' ": Samuel Johnson, *The Lives of the Poets: A Selection*. Oxford: Oxford University Press, 2009, p. 321.

53 "bitterness, satire, moroseness": Glendinning, p. 55.

53 "I got my giddiness": Wholley, Vol. 3, p. 120.

53 "What if I should add": Wholley, Vol. 2, p. 333.

53 "The giddiness I was subject to": Wholley, Vol. 3, p. 402.

54 "I have eat mighty little fruit": Jonathan Swift, *Journal to Stella.* Gloucester: Alan Sutton, 1984, p. 382.

54 "nasty steel drops": Swift, *Journal to Stella,* p. 430.

54 "a vomit": Swift, *Journal to Stella,* pp. 382–3.

55 "When the deafness comes on": Woolley, Vol. 4, p. 428.

55 "the noise of seven watermills": Woolley, Vol. 4, p. 524.

55 "a hundred oceans rolling in my ears": Woolley, Vol. 3, p. 121.

56 "One of these mistresses wanted an eye": Sheridan, p. 393.

57 "seraglio of very virtuous women": Boyle, p. 84.

57 "made a mess of two women's lives": Richard Ellmann, *James Joyce.* Oxford: Oxford University Press, 1982, p. 545.

57 "I long to drink a dish of coffee": Wholley, Vol. 1, p. 437.

58 "If you are in Ireland while I am there": Wholley, Vol. 2, p. 72.

58 "I was born with violent passions": Wholley, Vol. 2, p. 352.

58 "Cad assures me": Wholley, Vol. 2, p. 385.

58 "He could praise, esteem, approve": Jonathan Swift, *The Complete Poems*, Pat Rogers, ed. London: Penguin Books, 1983, p. 144.

58 "I really believe that it was a passion": Pilkington, p. 45.

59 "But what success Vanessa met": Swift, *Complete Poems*, p. 151.

59 "the concealed, but undoubted wife of Dr Swift": Boyle, p. 22.

59 "Stella, whom he has so beautifully praised": Pilkington, p. 280.

60 "Swift made no reply": Sheridan, p. 312.

60 "the excessive coldness of his nature": Boyle, p. 117.

60 "was one of the cleanliest men in his person that ever lived": Sheridan, p. 396.

61 "cleanliness in the first": Wholley, Vol. 1, p. 143.

61 "Strephon who heard the foaming rill": Jonathan Swift, *The Works of Dr. Jonathan Swift*, Vol. 7. London: C. Davis, 1754, pp. 213–5.

61–62 "And first, a dirty smock appeared": Swift, *Works*, Vol. 7, pp. 161–6.

62 "regularity was peculiar to him": Boyle, p. 67.

63 "in his friendships": Boyle, pp. 207–8.

63 "A young healthy child": Jonathan Swift, *Major Works*. Oxford: Oxford University Press, 2003, pp. 493–4.

64 "Deaf, giddy, odious to my friends": Swift, *Complete Poems*, p. 543.

64 "a monkey overthrow all the dishes": Woolley, Vol. 3, p. 295.

64 "peevish, fretful, morose": Glendinning, p. 218.

64 "despotic power": Boyle, p. 84.

64 "This wrong turn in his brain": Pilkington, pp. 316–7.

64 "he was a very rough sort of a tutor": Pilkington, p. 45.

65 "Instead of being vexed": Pilkington, p. 309.

65 "He asked the company": Pilkington, p. 310.

65 "He threw me down": Pilkington, p. 281.

65 "You, fellow with the blue string!": Pilkington, p. 317.

65 "the most mortifying sight I ever beheld," "dead to all natural affection": Swift, *Gulliver's Travels,* pp. 243–4.

65 "My memory is going fast": Woolley, Vol. 4, p. 103.

65–66 "I have entirely lost my memory": Woolley, Vol. 4, p. 490.

66 "About the year 1736": Sheridan, p. 269.

66 "his friends found his passions so violent": Boyle, p. 246.

67 "as noted by psychiatrist Paul Crichton": Crichton, *Lancet* 1993, Vol. 342, p. 874.

67 "loaded with water": M. Lorch, "Language and Memory Disorder in the Case of Jonathan Swift: Considerations on Retrospective Diagnosis," *Brain* 2006; 129:3127–37.

68 "The torture he was in": Wholley, Vol. 4, p. 664.

68 "He gave the little wealth he had": Swift, *Complete Poems*, p. 498.

69 "Swift has sailed into his rest": W. B. Yeats, *Yeats's Poems*. Dublin: Gill and Macmillan, 1989, p. 361.

4. Some Sweet Poisoned Breeze Had Passed Into Her Lungs: The Brontës and Tuberculosis

BOOKS

Barker, Juliet. *The Brontës*. London: Phoenix, 1995.

Barker, Juliet. *The Brontës: A Life in Letters*. Woodstock, New York: Overlook Press, 1998.

Benson, E. F. *Charlotte Brontë*. London: Longmans, Green and Co., 1932.

Brontë, Charlotte. Biographical Notice of Ellis and Acton Bell. In: Emily Brontë, Anne Brontë, *Wuthering Heights and Agnes Grey*. London: Smith, Elder, and Co., 1870.

Chitham, Edward. *A Life of Emily Brontë*. Cambridge, Massachusetts: Blackwell Publishers, 1987.

Constable, Kathleen. *A Stranger Within the Gates: Charlotte Brontë and Victorian Irishness*. Lanham, Maryland: University Press of America, 2000.

Gaskell, Elizabeth. *The Life of Charlotte Brontë*. London: Penguin Books, 1997.

Gordon, Lyndall. *Charlotte Brontë: A Passionate Life*. New York: W. W. Norton, 1995.

Green, Dudley. *Patrick Brontë: Father of Genius*. Stroud, Gloucestershire: Nonsuch Publishing, 2008.

Green, Dudley, Patrick Brontë: Father of Genius. Stroud, Gloucestershire: Nonsuch Publishing, 2008.

Miller, Lucasta. *The Brontë Myth*. New York: Alfred A. Knopf, 2003.

Tully, James. *The Crimes of Charlotte Bronte*. New York: Carroll & Graf, 1999.

ARTICLES

Ates, O., Dalyan, L., Müsellim, B. et al., "NRAMP1 (SLC11A1) Gene Polymorphisms that Correlate with Autoimmune versus Infectious Disease Susceptibility in Tuberculosis and Rheumatoid Arthritis," *International Journal of Immunogenetics* 2009; 36:15–9.

Aydin, I. O., Ulusahin, A., "Depression, Anxiety Comorbidity, and Disability in Tuberculosis and Chronic Obstructive Pulmonary Disease Patients: Applicability of GHQ-12," *General Hospital Psychiatry* 2001; 23:77–83.

Baron-Cohen, S., "Testing the Extreme Male Brain (EMB) Theory of Autism: Let the Data Speak for Themselves," *Cognitive Neuropsychiatry* 2005; 10:77–81.

Boelaert, J. R., Vandecasteele, S. J., Appelberg, R., Gordeuk, V. R., "The Effect of the Host's Iron Status on Tuberculosis," *Journal of Infectious Diseases* 2007; 195:1745–53.

Brosch, R., Gordon, S. V., Marmiesse, M. et al., "A New Evolutionary Scenario for the *Mycobacterium tuberculosis* Complex," *Proceedings of the National Academy of Science USA* 2002; 99:3684–9.

Cohen, A., Mehta, S., "Pollution and Tuberculosis: Outdoor Sources," *PLoS Medicine 2007*; 4:e142.

Craig, J., Baron-Cohen, S., "Creativity and Imagination in Autism and Asperger Syndrome," *Journal of Autism and Developmental Disorders* 1999; 29:319–26.

Donaghue, H. D., "Insights Gained from Paleomicrobiology into Ancient and Modern Tuberculosis," *Clinical Microbiology and Infection* 2011; 17:821–9.

Gutierrez, M. C., Brisse, S., Brosch, R. et al., "Ancient Origin and Gene Mosaicism of the Progenitor of *Mycobacterium tuberculosis*," *PLoS Pathogens* 2005 Sep;1(1):e5.

Ingudomnukul, E., Baron-Cohen, S., Wheelwright, S., Knickmeyer, R., "Elevated Rates of Testosterone-Related Disorders in Women with Autism Spectrum Conditions," *Hormones and Behavior* 2007; 51:597–604.

Kline, S. E., Hedemark, L. L., Davies, S. F., "Outbreak of Tuberculosis Among Regular Patrons of a Neighborhood Bar," *New England Journal of Medicine* 1995; 333:222–7.

Knickmeyer, R., Baron-Cohen, S., "Fetal Testosterone and Sex Differences," *Early Human Development* 2006; 82:755–60.

Lamar 2nd, J. E., Malakooti, M. A., "Tuberculosis Outbreak Investigation of a U.S. Navy Amphibious Ship Crew and the Marine Expeditionary Unit Aboard, 1998," *Military Medicine* 2003; 168:523–7.

Lerner, B. H., "Can Stress Cause Disease? Revisiting the Tuberculosis Research of Thomas Holmes, 1949–1961," *Annals of Internal Medicine* 1996; 124:673–80.

Lin, H. H., Ezzati, M., Murray, M., "Tobacco Smoke, Indoor Air Pollution and Tuberculosis: A Systematic Review and Meta-analysis," *PLoS Medicine* 2007; 4:e20.

Mackowiak, P. A., Blos, V. T., Aguilar, M., Buikstra, J. E., "On the Origin of American Tuberculosis," *Clinical Infectious Diseases* 2005; 41:515–8.

Martineau, A. R., Honecker, F. U., Wilkinson, R. J., Griffiths, C. J., "Vitamin D in the Treatment of Pulmonary Tuberculosis," *Journal of Steroid Biochemistry and Molecular Biology* 2007; 103:793–8.

Mason, C. M., Dobard, E., Zhang, P., Nelson, S., "Alcohol Exacerbates Murine Pulmonary Tuberculosis," *Infection and Immunity* 2004; 72:2556–63.

Tobacman, J. K., "Does Deficiency of Arylsulfatase B Have a Role in Cystic Fibrosis?" *Chest* 2003; 123:2130–9.

Todd, J., Dewhurst, K., "The Periodic Depression of Charlotte Brontë," *Perspectives in Biology and Medicine* 1968; 11:208–16.

Zink, A. R., Sola, C., Reischl, U. et al., "Characterization of *Mycobacterium tuberculosis* Complex DNAs from Egyptian Mummies by Spoligotyping," *Journal of Clinical Microbiology* 2003; 41:359–67.

70 "offensive fragments": Gaskell, p. 55.

70 "indifferent potatoes": Charlotte Brontë, *Jane Eyre*. London: Penguin Books, 2003, pp. 61–2.

71 "I perfectly remember": Barker, 1995, p. 126.

72 "too dull and heavy": Gaskell, p. 57.

73 "clever and good-hearted": Green, p. 46.

73 "a very earnest man": Barker, 1995, p. 36.

74 "a little eccentric": Green, p. 16.

74 "untidy," "eyes of a half-tamed creature": Chitham, p. 26.

74 "internal cancer": Gaskell, p. 40.

74 "O God, my poor children!": Barker, 1995, p. 104.

75 "in a remote district": Biographical Notice, pp. v–vi.

75 "very retired habits": Barker, 1995, p. 47.

75 "did not require companionship": Gaskell, p. 44.

75 "we were wholly dependent": Biographical Notice, p. vi.

75 "charity-children": *Jane Eyre*, p. 60.

75 "Canadian temperature": *Jane Eyre*, p. 88.

75 "nauseous mess": *Jane Eyre*, p. 56.

75 "semi-starvation": *Jane Eyre*, p. 89.

76 "a harsh man; at once pompous and meddling"; "starved us . . . and bored us"; "evening readings from books of his own inditing": *Jane Eyre*, pp. 141–2.

76 "the illness which is removing me is not painful; it is gentle and gradual": *Jane Eyre*, p. 94.

76 "A doctor treated her": For a DIY guide to blistering, see Samuel

Cooper, David Meredith Reese, *A Dictionary of Practical Surgery*. New York: Harper and Bros., 1836.

80 "People never die of love or grief alone": Charlotte Brontë, *Shirley*. London: Penguin Books, 1984, p. 205.

82 "Ronald Macelgin, Henry Angora": Barker, 1995, p. 451.

82 "very old-fashioned clothes"; "like a little old woman, so short-sighted that she always appeared to be seeking something"; "very shy and nervous, and spoke with a strong Irish accent"; "very ugly": Gaskell, pp. 78–9.

82 "In this struggle": Barker, 1995, p. 236.

83 "wretchedly ill," "Neither the pain": Barker, 1995, p. 280.

83 "heavy gloom," "mental and bodily anguish": Barker, 1995, pp. 288–9.

83 "neither she nor her sisters were naturally fond of children": Gaskell, p. 127.

83 "genius as something higher even than Charlotte's"; "had a head for logic"; "her stubborn tenacity of will"; "egotistical and exacting": Gaskell, pp. 166–7.

84–85 "peculiar music"; "My sister Emily": Biographical Notice, p. vi.

85 "poor, obscure, plain, and little": *Jane Eyre*, p. 284

86 "the slight astringencies in her character": Gaskell, p. 422.

86 "Charlotte-as-bitch": Miller, p. 149.

86 "strong passions and weak principles": Gordon, p. 72.

86 "blithe and gay": Barker, 1995, p. 370.

86 "morbid man, who couldn't bear to be alone": Barker, 1995, p. 357.

87 "daily troubled pleasure": Benson, p. 150.

87 "months of such utter sleeplessness": Barker, 1998, p. 191.

87 "Emily's cough and cold": Barker, 1998, p. 211.

87 "self-absorbed moroseness": Emily Brontë, Anne Brontë, *Wuthering Heights and Agnes Grey.* London: Smith, Elder, and Co., 1870, p. 218.

88 "Emily hardly uttered more than a monosyllable": Gaskell, p. 162.

88 "could not easily associate with others": Chitham, p. 113.

88 "extreme reserve with strangers": Chitham, p. 114.

88 "seems not even to notice human beings, especially males": Chitham, p. 160.

88 "never showed regard to any human creature": Gaskell, p. 199.

88 "was not very flexible": Biographical Notice, p. xiii.

88 "impervious to influence": Gaskell, p. 122.

88 "head for logic"; "stubborn tenacity of will"; "She should have been a man": Barker, 1995, p. 392.

88 "never seems to have made a single significant friend": Miller, p. 185.

89 "the Major"; "unparalleled intrepidity and firmness": Chitham, p. 159.

90 "Day by day": Biographical Notice, p. xi.

90–91 "slow inflammation of the lungs"; "She is a real stoic in illness"; "quackery"; "It is usually best to leave her to form her own judgment."; "hollow, wasted, pallid aspect"; "pain in the chest and side"; "deep tight cough"; "rapid pant"; "Her pulse"; "emaciation": Barker, 1998, pp. 212–4.

91 "the known facts of their lives": Barker, 1995, p. xviii.

93 "Some sweet poisoned breeze": Charlotte Brontë, *Shirley*, pp. 399, 401.

93 "blue pills"; "my mouth became sore": Barker, 1998, p. 341.

93 "almost repulsive": Barker, 1995, p. 727.

94 "fatigue and excitement", "my cough has become very bad": Barker, 1998, pp. 390–1.

94 "continual faint sickness": Barker, 1998, p. 396.

94 "She has been confined to her bed": Barker, 1998, p. 397.

94 "weakness & sickness & frequent fever": Barker, 1998, p. 398.

95 "skeletal emaciation," "low wandering delirium": Barker, 1995, p. 771.

95 "I told you, Martha": Green, p. 263.

5. Dismal Labyrinth of Doubt: The Strange Death of Nathaniel Hawthorne

BOOKS

Baym, Nina. *The Shape of Hawthorne's Career*. Ithaca, NY: Cornell University Press, 1976.

Bridge, Horatio. *Personal Recollections of Nathaniel Hawthorne.* New York: Haswell House, 1968.

Delano, Sterling F. *Brook Farm: The Dark Side of Utopia.* Cambridge: Belknap Press, 2004.

DeWolfe, Howe. *Memories of a Hostess: A Chronicle of Eminent Friendships Drawn Chiefly from the Diaries of Mrs. James T. Fields.* Boston: Atlantic Monthly Press, 1922.

Hawthorne, Julian. *Nathaniel Hawthorne and His Wife: A Biography. Vol. 2.* Boston: Houghton Mifflin, 1884.

Hoyt, Edwin P. *The Improper Bostonian: Dr. Oliver Wendell Holmes.* New York: William Morrow, 1979.

James, Henry. *Hawthorne.* Ithaca, NY: Cornell University Press, 1997.

Lathrop, George Parsons. *A Study of Hawthorne.* Whitefish, MT: Kessinger Publishing, 2004.

Mellow, James R. *Nathaniel Hawthorne in His Times.* Boston: Houghton Mifflin, 1980.

Miller, Edwin Haviland. *Salem is My Dwelling Place: A Life of Nathaniel Hawthorne.* Iowa City: University of Iowa Press, 1991.

Nichols, Roy F. *Franklin Pierce: Young Hickory of the Granite Hills.* Philadelphia: University of Pennsylvania Press, 1958.

Parker, Herschel. *Herman Melville: A Biography. Vol. 2.* Baltimore: Johns Hopkins University Press, 2002.

Stewart, Randall. *Nathaniel Hawthorne: A Biography.* New Haven: Yale University Press, 1948.

Turner, Arlin. *Nathaniel Hawthorne: A Biography.* New York: Oxford University Press, 1980.

Wineapple, Brenda. *Hawthorne: A Life.* New York: Alfred A. Knopf, 2003.

Young, Philip. *Hawthorne's Secret: An Un-Told Tale.* Boston: David R. Godine, 1984.

ARTICLES

Davidson, J. R., Connor, K. M., Swartz, M., "Mental Illness in U.S. Presidents between 1776 and 1974: A Review of Biographical Sources," *Journal of Nervous and Mental Diseases* 2006; 194:47–51.

Eslick, G., "*Helicobacter pylori* Infection Causes Gastric Cancer? A Review of the Epidemiological, Meta-analytic, and Experimental Evidence," *World Journal of Gastroenterology* 2006; 12:2991-9. ·

Fallowfield, L., "Truth Sometimes Hurts but Deceit Hurts More," *Annals of the New York Academy of Sciences* 1997; 809:525-36.

Fei, S. J., Xiao, S. D., "Diet and Gastric Cancer: A Case-Control Study in Shanghai Urban Districts," *Chinese Journal of Digestive Diseases* 2006; 7:83-8.

Ferrari, E., Chevallier, T., Chapelier, A., Baudouy, M., "Travel as a Risk Factor for Venous Thromboembolic Disease: A Case-Control Study," *Chest* 1999; 115:440-4.

Gonzalez, C. A., Jakszyn, P., Gera, G. et al., "Meat Intake and Risk of Stomach and Esophageal Adenocarcinoma within the European Prospective Investigation Into Cancer and Nutrition (EPIC)," *Journal of the National Cancer Institute* 2006; 98:345-54.

Gonzalez, C. A., Pera, G., Agudo, A. et al., "Smoking and the Risk of Gastric Cancer in the European Prospective Investigation Into Cancer and Nutrition (EPIC)," *International Journal of Cancer* 2003; 107:629-34.

Holmes Sr., Oliver Wendell, "Hawthorne," *Atlantic Monthly* 14 (July 1864), pp. 98-101.

Howson, C. P., Hiyama, T., Wynder, E. L., "The Decline in Gastric Cancer: Epidemiology of an Unplanned Triumph," *Epidemiology Review* 1986; 8:1-27.

Imamura, Y., Yoshimi, I., "Comparison of Cancer Mortality (Stomach Cancer) in Five Countries: France, Italy, Japan, UK and USA from the WHO Mortality Database (1960-2000)," *Japanese Journal of Clinical Oncology* 2005; 35:103-5.

Jakszyn, P., Gonzalez, C., "Nitrosamine and Related Food Intake and Gastric and Esophageal Cancer Risk," *World Journal of Gastroenterology* 2006; 12:4296-303.

Kidd, M., Modlin, I. M., "A Century of *Helicobacter pylori*: Paradigms Lost—Paradigms Regained," *Digestion* 1998; 59:1-15.

Liebowitz, M. R., Ninan, P. T., Schneier, F. R., Blanco, C., "Integrating Neurobiology and Psychopathology into Evidence-Based Treatment of Social Anxiety Disorder," *CNS Spectrums* October 2005; 10(10):Suppl 13:1-11.

Lipowski, Z. J., "Somatization: The Concept and its Clinical Application," *American Journal of Psychiatry* 1988; 145:1358–68.

Ogren, M., Bergqvist, D., Wahlander, K., Eriksson, H., Sternby, N. H., "Trousseau's Syndrome—What is the Evidence? A Population-Based Autopsy Study," *Thrombosis and Haemostasis* 2006; 95:541–5.

Peery, T. M., "The New and Old Diseases: A Study of Mortality Trends in the United States, 1900--1969," *American Journal of Clinical Pathology* 1975; 63:453–74.

Schneier, F. R., Johnson, J., Hornig, C. D. et al., "Social Phobia: Comorbidity and Morbidity in an Epidemiologic Sample," *Archives of General Psychiatry*, April 1992; 49(4):282–8.

Stolt, C. M., Klein, G., Jansson, A., "An Analysis of a Wrong Nobel Prize—Johannes Fibiger, 1926: A Study in the Nobel Archives," *Advances in Cancer Research* 2004; 92:1–12.

Tsugane, S., Sasazuki, S., Koyabashi, M., Sasaki, S., "Salt and Salted Food Intake and Subsequent Risk of Gastric Cancer among Middle-Aged Japanese Men and Women," *British Journal of Cancer* 2004; 90:128–34.

98 "simple medicine as we treat each other to ice cream," "the shark's tooth is upon him": DeWolfe, p. 27.

100 "biographers have suggested that his illness was psychosomatic": Wineapple, pp. 26–8.

100 "walking unnecessarily on the Sabbath": Stewart, p. 22.

100–101 "I love Hawthorne, I admire him," "a peculiar and rather remarkable young man": Miller, p. 74.

101 "an absurdly shy sort of person": Miller, p. 404.

101 "He hates to be touched more than anyone I ever knew": Wineapple, p. 345.

101 "a fine ghost in a case of iron," "blushes like a girl," "girlish

diffidence," "the shyest grape," "I never had a young lady": Miller, pp. 4–8.

101 "could not lay a piece of butter upon a lady's plate": Miller, p. 6.

101 "He has but just stepped over the threshold of a hermitage": Miller, p. 344.

101 "he erected a tower as an adjunct to the house": James, p. 111.

101–102 "I am perfectly satisfied with this arrangement": Wineapple, p. 54.

102 "I charge myself pretty high with champagne": Miller, p. 403.

102 "I seldom venture abroad till after dark," "natural tendency for seclusion": Turner, p. 10.

102 "a beautiful soul in prison": Wineapple, p. 380.

102 "I should not like to live": Turner, p. 45.

102 "I doubt whether so much as twenty people": Mellow, p. 36.

103 "were as regular as possible": Mellow, pp. 37–8.

104 "the least gregarious of men": Lathrop, p. 84.

105 "But as for Rappaccini": Nathaniel Hawthorne, "Rappaccini's Daughter," *Tales and Sketches*. New York: Library of America, 1982, p. 982.

106 Melville may or may not have made some sort of advance on Hawthorne, as one of Hawthorne's biographers has suggested: Miller, pp. 357–63.

107 "a melancholy and pale wraith," "He was convinced": Parker, pp. 855–6.

107 "extremely ill": Hawthorne, *The Life of Franklin Pierce*. Boston: Ticknor and Fields, 1852, p. 104.

109 "utterly prostrated by depression": Miller, p. 415.

109 "Fever walks arm in arm with you": Nathaniel Hawthorne, *Collected Novels*. New York: Library of America, 1983, p. 912.

109 "dangerously insane": Miller, p. 525.

110 "an audacious attempt": Miller, p. 446.

110 "As dramatists and novelists repeat their plots": Nathaniel Hawthorne, *The Dolliver Romance and Kindred Tales*. Honolulu: University Press of the Pacific, 2003, p. 303.

110 "He never grew accustomed to it": Hawthorne, *Dolliver Romance*, p. 21.

111 "had been more or less infirm": Bridge, p. 176.

111 "There was no improvement": Julian Hawthorne, p. 329.

111 "very delicate health": Franklin Sanborn ms, Aug. 28, 1901, Concord Free Public Library.

111 "thin and pale," "nervous and delicate," "I am amazed": Julian Hawthorne, p. 333.

111 "His face was pale and wasted": Julian Hawthorne, p. 334.

111 "His limbs are shrunken": Mellow, p. 573.

111 "Dr Holmes would feel his pulse": James T. Fields, yesterday with Authors. Boston: James R. Osgood and Co., 1874, p. 121.

112 "proceeded to cup, and poultice, and blister": Turner, p. 387.

112 "When, at last, he reached home": Julian Hawthorne, p. 344.

112 "I feared that there was some . . . malignant—disease": Miller, p. 521.

113 "the careful physician": Michael Bliss, *William Osler: A Life in Medicine.* Toronto: University of Toronto Press, 1999, p. 265.

113 "What is your duty": William Osler, *Lectures on Angina Pectoris and Allied States.* New York: D. Appleton and Co., 1897, p. 142.

113 "The patient with carcinoma . . . should be told enough": Walter L. Palmer, "Gastric Neoplasms," in Russell L. Cecil, ed., *Textbook of Medicine.* Philadelphia: W. B. Saunders, 1941, p. 763.

113 "the use of his hands was impaired": Bridge, p. 178.

113 "He evidently had passed from that natural sleep": Bridge, p. 179.

113 "a dismal labyrinth of doubt": Hawthorne, *Collected Novels*, p. 202.

114 "mental causes are at the bottom of his illness": Wineapple, p. 370.

114 "He is a victim of dyspepsia": Miller, p. 512.

114 "partly mental": Miller, p. 515.

114 "One biographer has raised the possibility of syphilis": For syphilis and ulcerative colitis as suggested diagnoses, see Wineapple, p. 370.

114–115 "anaemia, general languor and debility": Thomas Addison, *On the Constitutional and Local Effects of Disease of the Supra-Renal Capsules.* London: Samuel Highley, 1855, p. 4.

115 "The illness was never diagnosed": Baym, p. 251.

115 "Stomach cancer was the most common cancer": William Osler, *The Principles and Practice of Medicine*. New York: D. Appleton, 1892, p. 376.

115 "rapid and feeble": Osler, p. 381.

115 "Patients with pain of pancreatic or retroperitoneal origin": William Silen, *Cope's Early Diagnosis of the Acute Abdomen*. 18th ed. New York: Oxford University Press, 1991, p. 31.

118 "One biographer speculates that Hawthorne died from the spread of tumour to the brain": Turner, p. 391.

118 "The seat of the disease": Bridge, p. 177.

6. Perilous Outpost of the Sane: The Many Maladies of Herman Melville

BOOKS

Andreasen, Nancy. *The Creating Brain*. New York: Dana Press, 2005.

Arvin, Newton. *Herman Melville*. New York: William Sloane Associates, 1950.

Davis, Merrell R. and Gilman, William H. eds, *The Letters of Herman Melville*. New Haven: Yale University Press, 1960.

Delbanco, Andrew. *Melville: His World and Work*. New York: Alfred A. Knopf, 2005.

Jamison, Kay Redfield. *Touched With Fire: Manic-Depressive Illness and the Artistic Temperament*. New York: Free Press, 1993.

Leyda, Jay. *The Melville Log: A Documentary Life of Herman Melville. Volume 1*. New York: Gordian Press, 1969.

Leyda, Jay. *The Melville Log: A Documentary Life of Herman Melville, 1819–1891. Volume 2*. New York: Gordian Press, 1969.

Miller, Edwin H. *Melville*. New York: George Braziller, 1975.

Mumford, Lewis. *Herman Melville.* New York: Harcourt, Brace & Co., 1929.

Parker, Hershel. *Herman Melville: A Biography. Volume 1: 1819–1851.* Baltimore: Johns Hopkins University Press, 1996.

Parker, Hershel. *Herman Melville: A Biography. Volume 2: 1851–1891.* Baltimore: Johns Hopkins University Press, 2002.

Robertson-Lorant, Laurie. *Melville: A Biography.* Boston: University of Massachusetts Press, 1996.

Rorabaugh, W. J. *The Alcoholic Republic.* New York: Oxford University Press, 1979.

Sealts Jr., M. M. *The Early Lives of Melville: Nineteenth-Century Biographical Sketches and Their Authors.* Madison, WI: University of Wisconsin Press, 1974.

Weaver, Raymond. *Herman Melville: Mariner and Mystic.* New York: George H. Doran Co., 1921.

Yatham, Lakshmi and Maj, Mario, eds. *Bipolar Disorder. Clinical and Neurobiological Foundations.* Oxford: Wiley-Blackwell, 2010.

ARTICLES

Agid, O., Shapira, B., Zislin, J., "Environment and Vulnerability to Major Psychiatric Illness: A Case Control Study of Early Parental Loss in Major Depression, Bipolar Disorder and Schizophrenia," *Molecular Psychiatry* 1999; 4:163–72.

Bell, L., "On a Form of Disease Resembling Some Advanced Stages of Mania and Fever," *American Journal of Insanity* 1849; 1:97–127.

Carrier, D. R., Deban, S. M., Otterstrom, J., "The Face that Sank the *Essex*: Potential Function of the Spermaceti Organ in Aggression," *Journal of Experimental Biology* 2002; 205:1755–63.

Fink, M., "Delirious Mania," *Bipolar Disorder* 1999; 1:54–60.

Kligerman, C., "The Psychology of Herman Melville," *Psychoanalytic Review* 1953; 40:125–43.

Kraines, S. H., "Bell's Mania," *American Journal of Psychiatry* 1934; 91:29–40.

Martin, P. M., Combes, C., "Emerging Infectious Diseases and the Depopulation of French Polynesia in the 19th Century," *Emerging Infectious Diseases* 1996; 2:359–61.

Merikangas, K. R., Jin, R., He, J. P. et al., "Prevalence and Correlates of Bipolar Spectrum Disorder in the World Mental Health Survey Initiative," *Archives of General Psychiatry* 2011; 68:241–51.

Nemeroff, C. B., "Neurobiological Consequences of Childhood Trauma," *Journal of Clinical Psychiatry* 2004;65 Suppl 1:18–28.

Otto, M. W., Perlman, C. A., Wernicke, R., "Posttraumatic Stress Disorder in Patients with Bipolar Disorder," *Bipolar Disorder* 2004; 6:470–9.

Peek-Asa, C., Zwerling, C., Young, T. et al., "A Population-Based Study of Reporting Patterns and Characteristics of Men Who Abuse Their Female Partners," *Injury Prevention* 2005; 11:180–5.

Pollack, M. H., Simon, N. M., Fagiolini, A. et al., "Persistent Posttraumatic Stress Disorder Following September 11 in Patients with Bipolar Disorder," *Journal of Clinical Psychiatry* 2006; 67:394–9.

Potash, J. B., Kane, H. S., Chiu, Y. F. et al., "Attempted Suicide and Alcoholism in Bipolar Disorder: Clinical and Familial Relationships," *American Journal of Psychiatry* 2000; 157:2048–50.

Schneck, J.M., "Karl Kahlbaum's Catatonia and Herman Melville's Bartleby the Scrivener," *Archives of General Psychiatry* 1972; 27:48–51.

Shih, R. T., Belmonte, P. L., Zandi, P. P., "A Review of the Evidence from Family, Twin and Adoption Studies for a Genetic Contribution to Adult Psychiatric Disorders," *International Review of Psychiatry* 2004; 16:260–83.

Shneidman, E. S., "Some Psychological Reflections on the Death of Malcolm Melville," *Suicide and Life-Threatening Behavior* 1976; 6:231–42.

van der Linden, S., van der Heijde, D., Braun, J., Ankylosing spondylitis. In: E. D. Harris Jr., ed. *Kelley's Textbook of Rheumatology*. 7th ed. Philadelphia: Elsevier Saunders, 2005.

Wilkinson, M., Bywaters, E. G., "Clinical Features and Course of Ankylosing Spondylitis, as Seen in a Follow-Up of 222 Hospital Referred Cases," *Annals of the Rheumatic Diseases* 1958; 17:209–228.

120 "To him seas were deeper": Sonia Orwell, Ian Angus, eds. *The Collected Essays, Journalism, and Letters of George Orwell. Volume 1: An Age Like This.* Harmondsworth: Penguin Books, 1970, pp. 42–3.

120 "Herman Melville is not well": Leyda, Vol. 2, p. 316.

121 "According to his brother-in-law": Peter Gansevoort and Thomas Melvill on Allan Melvill's terminal illness: Leyda, Vol. 1, pp. 51–2.

123 "very backward in speech": Leyda, Vol. 1, p. 25; "rapid progress": Leyda, Vol. 1, p. 32.

124–125 "Squeeze! squeeze! squeeze!": Herman Melville, *Moby-Dick*. New York: Penguin Putnam, 2003, p. 456.

125 "These females are passionately fond of dancing": Herman Melville, *Typee: A Peep at Polynesian Life*. New York: Penguin Books, 1996, p. 15.

125 "at the Marquesas": Parker, Vol. 1, p. 210.

125 "One of the most dreadful curses": *Typee*, p. 181. Melville on venereal disease in Tahiti: Herman Melville, *Omoo*. Evanston, IL: Northwestern University Press, 1999, p. 191.

127 "quite delirious," "written by a madman": Parker, Vol. 1, p. 619.

128 "very evidently showed": Edwin P. Hoyt, *The Improper Bostonian*. New York: William Morrow, 1979, p. 135.

129 "Hawthorne has dropped germinous seeds": Parker, Vol. 1, p. 755.

129 "I felt pantheistic then": Davis & Gilman, pp. 142–3.

129 "fifty fast-writing youths": Leyda, Vol. 1, p. 401.

129 "wrote . . . *Moby-Dick* under unfavorable circumstances": Sealts, p. 169.

130 "write those sort of books": Leyda, Vol. 1, p. 316.

130 "The word insanity is far too loose": Mumford, p. 231.

131 "There is a wisdom that is woe": Melville, *Moby-Dick*, p. 465.

131 "a mouthful of brains": Leyda, Vol. 1, p. 296.

131 "who in the rainbow": Herman Melville, *Billy Budd and Other Stories*. London: Penguin Books, 1986, p. 353.

131 "Go mad I cannot": quoted in Robertson-Lorant, p. 563.

131 "did not leave his room": Leyda, Vol. 1, p. 441.

132–133 "Poetic or artistic genius": Jamison, pp. 2–3.

133 "extraordinary cock": Herman Melville. *The Happy Failure: Stories*. New York: HarperCollins, 2009, pp. 71–4.

133 "Intrepid, unprincipled, reckless, predatory": Herman Melville, *Israel Potter: His Fifty Years of Exile*. Evanston, IL: Northwestern University Press, 2000, p. 120.

134 "constant working of the brain": Parker, Vol. 2, pp. 152–3.

134 "how very ill Herman has been": Leyda, Vol. 2, p. 521.

134 "dispirited and ill," "depressed and aimless": Delbanco, pp. 250–1.

134 "much overshadowed": Leyda, Vol. 2, p. 531.

134 "Melville has not been well, of late": Leyda, Vol. 2, pp. 528–9.

134 "twilight of the eyes": Robertson-Lorant, p. 269.

135 "tender as young sparrows": Leyda, Vol. 1, p. 289.

135 "horrid week": Parker, Vol. 2, p. 209;

135 episode in Jerusalem, Parker, Vol. 2, p. 314; in Rome, Parker, Vol. 2, p. 326–7.

135 Episode in October 1858: Robertson-Lorant, p. 409;

135 "acute attack of neuralgia in the eyes": Robertson-Lorant, p. 472.

135 "Papa has been": Leyda, Vol. 2, p. 728.

135 "dark glasses": Sealts, p. 181.

135 "first attack of severe rheumatism," "sciatica," "prescribed for him": Sealts, p. 169.

135 "On the whole, more harm than good is done by medication": Oliver Wendell Holmes Sr, "Currents and Counter-Currents in Medical Science," *Medical Essays 1842–1882*. Boston: Houghton Mifflin, 1895, p. 202.

136 "ugly attacks": Parker, Vol. 2, pp. 261, 286; "severe . . . crick in the back": Parker, Vol. 2, p. 374.

138 "stands erect": Robertson-Lorant, p. 412; "erect bearing": Robertson-Lorant, p. 561. Melville's loss of height: Parker, Vol. 2, p. 293.

139 "has generally been considered rather favorable": van der Linden, p. 1134.

139 "Of all therapeutic modalities": A Keat. Ankylosing spondylitis. In: J. H. Klippel, ed. *Primer on the Rheumatic Diseases*. 12th ed. Atlanta, GA: Arthritis Foundation, 2001, pp. 250–4.

139 "did not take very kindly to the lecture platform": Sealts, p. 134.

139 "a more painful infliction upon an audience": Parker, Vol. 2, p. 395.

139–140 "rheumatism-bound": Robertson-Lorant, p. 437; "laid up for several weeks with a neuralgic attack": Parker, Vol. 2, p. 484; "sudden & severe illness," Robertson-Lorant, p. 531.

140 "This prolonged agony": Sealts, p. 136.

140 "This recovery is flattering": Leyda, Vol. 2, p. 656.

141 "sister's case": Parker, Vol. 2, pp. 629–30.

141 "Although . . . it's difficult to determine": Robetson-Lorant, p. 370.

141 "shy temperament," "marked unwillingness": Sealts, pp. 106, 132.

141 "warmed-up": Parker, Vol. 2, p. 400.

141 "a disappointed man": Leyda, Vol. 2, p. 605.

142 "drink should be only small beer": For Locke on beer for boys, see: John Locke, *Some Thoughts Concerning Education*. Cambridge: Cambridge University Press, 1892, pp. 12–13.

143 "heartbroken": Leyda, Vol. 2, pp. 689–90.

143 "Suicidogenic": Shneidman, p. 232.

143 "Go mad I cannot": Herman Melville, *Clarel* Chicago, Northwestern University Press, 2008. p. 335

143 "In the flesh": Parker, Vol. 2, p. 757.

143 "frightfully nervous state": Leyda, Vol. 2, p. 747.

144 "hermit": Leyda, Vol. 2, p. 781; "shut himself up in his room": Parker, Vol. 2, p. 850; "Many visitors to that household": Sealts, p. 180.

144 "Herman could again": Leyda, Vol. 2, p. 767; "rheumatic gout": Leyda, Vol. 2, p. 785.

144 "vigorous body": Robertson-Lorant, p. 577; "thick-set figure": Leyda, Vol. 2, p. 796.

144 "his tall, stalwart figure": Sealts, p. 121; "walking back and forth": Sealts, p. 181.

145 "two attacks of erysipelas": Sealts, p. 169.

145 "cardiac dilatation": Leyda, Vol. 2, p. 836.

145 "The Late Hiram Melville": Parker, Vol. 2, p. 921.

145 "The poor man is out of his suffering": Leyda, Vol 2, p. 836.

7. Sex and the Dead: Brucellosis, Arsenic, and William Butler Yeats

BOOKS

Alldritt, Keith. *W. B. Yeats: The Man and the Milieu*. New York: Clarkson Potter, 1997.

Brock, Pope. *Charlatan*. New York: Crown Publishers, 2008.

Brown, Terence. *The Life of W. B. Yeats: A Critical Biography*. Oxford: Blackwell Publishers, 1999.

Commission on Life Sciences. *Arsenic in Drinking Water*. Washington: National Academies Press, 1999.

Emsley, John. *The Elements of Murder*. Oxford: Oxford University Press, 2005.

Fitzgerald, Michael. *The Genesis of Artistic Creativity*. London: Jessica Kingsley, 2005.

Foster, Roy. *W. B. Yeats: A Life. Volume 1: The Apprentice Mage*. London: Oxford University Press, 1997.

Foster, Roy. *W. B. Yeats: A Life. Volume 2: The Arch-Poet*. London: Oxford University Press, 2003.

Harris, H. J. *Brucellosis*. New York: Paul B. Hoeber, 1941.

Hemingway, Ernest. *Hemingway and the Mechanism of Fame*. Columbia, South Carolina: University of South Carolina Press, 2006.

Huddleson, I. F. *Brucellosis in Man and Animals*. New York: Commonwealth Fund, 1943.

Lyons, John B. *Thrust Syphilis Down to Hell and Other Rejoyceana: Studies in the Borderlands of Medicine and Literature*. Dublin: Glendale Press, 1988.

Maddox, Brenda. *Yeats's Ghosts*. New York: HarperCollins, 1999.

Murphy, William M. *Family Secrets: William Butler Yeats and His Relatives*. Syracuse, New York: Syracuse University Press, 1995.

Torrey, E. Fuller. *The Roots of Treason: Ezra Pound and the Secrets of St. Elizabeth's*. New York: McGraw-Hill, 1984.

Tuohy, Frank. *Yeats*. New York: Macmillan, 1976.

Saddlemyer, Ann. *Becoming George: The Life of Mrs. W. B. Yeats*. London: Oxford University Press, 2002.

ARTICLES

Atkins, P. J., "White Poison? The Social Consequences of Milk Consumption, 1850–1930," *Social History of Medicine* 1992; 5(2):207–27.

Breathnach, C. S., "Maud Gonne: An Indomitable Consumptive," *Journal of Medical Biography* 2005; 13:232–40.

Calpasso, L., "Bacteria in Two-Millennia-Old Cheese, and Related Epizoonoses in Roman Populations," *Journal of Infection* 2002; 45:122–7.

Chapman, C., "Across the Atlantic: Impressions of England, Ireland, and Anne Yeats," *South Carolina Review* 1999; 32:202–10.

Gillette, A., "The Origins of the Manifesto of Racial Scientists," *Journal of Modern Italian Studies* 2001; 6:305–23.

Jolliffe, D. M., "A History of the Use of Arsenicals in Man," *Journal of the Royal Society of Medicine* 1993; 86:287–9.

Lasky, T., Sun, W., Kadry, A., Hoffman, M. K., "Mean Total Arsenic Concentrations in Chicken 1989–2000 and Estimated Exposures for Consumers of Chicken," *Environmental Health Perspectives* 2004; 112:18–21.

Miller, N. L., Fulmer, B. R., "Injection, Ligation, and Transplantation: The Search for the Glandular Fountain of Youth," *Journal of Urology* 2007; 177:2000–5.

Miller Jr., W. H., Schipper, H. M., Lee, J. S. et al., "Mechanisms of Action of Arsenic Trioxide," *Cancer Research* 2002; 62:3893–903.

Miner, M., Siegel, L. S., "William Butler Yeats: Dyslexic?" *Journal of Learning Disabilities* 1992; 25:372–5.

Nicoletti, P., "A Short History of Brucellosis," *Veterinary Microbiology* 2002; 90:5–9.

Pappas, G., Akritidis, N., Bosilkovski, N., Tsianos, E., "Brucellosis," *New England Journal of Medicine* 2005; 352:2325–36.

Potter, N., "An Essay on the Medicinal Properties and Deleterious Qualities of Arsenic." In: Caldwell, C., ed. *Medical Theses of the University of Pennsylvania, Vol. 1.* Philadelphia: Thomas and William Bradford, 1805.

Przygoda, G., Feldmann, J., Cullen, W. R., "The Arsenic Eaters of Styria," *Applied Organometallic Chemistry* 2001; 15:457–62.

Seneta, E., Seif, F. J., Liebermeister, H., Dietz, K., "Carl Liebermeister (1833–1901): A Pioneer of the Investigation and Treatment of Fever," *Journal of Medical Biography* 2004; 12:215–21.

Sengoopta, C., "Dr. Steinach Coming to Make Old Young,": Sex Glands, Vasectomy, and the Quest for Rejuvenation in the Roaring Twenties," *Endeavour* 2003; 27:122–6.

Wainwright, C. W., "Melitensis Infection: Treatment with Neoarsphenamine," *Southern Medical Journal* 1937; 30:600–8.

Vassallo, D. J., "The Centenary of the Sinking of the Mediterranean Fleet Flagship, HMS *Victoria*. What Was the Role of Malta Fever?" *Journal of the Royal Navy Medical Service* 1993; 79:91–9.

Young, D. A. B., "Florence Nightingale's Fever," *British Medical Journal* 1995; 311:1697–1700.

150 "999 mediums out of 1000": Maddox, p. 5.

151 "It's certain that fine women eat": W. B. Yeats, "A Prayer for My Daughter," In: *Yeats's Poems* / Dublin: Gill and Macmillan, 1989, p. 296.

151 "the livest, most intelligent and unexplainable thing": Torrey, p. 25.

152 "galvanized, agile baboon": Torrey, p. 71.

152 "peering into infinity": Foster, Vol. 2, p. 101.

152 "was possessed of the most acute ear": Torrey, p. 71.

152 "Ezra Pound devotes perhaps one fifth": Hemingway, pp. 5–6.

153 "supernatural nagging": Foster, Vol. 2, p. 134.

154 "It is not easy to talk to him in a familiar fashion": Brown, pp. 14–5.

154 "had no interest in people as such": Fitzgerald, p. 70.

154 "the sort of person who has no small-talk at all": Foster, Vol. 2, p. 534.

155 "she merely had neurasthenia": Foster, Vol. 2, p. 135.

155 "What shall I do with this absurdity": W. B. Yeats, "The Tower," *Yeats's Poems,* p. 302.

155 "slight congestion of the left lung": Foster, Vol. 2, p. 353.

155 "Pain in the region of the heart": Foster, Vol. 2, p. 716.

155–156 "the haemorrhage in the lung": Foster, Vol. 2, p. 354.

157 "At the beginning of December": Details of Yeats's illness are taken from: George Yeats, Letts Diary for 1930, National Library of Ireland MS 30,759; and George Yeats, Letter to Oliver St. John Gogarty, February 9, 1930. M0273, Healy Papers, Stanford University.

157 "convinced it was 'febbre di Malta'": George Yeats, Letter to Gogarty, February 9, 1930.

158 "It does not result in garlic breath": H. Hörlein, "Über das Solarson," *Archiv für Dermatologie und Syphilis* 1921; 130:334–40.

158–160 "most stimulating," "Pende . . . was positive," "rheumatic pains," "a good deal of diarrhoea": George Yeats, Letter to Gogarty, February 9, 1930.

161 "depression of spirits": Huddleson, p. 93.

163 "They put arsenic in his meat": A. E. Housman, *The Collected Poems of A. E. Housman*. New York: Henry Holt, 1965, p. 90.

163 "merely for the sake": Thomas Fowler, *Medical Reports on the Effects of Arsenic, in the Cure of Agues, Remitting Fevers, and Periodic Headaches*. London: J. Johnson and William Brown, 1786, p. 82.

163 "sex and the dead": Tuohy, p. 196.

164 "strange second puberty," "Cadillac engine," "gland old man": D. Wyndham, "Versemaking and Lovemaking: W. B. Yeats' Strange Second Puberty," *Journal of the History of the Behavioral Sciences* 2003; 39:25–50.

165 "obviously crazy," "he deserves punishment": Torrey, p. 175.

165 "chutzpah and hubris," "I have lived all my life": Torrey, pp. 278, 280.

165 "We have here an antique cardio-renal sclerotic": Foster, Vol. 2, p. 570.

166 "It is a curious experience": Foster, Vol. 2, p. 550.

166 "It has been suggested": For hypertension and Yeats's brain, see: Foster, Vol. 2, p. 586.

166 "You think it horrible": W. B. Yeats, "The Spur," *Yeats's Poems*, p. 430.

166 "dropsy": Foster, Vol. 2, p. 642.

166 "Now that my ladder's gone": W. B. Yeats, "The Circus Animals' Desertion," *Yeats's Poems*, p. 472.

167 "Cast a cold eye": W. B. Yeats, "Under Ben Bulben," *Yeats's Poems*, p. 452.

8. Medical Misadventures of an Amateur M.D.: Jack London's Death by Hubris

BOOKS
Haley, James L. *Wolf: The Lives of Jack London*. New York: Basic Books, 2010.

Kershaw, Alex. *Jack London: A Life*. New York: St. Martin's Press, 1997.

London, Jack. *The Cruise of the* Snark. New York: Penguin Books, 2004.

London, Jack. *John Barleycorn*. New York: Modern Library, 2001.

Moore, J. E.. *The Modern Treatment of Syphilis*. Springfield, IL: Charles C. Thomas, 1933.

Sinclair, Andrew. *Jack: A Biography of Jack London*. New York: Harper and Row, 1977.

Walker, Franklin. *Jack London and the Klondike*. San Marino, California: Huntington Library, 1978.

ARTICLES
Bomback, A. S., Klemmer, P. J., "Jack London's Chronic Interstitial Nephritis," *Pharos* 2008; 71(1):26–30.

Dodd, F., "An Astrologer from Down East," *New England Quarterly* 1932; 5(4):769–99.

Kampmeier, R. H., "Syphilis Therapy: An Historical Perspective," *Journal of the American Venereal Disease Association* 1976; 3(2 Pt 2):99–108.

Norris, J., "The 'Scurvy Disposition': Heavy Exertion as an Exacerbating Influence on Scurvy in Modern Times," *Bulletin of the History of Medicine* 1983; 57(3):325–38.

Rinaldi, A., "Yaws: A Second (and Maybe Last?) Chance for Eradication," *PLoS Neglected Tropical Diseases* 2008; 2(8):e275.

Thorburn, A. L., "Paul Ehrlich: Pioneer of Chemotherapy and Cure by Arsenic (1854–1915)," *British Journal of Venereal Disease* 1983; 59:404–5.

Weismann, K., "Neurosyphilis, or Chronic Heavy Metal Poisoning: Karen Blixen's Lifelong Disease," *Sexually Transmitted Diseases* 1995; 22:137–44.

168 "In the meantime": London, *Snark*, p. 183.

168 "Jack has finally worn down": Sinclair, p. 232.

170 "badge of shame": Kershaw, p. 39.

170 "the spook house": Haley, p. 25.

170 "work best": Haley, p. 20.

173 "It was something inside of him": Kershaw, p. 98.

173 "long sickness": London, *John Barleycorn*, p. 156.

173 "But mine is no tale of a reformed drunkard": *John Barleycorn*, p. 185.

174 "Straight down": *Snark*, p. 217.

174 "I can recommend no finer sport": *Snark*, p. 95.

174 "And now all this strength and beauty": *Snark*, p. 106.

175 "monomaniac on the question of sores and sublimate": *Snark*, p. 185.

176 "My hands were twice their natural size": *Snark*, p. 195.

176 "caused them to break": *Snark*, p. 230.

178 "return of the Wasserman reaction": W. G. Stimpson, *Treatment of*

Syphilis. Comparison of the Number of Days' Hospital Treatment Required for Patients Suffering with Syphilis, with and without the Use of Salvarsan and Neosalvarsan. Washington: Government Printing Office, 1915, p. 10.

178 "the fetish of treatment": F. E. Cormia, "Over-Treatment in Syphilis," *Canadian Medical Association Journal* 1939; 40:445–8.

180 "chronic interstitial nephritis": Sinclair, p. 238.

181 "I would rather be ashes": Haley, p. 311.

9. An Infamous Private Ailment: The Venereal Afflictions of James Joyce

BOOKS

Baumann, Frederick. *Gonorrhea: Its Diagnosis and Treatment.* New York: D. Appleton and Co., 1908.

Budgen, Frank. *James Joyce and the Making of Ulysses.* Bloomington, Indiana: Indiana University Press, 1960.

Ellmann, Richard. *James Joyce.* Oxford: Oxford University Press, 1982.

Ferris, Kathleen. *James Joyce and the Burden of Disease.* Lexington, Kentucky: University Press of Kentucky, 1995.

Jackson, John Wyse and Costello, Peter. *John Stanislaus Joyce.* New York: St. Martin's Press, 1997.

Johnson, Alexander B. *Surgical Diagnosis,* Vol. 2. New York: D. Appleton and Co., 1909.

Joyce, James. *Finnegans Wake.* New York: Penguin Books, 1999.

Joyce, James. *A Portrait of the Artist as a Young Man* and *Dubliners.* New York: Barnes and Noble Books, 2004.

Joyce, James. *Ulysses.* New York: Vintage Books, 1986.

Joyce, Stanislaus. *My Brother's Keeper: James Joyce's Early Years.* Cambridge, Massachusetts: Da Capo Press, 2003.

Lyons, John B. *James Joyce and Medicine.* Dublin: Dolmen Press, 1973.

Lyons, John B. *Thrust Syphilis Down to Hell and Other Rejoyceana.* Dublin: Glendale Press, 1988.

Maddox, Brenda. *Nora: The Real Life of Molly Bloom.* Boston: Houghton Mifflin, 1988.

Schloss, Carol Loeb. *Lucia Joyce: To Dance in the Wake.* New York: Farrar, Strauss, and Giroux, 2003.

ARTICLES

Ascaso, F. J., Bosch, J., "Uveitic Secondary Glaucoma: Influence in James Joyce's (1882–1941) Last Works," *Journal of Medical Biography* 2010; 18:57–60.

Burns, J. K., "Psychosis: A Costly By-Product of Social Brain Evolution in *Homo sapiens*," *Progress in Neuropsychopharmacology and Biological Psychiatry* 2006; 30:797–814.

Edwards-Jones, V., "The Benefits of Silver in Hygiene, Personal Care and Healthcare," *Letters in Applied Microbiology* 2009; 49:147– 52.

Lyons, J. B., "James Joyce: Steps Towards a Diagnosis," *Journal of the History of the Neurosciences* 2000; 9:294–306.

Paton, A., "James Joyce: A Case History," *British Medical Journal* 1975; 2:636–7.

Panush, R. S., Paraschiv, D., Dorff, R. E., "The Tainted Legacy of Hans Reiter," *Seminars in Arthritis and Rheumatism* 2003; 32:231–6.

Sullivan, E., "Ocular History of James Joyce," *Surveys in Ophthalmology* 1984; 28:412–5.

182 "I called upon the bard Kinch": *Ulysses,* p. 176.

182 "It has been blurtingly bruited": *Finnegans Wake,* p. 33.

183 "John M'Intosh, M.D.": M'Intosh is a fictionalized physician, inspired by the man in the MacIntosh in *Ulysses.* Gogarty referred Joyce to Dr Mick Walsh; it is unknown whether Joyce was treated by him or another physician.

184 "A medical student": *Portrait,* p. 214.

184 "religion of terrorism": Stanislaus Joyce, p. 18.

185 "I would have been even more disastrous": Ellmann, p. 475.

185 "drunk precisely 3.97 days a week": Ellmann, p. 150.

186 "a man of small virtue": Ellmann, p. 6.

186 "There is a young fellow named Joyce": Lyons, *James Joyce and Medicine*, p. 56.

186 "slight gleet": Lyons, *James Joyce and Medicine*, p. 60.

189 "international eyesore": Ellmann, p. 412.

189 "more like a capital S than a capital Z": Ellmann, p. 270.

190 "ubiquitous anal eroticism": J. Mark Knowles, "Nora's Filthy Words: Scatology in the Letters of James Joyce," *New School Psychiatry Bulletin* 2006; 4(2):91–101.

190 "I sincerely hope": Budgen, p. 190.

191 "nervous collapse": Ellmann, p. 406.

192 "a quack doctor for the clap," "a dose": *Ulysses,* p. 126.

192 "hard chancre": *Ulysses,* p. 388.

192 "syphilisation": *Ulysses,* p. 266.

192 "more pox than pax": *Ulysses,* p. 271.

192 "pox and gleet vendors": *Ulysses,* p. 452.

192 "that foul plague Allpox," "a stout shield of oxengut": *Ulysses,* p. 324.

192 "No, it did lots of other things too": Ellmann, p. 110.

193 "nice and bespectacle": *Finnegans Wake*, p. 386.

193 "demand that I make of my reader": Ellmann, p. 703.

193 "crossmess parzel": *Finnegans Wake*, p. 619.

194 "One eyegonblack": *Finnegans Wake*, p. 16.

194 "punsil shapner": *Finnegans Wake*, p. 98.

194 "ructions gunorrhal": *Finnegans Wake*, p. 191.

195 "Whatever spark of a gift I possess": Ellmann, p. 650.

195 "The surviving evidence": Few records survive to help sort out Lucia's illness. In the Richard Ellmann Papers (McFarlin Library, University of Tulsa), Ellman's "Notes on Lucia" (Box 75), and Cary F. Baynes's "Notes on Lucia," Zurich, 1934, are helpful.

195 "The patient . . . prefers to live wholly in his or her inner world": Schloss, pp. 445–6.

196 "nerves," "*une interpretation*": Lyons, *James Joyce and Medicine*, pp. 212–4.

197 "*Finnegans Wake* will be my last book": Lyons, *James Joyce and Medicine*, p. 216.

198 "raglike": Lyons, *Thrust Syphilis Down to Hell,* p. 218.

198 "I couldn't do that to him": Ellmann, p. 742.

198 "Sure, if you've been married": Ellmann, p. 743.

198 "What is he doing there under the ground": Ellmann, p. 743.

10. "The Disease Which Was Bound to Claim Me Sooner or Later": Orwell's Cough

BOOKS

Bowker, Gordon. *Inside George Orwell*. New York: Palgrave Macmillan, 2003.

Crick, Bernard. *George Orwell: A Life*. Harmondsworth: Penguin Books, 1982.

Dormandy, Thomas. *The White Death: A History of Tuberculosis*. London: Hambledon and London, 1999.

Kayne, G. G., Pagel, W., O'Shaughnessy, L. *Pulmonary Tuberculosis*. London: Oxford University Press, 1939.

Meyers, Jeffrey. *Orwell: Wintry Conscience of a Generation*. New York: WW Norton, 2000.

Orwell, George. *Collected Essays, Journalism, and Letters of George Orwell*. Sonia Orwell and Ian Angus, eds. Harmondsworth, England: Penguin Books, 1970.

Orwell, George. *The Complete Works of George Orwell*. Peter Davison, ed. London: Secker and Warburg, 1998.

Orwell, George. *Diaries*. Peter Davison, ed. London: Harvill Secker, 2009.

Orwell, George. *Penguin Complete Longer Non-Fiction of George Orwell*. Harmondsworth: Penguin Books, 1983.

Shelden, Michael. *Orwell: The Authorized Biography*. New York: Harper-Collins, 1991.

Taylor, D. J. *Orwell: The Life*. New York: Henry Holt, 2003.

ARTICLES

Afzelius, B. A., Mossberg, B., Bergstrom, B. E., "Immotile Cilia Syndrome," in: Scriver, C. R., Beaudet, A. L., Sly, W. S., Valle, D., eds. *The Metabolic and Molecular Bases of Inherited Disease*, 8th ed. New York: McGraw Hill, 2001, pp. 4817–27.

Dally, A., "The Rise and Fall of Pink Disease," *Social History of Medicine* 1997; 10:291–304.

Doll, R., Hill, A. B., "Mortality of Doctors in Relation to Their Smoking Habits," *British Medical Journal* 1954; 1(4877):1451–5.

Hendry, W. F., A'Hern, R. P., Cole, P. J., "Was Young's Syndrome Caused by Exposure to Mercury in Childhood?" *British Medical Journal* 1993; 307:1579–82.

Marshall, G. M., Blacklock, J. W. S., Cameron, V. C. et al., "Streptomycin Treatment of Pulmonary Tuberculosis," *British Medical Journal* 1948; 2(4582):769–82.

Oermann, C.M., "Fertility in Patients with Cystic Fibrosis," *Chest* 2000; 118:893–4.

Ross, J. C., Gow, J. C., St. Hill, C. A., "Tuberculous Epididymitis: A Review of 170 Patients," *British Journal of Surgery* 1961; 48:663–6.

Rustad, T. R., Sherrid, A. M., Minch, K. J. et al., "Hypoxia: A Window into *Mycobacterium tuberculosis* Latency," *Cellular Microbiology* 2009; 11:1151–9.

Shepherd, M. P., "Plombage in the 1980s," *Thorax* 1985; 40:328–40.

Sole-Balcells, F., Jimenez-Cruz, F., de Cabezon, J. S., Rosello, A. S., "Tuberculosis and Infertility in Men," *European Urology* 1977; 3:129–31.

Strieder, J. W., Laforet, E. G., Lynch, J. P., "The Surgery of Pulmonary Tuberculosis," *New England Journal of Medicine* 1967; 276:960–5.

Vargas, M. H., Furuya, M. E., Perez-Guzman, C., "Effect of Altitude on the Frequency of Pulmonary Tuberculosis," *International Journal of Tuberculosis and Lung Disease* 2004; 8:1321–4.

Vree, M., Hoa, N. B., Sy, D. N. et al., "Low Tuberculosis Notification in Mountainous Vietnam is Not Due to Low Case Detection," *BMC Infectious Diseases* 2007; 7:109.

Wawersik, J., "History of Chloroform Anesthesia," *Anaesthesiologie und Reanimation* 1997; 22:144–52.

199 "As I warned you I might do": Orwell, *Complete Works,* Vol. 20, p. 159.

199 "However great the kindness": "How the Poor Die," Orwell, *Collected Essays,* Vol. 4, p. 271.

202 "the dirty work of Empire": "Shooting an Elephant," *Collected Essays,* Vol. 1, p. 266.

202 "chesty," "bronchial": Taylor, p. 26.

203 "In winter, after about the age of ten": "Such, Such Were the Joys," *Collected Essays,* Vol. 4, p. 396.

203 "Eric has a bit of a cough": Crick, p. 106.

205 "chesty," "a cough every winter.": Crick, p. 262.

205 "a dessert-spoonful of dark-colored blood," "I later learned," "if you had some disease": "How the Poor Die," *Collected Essays,* Vol. 4, pp. 262–4.

206 "taking on something!": Shelden, p. 243.

207 "He was so tall and always standing up": Shelden, p. 260.

207 "My first thought": Orwell, *Homage to Catalonia,* in *Complete Longer Non-Fiction*, p. 434.

207 "It entered the neck": For George Kopp's detailed description of Orwell's bullet wound, see *Complete Works,* Vol. 11, pp. 23–6.

207–8 "The wound was a curiosity": *Homage to Catalonia,* p. 439.

208 "In Spain, for the first time": Orwell, *Looking Back on the Spanish War,* in *Complete Longer Non-Fiction,* pp. 478–9.

209 "TB confirmed": Preston Hall Records, George Orwell Archive, University College London.

211 "this seems too reasonable": Shelden, p. 302.

211 "Cromwellian": Shelden, p. 328.

211 "drizzly": Shelden, p. 325.

211 "halfway between a girls' school and a lunatic asylum": Shelden, p. 348.

212 "I have a disease called bronchiectasis": Crick, p. 486.

212 "I am also sterile I think": Meyers, p. 242.

212 "was incapable of having children": Bowker, p. 163.

214 "What matters is being faithful": *Complete Works*, Vol. 18, p. 249.

215 "one of the many ill-judged decisions": Bowker, p. 364.

215 "good deal of rain" etc: Orwell, *Diaries*, p. 393-456.

215 "Writing a book is a horrible, exhausting struggle": "Why I Write," *Complete Works*, Vol. 18, p. 320.

216 "It is TB": *Complete Works*, Vol. 19, p. 273.

217 "The first time you did it": *Complete Works*, Vol. 19, p. 248.

217 "It seems there's a regular tradition": *Complete Works*, Vol. 20, p. 165.

217 "But the truly frightening thing": George Orwell, *Nineteen Eighty-Four*. Harmondsworth, England: Penguin Books, 1954, p. 218.

218 "rather like sinking the ship": *Complete Works*, Vol. 19, p. 320.

220 "a high-sounding name for aspirins": *Complete Works*, Vol. 20, p. 16.

220 "a well-built blonde lady": Bowker, p. 405.

220 "When I first saw him": Crick, p. 574.

221 "Any life when viewed from the inside": *Collected Essays*, Vol. 3, p. 185.

**Prepared by the
Ministry of Transport
and the
Central Office of Information**

First published 1969
Reprinted, with amendments,
March 1970

References in this book to the
requirements of the law, traffic signs,
road markings, etc.
are correct at the time
of going to press.

The Ministry of Transport Manual

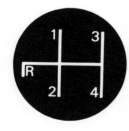

DRIVING

London: Her Majesty's Stationery Office 1970

Foreword

Somewhere among our millions of motorists there may be the perfect driver. It's possible. But unlikely. However long we have been driving, however experienced we may be, there is always something to learn. People who really take pride in their driving know this. It's one of the qualities of a good, safe driver that he recognises his own limitations. If safety is an attitude of mind, then humility is one of its main ingredients.

This manual is designed for all those who take their driving seriously. It is based on the Ministry's unique experience over more than thirty years of analysing, in detail, the everyday driving of millions of motorists. It answers many queries about points of technique or procedure which flood into the Ministry. It gives authoritative guidance.

Of course, good driving habits should be learned from the start. So the manual begins with learning to drive. But it isn't just an ABC for newcomers. Far from it. It has something to offer for every motorist, however experienced—and for instructors, too.

Anyone who has passed the driving test has shown that he knows the ingredients of safe driving. But all too often drivers let these standards drop in their everyday driving. This manual shows how they can keep the standards up—and improve them. It is an essential reference book for everyone with a genuine interest in driving.

Every year another million drivers take to the roads for the first time. Heavier traffic, more powerful and sophisticated cars, make good, safe driving more important than ever before. Higher driving standards are in all our interests. They make motoring not only safer but more enjoyable. Just reading *Driving* can't make a good driver. But it does point the way.

Acknowledgments

The Ministry of Transport extends grateful thanks to the following organisations for their help in supplying vehicles and equipment used in illustrations to this manual:

British Leyland Motor Corporation Limited

Ford Motor Company Limited

Rootes Motors Limited

Vauxhall Motors Limited

Contents

Chapter		Page
1	The good driver	1
2	Introduction to the controls of a motor car	4
3	The driving mirror	17
4	Beginning to drive: starting, changing gear and stopping	22
5	On the road	38
6	Approaching corners and junctions	58
7	Emerging at junctions	69
8	Traffic signs	93
9	Dealing with hills	104
10	Manœuvring	111
11	The open road	125
12	Other people	145
13	Keeping your grip	159
14	Motorway driving	175
15	Night driving	187
16	Making things a little easier	193
	Appendix I: The driving test	204
	Appendix II: Conversion table of equivalent speeds	213
	Index	214

1 The good driver

With the coming of the 'horseless carriage' at the end of the last century, a new era in personal transport was born. The early motorist certainly had his problems—perhaps the biggest one being whether his vehicle would start and then continue to go.

This problem has almost disappeared today, but others have taken its place. More traffic and faster vehicles mean that, however safe and reliable a car may be, its driver has to have much more driving skill than ever before. Today's drivers cannot escape their own direct and personal responsibility for the accidents that happen on the road every year.

What makes a good driver?

A good driver has many things in his make-up. Some of these, such as experience and skill, will come only in time. But others —just as important—must be part of him from the start. These qualities are a sense of responsibility for the safety of others, a determination to concentrate on the job of driving, patience and courtesy. Together, these become what is generally known as a driver's 'attitude'.

Not everyone is patient by nature or gifted with good powers of concentration. But because attitude is so important a part of safe driving, every driver must make a real effort to develop these qualities—and this effort must start from the very beginning of his first driving lesson.

Getting into the right attitude will be harder for some people than others. It can be more difficult than the actual business of learning to make the car go or stop. All the things which go to make up attitude are just as necessary for the experienced driver as for the learner. So, before we go any further, let us look at these qualities in a little more detail.

1

Responsibility

As a driver you must have a proper concern not only for your own safety and that of your passengers, but also for the safety of every other road user, including pedestrians. You can do this only if you pay close attention to the varying traffic situations as they develop. Then you can plan your own actions well in advance so that they do not cause danger or inconvenience to others. At times you may be tempted to make a rash move—don't.

Concentration

With responsibility goes concentration on the job of driving. You must concentrate all the time if you are going to be able to deal with present-day traffic. Nowadays this is usually heavy and fast-moving and there are possible dangers all around you. If you let your mind wander, even for a moment, the risk of making a mistake is increased enormously. And mistakes can cause accidents. If you are tired, upset or unwell, or even thinking about something else, you will take longer to react. It is better not to drive at all in these circumstances, but if you have to, make special allowances for them.

Anticipation

Concentration helps you to 'anticipate'. In motoring, anticipation means acting promptly to fit in with what other road users are doing, as well as being able and ready to alter your own course or behaviour as a situation develops.

To those who do not drive, this quality of anticipation has the appearance of being automatic—and this is what it should become. Experience and anticipation together will enable you to act to prevent possible danger from becoming actual danger.

Patience

It is very easy to get impatient, or lose your temper, when other drivers do something wrong, or you are caught up in a traffic jam. But if you do, you are well on the way to having an accident. Never drive in a spirit of retaliation or competition. If the incompetence or bad manners of another road user cause you inconvenience, don't let your annoyance, even if justifiable, override your good sense and judgment. Attempts to 'teach him a lesson' don't do any good: there is no better lesson than a good example.

Confidence

The degree of confidence a driver has in handling his vehicle is, in a sense, part of his attitude to driving. New drivers will, of course, be unsure of themselves. Confidence grows with experience. But a good driver never lets himself get over-confident. This leads to carelessness, risks and, eventually, accidents.

Planned tuition

All the things we have talked about so far—becoming a safe driver by developing a sense of responsibility, concentration, anticipation, patience and confidence—will depend very much on getting good instruction from the start. Drivers often begin to learn with a parent, relative or friend and this allows them to get lots of practice at low cost. But although some non-professional teachers can put over the details of car control and road procedure within a reasonable time, many good drivers are not good instructors. They can ruin a pupil's confidence by leading him into situations he is not ready for. In other words, they often teach him to run before he can walk. And, of course, not all parents, relatives and friends are good drivers anyway.

A planned approach is essential when teaching someone to drive. Ideally, each lesson should be phased to suit the pupil's development. There are no short cuts to being a good driver, either in time or money. There is no doubt that the best way to learn to drive properly is to have good professional tuition—and plenty of it. It will prove well worth while in the long run. But you need plenty of practice too.

Mechanical knowledge

So far we have said nothing about mechanical knowledge—how a car works. It is not necessary to know all the complicated details of car construction to be a good driver. But the more you do know the better, because if you know how the different parts of a car work, and what happens when you use the controls, you will develop a sense of car sympathy. This will not only make you a better driver, but add to your interest in driving. It will also prolong the life of your car. There are a number of very useful books which explain simply how a car works. It would repay you to get one of these and study it.

The new driver will learn to use the controls more quickly if he understands how they work. In the next chapter we give, in simple terms, a description of the foot and hand controls.

2 Introduction to the controls of a motor car

The main controls of a car can be conveniently grouped according to whether you use your feet or your hands to work them. The *foot* controls, reading from right to left, are: accelerator, brake, clutch.

The *hand* controls are: steering wheel, handbrake, gear lever.

(If you intend to drive a car with automatic or semi-automatic transmission you should see also Chapter 16.)

Learners will be told about the controls by their instructors, but here we shall look at each control in some detail because, simple though they may seem, each needs a particular skill. Proper understanding and use of the controls are 'musts' for safe driving. Every new driver must learn these skills thoroughly—however long it takes. Here again, the experience and knowledge of a good professional instructor are invaluable, if not essential.

Opposite, upper
RIGHT—This driver has adjusted the seat so that she can reach the controls easily and comfortably.

Opposite, lower
WRONG—This driver is seated too far back from the controls.

The driving position

Before you can begin to work the controls properly you must be able to reach them easily and comfortably. Always make sure that the driving seat is in the right position for you. You should be able to push the brake and clutch pedals right down without moving your body forward. At the same time you should be able to hold the steering wheel rim, lightly but firmly, with your hands at or between the positions corresponding to ten minutes to two, or a quarter to three on a clock face. Your body should be resting firmly against the back of the seat. You can check whether you have got the right position by pushing down any two of the pedals: your legs should be slightly bent at the knees—not stretched right out.

As to height, you must be able to see straight ahead without having to peer over the top of the steering wheel. If you are very short you may need a secure cushion to raise or support you —unless you have a car in which the height and slope of the driving seat can be adjusted.

Seeing properly to the rear through the driving mirror is another 'must'. But we shall deal with that more fully in the next chapter.

The foot controls

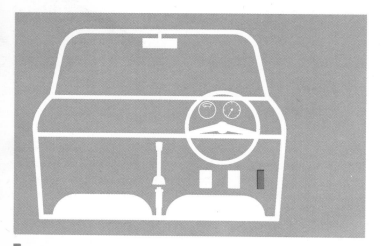

Accelerator

The accelerator (or gas pedal, as some instructors call it) is worked by the right foot. It is linked to the carburettor, a device supplying the correct mixture of air and petrol on which the engine runs. The accelerator controls the *rate* at which this mixture flows into the engine, and therefore the power output of the engine. The further the pedal is pressed down, the greater the power output and the faster the car goes. When you let the pedal up, or take your foot off altogether, the opposite happens and the car begins to slow down (unless you are going down a slope). This is because the engine is trying to run more slowly and is acting as a brake.

The accelerator pedal is very sensitive and new drivers usually find it difficult to get just the right amount of pressure on it. Getting the 'feel' of the pedal needs practice, to avoid jerky starts or a roaring engine.

■ Footbrake

The brake pedal, like the accelerator, is worked by the right foot. This is convenient, because in ordinary driving you don't need to use these two controls at the same time. The brake pedal is placed immediately to the left of the accelerator and should be worked with the ball of the foot.

Under normal driving conditions, this brake *only* should be used. (The other braking control, the handbrake, is dealt with later.) The harder the pedal is pushed down, the greater the braking effect and the more quickly the car will lose speed. In most situations only light pedal pressure is needed to brake safely and smoothly.

Training in using the brake pedal should include not only the application of the brake, but also practice in moving the right foot freely and accurately from the accelerator to the brake and back again without looking down at the pedals. This can be practised while sitting in the driving seat without the engine running.

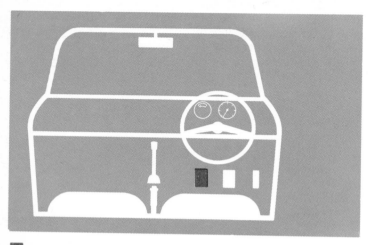

Clutch

The clutch is a device which allows the engine to run without driving the wheels. In its simplest form, it is made up of two plates. One of them turns all the time the engine is running; the other is linked to the wheels and is moved only when it is touching the first one.

When the clutch pedal is in its normal position the two plates are held together by strong springs so that the engine will drive the car. Pushing the pedal down separates the plates and breaks the link between engine and wheels.

To get a car on the move smoothly, the gap between these two plates has to be closed—but not too suddenly. This means letting the clutch pedal up until it reaches the point at which the two plates begin to come together. This point is called the 'biting point', 'point of contact' or 'take-up point'. With practice and experience, you will know just where it is. You will be able to feel it and also hear it, because the speed of the engine will drop.

Being able to sense this point is part of the secret of clutch control. The other part is being able to control the rest of the upward movement of the clutch pedal so that the two plates fit together without a jerk.

This needs lots of practice. You must be as careful to let the clutch pedal come up slowly as you are to use the accelerator gently. Ignoring these rules can cause a stalled engine or a jerky start.

The hand controls

 Steering wheel

This should be held lightly but firmly, with your hands at or between the ten-to-two or quarter-to-three positions. Always use both hands for the steering, except when you need one hand for another driving job. *Never* have both hands off the steering wheel at the same time. You will find that when the car is on the move it takes very little effort to turn the wheel. There is no need to grip it tightly.

The angle through which the front wheels can be turned is known as the 'lock'. The sharper the turn the more you will need to turn the steering wheel. When you turn it left or right as far as it will go you will be applying full left lock or full right lock.

The next rule to remember is not to cross your hands on the steering wheel when you are turning it. If you do you lose a lot of control over the steering, which can be dangerous. The correct way to steer round a corner is to feed the rim of the steering wheel through your hands with a pull-push movement. If you are turning left, the left hand should be moved to a higher position (but not past twelve o'clock) and the wheel pulled downwards, while the right hand is slid down the wheel. You can then push up with the right hand while the left hand, in turn, is slid up the wheel. (See Fig. 1.) If you are turning right the movements are reversed.

Where less steering lock is needed, hand movements may be shorter. For some changes of direction it may be enough to pull the wheel downwards and allow the rim to slide through the other hand.

As the turn is completed you must straighten up. To do this,

What the left hand does		What the right hand does
Slides up		
PULLS down		Slides down
Slides up		PUSHES up
PULLS down		Slides down

10

the steering wheel must be fed back through your hands in the opposite direction. We say 'fed back' because you must not let the wheel spin back on its own—there will be a tendency for it to do this. So keep control by *feeding the wheel back.*

▌ Handbrake

In this illustration the handbrake is shown between the two front seats. But it can be on the right of the driver's seat, or underneath the facia (dashboard).

The handbrake is provided to hold the vehicle still when it is halted or parked. In most cars the handbrake operates *only on the two rear wheels.* This is why it should not be used to stop the car while it is moving, except in an emergency such as the failure of the footbrake. Applying brakes to the rear wheels only can cause a nasty skid.

The handbrake is fitted with a catch to lock it in the 'on' position. To apply the handbrake you have to release the catch by pressing the button, or other fitment, on the end of the handbrake, pull it hard on, then release the button. The catch will now lock the brake in the 'on' position.

To release the handbrake, first pull it as if to apply it harder—this will release the catch more easily—then, still pressing the button, the handbrake can be moved to the 'off' position. (On some cars, twisting the brake handle takes the place of pressing a button.)

Fig. 1

Turning left (see text on pages 9 and 11).

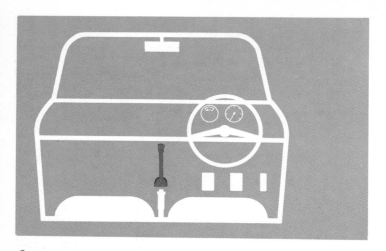

Gear lever and gearbox

The actual position of the gear lever will vary from car to car, but it is usually on the floor of the car on the left-hand side of the driver or on the side of the steering column below the steering wheel.

The gear lever is used to change from one gear to another. The gears, contained in a gearbox, enable the driver to match the engine power to the speed of the car and the load it has to move. For example, more power is usually needed when starting off, to get the weight of the car moving, than to keep the car at a particular speed on a level road.

The number of forward gears will depend on the make and model of the car. There will also be a reverse gear to drive the car backwards. Fig. 2 shows some of the possible arrangements which are sometimes marked on top of the gear lever. The centre part, marked N in the diagram, is known as neutral. Whenever the gear lever is moved out of one of the gear positions and into or through neutral, the link between the engine and the wheels is broken even though the clutch pedal is not pushed down.

To select the gear you need, you first have to push the clutch pedal right down. Then you can move the gear lever into the right position for the gear you want. You will see from Fig. 2 that whenever you change from one gear to another you always move the gear lever through neutral. New drivers should make a point of learning all the gear lever positions so that they know exactly which way to move the lever without having to look down at it. With practice, changing gear will become second nature.

The lowest, or first, gear is the most powerful. But it will drive the car only at slow speeds, and is used for moving off, manœuvring at slow speeds and climbing steep hills. After moving off you will have to use successively higher gears the greater the speed of

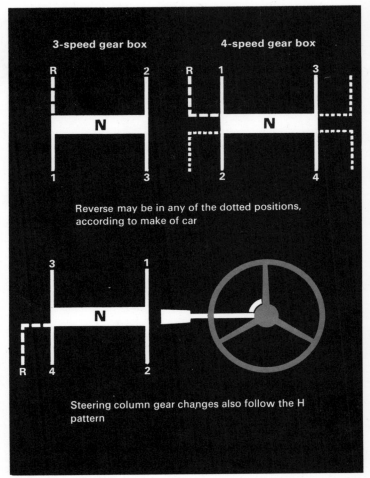

Fig. 2

Gear lever positions

the car—from first to second and so on until you get to top gear. This process is known as changing up. Top is the least powerful gear, but it gives the widest range of speeds. It is the third gear in a car having three forward gears, and the fourth in one with four. When you have to drive at a slower speed you should change to a lower gear. This is known as 'changing down'. We shall be referring to changing up and changing down a great deal—and explaining how to do it—in the following chapters.

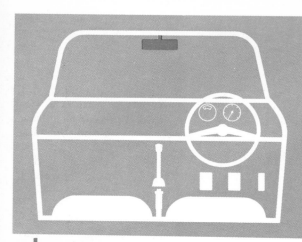

Driving mirror

The most vital and important visual aid is the driving mirror. This is usually fitted inside the car near the top centre of the windscreen. It is so important that the whole of the next chapter is about how to use it properly.

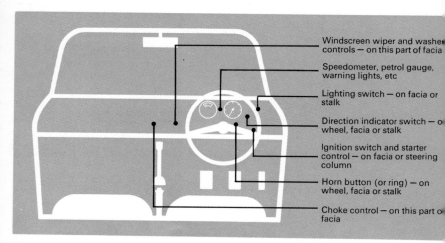

Windscreen wiper and washer controls — on this part of facia

Speedometer, petrol gauge, warning lights, etc

Lighting switch — on facia or stalk

Direction indicator switch — on wheel, facia or stalk

Ignition switch and starter control — on facia or steering column

Horn button (or ring) — on wheel, facia or stalk

Choke control — on this part of facia

Other controls

Visual aids

Most modern cars have dials and gauges on the facia below the windscreen. These tell you how the car is functioning. Apart from a speedometer and a petrol gauge, you may also have lights to warn you if something is wrong with the engine oil pressure or the electrical system; or to show that your headlights are on the main beam, or your direction indicators are switched on. Your instructor will tell you how to understand and act upon these visual aids.

Direction indicators

Most private cars, and an increasing number of commercial vehicles, are fitted with direction indicators. A few still have the semaphore-arm type where a lighted arm comes out of the side of the vehicle to show which way you intend to turn. But most modern vehicles have flashing indicators at both front and back, and some have them at the sides as well. All indicators are worked by a switch, usually a small lever, fitted on or near the steering column.

Most direction indicators are self-cancelling, which means that as you straighten up after a turn the signal switches itself off. But be careful. If your change in direction is only slight the self-cancelling device may not work and you will have to switch off the indicators by hand. After you have made a turn, check that your indicators are switched off—otherwise you will mislead other drivers, possibly with serious results.

It is especially important to do this if your indicators are not of the self-cancelling type and have to be switched on *and off* by hand. Most cars have either a warning light or an audible warning (usually a ticking noise)—or both—to show when the indicators are flashing.

Windscreen wipers and washers

Windscreen wipers keep the windscreen clear of rain, snow or fog. They are worked by a switch on the facia or in some other position within easy reach of the driver. With practice you should be able to switch the wipers on or off without taking your eyes off the road.

When the road is wet your windscreen will collect dirt, water and mud. In these conditions a windscreen washer is almost as necessary as the wipers. It is operated by a switch or button, which squirts jets of clean water on to the windscreen. By using it with the wipers, any dirt on your windscreen can quickly be washed off.

Never switch on your wipers when the windscreen is dry. If you do you will scratch the glass because there are always tiny specks of grit on it. And a scratched windscreen can add to dazzle at night and in strong sunlight. If you haven't a windscreen washer, use a sponge and plenty of water to clean the screen before wiping it dry. You won't be able to see properly through a dirty windscreen.

In time all windscreens are likely to get covered with tiny scratches. Prevent such damage for as long as you can by keeping the windscreen (and windows) clean and make a habit of washing the wiper blades as well.

Lighting controls

Your car will have two white side lights, two red rear lights, two red reflectors, a white lamp to light the rear number plate, and headlights for driving at night. The light switch normally puts the side, rear and number plate lights on together, and then switches the headlights on as well. There will be two settings (usually operated by a separate switch) for the headlights—main beam, and 'dipped' for use when the main beam would dazzle. As we have already said, most cars have a warning light to show when the headlights are on main beam.

Horn

The button operating the horn is often in the middle of the steering wheel on top of the steering column. But it may be on the end of the direction indicator switch, or on some other fitting that can be reached without taking either hand off the rim of the steering wheel.

Ignition switch and starter

Every car has a switch, usually operated by a key. This switches on the electrical circuits necessary to start, and run, the engine. There is generally a red warning light which comes on as soon as the key is turned to show that the circuits are connected.

In some cars the starter is combined with the ignition switch and is worked by turning the key further in a clockwise direction. In others there is a separate knob, switch or button which has to be operated after the ignition has been switched on. It is important to release the starter as soon as the engine starts, and never to use it when the engine is running. Otherwise serious and expensive damage can result.

Choke

All cars have some form of choke, which is a device to help start the engine when cold. By pulling the knob out you get more petrol into the mixture of petrol and air which the engine uses. How far you need to pull it varies from car to car and depends on how cold the weather and engine are.

Always remember to push the choke in again as soon as the engine warms up. If you don't you will harm the engine and waste petrol. The engine will also run unevenly and too fast; this could be dangerous, and will certainly make driving more difficult.

Some cars have automatic choke devices which do away with the need for a separate choke control.

3 The driving mirror

The correct and frequent use of the driving mirror is so vital to good driving that the whole of this chapter is devoted to it.

How to adjust it

You must get the best possible view through the mirror. In most cars you will be able to adjust the mirror so that it reflects three, if not all four, sides of the rear window. You can then see anything that is framed by these lines. But in most saloon cars some parts of the bodywork will get in the way and cause blind spots (see Fig. 3).

These blind spots can be overcome by fitting mirrors outside the car, either on the front wings or on the windscreen pillars. When properly adjusted, these mirrors will help you to see the side areas which are not reflected in the inside mirror. Even then, there may still be some blind spots, so this chapter also describes how to allow for these.

To set the inside mirror correctly, sit in your normal driving position and move the mirror, holding it by the edges to avoid fingermarks, until you get the best possible view through the back window (especially to the offside) without moving your head.

Adjusting outside mirrors is not quite as simple, even if you can reach one of them from the driver's seat. But you must get them set properly. This is easier to do if you get somebody to help you. Many of them have a spring-loaded joint, so that they should flick back into position if they are knocked. But they sometimes remain displaced after a knock so it is always worth checking them before you get into your car.

Most inside mirrors are made of flat glass, and being close to the driver's eyes they give a clear picture of the road behind.

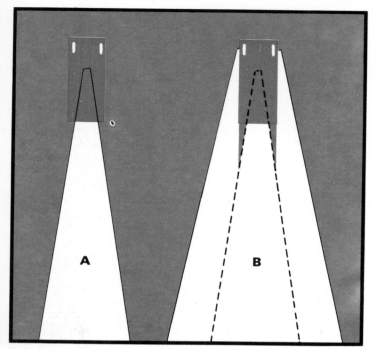

Fig. 3

How outside mirrors help to reduce blind spots

A   area seen with inside mirror only.

B   area seen with inside *and* outside mirrors.

Outside mirrors are usually made of curved (convex) glass, because they are farther from the eyes and this is the only way they can be made to cover a wider field of view.

It is more difficult to judge the position and speed of other vehicles when seen in a convex mirror, and you will need practice before you can do it accurately. You will learn more quickly if you make a habit of using the outside and inside mirrors together. Compare the different views they give of the same situation.

As an exercise, stop your car on the left of the road (choose somewhere sensible) and then watch the traffic approaching from behind through your mirrors. Try to pick out a slow-moving vehicle and then follow its progress until it passes you. As it gets closer, check what you see in the mirrors by looking round through the back window. Then compare what you see in the inside mirror with what you see in the outside one. The vehicle will seem smaller in the outside mirror than it does in the inside one. And because it looks smaller it will seem farther away than it really is. In other words, a vehicle seen in your outside mirror

A car seen in your outside mirror may be closer than you think.
In both these photographs the car is the same distance away, but it is
seen in a *convex* mirror (*above, top*) and a *flat* mirror (*above, lower*).

may be closer than you think. You can also practise this at suitable
times when you are actually driving, for instance, when you are
on a straight road and a vehicle is following at a steady distance.
But, of course, don't look round to check what you see!

How to use the mirror

The driving mirror is sometimes called the driver's third eye.
Even so, it is often sadly neglected. Just looking into the mirror
is no good. Proper USE of the mirror means looking in good time
and *acting sensibly on what you see.*

You must always use the mirror before signalling, changing
direction, overtaking, stopping normally, or opening your door.

Before moving off, make an extra check by looking round over your right shoulder.

This is one of the few driving rules that are not subject to any exception or qualification. There are three very good reasons for this rule. First, if you look in the mirror you will know what is behind you, how close it is, what it is doing. And you will know whether it is safe for you to make a manœuvre. Second, you must know what is behind you so that you can judge when to make your move. Third, you will know whether you need to give a signal to help drivers behind you. (You may need to give one to drivers or pedestrians in front of you, but that is a point we deal with in Chapter 5.)

The fact that you use the mirror to find out what is behind you, and whether it is safe to make the move you want to, means that you must not leave it too late before you look in the mirror. It is just as important that your signal, which follows your use of the mirror, should not be left too late either. If it is late other drivers won't have time to act on it. So the first rule is: use your mirror in good time.

This leads to the second rule, which summarises a really essential part of good driving—the safe routine of *mirror—signal—manœuvre* (MSM). This means: *never signal without first using the mirror; and do both well before you act*. We shall be referring to this basic routine frequently in the course of this book.

There are two further points to be made about the mirror. We have talked about using the mirror before making any manœuvre, but a good driver should always know as much about the traffic behind him as in front of him. So get into the habit of frequent glances in the mirror, because a lot can happen in a short time.

Finally, it is even more difficult to judge the speed and distance of following vehicles when seen through your mirror at night. This needs a lot of practice. And you will also have to get used to the headlights of following vehicles being reflected in your mirror. If they dazzle you it is better to move your head slightly than to move your mirror—you may forget to readjust it.

Looking round

We have already mentioned that, whatever mirrors are fitted to your car, there will almost certainly be some blind spots behind (see Fig. 3). So, before moving off, you must always look round over your right shoulder, after using the mirror, to make quite sure that you haven't missed anything. Incidentally, other drivers who see you do this will know that you are waiting to move off.

Summary

1

All mirrors should be properly adjusted.

2

Outside mirrors help to reduce blind spots.

3

Learn to judge distance and speed of vehicles behind you, as seen in your driving mirrors.

4

Always look in your mirror in good time before changing direction; and in good time to decide whether it is safe to make a move and if a signal is necessary. Remember the safe routine: *mirror—signal—manœuvre*.

5

Use your mirror—frequent glances. You must know as much about what is behind you as in front of you.

6

Before moving off, always make an extra check by looking round over your right shoulder.

4

Beginning to drive: starting, changing gear and stopping

Every car user should get into the habit of making regular checks of the vehicle he drives.

Every day he should check:

engine oil;

water in the radiator (if there is one);

that the windscreen and windows are clean.

It is also quite a good idea to make a point of walking round your car at least once a day to check that there is nothing obviously wrong—a tyre going down, for example.

Every week at least he should check:

tyres—to see that they are at the right pressures (the car owner's handbook will give these);

lights and indicators—to see that they are all in working order;

battery—to make sure it is topped up.

These checks are, of course, quite apart from the regular servicing checks that every car needs to keep it reliable and safe. Owners' handbooks show how often these are necessary for individual cars.

There is also a drill—rather like a simple form of 'cockpit drill' in aircraft—which you should use every time you get in your car. This is:

1 Are all the doors properly **closed and locked?**

2 Is your driving seat in the **right position?**

3 Are the mirrors clean and **properly adjusted?**

4 Have you, and your passengers, **put on your seat belts?**

5 Have you enough petrol?

Starting the engine

Having made these preliminary checks and settled yourself comfortably in the driving seat, you can now begin the drill for starting the engine (see Fig. 4):

1 Check that the handbrake is on by trying to pull it on further.
2 Check that the gear lever is in neutral. If it is, it will feel slack and you will be able to move it quite easily and fully from side to side.

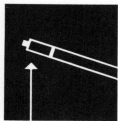

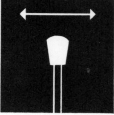

Handbrake on   **Gear lever** in neutral   **Choke** if necessary

Ignition: switch on by turning key (to 1st position only in most cases). This also puts on the ignition warning light.

Starter: turn key further; or use separate switch if fitted.

Engine running: release key (or switch) immediately; use accelerator as necessary; return choke as soon as possible.

Fig. 4
Engine starting drill

3 Pull the choke out if necessary. (You will soon know whether you need 'choke' for your car and, if so, when and how much.)

4 Switch on the ignition and check that the ignition light and oil warning light (if fitted) come on.

5 Operate the starter.

6 Release the starter key or knob as soon as the engine starts.

On some cars it may be necessary to press the accelerator while operating the starter. On others this would upset the air and petrol mixture and make the engine difficult to start. Instructors will be able to tell learner drivers what is best for their particular cars.

If the engine does not start first time, don't keep the starter motor going. Release the key or knob, wait a few moments and then try again. When the engine starts, the accelerator may need pressing *slightly* to keep the engine running. But, as soon as it runs smoothly, take your foot off the accelerator so that the engine is running at its normal 'tick over' or 'idling' speed. If the choke has been used, push it right in again as soon as the engine is warm enough to run without it.

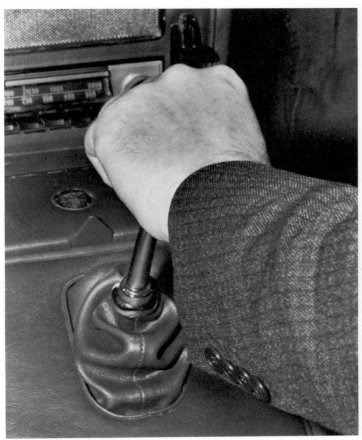

An important part of the starting drill is to check that the gear lever is in neutral. Hold the knob and not the stem, even when exerting sideways pressure.

The red ignition warning light will usually glow while the engine is ticking over. If it does not glow, this may be because the engine is running too fast. (Have you remembered to push the choke back?) But the ignition light should go out almost as soon as the accelerator is pressed down. Check that it does. The oil pressure warning light (if fitted) should also go out when the engine is running. If either light stays on, switch the engine off and have the system checked.

Moving off from rest

When you are sitting properly in the driving seat and the engine is ticking over smoothly, you are ready to get the car moving:

1 Press the clutch pedal right down with your left foot, and hold it down.

2 Move the gear lever from neutral into first gear. (If you can't get the lever into first gear, move it back into neutral,

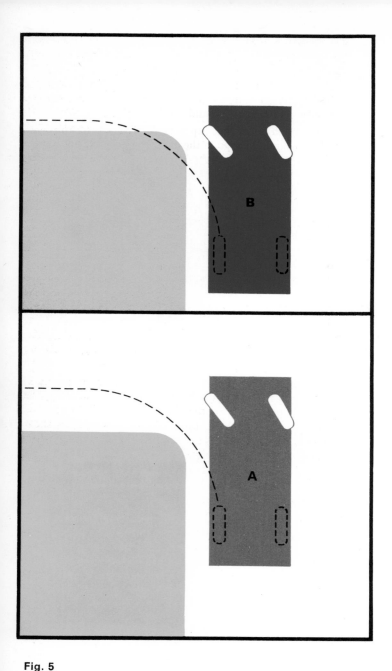

Fig. 5

You cannot steer your back wheels

and you must make allowance for this when turning corners. The
back wheels will not follow the front ones, but will take a short cut
along with the tail of the car, as shown in B. The correct position
for turning a corner is shown at A.

let the clutch pedal up, and then press it down again. Now try again to put the gear lever into first gear. You may need to do this more than once.)

3 Press the accelerator down slightly with the right foot and hold it there, perfectly steady. ('A lively, even hum' describes the noise your engine should be making at this point.)

4 Let the clutch pedal come up very slowly and smoothly until you hear a slight change in the engine noise. (This change in engine noise means that the clutch is at biting point—that is, the two clutch plates are touching—see page 8. With experience you will be able to 'feel' the biting point.)

5 Hold the clutch pedal *quite still* in this position.

6 Now make your final safety checks:
  (*a*) use your mirror;
  (*b*) then look round over your right shoulder—take your time.

7 Decide whether you need to give a signal to show that you are going to move off—ask yourself if there is any other road user (including pedestrians) anywhere near you who would be helped by a signal.

8 If a signal is necessary, give it, either by direction indicator or by arm. (The signal shown in the Highway Code for moving out to the right.)

9 When you are sure it is safe to move off, without getting in the way of anyone else (look round again if necessary), let the clutch pedal come up a *little* more—still slowly and smoothly. At the same time, release the handbrake—remember to put your hand back on the steering wheel straightaway. The car will begin to move.

10 Press the accelerator further gradually down to speed the car up; and at the same time let the clutch pedal come right up—still smoothly—and then take your left foot off it.

Getting these actions in the right order, and doing them smoothly and gently enough, are among the most difficult things a new driver has to learn. Don't hurry them. As with so much else, practice makes perfect. Once the knacks of holding the clutch pedal at biting point, and of not letting it up too fast, have been learnt the whole process of getting the car moving will soon become second nature. But you must get these right before you can make any further progress in learning to drive. Choose a quiet, level road for practising how to move off.

Steering

After learning the drill for starting the engine and moving off, it is as well to get some idea of the feel of the steering before going to the next stage—learning to change gear.

The best way to do this is to find a quiet, straight road. Go through the drills for starting the engine and moving off, and then practise steering the car, at slow speed, in first gear. Learn to keep the car moving parallel to the kerb, and fairly close to it—about three feet away. Don't look at the front of your vehicle; look well ahead and avoid jerky movements of the steering wheel.

When you can steer a straight course with both hands on the steering wheel, try it with only one hand. Again, practise this until you can steer a straight course with either hand. As you take one hand off the wheel, stiffen your other arm slightly so that you do not pull the wheel down and swerve.

The reason for practising steering with one hand is *not* so that you can drive like this, but because there will be times—for example, when you are changing gear or giving signals—when you will have only one hand free for steering. And it is most important that at these times you don't let the car wander from side to side.

Stopping

Having learnt how to get the car moving—even if only slowly in first gear—you should next learn how to stop it. Although you will be on quiet roads with little traffic in the early stages of learning to drive, the drill for stopping (except in an emergency) is always the same. So it is as well to learn it thoroughly from the beginning.

You nearly always have to use the footbrake at some time during the process of stopping. How much pressure you need to put on the brake pedal will depend on how fast you are going and how quickly you need to stop. But there is one golden rule: never jam the brakes on hard unless there is a real emergency.

You should always use the footbrake 'progressively'. This means that you should put a fairly light pressure on the brake pedal to start with, gradually increasing it as the brakes begin to act. Then, when the car has slowed enough, ease off the pressure so that it finally stops smoothly. There should be little or no brake pressure by the time the car actually stops. This is not only good and safe driving; it gives other drivers time to react, and prevents locked wheels and skidding; it also saves wear and tear on brakes, tyres and suspension.

Here is the drill for stopping:

1 Use the mirror.

2 Decide whether you need to give an indicator or arm signal to show that you are going to stop.

3 If a signal is necessary, give it.

4 Take your right foot off the accelerator (the engine will begin to slow down and this will help to brake the car, as explained in Chapter 2, page 7).

5 Move your right foot on to the brake pedal and push it down, lightly at first and then gradually harder.

6 Just before the car stops, press the clutch pedal right down

with the left foot. (This will disengage the engine from the driving wheels and prevent it from stalling.) Don't do this too soon, or you will lose the help of engine braking.

7 Ease the pressure on the brake pedal as the car stops (unless you are on a slope).

8 When the car has stopped, apply the handbrake.

9 Put the gear lever in neutral.

10 Take both feet off the pedals.

This is not a difficult drill, but like everything else it needs practice so that you can stop the car just where you want to. Pick out a particular point and see how near to it you can stop. It is better to find yourself stopping short than running past— you can always ease off the brakes and run forward a bit more. Pulling up at the kerb needs practice in steering too—both hands must be on the steering wheel.

In the next part of this chapter we shall be talking about changing into higher gears. Generally, you can stop the car without changing gear, although in some special situations, which we will discuss later, it may be necessary to change to a lower gear.

Changing gear

Having learnt how to get the car moving in first gear, and how to steer and stop it, you are ready to learn how to change up and change down—to which we referred briefly in Chapter 2.

As we said then, the purpose of the gears is to enable the driver to match the engine power to the speed of the car and the load it has to move. This is done by bringing different sizes of gear wheel into contact with the drive from the engine. And this, in turn, is done by moving the gear lever from one gear position to another.

Good gear changing depends on two things—knowing when to change, and knowing how to change. *When* is very much a matter of judgment and practice in matching the engine speed, by using the gears, to the work you are asking the engine to do. Until this judgment becomes second nature, as it will with experience, listening to the sound of the engine will help you to decide when you need to change gear.

There are no hard and fast rules about the speed at which you should change up from first to second gear; or down from third to second. This depends on the car you are driving and whether you are moving on the level, uphill or downhill. What we can say is that you should change up if you are going so fast that your engine begins to run too fast; and down if you are going so slowly that the engine begins to labour. Learners will, of course, be guided in this—as in all other matters—by their instructors. Guidance about the range of speeds for which the various gears on a car are designed will also be found in the owner's handbook— study this if you possibly can.

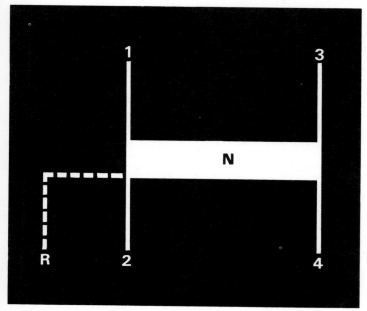

Fig. 6
A typical arrangement of gear positions

Now for *how* to change gear. First of all, as we said in Chapter 2, you need to know the various positions of the gear lever in your car without having to look down. Fig. 6 shows a typical arrangement of the gear positions in a car with four forward gears. Notice again the neutral area in the middle.

We have already been through the drill for getting into first gear and starting off. As your car begins to go faster, you need to change up through the gears, one by one. The drill is the same, whether you are changing from first gear to second, second to third, or third to fourth. Here it is, assuming that the gear lever is to the left of the driver:

Changing up

1 Left hand on the gear lever.
2 Press clutch pedal right down with the left foot and at the same time let the accelerator pedal come right up (but don't take your foot off it).
3 Move the gear lever to the next highest gear position.
4 Let the clutch pedal come up smoothly, and press the accelerator gradually. At the same time, put your left hand back on the steering wheel.

The reason for releasing the accelerator at stage 2 is to let the engine speed drop, because it needs to be lower to match the higher gear, and so give you a smooth gear change. Timing the movement of the gear lever, so that when the clutch pedal comes up the engine speed is just right for the new gear, is a matter of judgment which comes with experience. Once again, there are no hard and fast rules, but your judgment can be helped by listening to the sound of the engine at different road speeds.

The drill for changing down is very much the same. The main difference is that you need to raise the engine speed to get a smooth change instead of letting it drop. In detail the drill is:

Changing down

1 Left hand on the gear lever.
2 Press clutch pedal right down with left foot, at the same time keeping some pressure on the accelerator pedal.
3 Move the gear lever to the next lowest gear position.
4 Let the clutch pedal come up smoothly, and press down a little more on the accelerator pedal. At the same time, put your left hand back on the steering wheel.

How much pressure you will need to keep on the accelerator pedal at stage 2, and how much extra you will need at stage 4, will depend on the speed of the car and on how fast you need the engine to run to match this speed at the time you let the clutch pedal come up. Again, the sound of the engine will help you to judge this.

Once you get used to it, changing gear is quite a simple process. Nowadays nearly all cars have 'synchromesh' on all or most of the forward gears. This is a device which matches (synchronises) the speed of the gear wheels so that the teeth of the wheels are moving at the same speed when they mesh together. Although this means that it is easy enough to get the gear lever into the position you want, there are one or two points you should always remember about changing gear.

Never rush gear changing. Smooth, even movements are best. Never force the gear lever. It will need some pressure on the pull or push when you are moving it, because you are disengaging one pair of gear wheels (as you move from one gear position to the neutral position) and then working the synchromesh (as you move from neutral into the new gear position). But you will soon get used to this. Remember, smooth and even. This calls for a light but firm touch.

You will notice from the diagram of the gear lever positions that changing from first to second gear means moving the gear lever backwards in a straight line. It is a good idea to put a little pressure to the left on the gear lever as you pull it back, to make quite sure that it does not slip to the right (into fourth gear) as it goes through neutral. Similarly, when changing from third to fourth gear, a slight pressure to the right will prevent the gear lever from going across neutral into second gear. There is the same need for this slight sideways pressure on the gear lever when changing down from fourth to third, or from second to first.

Lastly—practise. Learner drivers can get to know the various gear lever positions and practise changing them when the car is standing still with the engine switched off. Sometimes the gear lever will not move freely from one position to another without the engine running. If this happens, leave it alone. A gear lever should never be *forced* into position.

Moving off at an angle

When your instructor is sure that you can move away safely and smoothly straight ahead, you next need to know how to move off at an angle from behind a parked vehicle. With kerbside spaces becoming scarcer every day, and vehicles parking closer, this is something that all drivers must know how to do.

The drill is the same as for moving off straight ahead, up to the stage where you are holding the clutch pedal at biting point (stage 5 of 'Moving off from rest', page 27). Then you go on to your safety checks. But you have to add another one: 'At what angle shall I have to move out, and how far will this take me out into the road?' The answer to these questions will depend on how close you are to the parked vehicle, and how wide it is. The fact that you will have to turn out into the road means that you will have to pay even more attention to other traffic—both from behind and coming towards you. But the last question is still the same: 'Will I get in anyone's way if I move now—and do I need to give a signal?'

When you are sure that it is safe to go, you can get the car on the move using the drill described in 9 and 10 on page 27. But at the same time you have to turn the steering wheel enough to clear the vehicle in front. Don't forget to allow for someone opening a door of that vehicle. Move out slowly, and straighten up as soon as you are clear of the vehicle in front. In particular, be ready to brake—a pedestrian may come out from in front of the parked vehicle.

Moving off uphill

When you can move off smoothly and safely on a level road, either straight ahead or at an angle, the next stage is to learn how to move off up a hill. The tendency will be for the car to roll backwards down the hill, and the steeper the hill the greater this tendency will be. To avoid rolling back, you must be able to use the accelerator, clutch and handbrake together—and properly. Choose a quiet road where the slope is not too steep to practise this. Later, when you have got the idea pretty well, you can try it on steeper hills.

Much of the drill for moving off up a hill is the same as for moving off on the level. But here it is in detail:

1 Press the clutch pedal right down with your left foot and hold it down.

2 Move the gear lever from neutral into first gear.

3 Now press the accelerator down with the right foot—a little further than when starting on the level—and hold it there, perfectly steady. (You need to have the engine running faster because it will have to work harder to move the car uphill than on the level.)

4 Let the clutch pedal come up very slowly and smoothly until the clutch is at biting point—when the engine note changes.

5 Hold the clutch pedal *quite still* in this position.

6 Now make your safety checks:
   (*a*) use your mirror;
   (*b*) then look round over your right shoulder.

7 Decide whether you need to give a signal to show you are going to move off.

8 If a signal is necesssary, give it.

9 Lift the handbrake and release the catch button. *At the same time* press the accelerator down a little more (how much more depends on the steepness of the hill) and let the clutch pedal come up a little more, very gently, until you feel and hear the engine trying to move the car forward.

10 Then release the handbrake smoothly.

11 As the car begins to move forward, press the accelerator down gradually to build up speed, and at the same time let the clutch pedal come right up, still smoothly.

The most common faults are letting the car roll back—because the handbrake has been released too soon; stalling the engine—because the handbrake has been held on too long, or the clutch pedal has been allowed to come up too quickly or too far, or the accelerator pedal has not been held down far enough (or any combination of these).

Try to follow the drill we have set out without rushing it—and practise it until you have really mastered it. When you can start up on a hill smoothly and without rolling backwards, practise doing it from behind a parked vehicle—in other words, at an angle. This means combining the drill with the one on page 32 for 'Moving off at an angle'.

Other points about stopping

We have told you how to stop and suggested practising until you are able to pull your car up, without violent braking, just where you want to. But there are two more equally important points about braking—knowing your 'stopping distance' and knowing the proper way to stop in an emergency.

Knowing your stopping distance

The Highway Code says, 'Leave enough space between you and the vehicle in front so that you can pull up safely if it slows down or stops suddenly.' Although most drivers will agree with this advice, very few seem to put it into practice. This is probably because they don't realise how far they will travel before they *can* stop. It is a 'must' for safe driving to know your stopping distance—that is, the distance your car will travel from the moment you realise that you must brake to the moment the car stops.

Stopping distance depends on five things:

1 How fast you are going.

2 Whether you are travelling on the level, uphill, or downhill.

3 The weather and the state of the road.

4 The condition of your brakes and tyres.

5 Your ability as a driver.

It can also be broken down into two parts—*thinking distance* and *braking distance*. *Thinking distance* depends on how quickly you react. Unless you are tired or unwell, the time it takes you to react will be fairly constant—well over half a second for most people. But the higher your speed the farther your car will go before you react. Even if you are going at only 20 m.p.h., you will travel about 20 feet before your brakes even begin to act. At 30 m.p.h. you will go 30 feet; at 40 m.p.h. 40 feet, and so on.

Speed has even more effect on *braking distance*. At a speed of 20 m.p.h. your brakes, even if they are good, will take about 20 feet to stop your car on a dry road. If you are going at 40 m.p.h. (twice the speed) they will take about 80 feet (four times as far). And this is on top of the thinking distance.

Many people drive much too close to the vehicle in front, or too fast for the road and traffic conditions. This is probably because they think they can pull up in a shorter distance than they really can. And this in turn is often because they cannot judge distances properly. It is all very well to be able to recite a table of stopping distances, but it isn't much good if what you think is 120 feet is really 80 feet.

How good are *you* at judging distance? Try it out. When you are walking in the street, pick out something ahead of you—a parked car or lamp-post—and estimate how far away it is. Then pace it out—a good stride is about a yard—and see how close your estimate was. Even if you are spot on first time, try it again with different objects at different distances.

The real point here is that you should not only know what your stopping distance is at various speeds, but you must be able to judge pretty accurately just what this is in terms of length of road as you are driving. Then you must apply this in deciding how far you should be behind the vehicle in front.

Finally—a very important point. Braking depends above all on how well your tyres grip the road surface. If the road is wet or the road surface is loose, your tyres won't grip so well and your braking distance will be quite a lot longer than on a good dry road. We shall go into this question of braking in bad weather in more detail later on. In the meantime, remember to leave *much more* time and room for braking in bad weather.

Stopping in an emergency

A good and safe driver should never have to brake really hard, still less to make a 'crash stop'. But emergencies do sometimes arise—for instance, a child may run into the road in front of you— so you must know how to stop really quickly. (This, incidentally, is why the 'emergency stop' is included in the Ministry driving test.)

The main thing to remember is that although you must brake hard you should still follow the rule of progressive braking—that is, pushing the brake pedal harder as you slow down. Here are some other points about emergency braking:

Keep both hands on the steering wheel—you need the greatest possible control over steering.

Avoid braking so hard that you lock any of the wheels— even if you don't skid sideways, a wheel sliding along the road is doing very little, if anything, to help stopping.

Leave the clutch pedal alone until just before you stop; this will give some help to your braking, and usually to stability as well.

Leave the handbrake alone. Most handbrakes operate on the back wheels only, and if you put extra braking on them you stand more chance of locking them and skidding. (Of course, if your footbrake fails to work, you will have to use the handbrake.)

If you are not moving on again straightaway after stopping, put the handbrake on and the gear lever in neutral, just as you would after a normal stop.

Many learner drivers tend to put too much pressure on the footbrake, and so lock the wheels. It certainly needs practice to get the right amount of brake pressure to stop the car without locking the wheels. But every driver should remember that the amount of brake pressure he can apply safely depends on the state of the road surface. If it is firm and dry, you can apply very firm pressure. If it is wet or loose, your tyres will have less grip and the wheels will lock more easily, so you cannot use as much pressure.

Finally, don't bother to give a signal if you are having to stop in an emergency. As we have said, you need both hands on the steering wheel. Nor need you make a special point of using the mirror before starting to brake. If you have been using the mirror properly, you should have a pretty good idea of what is behind you anyway. The most important thing, when you are faced with a real emergency, is to stop as quickly as you possibly can, with your car under full control.

Double declutching

You should be able to make a smooth change down into all your gears, including first. As we mentioned earlier, most cars have synchromesh on all or some of the forward gears. But if you don't have synchromesh on first gear, you have an extra problem in making a smooth change down into that gear because you have to do the matching of the gear wheel speeds yourself. You do this by 'double declutching'. Here is the drill:

1 Hand on the gear lever.
2 Push the clutch pedal right down and at the same time let the accelerator pedal come right up.
3 Move the gear lever to neutral and hold it there.
4 Let the clutch pedal come up, press the accelerator pedal quickly and release it immediately.
5 Push the clutch pedal right down and move the gear lever to the next lower gear position.
6 Let the clutch pedal come up, at the same time pressing the accelerator pedal.

The reason for engaging the clutch and using the accelerator at stage 4 is to speed up the gear wheel on the drive from the engine so that, when the gear is engaged at stage 5, the teeth on that gear wheel will be moving at the proper (higher) speed to engage smoothly with the teeth on the new gear wheel.

You will need to speed up the engine quickly by a sudden dab on the accelerator pedal at stage 4, rather than by a gradual pressure. How much you will need to speed up the engine will depend on how fast you are going. The higher your speed, the more you must speed up the engine. You will have to remember that the engine will begin to slow down while you are carrying out stage 5. So double declutching successfully depends very much on being able to make the various hand and foot movements reasonably quickly—a smooth rhythm is what is needed.

You can practise your first double declutching on a quiet, level road when going at a speed within the speed range of the gear into which you are going to change. Later, you can practise on slopes of increasing steepness.

Summary

1
The routine car checks: oil, water, clean windscreen and windows, tyres, lights and battery.
2
The 'cockpit drill'; doors, driving seat, mirrors, seat belts, petrol.

3

The drill for starting the engine.

4

The drill for moving off straight ahead; and the safety checks—using mirror and looking round.

5

The drill for stopping; progressive use of footbrake.

6

Changing gear—up and down; the need for smooth, unhurried movements. Learning the right gear to use for different speeds.

7

Moving off at an angle; the importance of proper steering.

8

Moving off uphill; using the handbrake to avoid rolling backwards.

9

The importance of knowing and judging stopping distances; and of not driving too close to the vehicle in front. Thinking distance and braking distance, and the effect of wet roads.

10

Stopping in an emergency. How to avoid locking the wheels.

11

Double declutching.

5

On the road

Anticipation

In Chapter 1 we say, 'In motoring, anticipation means acting promptly to fit in with what other road users are doing, as well as being able and ready to alter your own course or behaviour as a situation develops.' Now is the time to see how anticipation should be applied on the road. One dictionary definition of 'anticipate' is 'realise beforehand: use in advance'. Anticipation in the motoring sense is simply *making early use of the available information*. In anticipation lies the answer to most of the questions a driver must always be asking himself—questions such as: 'What am I likely to find?' 'What is he going to do?' 'Should I slow down or speed up?' 'Ought I to stop—where exactly?' and so on.

In any traffic situation, there are some things that are obviously going to happen. A driver who uses anticipation can quickly make his mind up what these are. He can then pay more heed to the things that *might* happen. Of course, he needs to check all the time that what he thought would happen *is* happening. And because the traffic situation will always be changing, this process of checking and rechecking must go on all the time.

Take an example. On a clear, dry day a driver on a stretch of dual carriageway with moving vehicles in both lanes will know that the cars around him are likely to continue on their way at about their present speed. He knows a great deal about what is happening, and what is likely to happen, around him. He can therefore concentrate on other things, such as how far to the next junction and the unexpected event for which any driver should always be ready.

Compare this with the situation of a driver on a cross-country journey who is using a dual carriageway (which happens to be

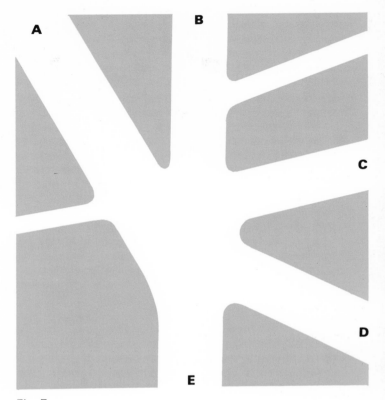

Fig. 7
There are many urban junctions like this one.

the by-pass to a small town). The route is strange to him; it is about a quarter to six on a wet weekday evening and it is getting dark. There are all sorts of vehicles on the road and a succession of roundabouts at each of which traffic is joining, leaving or crossing the by-pass.

This driver has a much more difficult job of anticipation because he cannot tell in advance what traffic and road situation he is going to meet. He may not even be sure of his route. If he is sensible he will be driving much more slowly than the driver in our first example because he needs more time to weigh things up.

A different kind of situation is illustrated in Fig. 7, where the junction lies just out of the centre of a country town and carries local traffic on all roads and through traffic on A—D. None of the roads is wide enough to take more than one vehicle in each direction.

A driver taking the simplest route from E to A can recognise the things likely to affect him reasonably easily. A driver going from A to E has a more difficult job, and drivers coming from B, C or D to A the most difficult of all.

What are the factors here which make the job of anticipation more difficult for some drivers than for others? First, the *direction from which other vehicles approach*. A car coming from A, for example, will not ordinarily affect a driver going from E to A, whereas one from C will. But if the driver from E can see C's right-turn indicator flashing he will have much more information.

The second factor lies in *what other drivers are doing*. If the driver from E can see that the one from C is not only signalling but *moving* in a particular direction, he knows more about his intentions. All this merely underlines the obvious fact that early and accurate information, conveyed by signals, lane selection, change of speed or other driving actions, makes good anticipation by other drivers possible because the two questions 'What is he going to do?' and 'What ought I to do about it?' are easier to answer.

This all adds up to the fact that a driver should not only pick out, from the traffic all around him, information that will or might affect his own actions, but he should also make it easy for other drivers to anticipate his own actions by making his intentions clear in good time.

The use of signals

There are basic signals a driver can and should give to help or warn other road users. Normally (but with one exception referred to later) these are given by direction indicators or brake lights, as shown in Fig. 8. A visual or audible warning system will tell you whether and when your direction indicators are working. But it is up to you to make sure that you have switched on the ones you intended to! Make sure, too, that indicator signals are cancelled when your movement has been completed.

If your vehicle is not fitted with direction indicators or brake lights, or if they are not working, signals can be given by arm as shown in Fig. 8. When using arm signals, give them clearly and decisively, using the full length of the arm. There is one situation in which an arm signal should be used—when slowing down or stopping for pedestrians to use a zebra crossing. Not only is this a positive warning to following drivers, but it helps the pedestrian to realise what you are doing—he cannot see your brake lights.

The important thing about signals, whether given by indicator or arm, is that they must be given *in good time* and for long enough for you to be as sure as you can be that other road users have seen and recognised them. You must allow other road users to see your signal, realise what you are going to do, and take their own action. This sounds fairly simple. But it isn't quite as simple as it sounds. There are times when a signal given *too* soon may confuse rather than help—for instance, when you are going to turn off and there are several turnings very close together. The general rule is:

'Give signals in good time, but watch out for situations which call for special care in timing.'

Drivers are sometimes in doubt about two questions: 'Should indicator signals be confirmed by arm signals?' and 'Should arm signals be confirmed by indicators?' The short answer to both questions is: 'Never as a routine'. For most intended changes of direction, an indicator is better than an arm signal. Usually, it shows up well and can be seen more easily (especially at night) and given for longer. But, again, there may be exceptions. For example, imagine that you are going to turn off to the right, but just before you get to the turning you need to pull out to pass a stationary vehicle parked on the left. You will have given a right-turn indicator signal well before you pull out. But an arm signal as well, after you have cleared the parked vehicle, could help a following driver to realise that you are going to stay out towards the middle of the road for your right turn.

Much the same applies to the other related question: 'Should I give a slowing down signal by arm as well as an indicator signal to turn left or right?' The important signal here, and the only one necessary, is the right- or left-turn indicator signal. This itself tells anyone behind you what you are going to do—which will include slowing down to make the turn. You must, of course, give the signal in good time, but it can't help anyone if you spend some of this time giving a slowing down signal before you turn. Indeed, it may confuse a driver behind you. A slowing down signal before your direction signal might make him think you are going to stop on the left—although in fact your real intention is to turn right. And if he begins to act on such a misunderstanding, both you and he could be in trouble.

Before leaving the subject of direction indicators, a further word of warning about the importance of timing your signals. The Highway Code now recognises the use of the left-turn indicators as meaning also 'I intend to stop on the left' (see Fig. 8). Be careful about using them for this purpose if there is a junction on the left and you are intending to stop *beyond* the junction. A driver waiting to come out from that junction might assume—though he should not—that you are going to turn left. It will usually be better not to use the indicators to indicate stopping until you are past the junction.

Another point about stopping—but this time concerned with giving signals early enough. Most drivers react quickly when they see the brake lights of the car in front come on. But brake lights do not light up until the brake pedal is pressed, and even then some downward movement of the pedal may be necessary before they come on. So there is always a time lag between the moment you decide to brake and the moment your brake lights tell a following driver that you are braking. So here is another good reason for beginning to brake in good time. Not only will you be able to reduce speed more gradually, but your brake lights will

Direction indicator signals

I intend to move out to the
right or turn right

I intend to move in to the
or turn left or stop on the l

Arm signals

I intend to move out to the
right or turn right

I intend to m
left or turn le

Fig. 8

The use
of signals

Arm signals to perso

I want to go straight on

Stop light signals

I am slowing down or stopping

o the

I intend to slow down or stop

This signal should be used when slowing down or stopping at zebra crossings

ntrolling traffic

want to turn left

I want to turn right

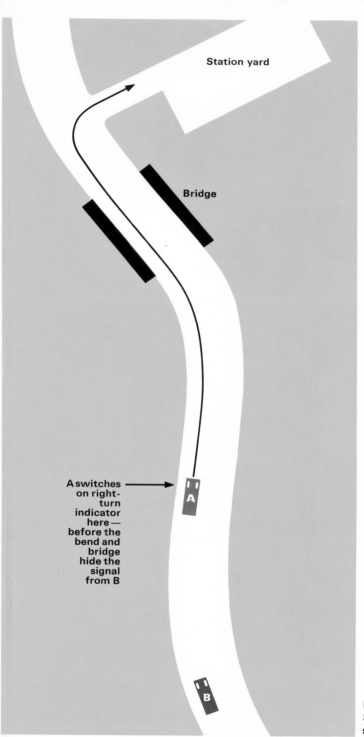

Station yard

Bridge

A switches
on right-
turn
indicator
here —
before the
bend and
bridge
hide the
signal
from B

Fig. 9
Sensible
signalling

come on earlier and so be more helpful to following drivers.

So far we have talked mainly about what signals to give and when. A point which sometimes bothers drivers is: 'Need I give a signal at all here?' It is sometimes said that if a driver positions his vehicle properly, everyone will know where he is going and what he is going to do; so no signals are necessary. But not every road user is another driver, and in any case positioning is only one of the indications of intention. Of course, if there are quite clearly no other vehicles anywhere near, and no pedestrians anywhere around, there is no need to give a signal. But if there is any doubt at all about whether a signal is necessary, it is better to be safe—give it.

Finally, remember that signals are not instructions to other road users. They are to tell them, in good time, what you intend to do. It is vital to use the correct signal and to make sure before signalling that what you intend to do is safe—by using your mirror first—*mirror—signal—manœuvre*.

Use of the horn

If you are driving properly and safely you will seldom need to use your horn. In fact, you should sound it only if you think that some other road user does not know your vehicle is there when he ought to. Remember that the legal description of the horn is 'the warning instrument'. On narrow, winding roads (which need great care anyway) the use of your horn will obviously help pedestrians or other drivers who cannot see or hear you coming. But don't use the horn when you should be taking some other driving action—slowing down for example.

When you do use the horn, consider how long you will need to sound it. For pedestrians or cyclists whom you intend to overtake. a short note is usually enough. It is not too alarming. Longer emphatic notes are usually more suitable when another driver does not know your vehicle is approaching and there may be an accident if he is not warned.

Above all, remember that using the horn does not give you right of way. Nor does it relieve you of the responsibility to *drive* safely. Neither is it a safety valve to let off steam about the failings of other drivers.

There are certain legal restrictions on the use of the horn. You must not sound it while your vehicle is stationary, or in a built-up area between the hours of half-past eleven at night and seven o'clock in the morning.

Headlamp flashing

The flashing of headlamps has the same meaning as the sounding of the horn, no more and no less. It lets other road users know that you are there. Headlamp flashing should not be used to give *instructions*, or to give information about your *intentions*. But it can be useful, especially on fast roads where there is a high noise level. Supposing, for instance, you are going to overtake and need to start the manœuvre from a considerable distance behind the vehicle in front. If you think that a warning is necessary, it is better to use your headlamps, even in daylight, than your horn which might not be heard.

The use of gears

The ability to change gear easily and smoothly is essential to good driving. Knowing when to change gear is just as important as knowing how to change, because to drive safely you need to use the right gear to match the particular traffic or road conditions. A lower gear gives greater control of the car in most situations. If you want to accelerate, you can do it more quickly in a lower gear. If you want to slow down, a lower gear gives a greater degree of engine braking.

Broadly speaking, the more powerful your engine the less frequently you will need to change gear. This does not mean that if you have a powerful car you do not need to use the gears, or that you have to change gear incessantly in a car with a small engine. Whatever car you drive, you must get to know how it performs and handles—uphill, downhill, round corners, loaded and unloaded. And this includes its performance in each of its various gears.

We shall be talking about automatic transmission in a later chapter. Here we shall deal with manual gear changes, in which the driver must always think for himself, weighing up the need for a change of gear and then making it. Get into the habit of thinking ahead about gears, which means sizing up the situation well in advance and knowing whether the gear you are in is going to be the right one for dealing with it. Sometimes, when overtaking for example, changing to a lower gear before you begin to pass will give the extra acceleration you may need in order to do it safely. Again, if you see that traffic ahead is likely to cause a check, change down in good time so that you can speed up more easily and smoothly as the situation clears.

The right gear to use will depend upon the situation you are in. The main thing is to make sure that the gear you use is the right one for the job. Driving in second gear and 'slipping the clutch' to keep the car moving, when you should really be in first gear, is bad driving.

When you increase speed, don't accelerate fiercely or for too long in the lower gears. This will only make a lot of annoying and unnecessary noise, and may harm your engine.

The clutch should always be let in as soon as possible after the gear lever has been moved into a new position. Driving with the clutch out is one kind of 'coasting'. This means that although the car is moving it is not being driven by the engine. (The other kind of coasting is to allow the car to run with the gear lever in

When a car is driven round a bend or corner, extra weight is thrown on to the front wheel on the outside of the curve. This overloading is increased if the brakes are applied at the same time.

neutral.) Any form of coasting is wrong, because it lessens the driver's control of the car, and particularly of steering and braking. Of course, technically a vehicle is coasting while a gear change is being made, or when the clutch is pushed out just before stopping. This is unavoidable. The important thing is to keep unavoidable coasting down to the shortest possible distance.

Some drivers, especially learners, worry too much about losing speed while they are changing gear and therefore tend to rush their gear changing, instead of doing it deliberately. In fact, a vehicle will normally keep moving for a far longer distance than is necessary to change gear.

All drivers should be able to change readily into bottom gear, even if it has no synchromesh, without having to bring the car to a stop.

The use of brakes

Proper use of the brakes is another vital factor in good driving. Yet many drivers (even some who call themselves skilled) do not seem to know the principles of safe and controlled braking. Braking systems on modern cars are good and efficient, but however well brakes are maintained they are only as good as the drivers who use them. And even good brakes cannot do the impossible.

A moving car is in its most stable condition when it is being driven forward at a constant speed and in a straight line. When the brakes are applied the balance of weight shifts forward. This means that the front tyres grip the road more and the rear ones less. Because the front tyres are gripping more, the car gets more difficult to steer. This change in weight towards the front, plus the greater difficulty of steering, makes it unsafe to apply the brakes hard except when travelling on a straight course. The harder a car is braked, the greater the shift in weight. The faster the speed at which it is braked, the more difficult it is to keep the car under full control.

Hard braking while on a *curved* course, such as a bend or corner, will have even more serious results. The weight of the car, and a considerable proportion of its momentum as well, will be thrown outwards as well as forwards. The tyre on the front wheel which is towards the outside of the curve will be considerably overloaded and will be gripping the road surface much more than the other tyres (see photograph on page 47). This extra grip can act as a sort of anchor and make the car go into a severe skid. Such a skid can be so sudden and unexpected that the car gets out of control. Skidding will be discussed more fully in a later chapter, but we have mentioned it here because harsh and uncontrolled braking is one of the chief causes of skidding.

Ideally, any slowing down should be gradual and smooth, by making the brake pressure light at first and then increasing it. You can get very near this ideal by good anticipation, so that you give yourself time to spread your braking over *a good distance*. The difference in safety and peace of mind of all concerned (including passengers) between braking a car to a standstill from 20 m.p.h. in, say, 60 feet, and stopping it from the same speed in half that distance is obvious. But this is what progressive braking is all about—and there is a dividend of reduced wear and tear on brakes, tyres, and car suspension.

Gentle and progressive braking goes with early braking. Late and fierce braking is the sign of a bad driver. Of course, you must always be ready to brake very firmly if the unexpected happens, but if you anticipate properly the need will seldom arise. Never drive so fast, or so close to the vehicle in front, that you would need to use full braking to keep out of trouble. If the driver behind you is too close, it is a good idea to drop farther from the vehicle ahead. This will give you more space for braking and therefore reduce the chance of a bump from behind because the driver who is following will also have more time to stop. If you spread out a bit, he may even follow your example.

To use the brakes properly, you need to take into account:

1 Your own speed of reaction.
2 The mechanical condition of your car—particularly the brakes, steering and suspension.

3 The type of tyres fitted, their condition and pressures.

4 The size and weight of your vehicle, and your load if any.

5 The gradient of the road and whether it has a camber or bend.

6 The weather and visibility.

7 The road surface—whether it is rough, smooth, loose, wet, muddy, or covered with wet leaves, ice or snow.

In other words, first know your car. Then, if you are driving with proper anticipation, and paying attention to the state of the surface of the road, you will have plenty of time and distance over which to spread your braking and so avoid skids. Prevention is better than cure. No system of skid control is so effective as driving in a way which keeps you out of skids.

Finally, a reminder about the brake pedal. When you take over a different car, get the feel of its brakes at the earliest opportunity.

The handbrake

Generally, when the vehicle is stationary the handbrake should be applied. When stopped at traffic lights or in a traffic block, for example, you should apply the handbrake and then put the gear lever in neutral. When it is clear that the wait will be very short (for instance, if you are in or behind a stream of traffic and the leading vehicles are beginning to move off) the use of the footbrake only may be safe and sufficient. But, as a general rule, you are safer with the handbrake on whenever your vehicle is stationary. However careful you are, a foot can slip off a pedal, especially if your shoes are wet. Or, if you are bumped from behind, your foot can be jarred off the brake pedal. (You may argue that if a moving vehicle runs into the back of another one which has stopped, the immediate effect will be less if the driver of the stationary vehicle has *not* applied the handbrake. This may be so, but what about the secondary effect? The vehicle that is hit would certainly be pushed further forward—much more violently, and possibly into another vehicle or a pedestrian.)

When you stop in a traffic stream, leave a good gap between your car and the one ahead, without undue waste of road space, of course. This will give you room to move forward a few extra feet if you see the driver behind coming up too fast to stop. It can certainly pay to keep an eye on the mirror while you are waiting to move off. When you are stopped on an uphill slope, there are other reasons for leaving a good gap. The car in front might run back before starting off.

The use of the handbrake when stationary is even more important in a car with automatic transmission. We shall look at the reasons for this in a later chapter.

Braking in general

To sum up, safe and controlled braking needs early appreciation of the traffic situation (anticipation), followed by gentle but firm and progressive application of the brakes so that you can spread your braking over the longest possible distance.

Learner drivers should regard the correct use of the brakes as one of the most important skills they will need to master. The fact that it is apparently so simple to press a pedal (or pull a lever) to make a vehicle slow down or stop tends to hide the fact that there are physical laws governing the momentum of a vehicle. As we have tried to show, the greatest safeguard for all drivers, new and experienced, lies in taking action in time and so 'spreading the load'.

Finally, remember that when you brake there will usually be other drivers who will be affected by your action. So apply the safe routine—*mirror—signal—manœuvre*. Always use your mirror before you brake (unless you are having to make an emergency stop) and consider whether a signal is necessary.

Driving ahead

On the road, as elsewhere, every picture tells a story. To be able to detect and interpret the vital clues in any driving situation, a driver needs to be alert and observant. Both these qualities call for continuous concentration, and no driver can be expert (which is another way of saying good and safe) unless he gives his driving undivided attention all the time. The good driver is constantly assessing the movement of *all* road users on the *whole* stretch of road on which he is travelling so that he can see things from an all-round point of view and is ready to react quickly and properly. The talkative man often becomes a silent one behind the wheel. This is simply because his mind is on his driving. But if you notice that the driver in front of you (or behind) is constantly talking and looking at his passenger—watch him. His mind cannot be entirely on his driving.

We have said before that good anticipation depends in the first place on early information. You get this by observing and judging the scene around you. As you drive, take in as much as possible of what you see in front, behind and to each side. Keep your eyes moving. Look well ahead and then near to you, and give frequent glances in the mirror. Keep a check from time to time on your warning and instrument lights. All this helps to make and keep you alert. Changing your field of view also helps to reduce eye strain.

Figure 10 shows some of the areas over which a driver's eyes should constantly be moving, according to the traffic and conditions through which he is passing. No other vehicles are shown in the diagram but there are obvious places which a driver must watch. As he approaches junction 3, for instance, the middle distance view (C) will be very important. But he must still watch the immediate area (A) and have time to spare for his mirror view (B) to see whether any vehicles have turned out of the

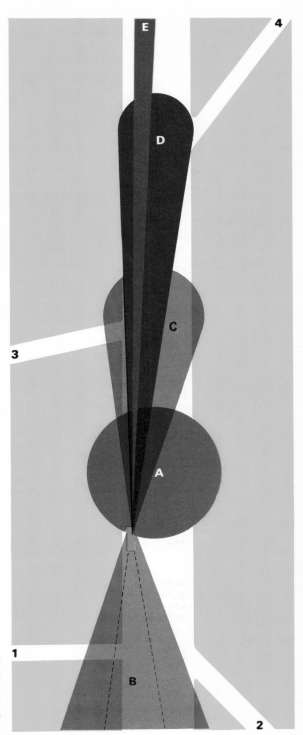

Fig. 10
The
changing
areas of a
driver's
vision

junctions (1 or 2) he has just passed. On top of this, he must take in view D to cover what is happening at junction 4, and also spare a glance for the long range view E. Truly, eyes everywhere! And the worse the weather, the more important—and the harder—these views are to pick out.

Here are some of the main things you should be looking for:
1 Other vehicles and pedestrians.
2 Signals given by other drivers.
3 Road signs and markings.
4 The type and condition of the road surface.
5 Movements by vehicles well ahead of you, as well as the one immediately in front.
6 Side roads or hills ahead—the building line at the side of the road may show these.

Keen observation can give you a lot of useful and varied information. The keener your search the better you will become at reading the road. The clues are there. It is up to you to find them, and use them. Especially in built-up areas, traffic conditions change rapidly and even the smallest detail is significant. Vehicles parked at the side of the road must be carefully watched. A driver who is apparently reading is unlikely to move off—but you cannot be sure that he or a passenger will not open a door suddenly. If someone runs out of a shop and gets into a waiting car, be ready for the driver to move quickly, perhaps without looking round. You may see only a puff of smoke from the exhaust, or the movement of his shoulder as he reaches for the gear lever. Small clues, but important ones which can be valuable to the observant driver. Keep a sharp eye on a driver who has stopped to set down a passenger. He may not use his mirror or look round before he moves off again.

All these pictures bring some message. Getting it properly and quickly often means the difference between a smooth reaction and 'panic measures'.

But however well you train yourself to observe, how much you see will depend on how *well* you can see—in other words, on your eyes. Ask yourself whether you can see as well today as you could, say, a year ago. Vision changes, and we tend not to notice a gradual worsening in our eyesight. It is sensible to have a regular check-up.

Some people have 'tunnel vision'. As the name implies, this means they can see only those objects which lie within a narrow field of vision directly ahead, and not those which lie to the left and right. To see objects in these areas they have to turn their heads, instead of just moving their eyes.

Your eyes are not your only source of information. Your ears can also warn you of what lies ahead. Everyone knows the warning of a fire engine or ambulance horn and bell. But how many drivers would take a factory siren or whistle as warning of a possible increase in traffic near the factory, especially cyclists? School hours, too, are a guide for the careful driver.

Reading the road thoroughly will give you plenty of time to plan, and prevent you from being caught unawares. It is an essential part of anticipation. And besides making your journey safer, it will also make it more interesting. This will help you to arrive relaxed—and in a good temper!

At first, new drivers will naturally be paying most attention to controlling their cars. But they should practise observation and teach themselves to read the road well. You don't have to be driving to practise this particular skill—you can do it as a passenger in a car or a bus.

Road positioning

Normally, you should drive well in to the left. This does not mean that you should drive in the gutter, but simply that you should not drive on the crown of the road. Just how far out from the side of the road you need to drive will depend on the road and the traffic on it. For instance, when driving in a town street where cars are parked at intervals along the kerb, weaving in and out between stationary cars is unnecessary and confusing to other drivers. It is therefore wrong.

Of course, we all have to 'get in' from time to time to help the flow of traffic. But, oncoming traffic and the width of the road permitting, you should normally drive in a line which keeps you clear of parked cars and leaves you room to deal with any of the dangers already mentioned—cars starting off, doors opening or children running out. It would be unsafe to drive very close to the kerb in a narrow street crowded with shoppers, many of whom will be walking or standing near the edge of the pavement. But if you can see in your mirror that the driver of a faster vehicle wants to overtake, and conditions permit, draw as far in to the left as you safely can and so give him as much room as possible.

The key to correct positioning is to be in the right position for the route you are going to take. You will then fit into the traffic flow and cause the least trouble to other road users. If you are turning left or going straight ahead, keep well to the left. If you are turning right, keep just left of the centre of the road.

The correct position for overtaking will depend on the circumstances at the time. This is one of the most dangerous manœuvres if it is not done properly. Always be very sure about what is involved and have things well worked out before going over the centre of the road. Remember that once you cross to the other half of the road you are on a possible collision course—in direct opposition to any approaching vehicle. (We shall be talking about overtaking in more detail in Chapter 11 and about some of the definite restrictions upon crossing centre or other lines marked on the road.)

The free flow of traffic depends very much on how accurately drivers position their vehicles. One thoughtless motorist can hold up streams of traffic. How often have you seen a lorry driver having to heave at his steering wheel just to get another six inches of clearance round somebody who could easily have stopped a yard further back or a foot to the right or left?

One-way streets

In one-way streets, position your vehicle according to whether you intend to turn left or right, or go straight on. If you are turning to the left, keep to the left of the carriageway. If you are turning right, keep to the right. If you are going straight on, be guided by the road markings. Where the road is not wide enough for a middle lane of traffic, you will have to choose the left or the right of the road. Having made your choice of lane, get into it as soon as you can, stay in it, but look out for other drivers who change lanes suddenly.

Traffic often moves very quickly in one-way streets, so keep your eyes skinned and watch out for vehicles overtaking you on each side. If you don't know the area in which you are travelling, you may reach your turn-off point before you expect it and not be able to get into the correct position for taking it without cutting across other drivers. If this happens, don't try a late dash. Drive on in accordance with your position and find another way back on to your route.

Lane discipline

Lane markings do two important things. They ensure that the available road space is used to the best possible advantage, and they guide traffic for the sake of safety. But they are no good for either purpose unless drivers keep to them. Keeping to the proper lane is absolutely vital in present-day driving.

Every road has lanes, whether marked or not. Where they are not marked (or where the markings are hidden), divide the carriageway into appropriate lanes in your mind's eye. Make it second nature to think in terms of lanes. Plan your course to avoid sudden changes and never move from one lane to another without good reason. Weaving in and out or straddling lanes or lane lines is bad driving. Once in your lane, stay in the *middle* of it until you *need* to move to another one.

Unless road signs or markings indicate otherwise, the drill is:

Driving along. Keep to the left-hand lane where conditions allow you to do so. Don't use the right-hand one just because you are travelling fast.

Before changing lanes. Check on the traffic behind (mirror) and signal your intentions in good time. If you find you are in the wrong lane, don't try a last-minute change—stay in it until you can get back on your route safely, even if it means going a bit out of your way.

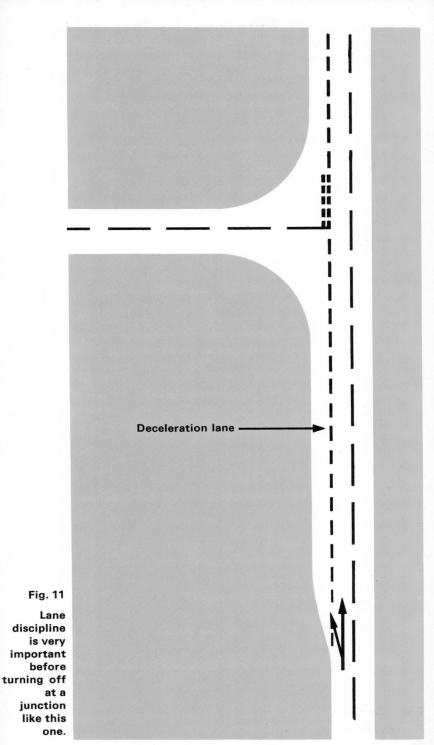

Deceleration lane

Fig. 11

Lane discipline is very important before turning off at a junction like this one.

Approaching a road junction. Look out for road markings or direction signs which may tell you which lane to take. Normally, when intending to *turn left* from a road with *two* lanes in each direction, stay in the left-hand lane. *Going straight ahead* you should normally keep to the left-hand lane unless signs or markings tell you otherwise. Using the right-hand lane defeats its own object if drivers ahead are turning right. When intending to *turn right*, move to the right-hand lane in good time. If you are turning left, don't drive up in the right-hand lane to try to steal a march on other drivers who are correctly positioned on the left. Equally, do not use the left-hand lane when turning right. Trying to change back to the proper lane at or near the junction is a risky business.

On a road with *three* lanes in each direction, when intending to *turn left*, stay in the left-hand lane. *Going straight ahead*, take the left-hand lane (unless there are filter-left traffic signals), or the middle lane. When intending to *turn right*, use the right-hand lane. (We deal with the approach to roundabouts in Chapter 7.)

Some junctions have a deceleration lane which gives you room to slow down for a left-hand turn without holding up vehicles that are not turning left. An example is shown in Fig. 11. Watch out for these and get into the left-hand lane in good time so that you can turn off into the deceleration lane as soon as you reach it.

Remember that every driver is entirely responsible for his car being in the right position on the road. The practical message of this chapter is: 'Stick to the rules; then everybody concerned knows what to expect.'

Summary

1

Anticipation—making continuous use of all that is happening on the road.

2

Signals—when and how to use direction indicators and/or arm signals; the safe routine—*mirror—signal—manoeuvre.*

3

Using the horn—a warning instrument.

4

Headlamp flashing—again a warning signal.

5

Using the right gear for the job—dangers of coasting and slipping the clutch.

6

Proper use of footbrake—the need for early and progressive braking; conditions to take into account.

7

The handbrake—when to use it.

8

Application of safe routine *mirror—signal—manœuvre* **when braking.**

9

Reading the road, ahead and behind.

10

Regular check on eyesight.

11

Road positioning—keeping well to the left; one-way streets; the importance of lane discipline.

12

Stick to the rules; then everyone knows what to expect.

6 Approaching corners and junctions

Corners

Steering

The purpose of the steering wheel is obvious—to turn the front wheels so that the car follows a curved course instead of a straight one. It is equally obvious that the more you turn the steering wheel, the sharper the curve your car will follow.

If this is all so obvious, why have we mentioned it? To give us a chance to say that different cars steer differently—you may have heard the terms 'understeer' and 'oversteer'. A full description of the causes and effects of these differences would be out of place here. What is important is that you should get to know the feel of your car, and how it behaves, when cornering. Don't assume that all cars are alike in this respect. Remember, too, that different loads and speeds will also affect steering—and so will tyre pressures.

Acceleration

The dictionary defines 'acceleration' as 'making quicker' or 'increased speed of motion'. But the accelerator doesn't only speed up the engine when necessary; it also (as mentioned in Chapter 2 under 'Accelerator') does the equally important job of keeping the engine speed at the level you want. The right engine speed is particularly important when it comes to cornering. More important still is road speed—that is, the speed at which your car is moving. Your correct road speed at a corner will depend on how sharp the corner is, whether there is other traffic about, and so on. There cannot be any hard and fast rules about this. You will have to judge for yourself both the proper speed for taking each corner, and the gear which is low enough for that speed.

Some things are certain. First, that your road speed should be at its lowest at the moment you begin to turn the corner. From then on, your car should be 'under acceleration'. This does *not* mean —as the dictionary definition suggests—that you should be going faster as you turn. It means that you should use the accelerator so that the engine is doing just enough work to be driving the car round the corner. In other words, the engine should be just under load. The lower the gear you use the more control you will have just where you may need it most.

Another certainty is that using the accelerator too much on a corner is not only bad driving, but dangerous. It can make tyres lose their grip on the road and so cause a skid. So, 'not too little, not too much'. The important thing is to know just how your car will behave, and to realise that different cars handle differently.

There are, of course, many kinds of corners. The first, and in some ways the simplest, is where no roads join, but the road itself turns, more or less sharply. As we shall see shortly, you have to be in the correct position to take the bend, and also pay attention to the right speed, the proper gear, and—as described above—steering and acceleration.

The second sort of corner is where one or more roads meet, in other words, a road junction. The same principles of steering and acceleration apply here too, as well as observation, anticipation, the use of signals, gears and brakes, road positioning and lane discipline, as discussed in Chapter 5.

Bends

Before dealing with junctions, let us look at bends. This is where the road changes direction, but without the complication of other roads joining it. Some bends are so sharp that they might just as well be described as corners—and, of course, a bend could become a corner to a driver who approaches it too fast!

Left-hand bends

Keep well to the left. Your view will be restricted, so reduce speed. One question to ask yourself is: 'What will I do if the last vehicle to take it has broken down just round the bend out of sight?' Another thought is: 'Suppose someone coming the other way *is* being crazy enough to overtake!' You *can* increase your vision by approaching the bend from a position towards the centre of the road, but this may well tempt you to take the bend faster than is safe. You will also be closer to any approaching traffic and this means less safety margin—especially if someone is coming the other way too close to, or over, the centre line. Finally, unless very careful use is made of the mirror you may mislead or inconvenience following traffic. So, keep well in to the left, slowing down as necessary.

Right-hand bends

A position well to the left will give you the greatest field of view into a right-hand bend. But don't let this tempt or encourage you to enter the bend too fast. On some right-hand bends the camber may tend to tip you towards the left side of the road. This will make the bend harder to turn than you expect. It is too late to find this out when you are in the middle of a bend and your brakes can't help you.

Speed on bends

Your speed should be lowest as you start to take the bend. Then, with your car under acceleration (the engine just pulling), you will have stability and full control. Your passengers will also feel safer and more comfortable.

Junctions

For the rest of this chapter we shall be talking about approaching junctions—a much more complicated business than the corners and bends we have discussed so far, although the same principles of steering and acceleration apply.

Junctions take many forms. Most necessitate some change of direction, if only for proper positioning. The more complex the junction, the more changes of course or direction you will have to consider and, if necessary, make. For example, turning to the left at a junction will almost certainly be simpler than turning to the right; and the difference between turning right from a main road into a side road and turning left into the main road at the same junction can be tremendous.

The possible layout of junctions can vary from a simple T in a village street (*top left*) in Fig. 12 to a complex road system (Fig. 13). Between these two extremes lie a great variety of Y junctions or forks, neat four-square crossroads, roundabouts of varying sizes and shapes, and the staggered or offset junctions where drivers must feel their way (such as in Figs. 14 and 15)—not to mention flyovers and underpasses.

Advance information

As with any other traffic situation, the good driver finds out as much as he can about the junction before he actually reaches it. When you sight a junction ahead the first thing to do is to use your mirror. Then weigh up the kind of situation you are approaching. Note any signs (especially direction signs) and road markings. This will give you all the advance information about the junction, what sort it is, what traffic is behind you, and about the position and course you should take to go through it correctly and safely.

Application of safe routine (MSM)

Dealing with junctions is very largely a matter of turning corners or steering round bends. And even if you are going straight ahead

Fig. 12
Junctions
Some variations on a theme ▶

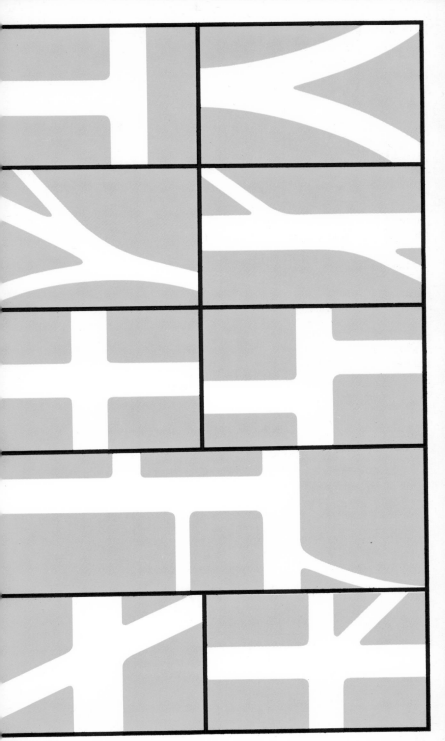

61

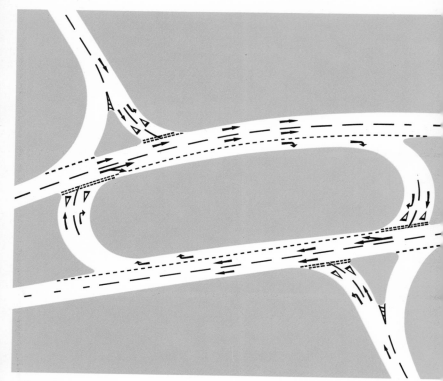

Fig. 13
A complex junction

with no need to do either, a junction is a hazard and you need
to take the same precautions as you would for any other hazard.
This is why the MSM routine (*mirror—signal—manœuvre*) should
be used for all junctions, from whatever direction you are entering them. So, when you are sure what sort of junction it is and
know what you need to do, use the *mirror* again, *signal* (if necessary) and follow with the *manœuvre* itself.

The junction routine (PSL)

We have just mentioned the MSM routine: there is another
which must be applied when you move from one road to another
through any sort of junction. It is PSL—*position—speed—look*.
In detail, the drill when approaching a junction is:

1 Take up position.
2 Adjust speed (by brakes and/or gears).
3 Look right, left, and right again *when you reach a point from
which you can see* whether there is anything in the other
roads—and stop if necessary.

To sum up so far, when you see a junction ahead use your mirror
and look well ahead. As you approach the junction apply the
three steps of the safe routine MSM—*mirror—signal—manœuvre*.

Break down the manœuvre itself into the three steps of the junction routine PSL—*position—speed—look.*

You will then be able to enter the junction with all the information that early observation has given you about conditions behind you and the hazard ahead. You will be on the right course and moving at the proper speed. Then, at the junction, look right, left, and right again and decide whether it is proper to go on or to stop.

In the next chapter we shall be looking in more detail at what a driver has to do *at* a junction in order to enter his 'new' road safely. But before going on, we will look more closely at the things a driver has to look for and consider when approaching a junction or similar hazard, as well as having a closer look at how to use the PSL routine.

Assessing a junction

This means answering a number of questions about it. Here are some, not necessarily in order of importance, which have to be answered for almost any junction:

1 'What sort of junction is it—crossroads, T junction, roundabout, or some other arrangement of roads?'

2 'Do I need to change my position in order to deal with it?'

3 'Are there traffic signals?'

4 'Is there a STOP sign on my approach road, or on any of the other roads?'

Whenever you approach a junction it is necessary to ask yourself what sort of junction it is. In this case, the car coming from the left must give way to traffic on the other road.

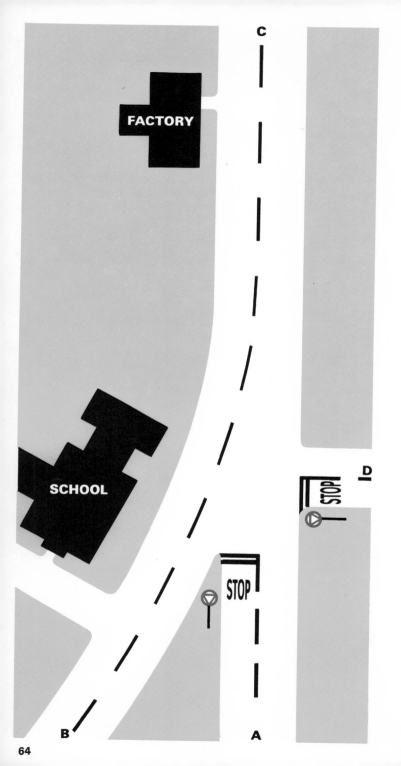

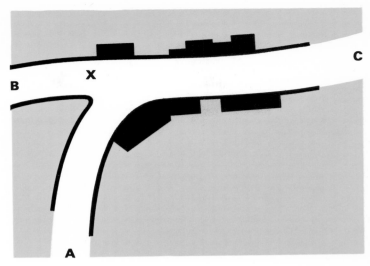

Fig. 15
High walls and buildings make for poor vision

5 'Is there a GIVE WAY sign? If not, where are the GIVE WAY lines?'

6 'Which seems to be the busiest road?'

7 'Is it obvious that I ought to stop anyway, or do I go forward until I *can* see whether or not to stop?'

Dealing with a crossroads can be quite complicated. All the junctions shown in Fig. 12, for example, are different, but nearly all of them might be regarded as crossroads by drivers who know them well. Yet, at many of them, a stranger will have to weigh up which is the main traffic stream and so 'feel his way'. (See Fig. 14.) And as we have seen, the main traffic stream may vary from day to day or even from hour to hour.

There are some junctions where you will be pretty sure that you should stop. Figure 15 shows such a junction—but the place at which you should stop to get a full enough view is not easy to find. A to C is the main road. There are high walls or buildings and no footways. If you are going from A to C you not only have to allow for the traffic from C to B, but also weigh up the risk from traffic going from B to C. Even with GIVE WAY lines at X, you still have to feel your way, because although any traffic coming from B should let you go first (and usually does) there

Fig. 14

An interesting junction Road A comes in on an up gradient while BC is the way to the coast. While this is a busy Y junction, school-children and factory workers use roads A and D. This means that there is often a crossroads in operation and two T junctions as well. Although there are STOP signs on A and D, this is very much a place where a driver must 'feel his way'.

may always be the odd vehicle that doesn't. GIVE WAY lines may be hard to see in bad weather.

Application of the MSM/PSL routines

Let us see how you should use these routines at the junction shown in Fig. 15, when you are going from A to C. First, use the *mirror* and *signal* with the right-turn indicator. You will know who is behind, and following traffic will know that you are going to turn right along road C. Next, the *manœuvre* of making the right turn at the junction. *Position* is obviously critical in such a narrow and restricted place, and *speed* must drop until you are moving so slowly that you just roll forward to make the stop which is obviously necessary here for you to have time to *look* right, left, and right again. You must 'feel your way' so that, in order to see properly, you do not get so far forward on A that you are to some extent in the way of a driver going from C to B. Incidentally, a driver going from C to B must be ready to feel his way forward too.

Narrow corners like this limit your field of vision, and there are many such corners in the streets of older towns. But similar conditions can arise at any junction of narrow roads. And if large vehicles are turning or unloading, there is need for a high degree of careful driving and accurate judgment from drivers. Very careful choice of *position*, low *speed* and a readiness to stop, with a most careful choice of stopping position from which to *look* without blocking other drivers unnecessarily, are all called for in such places.

At more complex road junctions (such as the one illustrated in Fig. 13), you should use the mirror as soon as you see the sign that indicates your need to change lanes or position for your route. Then signal and, provided you can do so safely, change lanes.

You are now ready to weigh up the junction itself or, if it is a very complex one, the first part of it. At most junctions there will be signs and other markings which will enable you to decide on your proper course right through the junction—but give yourself room to see them by leaving a good gap between yourself and the vehicle in front.

More about the junction routine (PSL)

PSL—position

Generally speaking, the earlier you get your vehicle into position the easier it is to do so. Early positioning also helps other drivers to know what you are going to do. Late positioning hinders the flow of traffic and can be dangerous.

In some situations you may need to change *speed* at the same time as you are changing position. In others you may need to change *speed* in order to change *position*, and then to make a further change of speed. But position should be the first thing you think of when approaching and negotiating a junction.

PSL—speed

The process of adjusting *speed* on the approach to a junction can vary in a number of ways. You may need to use the brakes and/or gears in differing order and proportions according to the circumstances. On a more or less level road it may be enough to release the accelerator and wait for your speed to drop. On an uphill slope a change down may be necessary. Again, you may already be in the right gear; or you may need to change down to help you slow down. All this will depend on the amount of traffic, the size and layout of the junction, and whether there are gradients and how steep they are.

You may see the point at which your own road joins another so far ahead that an upward change of gear is necessary to make a reasonably brisk drive to that point. Slip roads and acceleration lanes are examples of this.

Apart from the adjustment of speed to carry you far enough forward at a junction, there is the important question of bringing your speed down low enough to have time to carry out the next step of the routine—looking.

PSL—look

Look right, left, and right again *when you reach a point from which you can see*—and stop if necessary. It may seem too obvious to mention that it is useless to look right and left before you can see what you are looking for. Yet, looking before they can see the whole junction is a mistake made not only by learner drivers. Many an experienced driver has to get himself out of a tight place he should never have got into. Did he look? Did he look before he could really see? Did he allow for the fact that the pedestrians coming along the pavement were blocking his view? Did his adjustment of speed give him *time to look*—and time to stop?

To summarise, we have now looked at several sorts of junctions, including those which call for particularly careful judgment of speed and position where space is limited. We have seen too that a driver may find himself in a large system of road junctions where he actually drives from manœuvre to manœuvre within the same system, changing lanes here, turning or stopping there, and so on. This represents one extreme; between this and the simplest junction lie a multitude of others. But the routine of MSM (*mirror—signal—manœuvre*), with the third step—*manœuvre*—broken down into PSL (*position—speed—look*) is common to them all. The final action of looking—from a position where he can actually see into the whole junction—is essential before a driver can be sure that he can safely turn into, or cross, the junction.

Summary

1

The importance of getting to know how your car behaves in steering round a corner.

2

Judging the right gear and road speed at corners.

3

Cornering 'under acceleration'—not too little, not too much.

4

Keeping well to the left in both left-hand and right-hand bends.

5

Speed at bends.

6

Approaching a junction—the need for advance information; the particular importance of the *mirror—signal—manœuvre* and *position—speed—look* routines.

7

Assessing a junction—the questions to ask yourself.

8

More about the *mirror—signal—manœuvre* and *position—speed—look* routines.

7 Emerging at junctions

At every junction, a driver leaves one road and turns into, crosses or joins another one. This is what is meant by 'emerging'. In Chapter 6 we showed how a driver should deal with a junction up to the point at which he must *look*, and stop if necessary. But what exactly should he look for, and how does what he sees enable him to decide whether to wait or go on?

The most obvious thing to look for is the approach of traffic —particularly from the right, which is the greater danger. The decision to stop is sometimes made for you by STOP signs or traffic signals, or by a policeman or traffic warden. At other places it may be obvious that you will have to wait for a gap in a stream of vehicles before you can join or cross a road. At other times GIVE WAY signs and/or lines will remind you of the particular need to judge the speed and course of other vehicles. GIVE WAY does not necessarily mean that you must come to a stop, especially where you can see into the major road clearly so that you can fit in safely. But you must let vehicles on the major road go first, and not *enter* the junction unless and until you can do so without getting in their way.

If you have stopped at a junction you then have to make a second decision: When is it safe to go on? This may mean looking again and again. Even when traffic is controlled by signals, the green light means only that you may go on if the way is clear. You must still take special care if you are turning left or right and, in particular, you should give way to pedestrians who are crossing (see also Chapter 12). The same applies to junctions controlled by a policeman or traffic warden when you get his signal to move.

At any junction, therefore, you have to decide *whether* to wait or go on. If you stop, you will then have to decide *when* to go on.

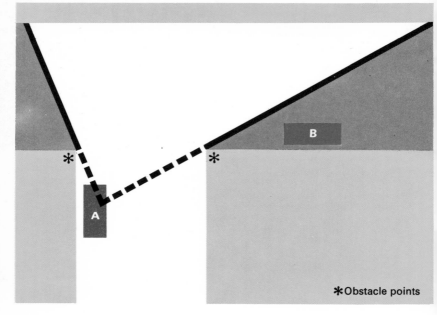

Fig. 16

Obstacle points and the driver's zone of vision

At every corner or junction there is some object or 'obstacle point'(✱) beyond which the driver cannot see. In the diagram above the obstacle points are shown as the corners of buildings at a T junction, but they could equally well be fences, hedges, trees, vehicles or pedestrians. The zone of vision opens up as the driver approaches the corner, but at the point A has reached, which is less than one car length from the corner, he still can't see B coming.

In all cases you need to have a full view. This brings us to the important subject of 'zones of vision'.

Zones of vision

A driver's field of view enables him to see a stretch of the road in front and behind him. His vision is normally limited only by other vehicles or buildings, or by the framing and pillars of the windscreen and windows of his vehicle. Sometimes his view can also be impaired by weather conditions, making it necessary for him to slow down or even stop.

Coming up to a junction is, in some ways, rather like running into a patch of fog. Consider the extreme case of a driver approaching a blind corner in a narrow street, with a lorry or bus behind him. His field of view almost disappears. In front he can see only a strip, a few feet wide, of the road he is to enter. Behind, only a large radiator. This can occur on any road, however wide, when a stream of traffic is approaching a junction. In fact, road

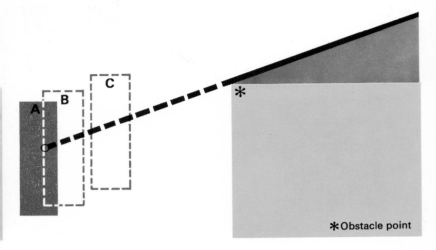

＊Obstacle point

Fig. 17

The nearer an object is to your eyes, the more it blocks your view
In the diagram above it is interesting to note that from A the driver
gets a view to the right while his car is still behind the obstacle line.
If he had approached the junction in positions B or C he would have
to be further forward before getting the same view. At position C his
car is as far in front of the obstacle line as it is behind it at position A.
Always be on the look-out for obstacle points which limit your zone of
vision. They need checking even at that most familiar corner—the one
at the end of the road where you live.

junctions are nearly always places where vision tends to be poor;
yet a good view into the other roads which make up a junction is
essential. This view into the other road or roads is called the
'zone of vision' (see Fig. 16).

Although the zone of vision gets wider as you get nearer the
junction, it is surprising—especially to learner drivers—how
close you must be before it widens enough for you to see far
enough into the other roads. Figs. 17 and 18 show why the last
few feet are so critical in giving you your zone of vision.

How far forward?

Once you have spotted the obstacle points and can begin to see
into the junction, you must decide how far forward to go. There
are two reasons for this. First, you must be far enough forward to
be able to *look*. Second, if you have to wait you must stop in a
safe position. So the answer to the question 'How far forward?' is:
With your eyes far enough forward to be able to look right, left, and

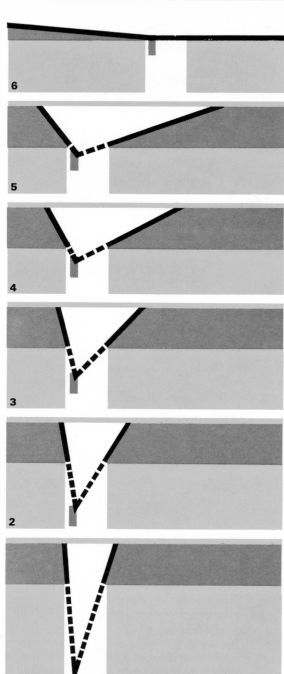

Fig. 18

Widening the zone of vision

Reading upwards from 1 to 5, each successive plan shows the car twice as close to the obstacle line. At 5 the car is 16 times closer than it was at 1, but the zone of vision into the major road has not increased very much. *Only when the driver's eyes are level with the obstacle line can he have a proper zone of vision so that he can look, and act, with confidence.*

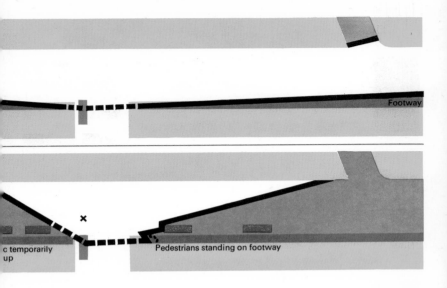

Footway

c temporarily up

x

Pedestrians standing on footway

Fig. 19

How far forward?

Above: The driver's zone of vision is satisfactory when the front of his vehicle is level with the kerb-line and his eyes are on a line with the buildings to left and right. *Below:* The same junction but with quite different conditions. The delivery van parked at the kerbside and the two or three pedestrians standing on the pavement form a screen to the right of the driver, and stationary vehicles block his view to the left. To see enough the driver needs to move forward until his eyes are at point X.

right again, so that you have a full view of the junction before deciding whether *to wait or go on.*

Fig. 18 shows such a position at 6. In the lower diagrams the zone of vision is shown widening as the car moves from positions 1 to 5. But even at 5 it is not wide enough. Notice that at position 6, where there is a proper zone of vision both ways, the driver's eyes are level with the right-hand obstacle point.

Notice that the reference is to 'eyes' and not to the front of the car. Obstacle points can vary from junction to junction. They can even vary at the same junction at different times, as is shown in Fig. 19.

Road width and the zone of vision

We saw in Fig. 17 that your distance from the right-hand obstacle point at a junction is important. Fig. 20 shows why careful positioning is so important, especially on a narrow road, and how little you can see until your eyes are level with the obstacle line. Then you have much the same view as you would have from a

Fig. 20. Zones of vision

The cars above are only one length from the obstacle line, but neither driver has more than a fraction of the zone of vision he needs in order to *look* properly.

In the diagram below, with the cars a length further forward, the zone of vision is still too narrow for the drivers to be able to *look* properly.

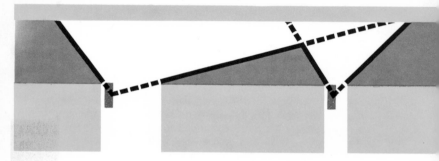

Now, with the drivers' eyes up to the line (*below*), they can see both ways and *look* to some purpose.

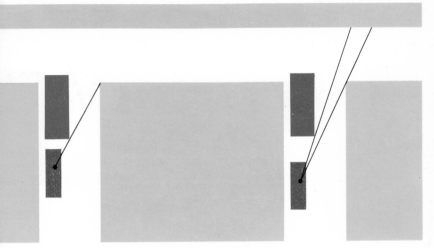

Fig. 21. The vehicle in front at junctions

This shows how your vision can be improved by careful positioning of your car. *Left:* In this position the following driver's zone of vision is completely blocked by the obstacle points. *Right:* From only a few feet further back, it is possible to see something of the road ahead, say, whether it is busy or whether it is a shopping street or bus route.

wider road. Observation, anticipation, positioning—getting far enough forward to *look* without blocking other traffic—all have to be judged very carefully when emerging from a narrow road.

The vehicle ahead

So far we have considered the zone of vision only when the road ahead is clear. A bus or large vehicle in front of you can reduce your zone of vision to nothing at a narrow junction, as Fig. 21 illustrates.

We shall be looking at the question 'How far behind the vehicle ahead?' in greater detail later on. The point to remember here is that, whatever the situation, the closer you are to the vehicle in front the less you will be able to see. At junctions it may also mean that you do not notice direction and other road signs or markings in time to act on them.

Watching for other vehicles

It is not always easy to judge the speed and distance of an approaching vehicle, especially if it is coming straight towards you. It is a little easier if it is coming at an angle or on a curve, because you will probably be able to 'time it' as it passes lamp-posts, telegraph poles and so on. Remember, too, that if the

Fig. 22. Dead ground

Anything on the road between A and B is hidden from the driver of the red car. Overhanging branches can have the same effect on roads without dips.

vehicle is coming downhill it may be travelling faster than you think. On the other hand, don't expect it to be crawling just because it is coming uphill.

Besides judging the speed and distance of vehicles you can see, don't forget that there may be other vehicles quite close that you can't see. Watch out for 'dead ground' where the road dips and a car can be hidden. An example of this is shown in Fig. 22. Look out, too, for overhanging branches which can hide a considerable stretch of straight road when they are leafy. Again, a car parked off the road, perhaps at an angle, can hide oncoming vehicles at a junction. This is really an obstacle point, but a car may come up and park while you are waiting at a junction, so be ready to re-assess your zone of vision and to move as necessary.

Finally, remember that poor weather conditions can complicate the whole business of *looking* at a junction, however wide and full your zone of vision would otherwise be. So take particular care to *make sure* before going on.

Wait or go on?

It is only when you have got into a position from which you can see clearly both ways into a junction that you can answer the question: 'Wait or go on?' If there is a vehicle coming from the right which is very close, the answer is obvious—you stop and wait. It may be equally obvious that any approaching vehicles are so far off that you can go on with perfect safety for everyone concerned. Where, however, a vehicle is coming towards you at such a distance or at such a speed that you have the least doubt about being able to go safely in front of it, you should stop and wait.

To put it the other way round, you must be careful to join or cross the path of an oncoming vehicle *only* when it is far enough away to make it quite safe for you to do so. To force other drivers to change their plans is a dangerous business. This is very much our basic practical message: Stick to the rules and everybody concerned knows what to expect. At junctions, the rules really mean that you should be prepared to fit in safely with other traffic by adjusting your speed or position (or both) and, if that is not enough, you should stop and wait.

Timing your approach

Most of the examples given so far have dealt with zones of vision in rather narrow and closed-in situations. Now let us look at the situation of two drivers on the same stretch of road, whose problems in timing and observation are quite different.

Fig. 23 shows the approach to a T junction in open country where visibility is so good (because there are no obstacle points) that you can spread its assessment, the safe routine (*mirror—signal—manœuvre*), and the junction routine (*position—speed—look*) over a long stretch of road. You can do the PSL steps over and over again. A complete MSM and PSL routine is needed again for the minor junction with the narrow road, B. After this you can resume the PSL routine to negotiate the T junction itself. The significant thing about this situation is that, because there is good visibility, speeds will tend to be high and you therefore need to know all the time what is going on at, and near, the junctions.

But this situation is very different from that of the driver coming out of road B. Immediately after entering road A he must fit in the whole process of assessing the junction—*mirror—signal—position—speed—look*—in the short distance between the exit from road B and the junction with road CD.

The new driver at junctions

Before we leave the subject of looking (and waiting) at junctions, a special word to learner drivers. As a learner, you will be conscious of other drivers lining up behind you at junctions. Don't let the fact that you are first in the queue influence your judgment about when to go on. What *you* see when you look must decide your action, and nothing else. After all, the chap behind you has been a learner too.

On the 'new' road

Having decided that it is safe to emerge at the junction, you go forward on to your 'new' road. At once you will have another set of questions to answer, varying with the sort of road it is and the traffic on it. They will include:

1 'What is behind me now?' (mirror).
2 'Do I need to adjust my position?' (lane discipline).

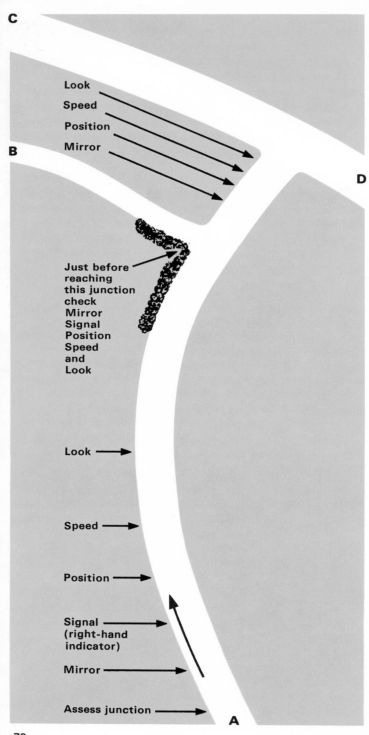

C

Look

Speed

Position

Mirror

B

D

Just before
reaching
this junction
check
Mirror
Signal
Position
Speed
and
Look

Look →

Speed →

Position →

Signal →
(right-hand
indicator)

Mirror →

Assess junction →

A

Correct positioning is vital when turning right. The situation illustrated calls for particularly careful judgment.

3 'Do I need to adjust my distance from the vehicle ahead?' (separation distance).

4 'Is my speed correct?' (signs and road and traffic conditions).

5 'Am I staying on this road?' (advance direction signs).

6 'Is it reasonable to overtake?' (observation—forward and rear).

The answers to all these questions concern *position* and *speed*. This, then, gives us the full routine for dealing with a junction: *mirror* and *signal*; followed by *position—speed—look* at the junction itself; and then *position, speed* again. Get in the habit of using this routine at all junctions. It will serve you well.

How *not* to join a new road

It may be very tempting when turning right on to a wider road, especially when there is little traffic from the right, to turn and drive along the centre of the road in the hope that you can fit into a gap in the traffic coming from the left.

This is very risky for a number of reasons. First, you will confuse drivers behind you. Second, the road may narrow, or there may be junctions or islands in the road further along. Third,

Fig. 23
Timing the junction sequence
Drivers coming along road A and road B have very different problems of timing and observation before joining road CD.

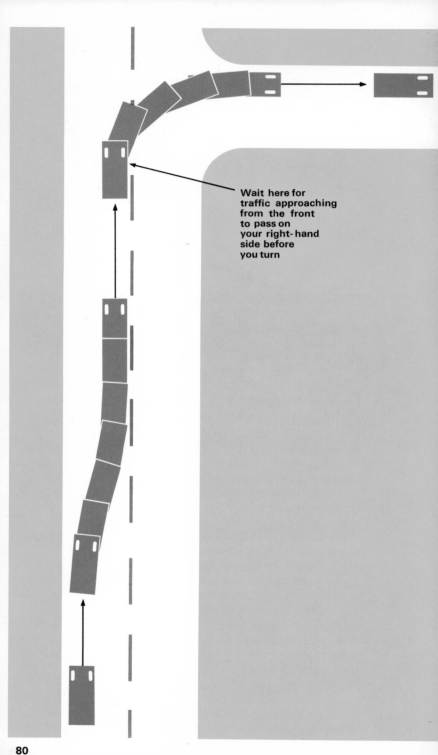

Wait here for traffic approaching from the front to pass on your right-hand side before you turn

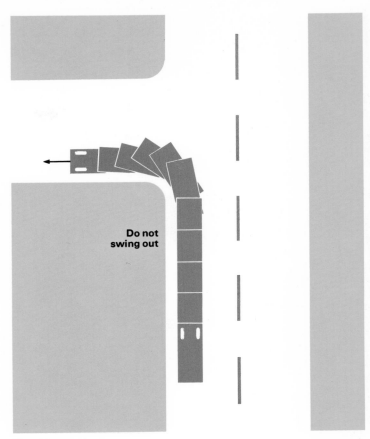

Do not swing out

Fig. 24

Turning right (opposite) and left (above) from a wide road
These two diagrams show the basic movements. Note the importance of correct positioning.

there may be no gap for you to fit into. So don't create an extra stream in this way.

You may also be tempted to pull into the centre of the road and wait there to complete the turn. This, too, is dangerous unless there is a central reservation with gaps (as on a dual carriageway) or the road is specially marked to allow it.

Turning into a road to right or left

The junction routine we have described should be used at all junctions. Some of the steps are less important, others more important, according to whether you are turning into a road to the right or left. If, for example, you are turning right out of a busy road, there is the job of actually finding the turn you want. Giving your signal and getting into *position* in good time becomes

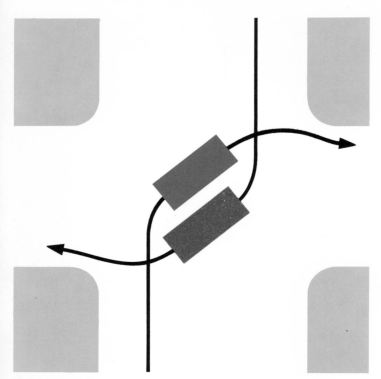

Fig. 25 (above)
Turning right (offside to offside)

Fig. 26 (opposite)
Turning right at a staggered junction (nearside to nearside)

At a staggered junction, as here, it is sometimes necessary to turn right by passing nearside to nearside. The disadvantage is obvious: each car blocks the other's view of oncoming traffic. ▶

essential—otherwise you may interrupt the traffic flow or even be forced to go on past your road. Looking, as always, is important. Don't begin a turn you can't complete. A sudden stop could have unfortunate consequences.

If you are going to turn to the left, watch out especially for cars parked, or about to stop, on the left. You don't want to get trapped behind them. Be very careful to look for cyclists or motor-cyclists coming up on your nearside.

If you are going to turn right, getting your *position* and *speed* correct is vital. You must look for traffic on the road you are joining as well as on the road you are leaving. Don't cross oncoming traffic until you can do so without causing it to change speed or direction. This will call for particularly careful judgment if the road is wide enough for two lanes of oncoming vehicles. Be

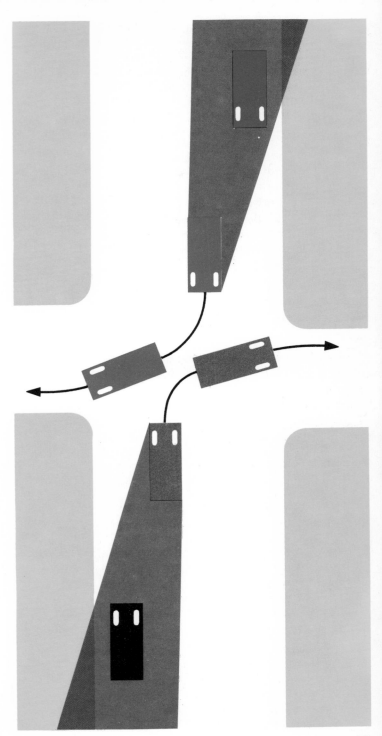

very careful where you stop and wait, because some of the oncoming vehicles may be turning right too. The correct positions for right- and left-hand turns are shown in Fig. 24.

Notice that Fig. 25 shows vehicles passing behind each other at a crossroads—or offside to offside. There are some junctions where the layout makes it more convenient to pass nearside to nearside, but this is less safe because each driver has his view of the oncoming traffic hidden by the other vehicle (see Fig. 26). The usual rule is offside to offside—but watch out for junctions where police control or road markings mean that you are intended to turn nearside to nearside.

Staggered junctions

At a staggered junction such as that shown in Fig. 26, you cannot turn right behind an oncoming vehicle that is also turning right (offside to offside). So be on the look-out for traffic hidden behind the leading vehicles—and be ready to stop.

Cutting right-hand corners

Fig. 27 shows what is meant by 'cutting a corner' when turning right. Always avoid this. It is dangerous because it reduces your zone of vision and puts you on the wrong side of the road.

When you are turning right out of a road which is only wide enough for one line of traffic in each direction, keep well over to the left (see Fig. 28).

Y junctions

These can be deceptive because some call for little change of direction. But if two drivers are approaching a junction on different roads, as shown in Fig. 29, and don't realise its importance, one at least will have to take very sudden—and therefore dangerous—action. Apply the PSL routine at Y junctions as you would at any other junction.

Pedestrians at junctions

Always be on the look-out for pedestrians and remember these two rules: *At pedestrian crossings controlled by lights or police* give way to pedestrians who are crossing when the signal to move is given. *When turning at a road junction* always give way to pedestrians who are crossing the road.

Fig. 27
Cutting right-hand corners
Three examples of bad driving.
A The driver approaches correctly but steers to the right too soon.
B The driver approaches in the wrong position.
C The driver takes his line from the wrong kerb.

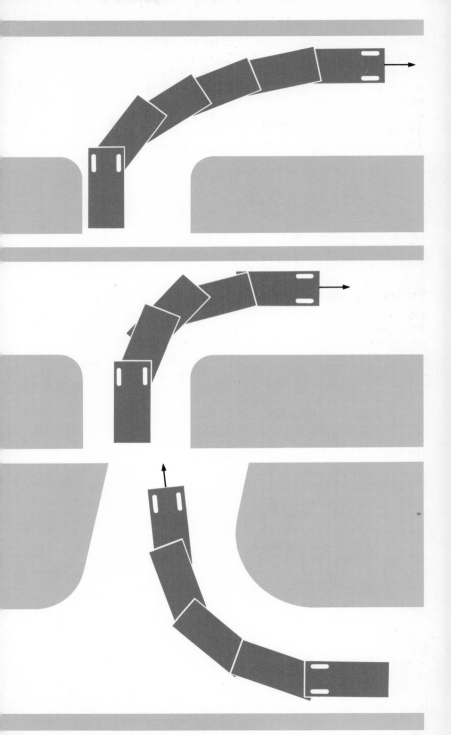

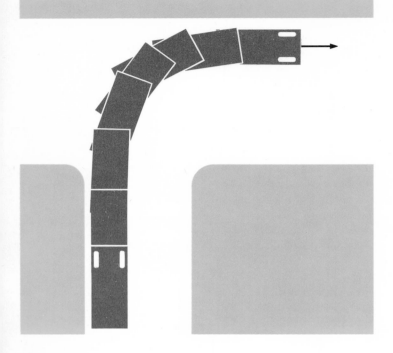

Fig. 28
Turning right out of a narrow road
This is the correct way. It leaves room for vehicles coming in.

Dealing with roundabouts

Roundabouts help traffic flow by mixing together several streams of vehicles. But this very function creates a situation in which a high level of information and anticipation is needed. The rules to remember are: the GIVE WAY rule, which defines who should wait and who should move on; and the 'driving procedure' rules, which tell you how to approach the roundabout and what course to take in it.

Give way

The GIVE WAY rule says that when you approach a roundabout you should normally give way to traffic from your immediate right to avoid causing any approaching driver to reduce speed, to alter course or to be put in any danger.

Since this is a general rule, upright GIVE WAY signs (on posts) are not placed at all roundabouts but the points of entry are marked by single broken white lines on the road. Fig. 30 shows three typical arrangements.

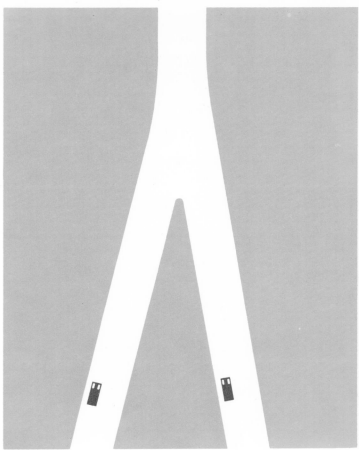

Fig. 29
Approaching a Y junction
Always apply the PSL routine as you approach the point where two roads merge. Failure to do so could force you to take hasty, and dangerous, action.

Occasionally, although a junction appears to have a roundabout, drivers on one or more of the roads into it are given a clear passage. At these exceptional places the GIVE WAY rule may be applied to drivers *in the roundabout;* double broken white lines are marked across the road in the junction (see Fig. 31), and there are upright GIVE WAY signs.

Driving procedure
The following rules should always be observed *unless* road markings indicate otherwise *or* the approach road and the roundabout itself are quite free of traffic.

When turning left
Approach in the left-hand lane; keep to that lane in the round-

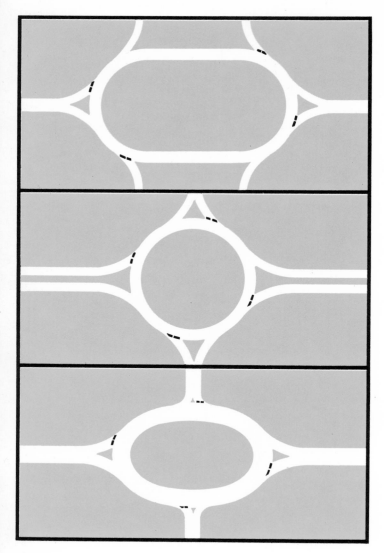

Fig. 30

Giving way at roundabouts

Typical arrangements, showing the entry points marked with broken lines (not to scale).

about and leave by it. Use the left-turn indicator on approach and through the roundabout.

When going forward

Approach in the left-hand lane; keep to that lane in the round-about. Use the left-turn indicator at the exit before the one you are going to take. If conditions dictate, approach in the right-hand

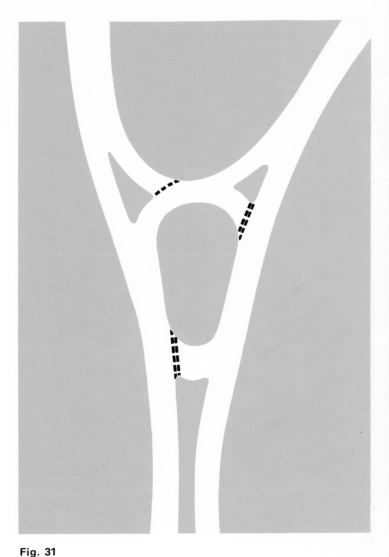

Fig. 31

Here, drivers *in the roundabout* are required to give way at two points marked by broken *double* lines.

lane; and keep to that lane in the roundabout. Use the left-turn indicator at the exit before the one you are going to take.

When turning right

Approach in the right-hand lane; use the right-turn indicator before entering the roundabout and maintain this signal while keeping to the right-hand lane in the roundabout; change to

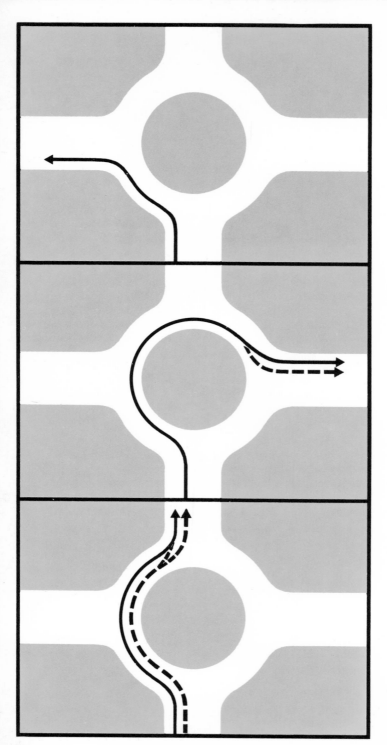

left-turn indicator at the exit before the one you are going to take.

Fig. 32 illustrates the correct courses to be followed including the proper choice of lane on the exit road. If you stick to these rules you will be letting other drivers know, by your course and signals, what you are going to do. And if they are observing the rules too, you will know what they are going to do. But note that they are not hard and fast. For instance, 'if conditions dictate . . .' means that you need to weigh up the situation and apply a degree of commonsense discretion. As we said earlier, roundabouts are places where traffic streams mix. So be prepared for other drivers to cross your path to leave by the next exit, and always be on the look-out for their signals.

Don't forget the other rules we have talked about: *mirror—signal—manœuvre* (MSM) and *position—speed—look* (PSL). You should apply these routines as much at a roundabout as at any other junction. Remember, too, that the signals for left or right turns must be given in good time so that other drivers are in no doubt about your intentions.

Summary

1

What to look for; deciding whether, and where, to stop before going on.

2

Zones of vision; recognising obstacle points; ways to get a full zone of vision.

3

How far forward? Far enough for a full view of the whole junction.

4

The importance of careful positioning on narrow roads etc., and of not being too close behind the vehicle in front.

5

Judging the speed of approaching vehicles; looking out for 'dead ground'.

6

Fitting in the routines—*mirror—signal—manœuvre* **and** *position—speed—look*.

Fig. 32.

Driving procedure at roundabouts

These diagrams show you how to turn left, right or go straight ahead at a roundabout. The recommended course is shown by a solid line. If conditions dictate, follow the course indicated by the broken line.

7

After entering a 'new 'road; the need to use the mirror and adjust speed.

8

Turning into a road on the left; signalling on approach; looking out for cyclists and pedestrians.

9

Turning into a road on the right; signalling on approach; crossing other turning traffic.

10

Roundabouts—the GIVE WAY rule; the drill for driving through a roundabout.

8

Traffic signs

Signs are an essential part of any road and traffic system. They tell you about rules you must keep and warn you about what you may meet on the road ahead. Signs may be words and picture symbols on roadside posts, lines and other markings on the road, beacons, bollards or traffic light signals.

To do its job, a sign must give you its message clearly and early so that you will have time to see it, understand it, and act on it. In the past many signs were too small to read or difficult to see and there were too few of them. But this has changed, and new-style signs are replacing the old ones.

In these new signs, symbols are used instead of words wherever possible, because they are more quickly seen and understood. Also, the similarity between our signs and those in the rest of Europe means that the British motorist on the Continent can understand the traffic signs even if he cannot speak the language—and vice versa.

The meanings of signs are much easier to understand if you know some of the simple rules about the shapes and colours used in designing them. To explain these rules, we will consider signs under five headings:

1 Signs that give orders.
2 Signs that give warnings.
3 Direction and other information signs.
4 Road markings (which can do any of these three things).
5 Traffic light signals.

There are also some special signs for motorways and other fast roads which we shall deal with separately in Chapter 14 under 'Motorway driving'.

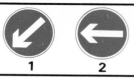

Fig. 33

1 Keep left   2 Turn left

Signs that give orders

Some of these signs tell you, as a driver, what you *must* do ('mandatory' signs) and others what you *must not* do ('prohibitory' signs). Most are in the shape of a circle.

Mandatory signs: Most of these have white symbols and borders on a blue background. Examples are given in Fig. 33. Notice the difference between the KEEP LEFT and TURN LEFT signs.

You must also obey such signs as the circular one with STOP in white on a red background sometimes found at road works, and the STOP—CHILDREN sign (the 'lollipop') carried by school crossing patrols. This has black lettering on a circular, yellow background surrounded by a red border.

Two signs in this group have a special design which includes a red triangle, point downwards. They are the STOP and GIVE WAY signs. These two signs are always accompanied by road markings, and, because they are at junctions, they are important for your guidance and everyone's safety.

The STOP **sign:** Fig. 34 shows the sign and road markings. Points to remember are:

Reason for sign: Usually, that the junction gives so limited a zone of vision that you must stop in order to be able to look properly.

Markings: The lines tell you how far forward you should go; in other words, they give you your final *look* position (in the junction routine *position—speed—look*).

What you must do: You *must* stop. You must not then drive on and enter the major road until you can do so without causing danger or making drivers on that road change speed or direction.

The GIVE WAY **sign:** Fig. 35(A) shows the markings at a junction where there is a GIVE WAY sign at the kerbside. Fig. 35(B) shows an alternative arrangement with only the two GIVE WAY lines. This is used at junctions where there is relatively little traffic. Here are the points to remember:

Reason for sign: GIVE WAY signs (or lines only) are being put at all junctions with major roads, unless they are controlled by STOP signs, traffic signals, or police, to show that main road traffic has priority.

Fig. 34
STOP sign

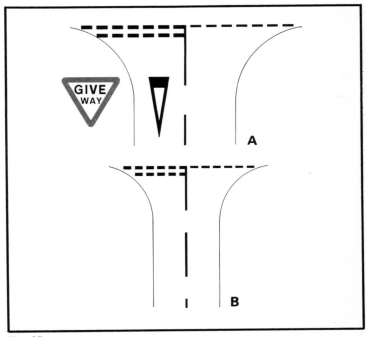

Fig. 35
GIVE WAY sign

Markings: The double broken lines across the road show you where you must stop, if this is necessary, to take your final look.

What you must do: Where there is a triangular GIVE WAY sign and lines across the road, you *must delay entering* the major road unless you can do so without causing danger to any driver on it or making him change speed or direction. If there are GIVE WAY lines only, you must still give way to traffic on the major road.

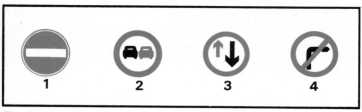

Fig. 36
Prohibitory signs
1 No entry   2 No overtaking   3 Give priority to vehicles from
opposite direction   4 No right turn

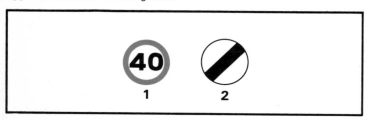

Fig. 37
1 Maximum speed limit   2 Maximum speed limit 70 m.p.h.

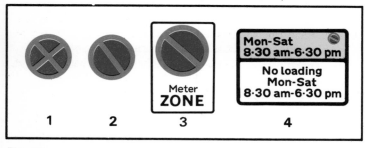

Fig. 38
1 No stopping ('clearway')   2 No waiting   3 Entrance to controlled
parking zone   4 Restrictions on waiting and loading

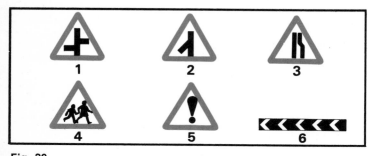

Fig. 39
Warning signs
1 Staggered junction   2 Traffic merges from left   3 Road narrows on
offside   4 Children   5 Other danger   6 Sharp deviation to left

Prohibitory signs: These tell you what you *must not* do. Fig. 36 shows some examples. They are easy to recognise by their circular shape and red border. The only exception is the NO ENTRY sign, which, although circular, has a red background instead of a red border.

The message is given either by picture symbols or by words and figures inside the red border. Sometimes the two are combined. Notice that the red symbols in the signs for NO OVERTAKING and PRIORITY TO VEHICLES FROM THE OPPOSITE DIRECTION show what you are *not* allowed to do. Similarly, a red bar across a symbol emphasises what you must not do (see the sign for NO RIGHT TURN).

Speed limit signs are an important example of prohibitory signs (see above); the 'Speed limit 70 m.p.h.' sign is also circular—plain white with a black diagonal bar across it (Fig. 37). Miniature versions of this sign are put on lamp-posts where the normal 30 m.p.h. speed limit for a built-up area does not apply. Similarly, miniature versions of the 40 m.p.h. sign may be put on lamp-posts. Lamp-posts without either of these signs are a warning that you are in a 30 m.p.h. area.

Then there are signs which tell you that you must not stop and wait at all, or that waiting is restricted in some way. In Chapter 10 we shall see that, before parking, a driver should always ask himself, 'Shall I be within the law?', so it is especially important to be able to recognise these signs when you want to park.

The general pattern for these signs is blue inside a circular red border. Examples are given in Fig. 38. The end of a clearway has the same sign as the beginning, but with the word END on a white plate underneath.

Where there are restrictions on waiting, the edge of the road is also marked with yellow lines. These may be continuous double or single lines, or a single dotted line. Short yellow marks on the kerb indicate where loading and unloading is restricted. Generally speaking, the more yellow paint there is the longer the restrictions apply. The actual times are shown on plates on posts or lamp-posts along the road.

Signs that give warnings

Warning signs tell you of dangers ahead. Their message is: take extra care and be ready to slow down or carry out some other manœuvre. Most warning signs (see Fig. 39) are triangular with a red border and a black picture symbol on a white background; some are rectangular with the message in white letters on a red background.

These signs warn you of some danger which you might not otherwise be able to see or recognise in time. The particular danger—a bend, hill, hump-back bridge—will be clear from the sign, but only you can decide what to do about it. What you cannot do safely is to ignore it.

Besides the obvious warning, these signs can give you other useful information. Here are some examples:

Junctions: These signs not only warn you that there is a junction ahead, but also tell you what sort it is; whether it is a crossroads, staggered junction or roundabout. Sometimes you can get information about the layout of a junction from advance direction signs. Notice the sign for merging traffic. This is really a warning of a Y junction. As more underpasses and flyovers come into use, so there will be more of these signs.

Narrowing roads: The warning sign in Fig. 39(3) shows which side of the road narrows; and every sign of this sort warns you against overtaking until you can size up the situation on the narrower stretch of road. Another form of sign for narrowing road is used where a dual carriageway becomes a single (two-way) carriageway, and here there is the extra message—watch out for oncoming traffic.

Children and schools: Signs showing children warn you of places such as playgrounds and recreation centres as well as schools. They call for extra care; children are apt to dash into the road suddenly. Where the sign relates to a school there will normally be a SCHOOL plate underneath it; or there may be a PATROL plate warning you of a children's crossing patrol some distance ahead. When you see these signs ask yourself if children are likely to be about. Is it their school arrival or leaving time?

Low bridge: However small your vehicle, this sign has a message for you too. It is to watch out for high vehicles coming towards you. They may have to use the middle of the road to get under an arched bridge.

Sharp change of direction: Black and white chevrons are used facing traffic at some roundabouts. They are also used where the road changes direction so sharply that a BEND sign would not be good enough warning. Another use is to show which way the main road turns at a T junction.

Hazard markers: Reflectors set on black and white posts are sometimes used to mark the edge of the road surface (carriageway) on embankments and hillsides. Sometimes they also show where the road narrows, or where there is an obstruction such as a bridge parapet or the corner of a building very near the edge of the road. The reflectors are usually circular but may be oblong. They show red on your left hand (nearside) and white on your right hand (offside).

Other hazards: The sign in Fig. 39(5) is used for any danger for which there is no special sign. It will usually have a plate underneath telling you what the hazard is, for example, gritting, tree-cutting and so on.

Directional and information signs

Directional signs: These help you to find and follow the

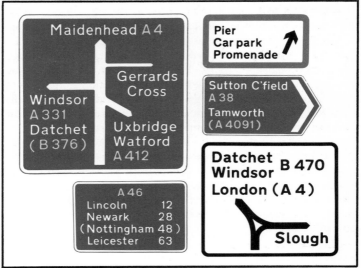

Fig. 40
Direction signs

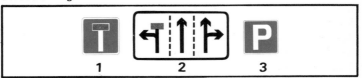

Fig. 41
Information signs
1 No through road 2 Appropriate traffic lanes at junction ahead
3 Parking place

road you want, or direct you to the nearest car park, station and so on. They are in different colours, depending on the importance of the road. Signs for important roads ('primary' routes), except motorways, have white letters and borders and yellow route numbers on a green background. Signs for other roads have black letters and numbers on a white background, and those for local places have black letters on a white background with a blue border.

Examples are shown in Fig. 40. Notice that each of the green signs is for a primary route; each has a different purpose. The first is an *advance direction sign* and you see this *before* you get to a junction. The second is a *direction sign* and this shows you the way to go *at* a junction. The third is a *route sign* to give you a check that you are on the right road *after* you have passed the junction. These signs also tell you distances and places on your route. Where there is a route number in brackets on the sign, this means that the road you are on leads to that route.

Information signs: These tell you where you will find parking places, telephones, camping sites, no through roads and so on. Examples are given in Figs. 40 (*top right*) and 41.

Road markings

Like other traffic signs, markings on the road give information, orders or warnings. They may be used with signs on posts or on their own. They have two advantages: they can often be seen when other signs would be hidden by traffic, and can give a *continuing* message as you drive along the road.

These markings help drivers to make full use of road space. Lane markings make lane discipline easier and so add to safety. Again the rule is 'the more paint the more important the message'. For example a single broken line across the road at the entrance to a roundabout shows where you *should* give way to traffic from your immediate right; a double broken line across the road at a junction or within a roundabout means you *must* give way.

Single STOP lines: A single continuous line across your half of the road shows you where to stop at junctions controlled by the police or traffic lights, at level crossings, swing bridges or ferries.

Lines along the road: The most important of these are double white lines. There are three sorts: those where both lines are continuous; those where the line on your side is continuous but the one on the other side is broken; and those where the line on your side is broken but the other one is continuous.

There are two general rules which you *must*, by law, obey where there are these lines. First, no waiting on the carriageway. Second, where the line nearest you is continuous you must not let any part of your vehicle go over it, except to enter or leave a side road or premises on the opposite side of the road, or because of circumstances beyond your control. This does not mean that you must never overtake when the continuous line is nearest you. You may be able to pass a small vehicle like a motor-cycle without going over the white line. Sometimes there is room for two lanes of traffic one way but only one the other way.

Where the broken line is on your side of the continuous white line you can cross the lines to overtake if it is safe to do so and you can get back on to your side of the road before there is another continuous white line on your side. Watch out for arrows on the road. They often tell you that you are coming to double white lines. Don't start overtaking when you see them.

At some very dangerous places, such as sharp bends and humps, the two continuous lines may be some way apart, with the space in between covered by diagonal lines. This is to give an extra safety margin; the rule is for all vehicles to keep off the diagonal lines.

Single broken lines along the road either mark the middle of the road or divide it into lanes. Sometimes they show the edge of the road—for example, across the mouth of a junction. Watch out for places where the gaps in the broken line become shorter. You will be coming up to a danger spot such as a junction, bend or island. Where there is particular danger, the broken line may change to a continuous single white line.

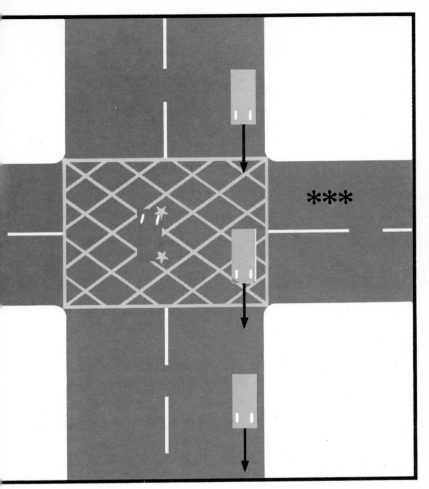

Fig. 42
Turning right at a box junction
Provided that your exit (✳✳✳) is clear, you may enter the box and wait there for a safe gap in the traffic.

Cat's-eyes: Like hazard markers, cat's-eyes are red on the left-hand side of the road and white elsewhere. Again, the nearer cat's-eyes are together the more important their message.

Hatched markings: Diagonal lines may be used to mark a safety zone to protect vehicles waiting to turn right. Keep off these hatched markings.

Box junction markings: You should never enter any junction if by doing so you will block it. At box junctions, which are marked with yellow criss-cross lines, you *must not* go into the junction unless the way through, and the mouth of your exit from it, are clear. There is only one exception to this rule, and that is if you want to turn right and the way through to your exit is blocked by oncoming traffic. In this case you may wait in the area marked with yellow lines until there is a gap in the traffic which allows you to cross over into your exit (see Fig. 42).

Words on the road: Words painted on the road surface, such as STOP, SLOW, KEEP CLEAR, and so on, usually have an obvious meaning. Where they indicate that a part of the road is 'reserved' for particular vehicles—buses or ambulances, for example—the message is 'Don't park here'.

Another kind of worded sign on the road surface is the destination marking near busy junctions which repeats the message given on advance direction signs about towns and road numbers. These signs are put well back from the turn so that you have time to see them, and get into the right lane. They are especially helpful when the advance direction sign is hidden by a large vehicle.

Lane arrows: These show you which lane to take for the direction you want to go. Where the road is wide enough for three lanes you may find each one arrowed for a different direction —the nearside lane for a left turn, the middle lane for straight ahead, and the outside lane for a right turn. Some arrows may be combined, depending on the amount of traffic using the junction. If the road is wide enough only for two lanes, the arrows have to be combined. Where there is a left-filter arrow at traffic lights, the filter (nearside) lane will be marked with the left-turn arrow and traffic going straight ahead or turning right will use the other lane, marked with a combined straight-ahead and right-turn arrow.

Left- and right-turn arrows are placed well before your turning point to guide you into the proper lane for turning. They are *not* intended to indicate the exact point at which you should turn. It is especially important to remember this at right turns.

Traffic light signals

Traffic lights usually have three lights which change in a fixed order: red, red with amber, green; then amber, and then red again. This means that when you see a traffic signal ahead you should know (as well) what the next signal will be.

The meaning of each signal is as follows:

Red means stop and wait at the stop line.

Red with amber means stop and wait. This is the safety margin for drivers on the other road to clear the junction and you must not go on until green shows.

Amber means stop unless you have already crossed the stop line or are so close to it that to pull up might cause an accident.

Green means that you may drive on if the way is clear. Take special care when turning left or right and give way to pedestrians who are crossing. Don't ever 'race for the line'. You must be ready to stop, especially if green has been showing for some time.

A green arrow means that you may go (filter) in the direction of the arrow. You may do this whatever other signals are showing.

Anticipation and the use of the *mirror—signal—manœuvre* and *position—speed—look* routines are just as important when you are coming up to traffic lights as at any other junction. Being prepared to stop, and getting in the correct lane—by paying careful attention to the lane markings—and the right gear, are specially important.

At some road works you may find traffic lights with only red and green lights. These have the same meaning as red and green at ordinary lights. Traffic lights—either the red, amber, green or twin flashing red lights—are also used to control traffic where low-flying aircraft cross the road, at swing or lifting bridges and at other places. They must always be obeyed.

Summary

1
Signs that give orders—what you must do; what you must not do. STOP and GIVE WAY signs and lines.

2
Warning signs—how to use them properly; points to remember about particular signs.

3
Direction signs—using them before and after junctions.

4
Information signs.

5
Road markings; double white lines and what they mean; words and arrows on the road.

6
Traffic lights—when to stop and when to go.

9 Dealing with hills

When a vehicle is being driven uphill the engine not only has to drive it along the road but lift its weight as well. Going downhill, the weight of the vehicle helps the engine to drive it along. In each case, the effect of the controls is different from what it is on the level. It is useful to look at the main differences and see how they affect your driving.

Going uphill (as compared with driving on level roads):

1 It is harder for the engine to make the car go faster.

2 The brakes slow the car down sooner.

3 If you reduce pressure on the accelerator, or if you declutch, your speed will drop much quicker than it would on the level. A change down may then become necessary and this must be done briskly so as not to lose too much speed.

4 When stopping, you can brake later and declutch later, but you must use the handbrake sooner to avoid rolling back.

Going downhill (as compared with driving on level roads):

1 Generally, it is harder to slow down and the brakes have less effect.

2 It is harder for the engine to slow the car down, and in the higher gears it will not do so at all.

3 If you declutch, the car will run faster.

4 Gear changes are more difficult and it is therefore important to be in the right gear before you begin to go downhill.

We dealt with moving away uphill in the basic driving sequences in Chapter 4. When it comes to dealing with hills in the ordinary course of driving remember the following points:

Fig. 43
Warning signs
1 Steep hill downwards   2 Steep hill upwards

Going up

1 **Look for signs.** The warning sign for a hill (upwards) will tell you how steep the slope is. The figures on it—say 1:6—mean that for every six feet (horizontal) the road rises one foot. (See Fig. 43.) The lower the second figure, the steeper the hill: 1 in 4 is steeper than 1 in 6. Extra signs on oblong plates may tell you the length of the hill or give you other information about it.

2 **Assess the hill.** Weigh up a hill as you would a junction and change down in good time if a change is necessary. If you cannot see much of the hill because the road turns, *change before the turn* because climbing and turning at the same time mean harder work for your engine. Also traffic tends to slow on hills, especially at turns.

3 **Speed.** Don't try to hang on to a high gear in an attempt to keep up your speed. Your car will climb better in a lower gear.

4 **Separation distance.** Keep well back from the vehicle in front. If you get close and the driver ahead slows down for some reason, you may have to make a sudden stop. Holding back may enable you to keep going gently while he regains speed. This is not only safer but it can help to avoid congestion.

5 **Overtaking.** Overtaking uphill is usually difficult. But where you are in mixed traffic on a straight upward gradient, perhaps on a dual carriageway, you might be able to overtake. But keep a look-out for others who are able to overtake easily, and don't balk them. One of the biggest dangers about overtaking on a hill (except on a dual carriageway) is that the traffic coming towards you downhill is nearly always going much faster than you are and is much less able to slow down or stop quickly. (See also Chapter 11.)

Going down

1 **Look for signs.** The steep hill (downwards) sign is a warning you must respect. As with the uphill sign, it will tell you the gradient. But this is more than information—it is part of the warning. There may also be an accompanying oblong sign about using low gear.

2 **Assess the hill.** Do this as soon as you can—the sign will help.

If you don't know the road, or conditions make it difficult to see, change down one gear right away and be ready for another change down if necessary *before* you begin the hill. (As with climbing, don't delay your gear changes.)

3 **Speed.** You will usually have to reduce speed to that of traffic ahead of you. Using your lower gears will help with this by giving you more braking power and control. The steeper the hill, the lower the gear.

4 **Separation distances.** Leaving a good gap is important because if you follow too closely and the vehicle ahead slows down you will have to brake very hard—and the driver behind you will get very little warning. A good gap gives you time to slow down more gently.

5 **Overtaking.** Overtaking downhill is safe only where there are no bends or junctions, where the visibility is good and you are *certain* that oncoming traffic will not be inconvenienced or endangered. Remember that just as you could not slow down easily, traffic coming uphill would have some difficulty in getting out of your way. (See also Chapter 11.)

Junctions on hills

When you leave a hilly road at a junction, or turn from a level road on to a hill, up or down, all the points mentioned so far become very much more important. Hills are not easy on car or driver and, as we have already seen, there are a great many driving operations to fit in when you go through a junction. Extra anticipation and considerable care are needed when dealing with a junction and a hill together.

Downhill junctions

When you are going downhill towards a junction, getting into the right position at the right speed needs the early use of mirror, signals, brakes, gears and steering. Remember the junction routine—*position—speed—look*. Your *look* will have to be made from a carefully chosen point at which you are ready to wait if necessary. Oncoming drivers will be climbing and, while their speeds may be easier to judge, you must be particularly careful not to balk them. If you are turning, don't move from your *look* position unless you are sure that you can complete the turn without blocking the oncoming traffic and causing a hold-up.

Uphill junctions

Again, it is important to judge your *position* and *speed* accurately when going uphill towards a junction, and to make correct use of mirror, signals, brakes, gears and steering. Your position will be particularly important to following drivers, especially if you are going to make a right turn. You will be very unpopular if you stop in the wrong position and force drivers behind you to stop unnecessarily.

Joining a hill at a junction

It is usually quite easy to turn left at a T junction into a road which runs uphill from the right. You can judge the speed of cars coming up the hill reasonably easily, and you don't have to cross any traffic stream. But if you are turning right and the road runs uphill from the left, you will find this much more difficult. Here you have to cross the traffic coming downhill from the right—probably quite fast—and at the same time fit into the flow of vehicles going uphill from the left without balking them.

Hills in town

What we have said so far applies to all hills, whether in town or country. But it is useful to look at some of the special conditions of hills in towns. First of all, there will be more pedestrians about. You need to take particular care at junctions when elderly people or young children are crossing the road uphill. Traffic speeds will be lower and vehicles closer together, making visibility that much poorer.

Traffic lights, school crossing patrols and pedestrian crossings will stop traffic on hills from time to time. This adds to the importance of using your mirror, recognising the sort of vehicle ahead of you, leaving a suitable gap when you stop, using your handbrake a great deal more than usual, and making sure that you are always in the right gear for the situation. You will be doing most of those things in towns anyway, but on hills they are all 'musts'.

Starting on a hill

Uphill: Apart from the need to co-ordinate the use of accelerator, clutch and handbrake, as described in Chapter 4, there are two other points that are worth mentioning here.

First, because you must avoid balking traffic climbing the hill, you must apply the *mirror—signal—manœuvre* (MSM) routine carefully and without undue haste. Second, you must allow for the fact that your car will be slower in pulling away and gaining speed than it would on the flat, so you will need a larger gap in the traffic if you are to fit in safely.

Downhill: This is a simpler operation because the weight of the car helps you to move away. (Faulty use of the accelerator, clutch or brake does not normally prevent the car from *moving away* on a downward slope.) But you must be careful to use the right gear for the slope of the hill to keep the car under full control. Remember, too, that drivers coming downhill from behind you will find it less easy to slow down or stop, so be sure that the gap is large enough before you move off.

Braking downhill

Don't rely on your brakes as the chief means of controlling your speed when going downhill. Overworked brakes get hot and may

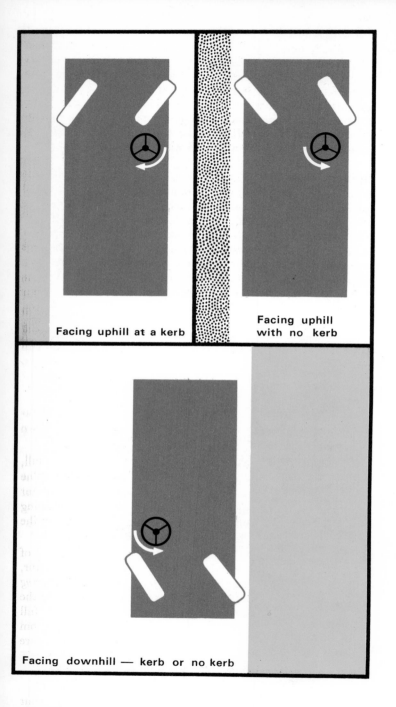

Facing uphill at a kerb

Facing uphill
with no kerb

Facing downhill — kerb or no kerb

Fig. 44.
Parking on a hill: how to set the front wheels

'fade' and lose quite a lot of their effect. Your chief means of controlling speed downhill should be the use of a lower gear; your footbrake should be regarded as an addition to your engine braking power in a low gear.

Get into a lower gear in good time and then be ready to slow the *engine* by braking the car with the footbrake. If the gear you are using is too high the *car* will run faster and speed up the engine. This is a signal to change down, but if you have left it as late as this you will have to brake very firmly to reduce speed enough to change down safely.

Because braking is best avoided on curves, use an even lower gear on a winding hill than you would on a straight one. You must do this *before* you begin to go downhill.

Parking on hills

It is far better not to leave your car standing on a slope. But if you can't avoid it, here are some points to remember.

Parking uphill: Stop as close as you can to the nearside kerb and leave your steering wheel turned to the right. Then, if the car should roll backwards, it will be checked by the front wheel coming against the kerb. If there is no kerb, turn the steering wheel to the *left*. Then, at least, the car will not run back across the road. (See Fig. 44.) Leave the car in first gear—with the handbrake firmly applied.

Parking downhill: Turn the steering wheel to the left, so that any forward movement of the car will be checked by the kerb. Leave the car in reverse gear and apply the handbrake firmly.

Parking with automatic transmission: Whether facing uphill or downhill, make sure the handbrake is on firmly *before* using the selector setting 'P' (park). This avoids risk of a locked transmission. If your car has no 'P' setting, turn your front wheels to the kerb (as above) and take good care to apply your handbrake firmly.

Leaving a gap: Moving in or out of a parking space is more difficult on a slope than on the flat and tends to take more room. So leave a bigger gap—it will help you and others.

There are more details about parking in the next chapter.

A final word

Whether for power to climb a hill, or for braking to control speed downhill, it is always important to get into the right gear in good time.

Summary

1

The difference between driving on the level and uphill or downhill.

2

Judging the hill; changing gear early; leaving a good

space behind the vehicle in front. The dangers of overtaking on hills.

3

Junctions on hills; the particular importance of the *position—speed—look* routine; judging the speed of vehicles on the road you are joining.

4

Special problems of hills in towns; the need to use the handbrake more.

5

Starting on a hill; the importance of the *mirror—signal—manœuvre* routine. Picking the right gap to fit into.

6

Braking downhill; the use of lower gears; using the footbrake for *assistance*; braking on winding hills.

7

Parking on hills; turning the front wheels to the kerb; leaving the car in gear; the necessity for leaving a larger space. Cars with automatic gears.

10 Manœuvring

This chapter covers the manœuvres of reversing, turning and parking.

Before carrying out a manœuvre in a particular place, there are three questions you must ask yourself:

1 'Is this a safe place?'

2 'Is this a convenient place?'

3 'Shall I be within the law?' (The answers to the first two questions will probably help to answer this one too, because traffic law is based on safety and convenience. There may, however, be cases where the law forbids a particular manœuvre for reasons which, although good ones, may not be immediately obvious.)

Your knowledge of the Highway Code, signs and other guidance and your own common sense will provide the answers. Then there is another question, the answer to which will depend very much on your experience and the vehicle you are driving:

4 'Can I control my vehicle accurately enough to use this particular place?'

Only you can answer this last question. For instance, if you are an experienced driver it may not worry you to reverse downhill for a reasonable distance. But if you are not so experienced you may feel unsure about reversing for even a yard or so downhill. The car you are driving and its steering circle may also influence your answer. But only when you can answer yes to all four questions can you be sure that the place you have chosen for your manœuvre is a suitable one.

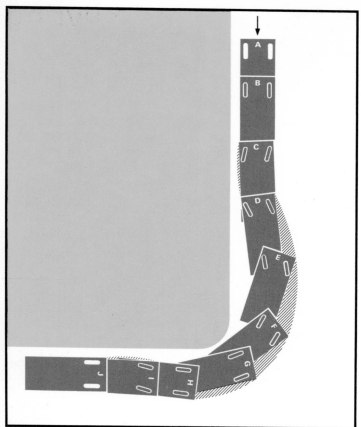

Fig. 45

The shaded part of the road shows how the car swings about as the steering wheel is turned. Most drivers take more room than this to reverse round a corner. At such close quarters a mistake could mean tyre damage against the kerb.

A Start—with wheels parallel to kerb.

B Moving back towards the corner.

C *Very slight* right lock here will steer back of car away from kerb.

D Back of car is now pointing away from kerb. Driver changes to left lock ready to turn corner.

E More left lock now as the car is really beginning to turn the corner.

F Some left lock is being taken off. Part of the car is round the corner— but not the steering end of it.

G Less left lock now and more of the car round the corner—but still not the steering end.

H The steering end is round the corner and all the left lock is off (wheels straight).

I Car moves very slowly while just enough right lock is put on to bring it parallel to the kerb.

J Car is in position at the kerb.

Reversing

Many manœuvres need reverse gear at some stage, so let us look first at the process of going backwards in a motor vehicle. Using reverse gear is obviously difficult for new drivers, not only because of the altered direction of travel but because the car steers differently; the front wheels become, in effect, the rear ones. (See Fig. 45.) When you drive forwards you can see the car turning with the steering. In reverse, you have to wait for the steering to take effect.

The first secret of manœuvring is to get the vehicle to move *slowly* enough. This way, the movements of the steering wheel will have the greatest possible effect. Don't turn the steering wheel while your car is stationary, but as soon as the car begins to move, however slowly, the steering wheel can be turned quite briskly. If your car has a small turning circle you will be able to change the angle of the front wheels quickly. The greater the amount of steering lock, the more important it is to move the car slowly. The second secret of manœuvring is to remember, all the time, which way your front wheels are pointing.

Reversing is not easy to master. Practice should begin with driving backwards in a straight line and then go on to turning corners and more complicated manœuvres.

How to sit

To reverse, you need to turn slightly in the seat. How much you turn will vary with your build and the car you are driving. When reversing straight back or to your left, you should hold the steering wheel with your right hand near the top (12 o'clock) and your left hand low on the wheel so that the rim may either slide through it or be gripped as necessary. If you find this position difficult because of your physical build or some other factor, hold the wheel at 12 o'clock with your right hand and sit so that you can steady your left arm on the back of your seat or along the back of the front passenger seat.

How to steer

One difficulty about steering, particularly in reverse, is to know just when to *begin* turning the steering wheel and when to straighten up. It is often helpful to move the steering wheel sooner than seems necessary. This, coupled with a slow speed, gives you time for unhurried control and time for checks to front and rear.

What to look for

Always check for other traffic before you drive backwards. Make quite sure there is nothing in your way—particularly children playing behind your car. Check all round—forwards, behind, over both shoulders and in your mirror. If you are in any doubt, get out (or ask your passenger to do so) to make quite sure. Keep a good look-out all the time you are moving backwards and always be ready to stop.

Before reversing, make quite sure that there are no children playing behind your car. If in doubt, get out and look.

Reversing into a side road on the left

Fig. 45 shows how a skilled driver can back round a corner, keeping very close to the kerb. Most drivers will probably need a bit more room than this—not least because any misjudgment could mean tyre damage against the kerb.

Remember these points about this manœuvre:

1 Although you must watch the line of the corner, you cannot follow it exactly.

2 When you have reached the point at which you are going to begin turning the steering wheel (C), check forward to make sure that your car will not swing out (D, E, F) into the way of approaching traffic.

Fig. 46

Reversing to the right

1. Do not drive across the road until this point is reached—and then only after full and proper observation.

2. Stop here, then reverse. Use a little left lock, then full right lock. (Compare with Fig. 45.)

3. By about this point, the front wheels should have been straightened.

4. Back well down the road, so that the normal position on the left can be reached well away from the corner.

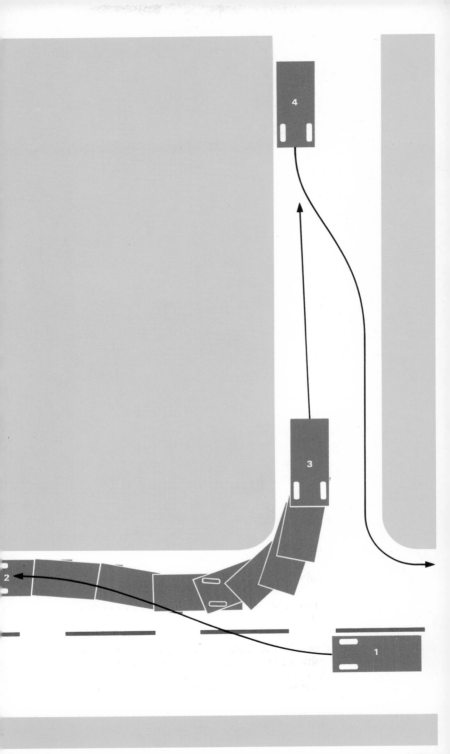

3 When you begin to see into the side road (E, F) look for vehicles coming along it.

4 At the same time, be ready to start to straighten up your steering.

5 Always keep to your own half of the road.

Reversing into a side road on the right

This is a useful manœuvre when there isn't a convenient turning on the left, or you can't see very well through the rear window. Fig. 46 shows that it is, in fact, two manœuvres. The first is to cross to the other side of the road (after passing the junction). As with any other change of direction, this needs full use of your mirror and proper judgment of position and speed. You should also take the opportunity to weigh up the side road as you pass it.

The second manœuvre is the turn itself. Sit so that you have a good view over your shoulder to the right and can see forward and to the left. Don't forget these checks: they are even more important here than in the left-hand reverse. Fig. 46 shows you, in detail, how to position your car.

Some more points about reversing

Besides asking yourself the four questions at the beginning of this chapter, remember also:

1 Not to reverse into a main road from a side road.

2 Not to reverse without making sure that it is safe to do so, even if it means getting help.

3 It is an offence to drive backwards on a road for such a distance as to inconvenience other road users. So keep your reversing as short as possible.

4 Whenever you reverse you must be ready to stop and give way to other road users.

Turning round

Every motorist has to turn round in the road at some time in his driving career. Here are three different ways of doing it.

Using a side road to turn and go back

This method is not so suitable for narrow or busy roads.

1 Find a side turning on your nearside into which you can reverse.

2 As you drive past the side turning, look down it and weigh it up. Then stop just past it.

3 Make sure the road is clear behind you, reverse round the corner. Stop close to the kerb, far enough back for you to be able to position properly for a right turn as you—

4 Drive forward, applying the junction routine (*mirror—signal—position—speed—look*) before driving out into your original road.

An alternative way is to drive into the side road on the left and then find another turning to reverse into. Or drive into the side road and then turn round in that road, using the manœuvre we describe next.

Turning in a road by using forward and reverse gears

This is a useful turn in culs-de-sac and roads where there are no side turnings or openings to reverse into. The drill is illustrated in Fig. 47.

The various stages of this turn are as follows:

1 Choose a place where there is good visibility, no obstruction in the road or on the pavement, and where you have plenty of room.
2 Stop on the left.
3 Make sure that the way is clear in front and behind—give way to passing vehicles.
4 Go *slowly* forward in first gear, turning your steering wheel *briskly* to the right. Aim at getting your car at a right angle across the road.
5 When the front of your car is about three feet from the kerb and still moving very *slowly*, change the lock by turning the steering wheel *briskly* to the left.
6 As your front wheels get near to the kerb, declutch and stop (footbrake). Put on the handbrake because of the camber or slope of the road. Select reverse gear.
7 Make sure again that the way is clear. Back slowly across the road. As you do this, turn the steering wheel farther to the left—if it will go. Then, as the back of your car nears the kerb (you will see this over your right shoulder), turn the steering wheel *briskly* to the right so that when you stop you will be on the right-hand lock ready to drive forward again.
8 Declutch and stop (footbrake). Put on the handbrake. Select first gear.
9 Make sure that the road is clear and drive forward.
10 You should then be able to straighten up on the left of the road. (If your vehicle is awkward to steer, or if you have had to turn in a narrow road, or where the camber is very steep, you may have to reverse again.)

Finally, be careful if you let your car overhang the kerb. This can be dangerous to pedestrians and there is a risk of hitting trees, lamp-posts, etc.

Making a U turn

This means turning your car right round in the width of the road. U turns are prohibited on motorways and in one-way streets, and on some other roads where there will be a sign—see Fig. 48—to tell you of the prohibition.

If you apply our four test questions about safety, convenience,

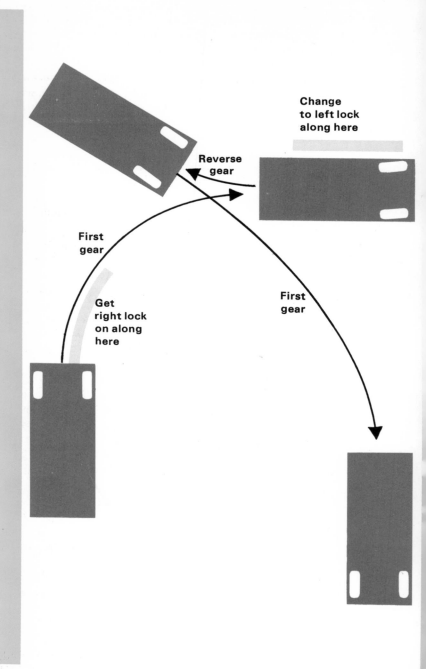

Change
to left lock
along here

Reverse
gear

First
gear

First
gear

Get
right lock
on along
here

Fig. 47
Turning in a road by forward and reverse gears

118

Fig. 48
No U turns

lawfulness and your own ability, you will see that a U turn isn't something you can do all that often. Nevertheless there are places where you can do it—and with some saving in time—such as little-used wide roads, or other quiet roads if your car is small or has an unusually small turning circle. But always remember that this is a manœuvre which other drivers do not ordinarily expect, so the safe routine of *mirror—signal—manœuvre* is particularly important.

Parking

Don't park on a road if there is somewhere else to leave your car. If you must use a road, choose a safe place. Before you leave a car anywhere, ask yourself the first three questions at the beginning of this chapter: Is it *safe*, *convenient* and *lawful*?

Some of the answers will be given by road signs and markings. These will tell you the places to avoid and whether there are restrictions at certain times or on particular days of the week. The question of safety will be answered by a knowledge of the Highway Code, which gives a list of places where you should not park, and by your own observation and common sense. Don't follow someone else's bad example.

Car parks

In a properly arranged car park there are markings to show you where to put your car. There are also arrows and signs to show the lanes you should take inside the car park. Always try to 'park pretty'; that is, squared up in the middle of the marked space.

In multi-storey, underground and indoor car parks, it is a good idea to use side lights whenever your car is *moving*—picking out moving cars among a lot of parked ones can be tricky in artificial light.

Unless you find a space at the end of a row, you will have to fit your car into a gap between two other vehicles. If the cars on either side are well parked you just have to centre your car between the lines. But if they are not carefully parked, make a check on the gap which is left for you before you move into it. You will have to leave enough room for you and your passengers to open the doors and, just as important, for the drivers and passengers of the cars on each side of you to open theirs. This question of room is all the more important with two-door cars.

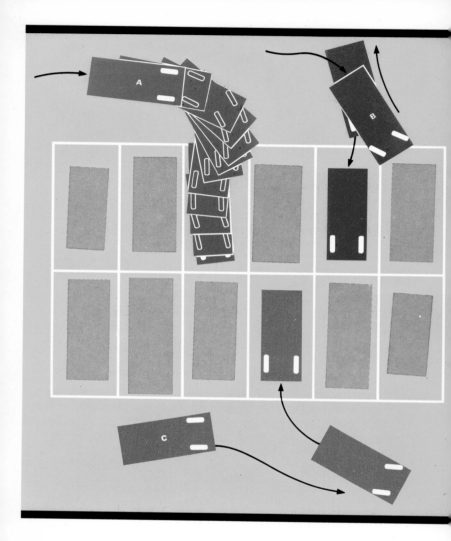

Fig. 49
Using a car park

A does a lot of steering at close quarters; even then he would do well to back out and straighten up.

B gets neatly into place.

C gets just as neatly into place, more simply, and is ready to go.

Parking a car accurately needs care, skill and practice. Everyone can be careful, but if you are short on skill or practice move your car *slowly* so that the steering has maximum effect. You will also have time to see and correct mistakes.

Sometimes the approach to a space in a car park does not give you enough room to 'square up' to it. Trying to get your car into a space in one go may involve very complicated movements of the steering wheel. See Fig. 49. A does a lot of steering at close quarters. He would do better to back out and straighten up as B has done. Better still, C has got just as neatly into place, more simply, and is ready to move out forwards. Car A made it in one go—but look at the position of the front wheels. Car B, on the other hand, nosed into the opening, moved back a bit, squared up, and drove in with the front wheels nearly straight. Except where cars are badly parked, leaving an odd-shaped gap to get into, it is nearly always best to reverse into a parking space, as C did. This gives you a better view when you drive out, especially important at night or if you have several passengers, and saves you from manœuvring with a cold engine. Even if you do have to manœuvre, you can do more of it in forward gear.

To sum up: before entering a car park use the mirror—and signal, if necessary. As you move forward, assess the park; notice its layout and markings, choose a space and see how other cars are parked. Use the mirror again, because car parks are crowded places and cars move quietly. Decide whether another signal will help, check your position carefully, keep your speed low and look again. Finally, 'park pretty', with your wheels straight.

Parking on the road

First, two general points. If there is a kerb try not to touch it when you park. Scraping the sides of your tyres will weaken them, with possibly disastrous results later. Secondly, don't leave your car so close to another that it will be difficult for you or others to get out again.

If there is plenty of room between parked vehicles you can, after using mirror and signal, draw into the side of the road and stop parallel and close to the kerb. But where the space between cars is not big enough for this, you will have to back in. You need a gap at least one and a half times the length of your car; even then you will only get in if you have a good steering lock (that is, a small steering circle). A gap of two car lengths will make the operation easier.

The most important step in this manœuvre is to go far enough forward before you stop. Drive past the gap and stop about half a length past the vehicle behind which you are going to park, parallel to it and about three feet away. When you have made sure it is safe to reverse you can then back into the gap, as illustrated in Fig. 50.

We have dealt with parking in some detail because it calls for care, and skill acquired by practice. If parking worries you, then practise it until you are really skilled. The advice given in this chapter should help you.

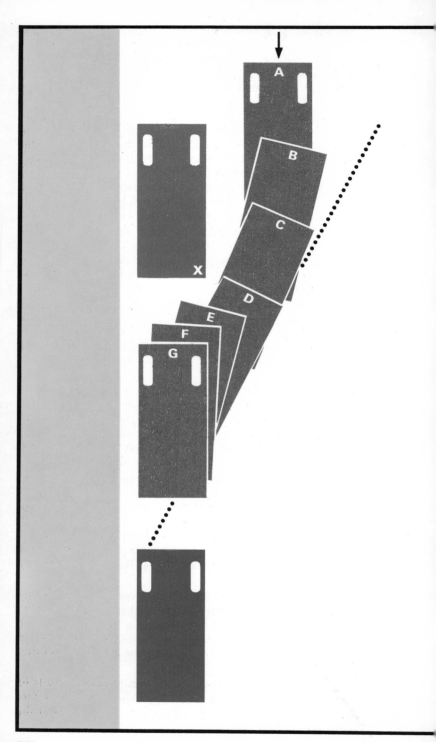

Fig. 50

Parallel parking in reverse gear. This takes advantage of a car's manoeuvrability when driven in reverse gear. When doing this you will be something of an obstacle, so the *mirror—signal— manoeuvre* routine is important. It is also vital to keep a look-out for traffic behind you.

A Drive forward and stop parallel to, and not more than three feet away from the blue car. Then reverse with slight left lock.

B Continue reversing with slight left lock but watch corner of the blue car at X.

C Continue reversing but straighten front wheels ready to change to right lock.

D As you clear the blue car, put on slight right lock and check the gap at X. Then put on full right lock. Your position here will bring the offside of the car in line with the nearside headlamp of the green car (see broken line in diagram). This should help you to judge your position and movements.

E With a large amount of right lock, you will swing in towards the kerb.

F Here you will be close to the kerb and the green car. Move the car very slowly and take off some of the right lock so that the front of your car does not swing in too far.

G Check your distance from the kerb and from the blue and green cars, adjusting as neccessary.

Before parking your car you must ask yourself: 'Is it safe? Is it convenient?' The driver of the second car to park in this road did not answer these questions properly, with the result that other cars have to thread their way through a narrow gap.

Summary

1

The questions to ask yourself before making any manoeuvre: 'Is it safe—convenient—lawful?' And 'Can I control my vehicle accurately enough?'

2

Reversing: the advantage of doing it slowly; the proper way to sit and steer; making the right safety checks.

3

Reversing to the left: where and when to look.

4

Reversing to the right: where and how to look.

5

Other points about reversing: don't back into a main road or for long distances; always be ready to stop.

6

Turning in the road: reversing into a side road; turning with forward and reverse gears; making a U turn (and where not to).

7

Parking: off the road if possible. Car parks: keeping to the markings; going in backwards; parking on the road; reversing into a gap.

11 The open road

Driving on the open road is largely a matter of putting together nearly all the advice in this book. Reading the road and anticipation obviously come into it. So do the proper and constant use of mirror and signals before making any manœuvre, and applying the proper routine at all junctions and other hazards. But there are some points which need special attention when it comes to open road driving, where speeds are usually on the high side, and these are dealt with in this chapter.

Stopping and separation distances

In Chapter 4 we talked about stopping distance and how this was made up of thinking distance plus braking distance. When driving on the open road it is essential to know and be able to judge your stopping distance at various speeds, because stopping distances get much longer the faster you go. So let's have another look at thinking, braking and stopping distances at speeds from 30 m.p.h. upwards, in good conditions on a dry road—and when conditions are not so good.

Stopping distances—in good conditions

When driving at	30	40	50	60	70	m.p.h.
your speed will be	44	59	73	88	103	feet per second
your thinking distance will be about	30	40	50	60	70	feet
your braking distance will be about	45	80	125	180	245	feet
your stopping distance will be about	**75**	**120**	**175**	**240**	**315**	**feet**

40 feet   **75 feet**   **120 feet**

20 MPH   **30**   **40**

Fig. 51
Stopping distances (red figures) get longer as speed increases
These are the stopping distances for a good car with good brakes on a

175 feet

240 feet

315 feet

50

60

70

dry road. On wet or slippery roads, or with poor brakes or tyres, they
are much longer still.

Fig. 52

The dial shows what miles per hour mean in feet per second. Note that you travel just about half as many feet per second again as miles per hour. In other words, at 20 m.p.h. you travel 30 f.p.s., at 40 m.p.h. you travel 60 f.p.s.

Stopping distances—in poor conditions

When driving at you should allow	30	40	50	60	70	m.p.h.
about	150	240	350	480	630	feet

Have a good look at the second line in the first table (see page 125); it gives speed in *feet per second*, as does the speedometer in Fig. 52. You will see that when driving at 60 m.p.h. you travel almost *90 feet every second*. This means that if your thinking time is half a second (much better than average) you will travel about 45 feet—the length of three or four popular cars—before you are able to *do* anything about braking. Then on top of this there is the distance before your brakes can bring you to a stop. The faster you are going, the longer this will be. It depends, too, on road and weather conditions—if they are bad, you cannot safely put so much pressure on the brakes.

These drivers are heading for trouble. They are following one another much too closely for their speeds of 40 m.p.h. and over.

There are two important points to remember about this. First, that your stopping distance is probably much longer than you think. Second, that, even with good anticipation, you will still travel quite a long way before you can turn the information you get from observation into action: and the higher your speed the further you will go before you can start that action.

So the good driver uses anticipation continuously to give himself room to work in; room to recognise a developing situation and room to act. The action may be no more than taking a foot off the accelerator and covering the footbrake; or it could mean applying the full safety routine of *mirror—signal—manœuvre*. Whichever it is, smooth driving—the hallmark of the good driver—is the aim.

If you have to take panic action because you have insufficient room to act smoothly, you are either going too fast or driving too close to the vehicle in front.

How big a gap?

How much room should you allow yourself when driving in a stream of traffic? The absolutely safe rule is to leave your stopping distance between your car and the one in front. But in heavy, slow-moving traffic, it is just not practicable to leave this sort of gap—40 feet (three to four car lengths) between vehicles moving at 20 m.p.h.—without a lot of waste of valuable road space.

So a sensible balance has to be drawn. Even so, if you are driving closer than your *stopping* distance you are taking a risk. The gap should never be less than your *thinking* distance—if it is, you are heading for trouble.

But out on the open road and going at a fair speed, it becomes much more important to keep a good gap. A collision at speed can obviously have serious results. Most people drive much too close to the vehicle in front (many even closer than their thinking

Below:
What a gap of 50 yards looks like when you are following a vehicle. You are still too close if you are doing more than 50 m.p.h.

distance). So if, in future, you leave more room than you have been in the habit of doing, you will almost certainly be doing the right thing. Your stopping distance is still the only really safe gap, but here again this is something of an ideal. A reasonable rule to apply in good conditions is a gap of *one yard for each m.p.h. of your speed.* (Do you know what 50 yards looks like when you are doing 50 m.p.h.?) On wet or icy roads, or if your tyres, brakes, or even your health, are below par, the gap should be much bigger. And when a vehicle overtakes you and moves into the gap ahead, lengthen the space again by dropping back.

Dual carriageways

These are becoming more and more common on main roads. A division between traffic going in opposite directions certainly helps vehicles to move faster and more safely, but there are a number of special points to remember about dual carriageways.

Fig. 53

This sign warns you that you are coming to a single carriageway and there will be two-way traffic ahead.

Use the lanes properly. (Have another look at the last part of Chapter 5.) Because traffic usually moves pretty quickly, it is vital to use the *mirror—signal—manœuvre* routine—and in good time. Keep to the nearside, except when overtaking (or in the few special cases mentioned on pages 141 and 142). Overtake only on the right. If there is a lot of slow-moving traffic in the nearside lane, there is no need to go back to that lane each time you overtake. It can be better to stay in the right-hand lane than to move in and out continually. But be sensible about this. Don't hog the outside lane and prevent others from overtaking you. Even if you are driving up to the maximum speed limit, it is not your business to stop others from going faster by staying in the outside lane. If the chap behind you is determined to exceed the speed limit, this could make matters worse by infuriating him and encouraging him to overtake on your left.

When you are going to turn right to leave a dual carriageway, use your mirror, signal and move over to the right in good time. Be ready to stop in the gap in the central reservation. *If you do, stop clear of traffic on both carriageways.* Watch out for and obey any road markings in the gap—the general rule is to keep to the left in the gap.

There will be warning signs to tell you when you are coming to the end of a dual carriageway: look out for the TWO-WAY TRAFFIC sign (see Fig. 53) and the warning to REDUCE SPEED NOW. You will almost certainly have to slow down and your speed will probably be higher than you think, especially if you have been on the dual carriageway for some time. So check your speedometer.

If you are crossing a dual carriageway or turning right on to it, you really have two roads to deal with. The first will be one-way from your right and the second one-way from your left. At some junctions you have to turn left before you can cross or turn right on to the second carriageway. Whatever the layout, be ready to stop in the central gap—clear of the traffic.

Positioning is usually simpler when turning left on to a dual carriageway, but even then you must be careful. Even if the slow lane is clear, take care not to swing out into the outside lane. Incidentally, if you are on a dual carriageway and see a vehicle ahead waiting to join it from a junction on the left, it is helpful to move over to the right-hand lane *if you can do so safely*. This will

Parking too near a corner can cause difficulty—and following through, as the blue car is doing, only adds to the difficulty.

let the driver join the carriageway without undue delay, and also give you an added safety margin.

Overtaking

Overtaking in the wrong place or at the wrong time is asking for trouble and is one of the major causes of death and serious injury on the roads. This is not surprising, as you are usually on a collision course with traffic coming the other way. So it is vital to pick your place and time carefully; to be sure, before you overtake, that you can get back to your side of the road safely, without getting in the way of vehicles coming towards you or those you are overtaking.

There are two sorts of overtaking. One is where you are passing stationary vehicles at the side of the road (or even obstructions such as road works). The other is where you pass a vehicle going your way.

Passing stationary vehicles and other obstructions

This is usually fairly straightforward but, like any other driving

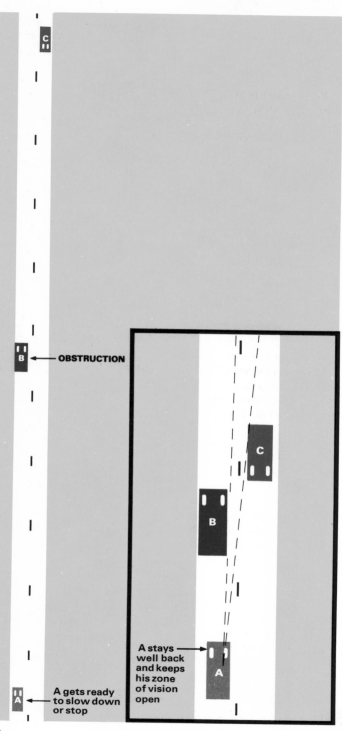

OBSTRUCTION

A stays well back and keeps his zone of vision open

A gets ready to slow down or stop

action, it needs thought. Fig. 54 shows a typical example. A can see the stationary vehicle or other obstruction at B on his side of the road. So the responsibility for deciding whether to go on or wait is A's. He should go on only if he can do so without making C slow down or stop. Otherwise, he must wait.

Put yourself in A's position. As soon as you sight B, use your mirror and then check that your speed is low enough to stop, if necessary, before you reach him. As you get nearer B, you can begin to assess what you see: whether C is slowing down or speeding up, whether B is still stationary or about to move away. Then you can make up your mind what you are going to do.

Having decided, check your *mirror* again, *signal* if necessary and then decide your *position*. If you are going to stop and wait, how close to B and how far in? If you are going to pass, how far out, and how soon to begin to pull out? Next, *speed*: is it time to brake for the stop, or to change down to move slowly towards B while C goes by, or to speed up and perhaps change down to, say, third gear to get briskly by? And finally, you must *look*—if you are stopping, to see whether it will be clear to go on after C has passed; or, if you are going on, to make sure that the situation has not changed since you made your decision.

If B is an obstruction such as road works you will also have to look out for workmen and their vehicles, and see what sort of road surface is ahead.

Obstructions on hills need special care. As we have already seen, gradients can affect braking, steering and acceleration, so you need an extra safety margin. Always try to act just that bit sooner on a hill. If you are going downhill and the obstruction is on your side of the road, begin your braking in good time. This will not only keep your driving smooth but will give drivers coming towards you a chance to see what you are going to do. If, on the other hand, you are going on, and perhaps accelerating, remember that if you should need to slow down again your braking will have to be that much heavier.

Finally, don't assume that you have right of way if the obstruction is on the other side of the road. It is much more considerate to let traffic, especially heavy vehicles, coming uphill have a clear run. You can start off again downhill more easily than they can uphill.

Overtaking a moving vehicle

Although you must pass a stationary vehicle in order to get on with your journey, you don't *have* to overtake a moving vehicle. So this brings up the first question to ask yourself: 'Is my overtaking really necessary?' If you decide that it is, you must then

Fig. 54

Waiting to pass an obstruction.

It is difficult to see round a large vehicle, especially if you are too close behind it (*above, top*). If you keep well back (*above, lower*) you can see the road ahead and make sensible decisions.

find a suitable place. Some places are never suitable, as the Highway Code shows us, and there are three main reasons for this. Firstly, you may not be able to see the road ahead; this happens at junctions, corners, the brow of a hill etc. Secondly, there may be a special need to allow for the movement of other road users; for instance, at pedestrian crossings, narrow roads and, again, junctions. Thirdly, when you overtake you are frequently travelling fast on the wrong side of the road for quite a long distance; this means that you cannot overtake safely unless you have a first-class zone of vision and are certain that you have weighed up all the foreseeable possibilities.

The speed of the vehicle you are going to overtake is very important. When you are coming up to a stationary vehicle, you know exactly where you are going to pass it (assuming it doesn't move before you get there). But when you are closing up behind a moving vehicle, it will cover quite a distance before you can actually pass it. How far it will have travelled will depend on the difference between its speed and yours. If you see a vehicle 200 yards ahead of you doing 15 m.p.h. and you are doing 30 m.p.h., you will have to go 400 yards—nearly a quarter of a mile—before you catch up with it. This means that you must not only be thinking well ahead, but that you must be assessing and re-assessing the traffic and the situation, in front and behind, throughout this quarter of a mile.

This assessment has to be linked with another judgment about speed—that of any vehicle coming towards you from the opposite direction. Here it is a matter not of the difference between two speeds, but of the sum of them. Two vehicles coming towards each other at 55 m.p.h. will be closing the gap between them at 110 m.p.h. They will get more than 160 feet closer to each other *every second*. So for every second you are going to be on the wrong side of the road you need, at these speeds, a pretty long stretch of clear road ahead of you. Overtaking takes much more than a second. And the smaller the difference between your speed and the speed of the vehicle you are overtaking, the more time and the longer stretch of clear road you will need. It is because so many drivers do not realise how much time and how much road they need to get past and back again to their own side of the road that there are so many fatal and serious overtaking accidents. Remember the golden rule: if in doubt, do not overtake.

Large vehicles present a particular problem, just because they are more difficult to see round. You need to keep well back to get a view of the road ahead so that you are ready and able to overtake as soon as a suitable moment arrives (see Fig. 55). You often see drivers bunched up behind a large lorry which they are unable to overtake because they are so close together they can't see that the road ahead is clear.

So play it right: leave a good space while waiting to overtake, and if another car fills the gap drop back again. You won't gain anything by sitting on his tail; you will only deny yourself the chance of having a good view of the road ahead, and help to build up a queue.

Another thing to remember about large vehicles is that their speed can vary quite a lot, particularly if they are loaded, between moving along on the level and going uphill or downhill. When you are behind a large lorry notice whether or not it is loaded. If it is you can expect its speed to drop, perhaps to a crawl, if there is a hill to climb ahead. But once over the top of a hill, a loaded lorry can pick up speed again very quickly, especially downhill.

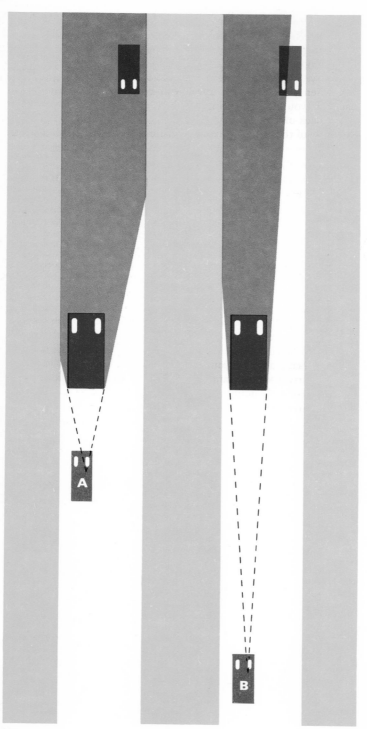

Remember these possible changes in speed differential when thinking about overtaking a lorry.

Other points about overtaking on hills have already been mentioned in Chapter 9—particularly that it is more difficult to slow down when going downhill; and that traffic coming towards you when you are going uphill will be approaching faster than usual. If you are overtaking uphill, give yourself time and room to get back on to your own side of the road well before you reach the brow of the hill. Your zone of vision will be getting shorter the closer you get to it, which means that a vehicle coming towards you could be on top of you very quickly.

On some long hills where the road is not wide enough for four lanes of traffic you will find double white lines dividing the road so that there are two lanes for traffic going uphill and only one downhill. In some places the line on the downhill side is broken. This means that you can overtake going downhill if it is safe to do so, but the uphill traffic in effect has priority. (See Fig. 56.)

Overtaking at the wrong time or place is particularly deadly on a road divided into three lanes, because the middle lane is used for overtaking in both directions. This middle lane is not an open invitation to overtake: on the contrary, it is most important here to make sure that the road ahead is clear far enough ahead. Never overtake when coming up to a blind spot like the brow of a hill; you could be on a collision course with a car which you can't see coming fast towards you from the other direction—and no sensible driver would want to do that. Many of these danger spots are marked with double white lines, so be on the look-out for advance arrows warning you to get over to the left.

On three-lane roads, junction signs and hatched markings in the middle of the road are particular warnings not to overtake. There may be traffic waiting to turn right or slowing down to turn left. So you must be ready to hold back.

Lastly, before overtaking anywhere, make up your mind what the driver in front is doing or is likely to do. He may be deciding whether he is going to overtake; or he may be content to drive at the speed of the vehicle in front of him. Perhaps he is going to turn off soon or can see something ahead which you can't. You can decide what he is going to do only by watching him—and the road ahead—for a while.

Fig. 55

Overtaking a large lorry

This diagram shows how getting too close behind a large vehicle makes it impossible to see far enough ahead. A's position is useless. B, who is keeping much farther back, has a much better view. If he moved *slightly* to the right, which he could do safely from this position, he would have a better view still.

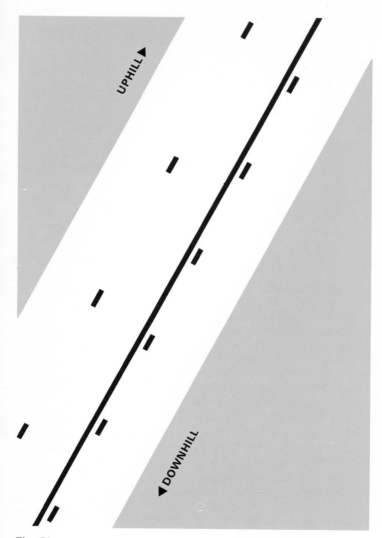

Fig. 56

Two lanes up and one down help overtaking up a long hill

Beware the driver ahead who is so close to the vehicle in front of him that he is constantly swinging in and out. He will be one of the impatient sort who doesn't give himself enough room to see ahead. Leave yourself plenty of room behind him—just in case he does something silly.

Steps to overtaking

Having looked at some of the particular problems of overtaking, we now sum up by giving the drill in detail. As you will see, it brings in the *position—speed—look* and the *mirror—signal—manœuvre* routines.

Position: near enough to the vehicle ahead so that you can pull out and overtake smoothly when you are ready, but not so close that you can't get a good view of the road in front of it.

Speed: fast enough to keep up with the vehicle in front and with enough in reserve to be able to pass it quickly. You may need to change down to give you extra acceleration when you are ready to start overtaking.

Look: assess the whole situation; in front, the state of the road, what the driver ahead is doing, any hazards, the speed and position of vehicles coming towards you, speed differentials and so on. Then the situation behind you, which means using your . . .

Mirror: never begin to overtake if another vehicle is overtaking you or is about to do so. When you are sure it is safe to overtake . . .

Signal: give a signal, if necessary, to show other drivers you intend to pull out. Even if there is no one behind you, a signal can be helpful to drivers coming towards you and possibly to the one you are overtaking.

Manœuvre: make a final check in front and pull out on a smooth easy line. Get past as quickly as you can. Then another check in the mirror to see that you are clear of the vehicle you have overtaken and then pull in again to the left, also on a smooth easy line to avoid cutting in.

You may have to do some or all of these steps several times before the right moment arrives. If, as you are about to overtake, someone overtakes you, then you must start the routine all over again. (Incidentally, never accelerate when someone is overtaking you.)

A last word of warning about overtaking. Many drivers seem to think that because the car in front has passed an obstacle or moving vehicle, it is safe for them to follow through. They seem to believe that the vehicle in front will protect them in some magic way. But it won't. The driver in front has more time to pull in out of the way of approaching traffic than you would have.

Always make your own decision about overtaking, based on what *you* see and what *you* know. The biggest virtue for any driver who wants to overtake is patience. If in doubt—hold back.

Overtaking on the left

Generally speaking, you should never overtake on the left. There are, however, a few exceptions to this rule. They are:

1 When the driver in front has signalled a right turn and has moved out so that you can pass him on the left. But make sure you do not get in the way of following vehicles coming up on your left. If there is a turning on the left as well,

141

watch out for anything moving into it across your path which may be hidden by the vehicle turning right.

2 When you are in the correct lane to filter left at a junction.

3 When there are queues of slow moving traffic, and vehicles in the lane on your right are moving more slowly than you are.

4 When it is safe to do so in one-way streets.

Level crossings

Level crossings with gates or barriers right across the road

Some crossings with gates or barriers across the whole width of the road are controlled by a gate-keeper or from the local signal box. The gates are closed to the road only when a train is coming. Where the crossing is not controlled, you will have to open the gates yourself. To do this, get out of your car, and look and listen carefully for any sound of a train. When you are sure that none is coming, open *both* gates and drive right across the railway on to the road on the other side. Then get out and shut the gates. Never stop on the crossing itself. At some of these 'open it yourself' crossings there are miniature red and green warning lights. If the red light comes on, a train is on the way. Keep clear of the rails until it has gone.

Crossings with barriers across half the road

Some level crossings have half-barriers which are worked automatically by approaching trains. As well as the barriers, this type of crossing has bells, amber lights and pairs of red flashing lights at the side of the road. There are telephones to the nearest signalman at the side of the road near each barrier.

The first warning of a train coming is the bell ringing and a steady amber light (where fitted) followed by twin flashing red lights. Then, within about eight seconds, the barriers come down across half the road. The train arrives soon afterwards. These crossings are designed to help the flow of road traffic. Properly used, they do this. But their safe use depends on everyone knowing how they work and keeping to the rules of proper behaviour. These are the points to remember:

1 Stop if the bells sound and the lights show as you approach the crossing.

2 Never zigzag round barriers when they are down (or coming down).

3 Stop as close to the stop line as you can.

4 Don't cross unless there is enough clear road beyond the crossing for your vehicle and any other one that you may be following on to the crossing.

5 Keep a reasonable distance behind the vehicle in front so that if it stalls on the crossing you don't get caught on the crossing as well.

6 If the barriers stay down and the lights continue to flash after a train has gone, it means another train is coming—wait where you are.

7 If after about three minutes the barriers stay down but no train appears, telephone the signalman to find out what has happened.

8 If you are crossing and hear the bells ringing (you won't see the lights, which will be behind you), keep going.

9 If your vehicle breaks down or stalls on the crossing and you have passengers, the *first* thing to do, in *any* circumstances, is to get all your passengers out and clear of the crossing. Then phone the signalman. If he says there is no train near, try to re-start your vehicle or to push it clear and tell the signalman when you have done so. If the bells start to ring, stand clear of the crossing. Don't waste time trying to re-start or to drive off on the starter before you get your passengers out.

10 If you break down on the crossing when you are alone in your car, try to start it again. But don't waste time. If you can't move it quickly, phone the signalman. In any case, stand clear of the crossing if the bells begin to ring.

Open level crossings

Some crossings without gates have flashing red lights as at half-barrier crossings. The rule is the same: don't cross when the lights are flashing. In very quiet places there are crossings with neither gates nor traffic signals. Here you should slow down as though you were approaching a crossroad, look both ways, listen carefully and cross only when you are sure it is safe.

Summary

1

Driving on the open road; the need for reading the road and anticipation; the constant use of mirrors and of the safe and junction routines.

2

The importance of knowing your stopping distances and being able to judge them accurately; making allowance for bad weather conditions.

3

Keeping good separation distances—how big a gap; enough room to work in; the importance of driving smoothly.

4

Dual carriageways; the proper use of lanes; keeping to the left except when overtaking; how to join and cross them.

5

Overtaking; picking the right time and place; passing stationary and moving vehicles; looking well ahead; the importance of judging speeds accurately; avoiding queues; how to pass large lorries. Overtaking on hills, three-lane roads and, exceptionally, on the left.

6

A drill for overtaking.

7

Level crossings.

12 Other people

Previous chapters have shown how much the good driver needs to watch other road users to decide on his own course of action and how important it is to fit in with the flow of traffic at junctions, roundabouts and so on. But 'other road users' means more than just the flow of traffic; it means everyone who is on or near the stretch of road you are on.

The good driver not only has to recognise what the other chap is doing or going to do, but must also understand his problems and difficulties and allow for them. To everyone else, we are the 'other people' and are grateful for help and consideration from them. Here are some general points which can help you to help others.

Cars and lorries

Large vehicles ahead turning left. As well as keeping well back from a large vehicle, remember that its driver may not be able to turn left without going out to the right first. So be very careful about moving up on the left; if you get so close that you cannot see his signals you may get caught out. Goods vehicles often have to turn into gateways and yards on the nearside, and the narrower the opening the more likely it is that the driver will have to go out to the right first. So watch out for these vehicles turning left, especially if they are long ones or articulated. Be ready to stop to give them room—and don't try to get past on the left—you could get caught.

Standing vehicles. We have already looked at most of the problems caused by stationary vehicles. No road is wider than the gap between a stationary vehicle and the kerb opposite. The real message of a stationary vehicle on the road, however far ahead, is 'road narrows'. (See Fig. 57.)

145

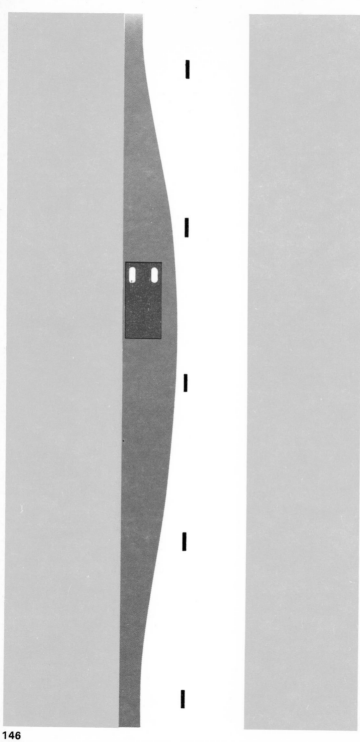

Be prepared for large vehicles to move out to the right before turning left.

Gaps for turning vehicles. You can often help other people (and yourself, in the long run) by stopping a little short to allow space for other vehicles to turn while you are waiting. At traffic lights, for example, a line of waiting vehicles may overlap a side turning farther back (see Fig. 58). Leaving a gap costs you nothing; it is not only good manners but it will reduce congestion. If you are waiting at A and there is a vehicle immediately ahead, leaving no gap, you can sometimes let a waiting driver turn in or out ahead of you by holding back when the gap does open. There are no rights of way about this; it is a matter of anticipation and fitting your actions to the circumstances.

Behaviour at junctions. You may know how to deal with a junction properly, but other drivers don't know that you know. An eyes-down, last-minute-braking approach to a junction is not only bad driving in itself, but can alarm other drivers and lead them into panic action. Your actions should speak for themselves. A well-controlled approach to a junction tells everyone that you are aware of the situation and are dealing with it properly.

Cutting in. To cut in is to force yourself into a stream of traffic in such a way that another driver has to get out of your way. It's a bad fault, most often caused by ill-judged overtaking or an unsuccessful attempt to pass which forces the driver to get back in lane regardless. If you see this situation building up, you can help to prevent an accident by being ready to drop back. Follow

Fig. 57

A standing vehicle tells you: 'road narrows'

Because the shaded part is lost, road width may be down to half.

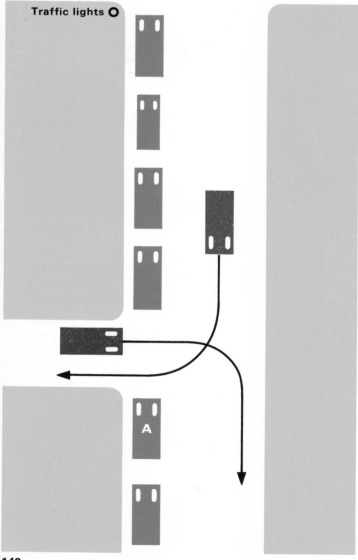

Traffic lights O

A

the overtaking routine properly yourself, and you will avoid any need to cut in.

Left-turn indicators at a junction. While waiting to emerge at a junction, you often see a vehicle coming from the right showing a left-turn indicator. Don't assume that it *will* turn left. Wait and be sure. The driver *may* be going to turn left; but he may also be going to stop on the left either before or after he gets to the junction—or he may have forgotten to switch off his indicators. If the vehicle is a large one it may be hiding others coming up much faster behind it, or even overtaking it.

Buses and coaches

Look for bus and coach stopping places so that you will be ready to pull in, stop or pull out. Notice the design of bus shelters and stops so that you can spot them quickly, wherever you are. At busy times when bus traffic is heavy, there is a particular need to be ready to allow for buses stopping or pulling out—so use your mirror frequently and keep your speed well in hand.

When driving behind a bus or coach watch for passengers moving towards the door. This will often warn you of a stop ahead. Similarly, if you are held up behind one of these large vehicles at a stop and are thinking about whether to pass or wait, a rough count of the waiting passengers will sometimes help you to decide.

Remember that the bus or coach driver, although helped by sitting higher than you, has a much larger vehicle to handle and is handicapped by poorer vision behind him. So be patient, especially if there are several buses together.

Near roundabouts and other junctions remember that a bus or coach is more difficult to manœuvre than a car. For a number of reasons, a change of lane will take more time and space for a bus than for you.

Cyclists

Look out for cyclists and make allowances for the differences between your means of travel and theirs. The younger they are the more closely you should watch them and be ready to slow down or stop. A cyclist glancing round is a signal to you that he may be going to move out or turn.

Cyclists may make sudden sideways movements; give them plenty of room when you pass them.

Cyclists are affected by cross-winds, particularly at side turnings, near tall buildings or at such places as low bridges.

In headwinds or in wet weather cyclists tend to keep their heads down. This creates risk; be alert for it and for the danger of cyclists skidding (side-slipping) on smooth wet surfaces.

Fig. 58
Leaving a gap for turning vehicles.

Cyclists going uphill have difficulty. Be ready for them to slow down or to stop and get off.

Cyclists with bulky loads. Cyclists are sometimes tempted to ride when carrying light but bulky objects. This can seriously affect their control and balance and even their vision. So be wary.

When you are going to turn left, and especially if you have to wait at the corner, look out for cyclists who may have moved up between you and the left-hand kerb (or who may be using a cycle-track).

Before turning left, look out for cyclists moving up between you and the kerb.

Motor-cyclists (including moped and scooter riders)

Much of what we have said about cyclists applies also to motor-cyclists, although some of them will be less affected by weather conditions and hills. There are many situations in which a two-wheeled machine is less stable than a car, so leave plenty of room, especially for riders on less powerful machines.

In many places motor-cyclists will be able to go on when there is no room for your car. Don't let this irritate you or encourage you to push forward when you shouldn't. As with cyclists, be on the look-out for motor-cyclists who move up on your left when you are preparing or waiting to turn left.

Pedestrians

Pedestrians are not just 'traffic'—they are people, and the younger they are the faster they are likely to move or change direction. Those with prams, the elderly, the blind and the infirm all need your special care and consideration. They depend on you for their safety.

When you choose a place to stop and park your car, give a thought to pedestrians. Might it prevent a mother from getting her pram up or down the kerb? Would its position puzzle or confuse a blind person—for instance, by overhanging the kerb or blocking his path?

In busy shopping areas, watch out for pedestrians stepping out between parked cars. This is especially common in wet weather when shoppers are apt to make a sudden dash across the road.

Turning corners. Always give way to people who are already in the road when you turn a corner.

On country roads where there are no footpaths pedestrians, perhaps with children, a pram or an animal, may be coming towards you on your side of the road on a left-hand bend. Be on the look-out and keep your speed down. Remember too that cyclists become pedestrians on hills which are too steep to ride up.

Where vehicles are parked at the kerb or held up in a traffic stream, watch out for pedestrians who may step out between them. Elderly people and children are apt to do this and it is common in shopping streets, especially in wet weather. So keep

At pedestrian crossings give way to anyone with a pram.

your eyes open and *keep your speed down*. Nearly a quarter of all pedestrian accidents happen near parked vehicles.

Don't use your horn too close to a pedestrian who appears not to have seen you. A quick tap, in good time, is best. If he has already moved out of your path, don't sound the horn at all. It could startle him into stepping back. On this point of considering others, don't use the starter and rev your engine just as an elderly pedestrian is level with you, especially when streets are slippery. Wait a second; it can make all the difference.

Pedestrians at crossings

People on foot have certain rights of way at pedestrian crossings but they are safe only if drivers keep to the rules and do the right things. Never overtake when you are approaching any sort of pedestrian crossing, and have your speed well in hand so that you are ready to slow down or stop to give way to pedestrians.

Zebra crossings. Uncontrolled or zebra crossings have flashing orange beacons as an advance warning. The crossing itself is marked by black and white stripes and there are studs across your half of the road 15 yards before the actual crossing to provide an area free of parked vehicles so that everyone has a clear view. In one-way streets the studs run from kerb to kerb.

You must allow free passage to any pedestrian on the crossing. The approach to a pedestrian crossing is another place where the *mirror—signal—manœuvre* routine needs to be applied. Another thing to remember is that the 'signal' part means the arm signal for slowing down or stopping. The Highway Code tells pedestrians to allow drivers ample time to give way, especially if the road is wet or icy. A good practical rule for drivers is: Where people are waiting on the pavement, let them wait; but where they are crossing, let them cross. As with many good rules, there is an important exception and this is where a mother is waiting at the kerb with a pram. She cannot safely stand on a crossing holding a pram, but let her cross just the same.

Some zebra crossings are divided by a central island, and then each half forms a separate crossing.

At pedestrian crossings, controlled by light signals, or the police, you must give way to people who are still crossing when you get the signal to move. At some crossings, where pedestrians can use push-buttons to start the signal sequence, you will not see the red-with-amber signal before the green. Instead, there will be flashing amber. This means that you must give way to pedestrians on the crossing, but otherwise you can go on.

All pedestrian crossings should be left free during traffic hold-ups. Stop before you reach the crossing if you can see that you won't be able to clear it.

Wherever there are pedestrians:

1 Give yourself more time to stop if the road is wet or icy.
2 Always give children, the elderly, the blind or infirm plenty of time to cross the road.
3 Never signal to pedestrians that you are giving way to them. (There is no authorised signal for this, and it is dangerous to wave invitations to them to come into the road because you cannot be sure what other drivers may do.)
4 Stick to the rules, then everyone knows what to expect.

Children

The very young lack experience of traffic, and even the older ones are unlikely to be good judges of speed and distance. They are all apt to do things unwisely and without warning. So whenever you see a child on the footpath or the road—take *extra* care. You have to do for the child what it may not yet be able to do for itself— take proper care. Over 750 children are killed on the roads each year and there are no more useless words than 'I didn't have a chance'.

Young pedestrians. Although children are trained at school and elsewhere to walk on the footpath and to use pedestrian crossings, they do forget. So watch them carefully as you approach and as you pass. Give them plenty of time on crossings.

Children at play. Children playing near roads are especially likely to forget the traffic. Think for them, particularly near ice-cream vans, window displays, street traders' stalls and so on.

A child running is a signal of danger to the child himself, to you and your passengers, and to drivers who may be following you. Be ready to take action *in good time* so that you don't have to brake suddenly.

Child cyclists. Children on bicycles need plenty of room. Give them a wide berth when you are passing and always be ready for them to change direction suddenly.

School times. Get to know school times in your area; these are the danger periods for children. Watch out for children on foot or on cycles, especially on dark winter mornings and afternoons. Keep a look-out for school buses, particularly in country districts.

Warning children of your approach. Children often take more notice of a repeated tap-tap on the horn than they do of a loud blast, which can go 'over their heads'.

Reversing. The Highway Code warns you to make sure that there are no children behind your vehicle before you reverse it. Make sure—even if it means getting out to look.

Children as passengers. Children are safer in the back. Make sure that they are *seated* and, if they are old enough, that they wear a proper safety harness or seat belt. If they are not old enough for this, they should be held by a passenger who is wearing a belt or harness, or fastened in a cot which is itself firmly fixed. Be specially careful to lock the doors, and teach your children not to fiddle with locks.

Animals

The animals you are most likely to meet on the road can be divided into two groups: dogs and cats in towns and cities; and horses, cattle, sheep and led animals in smaller towns and the countryside.

Dogs. When you see a dog, notice whether it is on a lead. If it is not (or if you can't see for sure) use your mirror and then keep an eye on the dog. If it runs into the road do your best—but don't swerve or stop regardless and endanger other people.

Cats can usually look after themselves but they do sometimes make a high-speed dash across the road. Be ready to ease your foot off the accelerator pedal—but no emergency stops.

Horses. When you see a horse and rider, slow down, avoid making unnecessary noise, and leave plenty of room. A group of riders may mean a riding school and children learning, so go easy and be ready to stop or crawl past. If you see a string of horses near racing stables, look for signals from the first and last riders. Led horses may be coming towards you on your side of the road; be prepared for this, especially on left-hand bends in horse-riding country.

Other animals. Always reduce speed and be ready to stop. Be patient, even if animals block the road while they are being moved, and respect the signals of the person in charge of them.

Signs about animals. In some areas you will see warning signs about ponies, deer or other animals which may come on to the road. Watch out for them, especially at dawn or dusk and other

Opening a car door without due care can maim or kill a passing cyclist.

times when it is difficult to see—in dazzling sunshine, mist and heavy rain.

Animals at night. Look out for any lights which may warn you of animals on the road. Herdsmen sometimes rely on the lamps of their own bicycles.

The dog in your car. If you take a dog with you train him not to clamber about. If you can't do this, tie him up. At all events— no climbing about and no touching the driver.

Car doors

Closed car doors won't hurt anyone. Open, they can be a menace and can even kill a passing cyclist. When you stop, always link *doors*, *cyclists* and *pedestrians* in your mind.

Opening doors on the pavement side of the car can be a real danger to pedestrians, especially the very young or the elderly.

Don't open your driving door without first using your mirror and looking round to double-check behind. Even then, open it carefully.

With a four-door car, make a rule that no one inside the car should open the rear door nearest the traffic.

If there are children in the car, have some rules about who opens any door—and when.

Summary

1

Making allowances—large vehicles ahead turning left; standing and turning vehicles.

2

Buses and coaches; making allowances for them; stopping places.

3

Cyclists and motor-cyclists; why they need plenty of room.

4

Consideration for pedestrians; correct procedure at crossings.

5

The need to be especially careful where children are about; making them safe as passengers.

6

Dealing with cats, dogs and other animals.

7

The need for care when opening car doors.

13 Keeping your grip

Tyres

The tyres of your car are, or should be, your only contact with the road. The area of contact is small—little more than the size of the sole of a man's shoe for each tyre. This chapter shows just how hard that small area of tyre has to work and what you can reasonably expect it to do for you.

Tyres won't do their job properly and safely unless they are in good condition—and this includes the spare. They can easily be damaged and, of course, they wear out. So they need to be treated with care, as well as checked, maintained and replaced when necessary.

How to save wear and tear

Keep your tyres at the correct pressures. Few things wear them out more quickly than running them too soft. This allows too much flexing, or bending, of the tyre walls (sides) and so makes the tyre overheat. Wherever possible, avoid driving through potholes and breaks in the road surface. If you can't avoid it—for instance, where the road is being repaired—you will save wear and tear by slowing down. Don't drive over kerbs or scrape your wheels along them when manœuvring. This can cause damage to the walls of the tyres and lead to tyre failure later on. You can also save wear on the treads by avoiding high speeds, fast cornering and heavy braking.

Tyre pressures

Except for the obvious flat, you can't guess pressures by just looking at the tyres. Use a reliable pressure gauge to check your tyres, at least once a week, when they are cold. (Don't forget the spare, and remember to put the valve caps back.) Your car handbook will give the recommended pressures. It will also tell you whether the tyres need different pressures for different conditions. In general, pressures should be higher for a heavily loaded car or if you are going to drive at high speeds for long periods. Remember that it is an offence to use a car with a tyre not properly inflated.

Checking the condition of your tyres

Don't let oil or grease remain on your tyres. Anything caught in the treads—stones, glass, tacks—could work in and cause damage, so check from time to time and remove anything of this sort.

Tyres must be free from cuts and bulges. When you check your tyre walls, don't forget the inner ones (those facing each other under the car). The gripping power of a worn tyre is much reduced, particularly on wet roads. So see that all your tyres have a good depth of tread right across and all round them. (One millimetre of tread across at least three-quarters of the width and all round the tyre is the absolute minimum legal requirement.)

Uneven wear of the tread, either across or round the tyre, may be due to a mechanical defect. The wheel alignment may be wrong or the wheels out of balance, or there may be a fault in the suspension or the braking system. As soon as you see anything of this sort, have your car checked and the defect put right, and a new tyre fitted if necessary.

Replacing tyres

When you are thinking about replacing tyres, you need to distinguish between the two main types of tyre in general use—*cross-ply* and *radial-ply*. In cross-ply tyres the cords making up the tyre carcass run diagonally across it, with alternate layers at opposite angles, forming a kind of trellis. Radial-ply tyres have all the cords running at right angles across the tyre, resulting in thinner and more flexible walls. There are also differences in the way the tread of radial-ply tyres is built up, giving extra grip, especially in the wet.

A new car is normally fitted with the same type of tyre all round. If you change tyres one or two at a time, keep to the same type.

It is never safe to put radial-ply tyres at the front with cross-ply at the rear. There are no exceptions to this rule and it applies whether the car has front-wheel drive or rear-wheel drive. And don't mix cross-ply and radial-ply on the same axle. (See Fig. 59.)

Apart from its dangers, mixing radial- and cross-ply tyres obviously makes rotation of tyres (if recommended for your car) difficult if not impossible. So the answer is to keep to the same type of tyre all round. If you want to change your type of tyres, change them all if you can—all cross-ply or all radial-ply. If you have to mix types, the radial-ply tyres must go on the back wheels. Even so, the car will handle differently from the way it would with the same type of tyre all round.

CROSS-PLY

on all 4 wheels
— this is SAFE

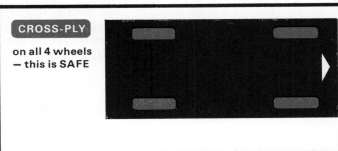

RADIAL-PLY

on all 4 wheels
— this is SAFE

RADIAL-PLY

on REAR;

CROSS-PLY

on FRONT —
this is the only
safe mixture;
but it is not
suitable for
high-
performance
cars

RADIALS ALL ROUND — or on REAR ONLY

NEVER put RADIALS on front only or on the same axle as
CROSS-PLY

Fig. 59
Cross- and radial-ply tyres

When you replace a tubeless tyre, have a new valve fitted to the wheel. Some punctures in these tyres can be 'stopped' with rubber plugs—but this is only a temporary repair, so keep your speed down until you can get the tyre looked at thoroughly.

If you follow this advice you should always have a good set of sound and effective tyres, which will hold the road well and help you to brake firmly. Even so, they cannot do the impossible. Your safety will still depend on your handling of the car. This is particularly true when roads are wet or icy because, however good your tyres are, they cannot grip so well in these conditions. So while on the subject of tyres and grip, let us look at what happens when you lose grip and skid.

Skidding

There are three factors in a skid; in order of importance, the driver, the vehicle and the road. Skids are more likely in some places than in others, but the part the road plays in a skid is not much more than providing somewhere for it to take place.

But skids do not just happen. They result from what a driver does with his vehicle. The driver who says 'I had a skid' (as though fate took a hand) really means 'I made a skid'. For instance, if a car is going steadily along a level road where there are no junctions, bends or traffic, there need be no skid, however slippery the road, as long as these conditions last. It is when a driver alters his *speed* or *direction* that he may skid. In other words, the risk comes when the car is being slowed down or speeded up, turned or driven uphill or downhill.

A car skids because the driver is asking more from it in braking (or acceleration) and/or steering than is possible with the amount of grip the tyres have on the road at the time.

Skids caused by braking

In Chapter 5 ('The use of brakes') we said that harsh and un-controlled braking is one of the chief causes of skidding. Why is this? Mainly because heavy braking can lock the wheels. Brakes have their greatest stopping power when the wheels are nearly, but not quite, locked. But braking throws the weight of a car forward. The heavier the braking the more the weight is thrown to the front and the less there is on the rear wheels. The less weight on the rear wheels the less their grip and the more likely they are to lock. Then, unless braking is eased off, the front wheels lock too. The fact that the rear wheels lock first means that the car tends to swing, if not to spin.

The proof of all this is that uncontrollable skids can be produced, even with good tyres on dry roads, by drivers who do not leave themselves enough stopping space and then brake harshly (and keep on braking) in an attempt to stop somehow. A car so treated cannot run straight for long; and as soon as it begins to

This tyre has a good tread—but it cannot grip so well on a wet, smooth road surface. In these circumstances your safety will depend upon how you handle the car.

swing it has only to touch something to be in danger of turning over.

Skids caused by steering

We also mentioned in Chapter 5 that when a car is turned more weight is thrown on to the front wheel on the outside of the curve. Not only is steering affected, but the lessening of weight on the back wheels can cause them to lose grip and slide.

Skids caused by acceleration

Sudden or heavy use of the accelerator—especially in the lower gears—can cause the driving wheels to spin on the road surface instead of gripping it and driving the car. Unless the accelerator pressure is very quickly eased off, the car could go into a skid because of this wheelspin.

Skids caused by braking and steering

To combine two possible methods of producing a skid—wrong braking and wrong steering—is to ask for real trouble. If your tyres are only just gripping while you are cornering and you then start to brake (or if they are only just gripping while you are braking and you then start to corner), locked wheels and a skid are inevitable. You can't expect your tyres to do the impossible.

The answer to all this is simple—and has already been mentioned. Give yourself plenty of room to work in. The other point to remember is that when roads are wet or icy your tyres have less grip to start with. So you must brake, steer and accelerate very

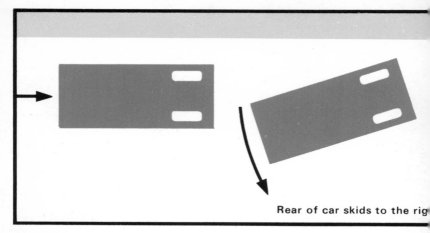

Rear of car skids to the rig

Fig. 60
Steering 'into' a rear-wheel skid

much more gently in these conditions because your 'grip margin' is that much smaller. The best way to give yourself time to do this is to keep your speed down. We go into these points in more detail later in the chapter.

Avoiding skids

However skilful you are, the result of skidding must, in today's traffic, be largely a matter of pure chance. There is no system of skid control so effective as driving in a way that will avoid them. Drivers not only make skids but, having made them, can make them much worse. Here is some advice on how to avoid skids:

1 *On very slippery surfaces your stopping distance can be as much as ten times longer than on a dry road.*

2 Be on the look-out for signs of slippery roads. Any wet road should be regarded as being slippery. Rain, ice and packed snow are obvious causes of slippery roads, but they are not the only ones. Frost can linger in shaded places well on into the day; wet mud can be almost as slippery as ice at any time of the year. Loose surfaces and wet leaves on the road are other danger signs. (See 'Anticipation' in Chapter 5 and 'Weather and vision' on page 166.)

3 When you suspect that the road is slippery, keep your speed down. Your brakes will not get you out of trouble when tyre grip is poor. *They are far more likely to get you into it.* It helps to use engine braking by changing down in good time. but be very careful with the accelerator and clutch. Misused, they can cause skids too. (See 'Wet roads', 'Braking on snow and ice' and 'Climbing hills on snow and ice' later in this chapter.)

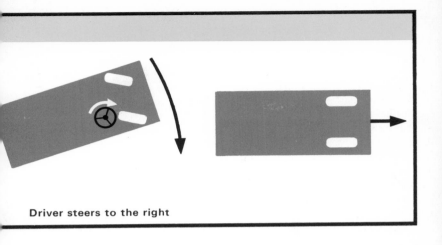

Driver steers to the right

4 Keeping your car in good condition will help to avoid skids. Brakes that snatch or pull unevenly are dangerous in slippery conditions. An accelerator pedal linkage which is jerky can cause wheel spin.

Dealing with skids

If you should find yourself in a skid while braking, the first thing to do is to *release the brake pedal altogether*. This is more easily said than done, because the natural tendency is to try to stop the car by using the brake still more. Drivers often 'freeze' with the right foot hard down on the brake and hang on, all through a skid, with the wheels locked. This only makes matters worse. In any skid, keep off the brakes.

A skid may be no more than a slight slide of the rear of the car, which can be felt rather than seen. This can be corrected by a slight movement of the steering wheel in the same direction as the skid (and perhaps by easing off the accelerator as well) to bring the front and back wheels into line again.

If the skid has developed beyond the stage of a slight slide, easing off the accelerator is more important, and more definite steering into the skid is needed. This means that if the *rear* of your car is going *left* you should *steer* to the *left* to bring the front wheels into line with the rear ones. If the *rear* of your car is going to the *right*, *steer* to the *right*. (See Fig. 60.) But beware of over-correction by too much steering movement of the front wheels, which will lead to another skid in the opposite direction. If the front wheels seem to be sliding instead of, or as well as, the back ones, release the accelerator and don't try to steer the car until they regain some of their grip. With a front-wheel drive car, too much power can produce a front-wheel skid, but easing the accelerator will usually help to correct this.

Weather hazards

Weather hazards can range from no more than having to put a vizor down against the sun to being completely stuck in a snow-drift. Having your car, and its equipment, in good condition and properly adjusted can be more than half the battle. In bad weather it is even more important that your tyres should be sound, have good treads and be properly inflated, because their grip on the road will be less and you cannot afford to lose any more of it by having tyres below par. Similarly, the effect of brakes badly adjusted or out of balance will be worse because the tyres have less grip. This could lead to the car pulling to one side when braked, or to braking in jerks ('snatching and grabbing').

As far as your driving is concerned, weather has to be reckoned with just as much as the amount of traffic. Even on a short journey the weather may vary so much that constant alertness is needed. Daytime mist, for example, may be fairly easy to deal with if the sun is out overhead so that there is a good background of light. But on the other side of the hill the same mist can be freezing on your windscreen in a matter of seconds.

Common sense gives—or should do—the most important of all weather rules. On wet or icy roads, or in fog, keep your speed well down. The worse the conditions the slower your speed, is a good summary, but it is only the beginning of the story of bad weather driving. The rest of this chapter fills in the detail of the ways in which you can, whatever the weather, still keep your grip.

Weather and vision

The biggest single danger to any driver is being unable to see properly. One of the ways in which weather often makes vision poor is by causing the inside glass of your car, including the mirror, to mist up. Misting has many causes, from winter fog to a sudden shower on a summer day. You can do a lot to overcome misting by keeping the inside glass clean, by wiping it dry before you start out, and by making the best use of your demister and any other means of ventilation, including open windows.

There are many anti-mist (and anti-frost) accessories available —liquid for the glass, prepared cloths, panels for double glazing the back window, and electrically heated glass. Best of all is plenty of warm dry air. You won't have this when you start up from cold, so experiment to find out what suits your particular car. Whatever you use, it is sensible to keep a piece of clean dry wash leather or suitable cloth handy so that you can dry the inside of the windscreen when necessary. If the inside of the rear and side windows need wiping, get your passengers to do it. If you haven't any passengers, stop and do it yourself. When it is very cold the outside of the glass may ice up. This can, and should, mean delay until the ice or frost has been melted off.

Study your car handbook so that you know how to get the very best out of any ventilating and heating system fitted. Whatever you do, don't drive unless you can see properly all round. Treat any other cars you see which are misted up as special hazards.

Rain and vision

Apart from misting up the windows inside the car, rain can cause loss of vision by obscuring the outside of the screen and windows. The cleaner you keep the glass of your car, the sooner the wipers will be able to clear the outside of the screen, and the less you will be hampered by wet and dirty side and rear windows. (Keep the washer bottle topped up.) At higher speeds some windscreen wiper blades lose their pressure on the windscreen, or even lift off, and this affects vision very severely.

Wet roads

When roads are wet, braking distances increase because tyre grip is reduced. Give yourself much more room for slowing down and stopping. Water on the road makes a slippery film, especially after a spell of dry weather.

Your allowance for braking distances when the road is wet should be *at least doubled*. Be on the look-out for differences in road surfaces which may reduce the grip of your tyres still more. The smoother your tyres the greater the increase in braking distance on a wet road.

Surface water

Rain can be so heavy that it forms a thin sheet of water all over the road. Even good tyres cannot grip through this. The surface water can then build up under the tyres so that your car is just sliding forwards, not in contact with the road at all. This is called aquaplaning. In this situation you would have no control at all over steering or braking. The higher your speed on a road as wet as this, the more likely you are to aquaplane. This just reinforces the advice—slow down in the wet.

Quite apart from keeping proper control on wet roads, there is another reason for slowing down which marks the good and considerate driver. Driving too fast through pools of water can drench pedestrians and also smother other people's windscreens, if not your own. Water thrown up under your car can affect your brakes and, spread around under the bonnet, it can stop the engine. There is no profit in plunging through puddles.

Floods

Don't rush things. Stop and find out how deep the water is. If it is not too deep and you decide to drive through, notice if there is a camber on the road so that you can keep to the shallowest part of the water. Drive through in first gear as slowly as you can, but keep the engine speed high and steady. Slip the clutch to keep the engine speed up but the actual speed of the car down. You will have to strike a balance. If the engine speed is too low you will

Fog is one of the most dangerous weather conditions a driver has to face. An accident to one vehicle may so quickly involve many others. The first and best precaution in mist or fog is to slow down.
(*Photographic material courtesy of Uniroyal Limited*)

stall. If you go too fast you may build up too much of a wave and water will get over the engine.

As soon as you have driven through a stretch of flooded road, try your brakes. You will probably find that they are of little use because they need drying out. You can do this by driving very slowly with your left foot pressing lightly on the brake pedal. Make sure your brakes are working properly again before going back to normal speeds.

Fords

Watch out for a depth gauge; in winter especially there can be

Above, top
Don't let mist or fog on your windscreen make it more difficult for you to see.
Above, lower
Use your windscreen wipers.

quite a depth of water. Otherwise, use the same technique as you would for a flood. At the far side there may be a sign reminding you to try your brakes; in any case remember for yourself to try them out, and dry them out if necessary.

Fog

Fog is not only frustrating but is also one of the most dangerous weather conditions a driver has to face, because an accident to one vehicle can so quickly involve many others. Because fog reduces a driver's ability to anticipate and react to changes of situation ahead, the first thing you must do is to reduce speed. *You must*

Use headlights in daytime mist or fog. The side lights on the overtaking car show up only when the outline of the vehicle itself can be seen.

be able to stop well within the distance you can see to be clear. The second is to make sure that none of the fog is being created or carried on your own screen, inside or out. Use the demister and windscreen wipers to take care of that—and keep them going.

Lights in fog

In daylight, use headlights when it is misty or foggy; they can be seen from a far greater distance. Side lights may not be seen by other drivers or pedestrians until your car is itself visible—which is too late. Headlights on full beam will not usually dazzle or inconvenience other drivers in daytime mist or fog. *At dusk*, and at other times when overhead daylight is poor, use dipped beams.

In darkness you may have to depend entirely on fog lamps, but foggy or misty conditions can change quickly, so do not settle down to fog lamps only. You may find that over some stretches dipped beams will give a better view ahead. Adapt your choice of lights as conditions vary.

Following another vehicle in fog

Leave yourself plenty of room for stopping. There may be

something ahead *which you cannot possibly see*, which will mean an emergency stop for the vehicle in front. Space is vital because you will first have to see and recognise that the vehicle ahead is stopping or has stopped, and then you still have your thinking and braking distances to allow for. Make up your own mind about a safe speed—and keep to it. Don't be tempted to keep up with the vehicle in front just for the sake of it. 'Follow my leader' can be a dangerous game in fog.

Another pitfall is that when you are driving behind another vehicle the fog will seem less thick than it really is, because some of it will be displaced by the other vehicle. Resist the urge to overtake, which is highly dangerous in fog. If you start to overtake, you may find that visibility ahead is much worse than you think.

Finally, another point about lights when you are following a vehicle. Don't use lights which shine so far forward that they cast a shadow of the vehicle ahead on the fog in front of it. This can make things very difficult for its driver.

Junctions in fog

Turning at a junction in fog, especially to the right, needs a lot of care. Lower your windows so that you can hear, start the indicators well beforehand and make the greatest possible use of your car lights. If you have to wait for other vehicles to pass before you can turn, keep your foot on the brake pedal so that your stop lights are on as an extra warning to following traffic. Use the horn and listen for possible answers. Don't turn until you have made as sure as you can that it is safe.

Road markings in fog

A fog lamp may pick out reflective studs (cat's-eyes) well, but generally it is not so easy to recognise other road markings in fog. Local knowledge, gained from earlier observation, particularly of edge of carriageway or similar markings, will help you tremendously. When you can see lane lines or studs, try to keep centrally between them. But don't mix up lane lines and centre lines. Driving right up to the centre line could put you too close to someone coming the other way and doing the same thing. (Details of how line markings vary are given on page 100 in Chapter 8.)

Parking in fog

Never park on a road in fog. Find an off-street parking place. If your vehicle breaks down, or if you have to leave it for any reason, get it off the road if you possibly can. If you can't do this, never leave it without warning lights of some kind—or on the 'wrong' side of the road.

Snow and ice

Falling snow, like rain, can have varying effects on driving. Sometimes it melts on the windscreen or doesn't lie on the road at all. At other times traffic churns it up and keeps it slushy, especially in the daytime on busy roads, or if the road has been gritted or salted.

Except in heavy snow-storms, falling or freshly fallen snow does not usually cause much difficulty, provided you are sensible and remember four points. First, once again, that you need to increase the gap between you and the vehicle in front. Second, that sticky snow can pack behind the front wheels or round brake linkages under the car and so affect steering and braking. So test your brakes, very gently, from time to time. Third, that your wipers, even when helped by the heater, may not be able to sweep a lot of snow clear, and you may have to stop and clear the windscreen by hand. Fourth, that you may be getting packed snow on your lamp and indicator glasses. This will need clearing away, especially if you are driving at night.

Always clear your rear window before you start driving, and then keep it clear.

Overnight freezing of already packed-down snow usually results in an icy surface, particularly on less well-used roads. Driving on ice has been compared with walking on eggs. Certainly this gives the right idea. Every control—brakes, accelerator, steering, clutch and gears—must be used very delicately. Roads are often more slippery when it is just beginning to freeze (or thaw) and there is both ice and water on them. Another danger is glazed frost, caused by rain freezing on roads as it falls. You will not be able to see this 'black ice' on a wet road. The first warning of it may be that the steering feels light. So when there is any risk of this, keep your speed well down.

Braking on snow and ice

Anything except the most gentle braking will lock the wheels on ice. If your front wheels lock you cannot steer the car, and if you can't steer you can't keep out of trouble.

Braking distances on ice can easily be *ten times* as much as normal. Downhill braking, especially to a stop, calls for careful control of speed both before you reach the hill and while you are on it. Get into a lower gear earlier than usual, allow your speed to drop and, if necessary, use the brake pedal, gently and early, to keep your speed down to what you can control.

Corners and bends on snow and ice

Your front wheels are even more likely to lock if you brake while you are turning. Time your driving so that you do not have to touch the brakes at all *on the corner*. Take corners at a steady speed, in as high a gear as you reasonably can.

Be delicate with the accelerator pedal and leave the clutch alone as much as you can. Steer smoothly; sudden movements of the steering wheel must be avoided at all costs. This also applies to straightening up after the turn, which calls for just as much delicacy in handling the controls.

Starting off on snow

If you have wheelspin when trying to start off in deep snow, don't go on racing the engine. This will only dig the wheel or wheels in deeper. Try moving your car slightly backwards and then forwards to get out of the rut. Use the highest gear you can for the conditions.

Climbing hills on snow and ice

Although speed generally must be kept down on slippery roads, the loss of momentum going uphill may mean that you won't get up at all. Trying to regain lost speed may cause such severe wheelspin that you lose control. If you have to stop, it may be very difficult to start again. Here again, leave a good gap behind the vehicle in front. Then, if it stops on the hill you will have at least a chance to keep going while it re-starts or, possibly, to pass it. Traffic that is well spaced out helps to avoid queues and hold-ups on slippery roads.

Use the highest gear you reasonably can. This gives the least increase in speed of the driving wheels for any given movement of the accelerator pedal, and reduces the chance of wheelspin. If some wheelspin is unavoidable, the less you have of it the better. Don't try to rush a hill with the idea of changing down on the way up. Choose the best gear for the whole climb and make it in that gear. Changing gear on the way up is not easy. Even for the best driver, it needs very delicate footwork to avoid wheelspin and loss of speed.

Other vehicles on snow and ice

No driver wants to see a vehicle coming towards him that is obviously out of control. But it does happen. In some situations there may not be much you can do about it. Your main thought will naturally be to get out of the way, either by steering or braking. But as we have seen, both are dangerous in icy conditions. Make use of engine braking if there is time and, if you must use the brake pedal, do it as gently as you can. But whatever you do, don't make matters worse by trying to steer and brake at the same time.

Summary

1

The need for good tyres; regular checks; saving wear and tear.

2

Radial-ply and cross-ply tyres; the dangers of mixing them.

3

Skids—how they are caused and how to avoid them; correcting skids.

4

Driving in bad weather; leaving a bigger gap and driving more slowly on wet or icy roads.

5

Floods and fords; how to deal with them.

6

Driving in fog; speed and spacing; use of lights.

7

Snow and ice—the main problems.

14 Motorway driving

There are no ordinary junctions, sharp bends, roundabouts, steep hills or traffic lights on motorways. Traffic is less mixed than on other roads; it is all one-way and the slowest vehicles are excluded. Traffic can therefore safely travel faster over longer distances, but this makes lane discipline even more important than on ordinary roads.

The driver on a motorway

What about the driver in all this? As with driving on any road, you need to be fit. It is particularly unwise to go on to a motorway if you are at all below par. This is not only because alertness is so important for motorway driving, but because parking is prohibited and if you need to rest you may have to go quite a long way before you get to an exit point or a service area where you can stop.

The higher speeds on motorways mean that you need more time for almost every driving action. In other words, you need to give yourself bigger margins than on ordinary roads; bigger margins of roadworthiness and of space between your car and the one in front. This chapter describes why these bigger margins are so important.

Your vehicle on a motorway

Before using a motorway make quite sure that your vehicle is in good order, especially the tyres. See that your tyre pressures are high enough. Instruments and warning lights are important too, because higher speeds over long distances increase the risk of mechanical failure. Check that you have plenty of petrol, oil and water. Motorway speeds use them up faster and to run out of any of them can be dangerous, inconvenient and costly.

Joining a motorway : The slip road leads into an acceleration lane. Watch the traffic on the motorway and adjust your speed so that you can join the left-hand lane in a suitable gap.

Don't flog your car. Choose a steady speed (within the speed limits) which suits you and your vehicle and the weather conditions.

Getting on to a motorway

Motorways usually start at a roundabout, unless a main road becomes a motorway. Elsewhere you will get on to them by a slip road which leads into an acceleration lane. This lane is an extra piece of road from which you can see, and adjust to, the motorway traffic and its speed before you become part of it. *You must give way to traffic already on the motorway, taking your place only when there is a suitable gap in the left-hand lane.* Once you have joined the motorway stay in the left-hand lane until you have had time to judge and get used to the speeds at which the traffic is moving.

Seeing on a motorway

Don't put unnecessary difficulties in the way of being able to see properly. Start out with clean mirrors, screen and windows. Use the washers, wipers and demisters freely whenever necessary. Keep your eyes moving so that you can see things, near and far, to the front and rear. Use your mirror even sooner than you would on an ordinary road and check it more often, because the higher motorway speeds are more difficult to judge and situations develop very quickly. Any increase in the number of vehicles you can see ahead may mean that traffic is slowing down for some reason—a warning to you to reduce speed until you are sure just what is happening.

Being seen on a motorway

Your car is often visible to other drivers on a motorway much earlier than it would be on an ordinary road. It needs to be, because of the higher speeds. If the daylight is at all poor use your side and rear lights at least. If it is hazy or misty in daytime use your headlights.

Ventilation

Driving on a motorway can get monotonous and cause drowsiness. Avoid this by making full use of whatever ventilation system you have. Keep the car warm but well aired. If you still feel drowsy keep a window open until you can get to a service area. There, open all the windows. Better still, get out into the air for a while.

Spacing

A gap of at least one yard for each m.p.h. of your speed is an absolute minimum. If the road is wet or icy the gap should be much longer. In the worst weather conditions you could need up to ten times the stopping distance that you do for a dry road.

Headlamp flashing

The higher noise level on motorways, particularly in wet weather, may prevent other drivers from hearing your horn. Flashing your headlamps is usually a better warning of your presence when one is necessary. By the same token, be alert for such a warning yourself.

Changing lanes on a motorway

Change lanes only when there is need. Keep in the middle of the lane you are using and don't let your car wander from side to side or into another lane.

When you do need to change lanes use the *mirror—signal—manoeuvre* routine, remembering how quickly vehicles may come up behind you. This routine is vital for motorway safety. Start it much earlier than on an ordinary road so that your indicators are seen well before you start your move. This should tell all who can see them that a shift in the traffic pattern is coming, even though they may not be able to see why, and give them time to prepare for it.

Two-lane discipline

On a two-lane motorway the normal driving position is in the left-hand lane. The outside (right-hand) lane is for overtaking.

Three-lane discipline

The normal driving rule still applies—well to the left; that is, in the left-hand lane. But if there are so many slower moving vehicles in that lane that you would be moving in and out repeatedly, you may stay in the middle lane. The outside (right-hand) lane is for overtaking; it is *not* 'the fast lane'. Don't stay in it any longer than is needed to move out, overtake and then move in again, all with a good safety margin.

If you are towing a caravan or any other kind of trailer, or driving a heavy goods vehicle, you must not use the right-hand lane. This restriction does not apply in exceptional circumstances such as the temporary closing of one or more of the inner lanes.

Braking

Because of the high speeds on motorways any braking must be unhurried, progressive and properly spread out. The need to spread your braking adds point to the importance of proper spacing, which has already been mentioned. And *mirror* first— every time.

Overtaking

This is almost entirely a matter of proper spacing and good margins. The *position—speed—look* routine is the first thing to think about. The correct *position* is well back from the vehicle you are going to overtake, so that you can move out on a smooth, easy course when you are ready. No sudden lurch to the right.

Next, *speed*: are you going fast enough, or can you accelerate enough, to overtake without balking anything coming up faster behind you? Then, *look*—ahead to make sure there is nothing to prevent you from overtaking safely (a lane closed for repairs, for example) and behind you.

Mirror checks are vital on a motorway; and remember that vehicles may be coming up from behind much faster than you think. Next, *signal*—well before you start to move out. (We have all seen drivers who start their signalling dangerously late, when they are already the best part of the way into their new lane.) After a final mirror check, pull out smoothly into your overtaking lane, get past and back into the left as soon as you can, taking care not to move in too soon in front of the vehicle you have passed. Be particularly careful to see that indicator signals are cancelled after you have finished overtaking. The comparatively slight movements of the steering wheel may not be enough to work a self-cancelling device.

Normally you should never overtake on the left. But where the traffic is moving in queues in all lanes, and the traffic on the right is going more slowly than you are, you may maintain the speed of the traffic in your own lane and so pass on the left.

Changes in traffic conditions

In deciding when to carry out a manœuvre, and how much margin to leave, remember that traffic conditions can vary on motorways

Leaving a motorway: The deceleration lane and slip road at a motorway exit give you time and space to begin to adjust to the lower speeds on an ordinary road.

as much as on any other road. Some stretches attract considerable rush hour traffic where they run near towns. Other stretches may have no particular rush hours. Differences of this sort are likely to have much more effect on two-lane motorways.

Leaving a motorway

If you are not going to the end of the motorway you leave it by moving left from the inner lane into a deceleration lane (extra strip) which takes you on to the exit road.

Don't rush this in any way. Use your mirror, and signal in good time. There are plenty of signs to help you with your timing so that you can give yourself the necessary margins. One mile before the exit (unless, unusually, there are exits very close together) you will see a sign for the junction with road numbers. At half a mile another sign with place names as well. Farther on there will be 'count-down' markers at 300 yards, 200 yards and finally 100 yards before the beginning of the deceleration lane. Use this succession of signs and markers to spread your use of mirror and indicators, your change of lane and speed—and if necessary your braking. This will leave a margin all round for yourself and the other drivers affected by your action.

Unless you are already in the left-hand lane, the first step is to get into that lane. On a three-lane motorway this may mean more than one lane change. If so, you must follow the *mirror—signal—manœuvre* routine for *each one*. Don't move to the left more than one lane at a time, and don't cut straight across from an outside lane into the deceleration lane. Move into the deceleration lane so that you can slow down before you join the exit road. If you miss your turn-off point you must carry on until you reach the next one. Never reverse, turn in the road or cross the central reservation.

There are END OF MOTORWAY signs at all exits from these roads. Remember that these also mean that the road you are joining is subject to different rules, so watch for any signs which tell you what these are—speed limits, dual carriageway or two-way traffic and so on.

Speed when leaving a motorway

After some miles of driving on a motorway your judgment of your own speed will almost certainly be affected. Nearly everyone underestimates—40 or 45 m.p.h. may seem more like 20. Use your speedometer, especially when you get on the exit road from the motorway, and until you have had time to readjust to the slower speeds on ordinary roads. This readjustment takes several minutes.

Weather on motorways

All that was said in Chapter 13 about driving in poor weather conditions applies even more strongly on motorways. For instance, wet weather can make visibility much worse because vehicles (especially big ones) travelling at higher speeds throw up more spray, particularly on exposed stretches.

Never drive at fine-weather speeds when conditions are poor. Use side lights in the daytime and headlights if necessary. Keep your speed down and leave much longer gaps; you need a bigger margin because braking distances are far longer on wet roads. If there is a danger of frost or ice, notice the feel of your steering. Any lightness is a danger sign. A *very* gentle touch on your brakes occasionally, to see how they respond, is a sensible precaution.

Cross-winds are another motorway hazard. They may affect

your steering much more than on ordinary roads. If the wind is coming from your left, be especially careful when passing a large vehicle. A sudden gust as you come out from the shelter of the vehicle could make your car swerve to the right. Wind effects are also increased as you come out of the shelter of bridges or high embankments.

When there is a fog on a motorway the only safe rule is that *you must be able to stop well within the distance you can see to be clear*. Fog affects not only visibility but also judgement of speed and distance so, once again, *reduce speed*. Even if other drivers are ignoring this elementary safety rule, there is no reason why you should. Unless the fog is so thick that visibility restricts you to an absolute crawl, you can easily find yourself speeding up without realising it, so glance at your speedometer occasionally.

Motorway signals

There are signal lights on motorways to warn you of such dangers ahead as accidents, fog or the risk of slippery roads. The earlier type of warning, at one-mile intervals, consists of two amber lights, one above the other, which flash alternately to convey the general message—'Danger ahead—slow down to 30 m.p.h. or less'. These are being replaced by later types. On rural (country) motorways, these newer signals, which are at two-mile intervals, have a double pair of amber lights flashing alternately and an illuminated symbol giving advised maximum speeds or information about closed lanes. On urban (town) motorways these new signals are fixed overhead at shorter intervals. They have red flashing lights to indicate STOP (for closed lanes), or flashing amber lights with illuminated symbols to show the lane to be taken, or the advised maximum speed. (See Fig. 61.)

Some motorways may have other special signals—warning of high winds on the Severn Bridge, for example. Whichever type of signal is in use:

SLOW DOWN if you see flashing amber lights—to the advised speed, or follow the course shown.

STOP if the flashing amber lights change to flashing red lights.

If you do not have to stop, be ready, when you see the danger itself, to slow down still more; to a crawl if necessary.

Look out for police notices and diversion signs.

Remember that fog can drift rapidly and is often patchy. Even if it seems to be clearing there can be a sudden thick patch ahead.

If you can see that you need to slow down or stop, start to do so much sooner than usual and treat all controls gently, especially the brakes.

Keep below 30 m.p.h. or other advised maximum speed until you are satisfied that it is safe to go faster again.

Motorway signals above lanes

Earlier type signals

The flashing amber lights tell you that an advised maximum speed of 30 m.p.h. is in operation, and warn of danger ahead (such as accident, fog or risk of skidding).

Fig. 61

Motorway signals beside the carriageway

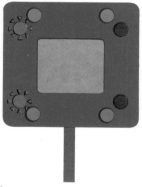

At entrances

These signals may have red as well as amber lights. If flashing amber lights change to flashing red lights YOU MUST STOP AT THE SIGNAL.

On central reserva

This signal is showing a advised maximum speed 20 m.p.h. (other speeds may be shown).

...en amber lights flash above your lane, one of these symbols will tell you ...

... move to the
...e on your left

... move to the
lane on your right

... leave motorway
at the next exit

... the advised
maximum speed
(other speeds
may be shown)

...e flashing amber lights change to flashing
lights YOU MUST STOP AT THE SIGNAL.

This symbol
(which appears
without flashing
lights) tells you
that the lane is clear.

...hen amber lights flash you will see an advised maximum speed
...one of the following symbols which will tell you ...

right-hand lane
...sed

... left-hand and
middle lanes
closed

... right-hand and
middle lanes
closed

left-hand lane
...sed

... left-hand lane
closed

... right-hand lane
closed

This symbol
(which appears
without flashing
lights) tells you
that the road is
clear.

Fig. 62
Emergency telephone

Fig. 63
Motorway junction sign
with inset junction number

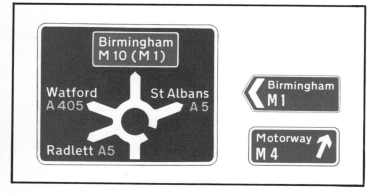

Fig. 64
Motorway signs

Stops on motorways

Apart from the flashing red lights just mentioned, you may also be signalled to stop by the police or by an emergency traffic sign. Otherwise, you are allowed to stop on the carriageway only if by doing so you will prevent or avoid an accident. If you do have to stop on the carriageway, and if your vehicle is equipped so that you can switch on all the direction indicators to flash together, do so as a warning signal.

The hard shoulder at the side of the motorway is for use only in emergency—not for sightseeing stops, picnics or taking a rest. If you break down, get your vehicle on to the hard shoulder as soon as you can. If the breakdown affects your control of the car, try to keep it in a straight line while you lose speed. Avoid hard braking if at all possible, and aim at steering gently on to the hard shoulder. When you get there don't open the offside doors. Warn your passengers of the danger of passing vehicles, and keep children and animals off the carriageway—in the car if possible.

Emergency telephones

There are emergency telephones connected to a police control point on most stretches of motorway, usually at one-mile intervals. If you need a telephone, look at the marker posts along the hard shoulder—they are usually 110 yards apart—for a telephone symbol with an arrow (see Fig. 62). This will show you the way to the nearest telephone.

Parking

The only parking places along a motorway are the specially provided service areas. When you go into a service area be very careful about your speed. Getting down to car park speeds will seem like crawling after motorway speeds. Be as careful about your passengers, especially children and animals, as you would on the hard shoulder. Other drivers will be coming very close after driving at motorway speeds and spacing. Parts of the service area are carriageways, so when you get out of your car turn yourself into a careful pedestrian and look after children and animals.

The only exit from a service area is back on to the motorway. The joining procedure is the same as at any other slip road and acceleration lane.

Motorway signs

The signs which direct you from ordinary roads to motorways have white letters and figures on a blue panel, usually with a white border. You may see these blue panels either as separate signs or included in larger signs of various colours.

The map-type advance direction signs and count-down markers on the motorways themselves have already been mentioned. Other advance direction signs give information about service areas. All advance direction signs on motorways are very much larger than those on ordinary roads so that you can read them from a greater distance—a constant and practical reminder of the need for good margins for error (see Figs. 63 and 64).

You will notice from Fig. 63 that each motorway junction has an identifying number. These numbers (which are included on up-to-date road maps) are there to help you to plan and follow your route.

Motorways at night

The next chapter deals with driving at night, wherever you are. Nearly all of it applies to motorway driving, but take special note of 'Your eyes at night' on page 187. The point about giving your eyes time to begin to adapt to darkness is an important one if you have just come out of a well-lit service area.

Here are some special points about motorways at night:

1 Speeds and distances are more deceptive than on ordinary roads.

2 Dazzle can still be a problem for oncoming drivers, especially if you are on a long left-hand bend. Use dipped beams if dazzle is likely.

3 If you are dazzled and have to slow down, remember the traffic behind—don't brake too suddenly.

4 Judging the speed and judging the distance of other vehicles are both more difficult *on a motorway and at night*. This means that changing lanes, whether to pass other drivers or to leave the motorway, needs special care. Use your indicators sooner—that is, for longer periods. If you have any doubt at all about the safety of a particular manœuvre, don't make it.

Summary

1
Making sure that you and your vehicle are in good shape.

2
Joining a motorway.

3
Seeing and being seen.

4
The importance of good spacing and early signalling.

5
Lane discipline and overtaking.

6
Leaving a motorway; checking your speed.

7
Bad weather driving on motorways.

8
Emergency warning signals, stops and telephones.

9
Special points about night driving on motorways.

15

Night driving

Even in perfect weather and with good headlights properly adjusted, you cannot see as far or as much at night as you can in daylight. So you cannot possibly know as much about what is ahead of you and around you. The night-time need is therefore for even more alertness and a realisation that you cannot safely drive as fast as you would do in daytime.

So far as driving is concerned, the word 'night' includes the periods of dusk and dawn—not just the hours between official lighting-up and switching-off times. Towards dusk it may well be wise to put your lights on before lighting-up time, even if it is not legally necessary. Be guided by the conditions. It is not a bad thing to be the first to switch on (even if this does produce reproachful switchings on and off by other drivers who seem to think you have put your lights on by mistake). In the mornings the opposite applies. Don't switch off until you are sure that other drivers can see you and that you will be just as safe without lights. Even the colour of the car comes into this. If yours is dark— navy blue, brown, grey and so on—switch on earlier and switch off later.

Apart from being able to see your car more easily, other drivers will be able to tell, from seeing your lights, *which way* you are going—very important in conditions of changing light.

Your eyes at night

The need to have your eyesight checked regularly was mentioned in Chapter 5. Night driving in particular may show a need for a check. Can you really see as well as you would like to? Could your eyes be partly to blame? If you have doubts, this is the time to get a check.

On dark nights you may have no more visibility than this on an unlit road. Under these conditions the rule is: if you cannot stop well within the range of your lights you are going too fast.

Fig. 65

Headlights on bends

Driver A, on a right-hand bend, is about to dip.
Driver B, on a left-hand bend, needs to dip much earlier.

Even if your sight is perfect your eyes will take some time to adapt to darkness. Don't come out of a brightly lit building and drive off straightaway. Give your eyes time to begin to adjust; closing them for a moment or two helps. Wait at least a minute or two before you start driving. You can fill in the time usefully by wiping your lights, windscreen, mirror and so on, and your spectacles if you wear them. The windscreen is particularly important—a clean screen cuts down dazzle.

Your vehicle lights

At night vehicle lights replace most of the many daylight sources of information about what is ahead. They also tell other road users about your movements. Your safety therefore depends on them, so keep them in proper order and use them sensibly and with consideration for other people. Get the most out of them by such simple precautions as a wipe over after daylight driving on wet roads. Check them before any long journey.

The adjustment and setting of headlights is important and these too should be checked periodically. Whenever a light fault occurs get it put right straightaway—a new bulb or whatever it is. If you don't you will be a danger to yourself and others.

Speed at night

Speed limits apart, the general rule about never driving so fast that you cannot stop well within the distance you can see to be clear means, at night, 'within your lights'. If you cannot stop well within the range of your own lights (or of other available lighting) you are going too fast. Try it out in a suitable place. Look for an object which is just within the range of your lights and then see if you can stop by the time you get to it. This test may give you something of a shock if you try it with *dipped* headlights on an unlighted road. It will certainly show how much easier it is to pick out white or light coloured objects than darker ones. It will also show the value of a good look ahead before you dip your headlights for a driver coming towards you.

Auxiliary driving lamps can help you pick out pedestrians or cyclists when you are on dipped beams. But it is most important for such lamps to be properly aimed—well to the left and only just high enough to give you a slightly earlier view, without dazzling oncoming drivers.

Meeting other vehicles at night

The lights of another vehicle usually tell you its direction of travel. They may tell you very little about its speed. Lights coming towards you should raise a number of questions in your mind. These will vary with the sort of road you are on—but here are some of the chief ones:

1 How far away is he—and how fast is he coming?

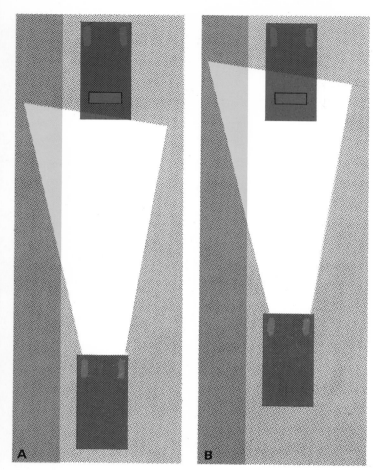

Fig. 66
Following on dipped headlights

Correct (A)
(provided that your speed is low enough.)

Wrong (B)
—front driver is dazzled through his rear window.

2 Is this the sort of road where I should slow down while we pass each other?

3 How soon should I dip?

4 How far ahead can I see before I dip?

5 Before I dip, is there anything in the way on my side of the road—stationary vehicles, cyclists, pedestrians?

On roads where headlights on full beam are necessary, dip soon enough to help oncoming drivers and riders, but not too soon.

Dipped headlights cut down your range of vision, so dip just before you would begin to dazzle the other person. Look along your left-hand verge—not directly at oncoming headlights. Before you dip, check the road ahead as far as you can see, slowing down if necessary. This is all assuming the driver coming towards you dips too. If he doesn't, slow down or stop if necessary.

Dip earlier going round a left-hand bend, because your headlight beams will sweep across the eyes of anyone coming towards you. On a right-hand bend this doesn't happen so soon—and may not happen at all, depending on the bend. (See Fig. 65.)

Overtaking or following at night

The need for lower speeds at night, and the fact that you can see less than in daylight, make overtaking more difficult and less common. Less chance to overtake makes it all the more important to follow other vehicles correctly. When you come up behind another vehicle, dip your lights in good time so that the beam does not dazzle the man ahead, either through his rear window or by reflection from his mirror. If you are being overtaken, dip your headlights as soon as the other vehicle passes you.

If you drive too close, even dipped beams will dazzle the driver ahead. So the drill is: first dip, then make sure that you are far enough back for your dipped beams to fall clear of his rear window, if not of his car. In any case, you should be keeping a proper separation distance for your speed. (See Fig. 66.)

Where it is possible to overtake but there is oncoming traffic (on a dual carriageway, for example) don't use full beam in the face of oncoming drivers.

Built-up areas at night

Use dipped headlights in built-up areas, unless the street lighting is very good. Notice any changes in the level of street lighting and, as far as you can, adjust your own lights to suit. Watch out for pedestrians, especially those with dark clothing. They can be difficult to see, particularly where street lighting is patchy.

Junctions at night

If you are waiting at a junction, don't keep your foot on the brake pedal (except in fog). Close to, your brake lights can be dazzling, so use the handbrake. Sometimes—especially while waiting to make a right turn—you may feel that your rear indicator is dazzling the driver behind you. But don't switch it off unless you are sure that you will not mislead anyone by doing so. If you do switch off, remember to put it on again before you move off and turn.

Lights when stationary

Never leave your car on a road at night without lights (unless there are special arrangements about parking and vehicle lighting). It is best to try to find somewhere off the road to leave it. If you can't, leave your lights on—and remember that your vehicle must not stand on the right-hand side of the road (except in a one-way street).

Switch off your headlights when you stop, even if you have only stopped to set down a passenger. The fixed glare of stationary headlights can be very dazzling.

Warning instruments at night

The law says that you must not use the horn between 11.30 p.m. and 7 a.m. in a built-up area. If you need to warn other road users of your presence, flash your headlights. But remember, this is only a warning; it does not give you right of way.

Noise at night

Remember the neighbours—and children who may be asleep. Close your car doors quietly and don't rev your engine unnecessarily.

Summary

1

Your lights and your eyes.

2

Speed at night.

3

Meeting and overtaking other vehicles.

4

Driving in built-up areas.

5

Lights when stationary.

6

Noise at night.

16

Making things a little easier

Most jobs become easier if they are done properly, and driving is no exception. But it involves taking a little more care in the first place to save trouble later on. This chapter suggests some of the ways—many of them quite small in themselves—in which a driver can help himself and other road users. It also includes some advice for disabled drivers.

Automatic transmission

A vehicle with automatic transmission has no clutch pedal. It has instead a system that not only senses the need for changes to higher or lower gears, but makes such changes for itself. So a driver does not have to worry about the repeated decisions and movements involved in normal gear changing. This not only makes the physical job of driving that much easier but should allow a driver to give more attention to such things as earlier observation and better anticipation.

But that is not the whole story. Generally speaking, an automatic transmission changes to a higher gear as road speed rises and to a lower one as it falls. But it also takes into account the load on the engine so that (for example) it changes down, if necessary, for uphill work. But there are times when you need a low gear although your speed is constant and the engine load is light—as when you are going down a long steep hill. The automatic transmission will not necessarily choose the right gear in these situations, so you need to know how to use the particular type of controls fitted to your car to best advantage.

Selection and control of drive

Most automatics have a small selector lever, and there is usually one position or setting which corresponds to *neutral* on an ordinary gearbox. (One type, dealt with later, is an exception.) With the engine running, the selector can be moved between *driving* and *reversing* positions. These three positions are basic to most types and are often labelled D—for drive, N—for neutral, and R—for reverse, arranged in that order. Having started the engine with the selector at N (neutral), then with the lever moved to D (drive) you need only take the brakes off and press the accelerator pedal for the car to move forward. It will then continue moving, changing gears as necessary, as long as there is enough pressure on the accelerator pedal. When there isn't, the car will slow down, change down and eventually stop (except downhill).

Because an automatic transmission is sensitive to both speed and load on the engine, heavy acceleration delays upward gear changes until the car has built up more speed. This is because hard acceleration on the flat can put much the same load on the engine as climbing a steep hill. The mechanism can only measure the load and then change gear accordingly. On one popular 1600 c.c. family car, automatic transmission makes the change up from first gear at any speed between something under 10 m.p.h. to just over 40 m.p.h., according to accelerator pressure. With most automatics, the lower the speed the smoother the change.

L (lock-up or hold)

This position on the selector enables you either to keep in a low gear or to use a lower gear. In heavy slow traffic you might find that if you were using D there would be unnecessary upward and downward automatic gear changes. Using L would override the automatic mechanism and keep you in the lower gear. Similarly, if you want to change to a lower gear—for example, to go down a long steep hill—you need to use L.

Many automatic transmissions have three forward gears; the L position is usually arranged to give you, or to hold, either the middle or the lowest of these. If you select L when in second gear, it will, with most types, hold that gear only at speeds above about 5 m.p.h. If speed drops so low that bottom gear comes in, the L position will then hold the transmission down to that gear. In other words, there will be no change back to second gear—unless, of course, you select D again.

Some automatics have only two gears, others four. The lock-up arrangements on some versions allow any gear to be selected and held; on others, any gear except top may be held.

Kick-down

Many automatics have a form of foot control called 'kick-down'. A short sharp pressure right down on the accelerator pedal, past the fully open position, causes a quick change down to the next lower gear. This ability to override the automatic mechanism is very useful for quick acceleration when you need it—for over-taking, for example. To return to the higher gear again you merely ease the pressure on the accelerator pedal.

P (park)

This is a selector position, provided on many automatics for use when parking, which mechanically locks the transmission. When used, it should be selected with the car stationary and the engine stopped. (It is possible to re-start the engine with the selector lever in this position.)

Variations of selector positions

We have now looked at the five main selector positions which are found on a wide range of cars with automatic transmission. But there are many variations between different models. For example, on some cars separate markings such as D1 and D2 take the place of the D (drive) position. D2 cuts out bottom gear when moving away and gives a very smooth slow take-off in the second of the three gears—obviously very useful on slippery surfaces and in bad weather. The many other variations will be explained in the handbook for the particular car. With all automatics, it is important to study the handbook so that the fullest and safest use of all the facilities given by the particular transmission can be obtained. Some types of automatic transmission give a driver just as much opportunity for intelligent use of gears as ordinary manual transmissions.

If you haven't driven an automatic before, do your homework on the handbook. Practise and learn the selector positions by heart so that you don't have to look down at them. The makers will have put in various stops or notches to make the selector moves easy and accurate. Some points are simple: for example, if your engine stops you will need, with most types, to move the selector to neutral in order to re-start and then back to whatever setting you need for moving away. But other points may need a bit more study. As we said at the beginning of the chapter, you need to take a little trouble to start with to make the best of the advantages an automatic can give.

Before leaving the subject of selector positions, mention should be made of another type of automatic which has belt drive with pulleys that expand and contract with varying speed and load. This gives variable gear ratios with no changes as such. The lever is pushed forward for *drive* and pulled back for *reverse*. The upright position of the lever between drive and reverse corresponds to neutral. This transmission has the peculiarity that the selector lever must be in either the drive or the reverse position—and not in between them—when the engine is started. *This makes the use of the handbrake essential for safety*, especially when the choke is being used and engine revs are therefore higher.

One useful feature of this particular type is a pull-out knob which can be used to put the car into the lowest available gear ratio, and to keep it there, giving a much higher degree of engine braking on very steep hills.

The importance of the handbrake

In Chapter 5 we said that, as a general rule, the handbrake should be on whenever your vehicle is stationary. With no clutch pedal, this is even more true. If the selector lever is at D, L or R (or an equivalent position) an automatic will move off under power if the accelerator is pressed—accidentally or on purpose—unless the brakes are on. If the choke is in use (and it may be an automatic choke) making the engine revs higher, an even lighter accelerator pressure can move the car away.

Another reason for using the handbrake is what is known as 'creep'. This happens if the tick-over or slow running of the engine gives enough drive to move the car gently forward. The brake is necessary to keep it still. When you drive an automatic which is new to you, check it for a tendency to excessive creep, and have the tick-over adjusted if necessary. Do the check on the level (not uphill) and remember that the effect will be even greater downhill. Don't rely on creep to hold the car on an upward slope however well it may balance with the gradient. The car could roll back without warning if the engine stopped for any reason. The safe rule is: *put your handbrake on whenever you pull up.*

Right-foot-only

The common term 'two-pedal car' rather suggests that you use one foot for each pedal. It is true that when you are manœuvring an automatic, using hardly any accelerator and only a touch on the brakes, one foot on each pedal is convenient—and safe.

But when driving along, the advantage lies entirely in using the right foot only for both accelerator and brake pedals, just as you do in a car with normal transmission. Right-foot-only develops, or helps you to maintain, anticipation; it gives all the safety factors which lie in the early release of the accelerator pedal and in early and progressive braking; it avoids the instability and wear and tear produced by braking against acceleration. There is the added advantage that there is nothing to learn or unlearn when you change from an automatic to a non-automatic, or vice versa. So tuck your left foot away.

Other points to watch

The greater need for using the handbrake when stationary has already been mentioned. There are other points that need watching, mainly because the accelerator has such a direct effect. One particular danger—apart from excessive creep—is when the tick-over is set too fast, so that the engine keeps on driving the car at what may be too high a road speed for the situation. Even

When driving an automatic, use your right foot only. It is best to tuck your left foot away.

with your foot off the accelerator you could, for example, find yourself approaching a junction much too fast.

Automatics sometimes change up as you approach a corner because of reduced pressure on the accelerator. The answer is to slow down *before* the corner, then accelerate gently as you turn. As mentioned in Chapter 6, the accelerator should be used so that the engine is doing just enough work to be driving the car round the corner. This is especially important with an automatic. For very difficult corners—steep downhill ones, for example— the use of L (lock-up) will usually help, but the accelerator pedal must still be used very gently. The possible need to use lock-up selector positions for going down very steep hills has already been mentioned, but, as with low normal gears, it is important that they should be selected in good time.

Automatic systems vary a great deal in the amount of engine braking they give in some (or all) of their selector positions. Generally, the slowing effect tends to be less than it is with ordinary transmissions. Check this for yourself when you take over an automatic.

Finally, the fact that it is physically easier to drive an automatic may lead you to drive faster, perhaps unconsciously. This calls for even more anticipation and earlier observation, as well as an earlier *position—speed—look* (PSL) routine. Particularly if you are a new driver, take care that driving without clutch and gears doesn't lead you into over-confidence.

Semi-automatics and pre-selectors

In a car with semi-automatic transmission (as distinct from one with automatic transmission which itself senses the need for a gear change and makes it), the driver has to decide when a gear change is necessary and which gear to choose. The change is made simply by moving the gear lever to the position for the chosen gear. As soon as the slightest pressure is applied to the gear lever the mechanism takes over and does the necessary declutching automatically. There is no clutch pedal. When the gear lever is released the clutch is let in automatically.

'Pre-selector' transmissions, mostly found on buses and coaches, have a lever by which the driver can select gears in advance, ready for later changes. With this type, no gear change takes place until a gear-change pedal is pressed and released. A single push on this pedal sets off the process of declutching, changing into the gear already selected and then re-engaging the drive automatically. Again, this is not a clutch pedal.

Overdrive

Overdrive, fitted as an extra on some cars, can do a good deal to make things easier—perhaps more for the engine than for the driver—particularly on faster journeys. It gives an extra gear, higher than the normal top gear, in which the engine turns more slowly for the same road speed. A four-speed box can have overdrive on both third and fourth gears, giving six gears in all— one between normal third and top and one higher than top. These extra gears, which are usually engaged by no more than the flick of a switch, do not necessarily make the car go faster, but they can save wear and tear (even though some acceleration may be lost).

The disabled driver

The need for easy transport encourages many disabled people to make remarkable efforts; and those who drove before they became handicapped are often spurred on to learn new skills in order to master vehicles and drive them safely. Disabilities can vary so much and call for so many different sorts of adaptations to the controls that it is not possible to mention them all here in detail. But we do describe some of the possibilities in fairly general terms.

Two-pedal cars

Automatic transmissions can be a great help to drivers with physical handicaps, simply because there is less work for feet and hands to do. Using the good foot for both accelerator and brake pedal can put the driver with a leg or foot disability on almost equal terms with the driver who has the use of both feet. An arm too weak to work normal gear levers may be quite capable of using small and easily moved selector levers, as well as doing its share of steering. Semi-automatics reduce footwork too, and disabled drivers may find the special gear levers easier to use when there is no clutch to be operated as well.

Adapted cars

Apart from the help which automatic transmissions can give disabled drivers, there are many cases where conventional controls can be adapted to overcome driving difficulties. These adaptations can range from re-positioning one item—even the horn button or the dip switch—to fitting one of the proprietary systems of full adaptation which cater for leg or foot disabilities by giving hand control over accelerator, clutch and what would normally be the footbrake.

An arm or hand disability may be overcome by such fittings as a steering wheel device to which an artificial hand can be linked, leaving the good hand to do more work. Even a severe arm injury can sometimes be overcome by specialised equipment. In exceptional cases this can include special controls and even arrangements for the steering to be done by the driver's foot, although such things can be costly. Some disabilities which restrict the movement of the driver's body can be met by such relatively simple means as fitting extra mirrors, a specially padded seat or by lengthening the pedals. But others may be so severe that it has to be accepted that safe driving is impossible.

Do you fit your car?

This brings us back to fitting the car to the driver. Does your build affect your driving? If you are unusually tall the mirrors may need some re-arrangement to give you a full view, or you may need an extra one. If, on the other hand, you are very short, you may find some cars difficult to drive because of high facias or small pedals; or again you may need to re-position or add to the mirrors.

Your physical build may affect only certain driving operations; in this case you may need do no more than adapt your driving method slightly to overcome the difficulty. In Chapter 10 we mention reversing as one of the times when your physique may affect your way of steering.

Good habits

Good habits are as much a part of safe driving as good technique. Most drivers have their own pet good habit which they recommend to other drivers. You may find yours among the following, or you may think some of them too obvious to mention. But they are all important—as habits—to good driving and to safety.

More haste, less speed

Even getting up early enough can be part of the story. If you don't start in time you may be tempted to hurry on the journey. Hurrying leads to mistakes, and mistakes can lead to accidents. Accidents mean arriving late—or even not at all. Leave in good time so that you don't have to rush.

Planning your journey

A map or road book will often show you the way round a town rather than through it. Give a little thought to rush hours and keep out of towns at difficult times.

Adapt your plan to weather conditions if possible. Mist or fog may mean a later start to a morning journey or an earlier start to an afternoon one to get you in before dark. Try to avoid driving in fog if you can, and so leave more room on the road for those who must be out in it.

If you like to run to a schedule on a long journey, plan it on the generous side. You will then probably find yourself running ahead of time instead of late and avoid any temptation to feel that you must catch up at all costs.

Regular daily journeys

If you drive to work every day, leave yourself more than the bare time for the journey, especially if you have no regular parking place and have to look for one. Don't be too thrusting or drive too fast just because you know the route well. Try to keep home and business worries out of your mind. They may creep back during traffic hold-ups, but switch them off before you move off again.

Your home ground

Don't let familiarity breed contempt. One day there *will* be something there.

Clothes

Comfortable clothes can make all the difference, especially on a long journey. Shoes are important too. Slippery soles are a menace on brake and clutch pedals. Shoes that are too wide can cause you to operate the accelerator by mistake at the same time as the brake pedal. For women, driving is certainly one of the occasions when shoe comfort is much more important than fashion. It is a sound idea to keep a pair of comfortable shoes— even if they are old ones—in the car.

Rest and refreshment

Don't go too long without a rest or try to press on if you are tired or in need of refreshment. (See also Chapter 14—Motorway driving.)

Health

Health affects driving; even a cold can put you below par. If you must drive when you are feeling under the weather, keep your speed down and give yourself more time to react.

Drugs and medicines

Always check with your doctor whether a medicine you may be taking will affect your ability to drive. And take his advice if he warns you against driving.

Drinking and driving

Apart from the penalties, these two things just do not mix.

Necessary stops

Don't be tempted to put off stops for natural functions. If you do, it will usually be at the expense of your concentration and safety.

Smoking

Smoking presents difficulties when you are driving. Lighting up, smoke, ash and so on all involve risks, even if you feel that smoking helps you to concentrate. If you really must smoke, remember the risks. Lighting a pipe certainly means a stop.

Radio

Listening to a car radio is a matter of taste and utility. Road bulletins, for example, can be very useful. But serious listening could affect your concentration.

Talking to passengers

Even at the risk of seeming rude, be ready to drop out of any conversation if the road needs more attention—or if an argument seems to be developing!

Clear windows

Like misted windows, stickers on the glass and dolls in the back window don't help anyone—except possibly as a warning to other drivers!

Seat belts

You are twice as safe wearing a seat belt as you are without one. Always wear your seat belt when you drive, and get your passengers to do so—even for the shortest journey. Safety apart, the steadying effect of a belt can help to prevent tiredness for both driver and passenger. Children should always ride in the back of the car, with a harness or belt, or in a safety seat, if possible.

Advance warning triangles

Get into the habit of carrying one of these red reflecting signs. Use it to warn other road users if your car becomes an obstruction as a result of a breakdown or accident. Stand the triangle on the road, usually in the same lane, well back from your car.

On a straight and level road the triangle should be at least 50 yards away from your car (although 100 yards is better). On a dual carriageway or motorway it should be 150 yards away *at least*. A warning triangle does not excuse your vehicle from stand-

At a busy junction like this one all works smoothly provided everyone does the right thing. Do you *always* stick to the rules?

ing in a dangerous position unnecessarily, and it is *not* a substitute for vehicle lights at night.

Where the road is not straight and level, be careful to put the triangle where an oncoming driver will see it *before* he comes to any bend or hump in the road. Where the road is so narrow or winding that the triangle might be run over, put it on the edge of the nearside verge or footpath.

Don't forget to take the sign with you when you can move your car.

Soft ground

If you have to go on to soft ground to turn (or for any other manœuvre) don't let your *driving* wheels get on to it. Keep them on the road, or other hard surface, so that they don't dig in.

Litter

Don't throw anything out of your windows.

Acknowledging courtesies

It doesn't cost anything, and it makes things more pleasant, to acknowledge courtesy and help from other road users.

A last word

Finally, worthwhile experience takes time to acquire. Driving is no exception, and no one has ever 'seen it all'. You may be a new driver, recently freed of your instructor by having passed the test, or you may have had years on the road. Whatever stage you have reached as a driver, you will always be getting more experience from watching other people on the road. Judge the *quality* of what you see. Looking for and copying only the best of what you see will go a long way towards making (or keeping) you a good driver. It is easy, and perhaps natural, for drivers who took their test a long time ago—or who perhaps have never taken one—to be critical of less experienced drivers. But just how critical are you of *your own* driving? Do you always stick to the rules so that everyone knows what to expect?

New driver or old, the responsibility is yours; the road is no place for impatience, exhibitionism or selfishness. Your attitude to driving is as important as a detailed knowledge of the finer points of driving technique. This book has described, in some detail, the techniques necessary for good, safe driving. A proper attitude of mind is something that only *you* can develop. And here we come back full circle to Chapter 1 where we said that a good driver needs a sense of responsibility, concentration on the job of driving, patience and courtesy.

Summary

1
Automatic transmissions: what they do and how they help; getting the best out of them; the functions of the controls—drive, lock-up, kick-down, park—and how to use them; the importance of the handbrake; guarding against 'creep' and too fast tick-over; right-foot-only; using the accelerator gently; avoiding over-confidence.

2
Semi-automatics: how they differ from automatics. Pre-selectors.

3
Overdrive: its value on long, fast journeys.

4
Problems—and some solutions—for the disabled driver.

5
Do you fit your car? How your build can affect your driving.

6
Good habits: learning to acquire them yourself and recognise them in others. The right attitude to driving.

The driving test

For most learner drivers, the driving test looms ahead as a major hurdle. It is also a general source of conversation whenever drivers are gathered together. There are probably more tall stories about the driving test than about any other motoring subject; the most remarkable thing about these stories is the number of times the old ones crop up again, years after they were first heard, in new and exaggerated forms. So although this book is directed to all drivers, it would not be out of place to describe, in this appendix, how the Ministry organises driving tests and exactly what the examiners are looking for.

There are about 400 centres, some of which are 'occasional'—that is, opened according to demand on one or more days each week, and staffed by examiners travelling from the permanent centres. There are about 1,500 driving examiners, all of whom have had to pass a very strict selection process, followed by at least six weeks' training. In the course of this training the Ministry makes sure that their driving is of a consistently high standard, and also that each examiner knows exactly the things he is expected to look for during a driving test.

Driving test centres are chosen with equal care. It would be nice to have centres and examiners to match the public demand town by town. But this is just not possible, because the centres have to be at places where there is enough parking space for candidates and where there are enough test routes which can be reached from the centres. Routes are carefully chosen to make sure that they are all roughly comparable—the same proportion of right and left turns, hills, pedestrian crossings and so on. The object of all this is to make sure, as far as possible, that all candidates in the driving test have to cope with the same sort of conditions whether they take the test in Inverness or Penzance.

The work that examiners do in actually carrying out tests is checked continuously by supervising examiners, who go out on driving tests and check the detailed records that examiners make of their tests. All this is to make as sure as possible that every candidate for the driving test has a proper and equal chance of showing the examiner, in the words of the Regulations, 'that he is competent to drive without danger to and with due consideration for other users of the road . . .'. This is *all* the examiner is concerned with. He is not concerned with whether the candidate is a man or a woman, old or young. Examiners do not have any quota of passes and failures, and there is certainly no truth in the story that 'they never pass anyone on Thursday afternoons'.

Now for the test itself. You can take the driving test at any one of the Ministry's centres. You send your application, with the fee, to the Traffic Area covering the centre at which you want to take the test. A few days later you will get an appointment card showing the date and time arranged for your test. If you cannot keep this appointment, let the Traffic Area know as soon as you can. If you cannot give three clear days' notice, so that the appointment can be given to someone else, you will have to pay a fee for another appointment. Allow yourself plenty of time to get to the test centre. If you are late—for instance, because you had difficulty in parking—the examiner may not be able to take you. He has to keep to a timetable for the sake of the other candidates.

The first part of the test is easy. The examiner meets the candidate in the waiting room, where he gets his signature and sees his driving licence. On the way to the car he will ask whether the candidate is disabled in any way. Then he will carry out the eyesight test by asking the candidate to read a number plate. This will be at a distance well above the standard actually required. He will only come down to the exact distance (which will be measured with a tape, if necessary) if the candidate's eyesight is obviously borderline. Incidentally, every candidate should have checked for himself that his eyesight is up to the required standard. If it is not, he will have been committing an offence when driving anyway. The standard is to be able to read a number plate with the old $3\frac{1}{2}$-inch letters at a distance of 75 feet, or a plate with the newer, smaller symbols at 67 feet.

Next comes the actual driving part of the test. This will last about 30 minutes and falls into four parts:

1 Some straightforward driving to allow the candidate time to settle down and to help overcome 'test nerves'.

2 A section leading up to the emergency stop.

3 The manœuvres—reversing, turning and so on.

4 Driving on busier roads.

Before we discuss the actual requirements of the test in detail, here are two general points. First, the thing that candidates seem to notice most about the examiner is that he does not chat during the drive as an instructor would. The Ministry knows that some candidates would prefer the examiner to talk more. But others would not, and it is really better that candidates should be left alone to concentrate on the job of driving without having to worry about keeping up a conversation. So examiners keep their talking to the minimum necessary to let the candidate know what he is required to do—turn right, pull up and so on. Directions are given in plenty of time.

Second, the manœuvres. These are included as part of the driving test not because drivers will be doing them regularly in the course of everyday driving, but because they are very good exercises in control. For instance, turning in the road requires the use of all the controls—steering, accelerator, footbrake, handbrake and clutch—and the driver also has to keep a proper look-out at the same time.

Before driving off, remember your cockpit drill—doors, driving seat, mirror, seat belt, petrol. As the test proceeds, the examiner will make notes on his pad. Don't let this put you off. Concentrate on your job of driving, as the examiner will be concentrating on his. You start with a clean sheet, and although the examiner will be noting your mistakes he will disregard the minor ones. After all, few people can put up an absolutely faultless performance at anything when they have a critic sitting beside them. It is part of the examiner's job to decide whether mistakes are minor or serious in degree. A minor one does not result in a failure but a serious or dangerous one does.

The practical test

After you have both settled in your seats, the examiner will ask you to start up and drive away when you are ready. From then on, he will be marking your performance on his sheet, so it is useful to go through the points he will be looking for, as they are shown on the Statement of Failure given to unsuccessful candidates. All the driving techniques and procedures necessary to ensure success in the driving test have been described in this book. We shall refer back to them so that you can study them in detail and avoid failure points, or correct them if you collect a Statement of Failure after a test.

The first thing the examiner will want to see is that you—**Take suitable precautions before starting the engine.** This means, after the cockpit drill, making sure that the handbrake is on and the gear lever in neutral. (Study: Chapter 2—Handbrake; gear lever and gearbox; and Chapter 4—Starting the engine.)

Next, remember the drill for moving off as explained in Chapters 2, 3 and 4. You will be expected to do this smoothly, co-ordinating the handbrake, clutch and accelerator properly; and to move off safely, without causing danger or inconvenience to anyone else on the road. This applies to every start you will have to make during the test, whether straight ahead, on the level, uphill, or moving out from behind a stationary vehicle. Any fault here will be marked under the heading—**Move off smoothly/ at an angle/on a gradient/on the level/straight ahead.** Remember too the other important thing about moving off safely —the look behind (Chapter 3). If you don't do this you will be faulted under the heading—**Look round before moving off.**

Throughout the test the examiner will be looking for reasonably smooth use of the controls. In other words, he will expect you to —**Make proper use of/accelerator/clutch/footbrake/gears/ handbrake/steering.** This means using the accelerator and clutch properly together to get a reasonably smooth start; using your footbrake firmly without being too harsh or sudden with it; being in the right gear according to the conditions and your road position; and changing gear in good time where you can see that it is going to be necessary—for instance, before going uphill or downhill, or before turning a corner. Incidentally, 'coasting' round a corner in neutral or with the clutch pedal held down is regarded as a serious fault because it reduces your control over the car. The proper use of these controls is so fundamental to good driving that a large part of this book has been devoted to it— there are many references in Chapters 2, 4, 5, 6, 9 and 10.

During the whole time you are driving the examiner will be building up a picture of your ability and common sense as a driver. There are five 'road behaviour' points which go towards making up this picture. The first is your general sense of position- ing for normal driving. The examiner will expect you to— **Keep well to the left in normal driving**—that is, except when you intend to turn right, overtake or pass parked vehicles or any other obstruction in the road. This does not mean driving along with your nearside wheels in the gutter. You need to choose a happy medium between this and being too far out towards the middle of the road. Where there are lane lines marked on the road, keep in the middle of your lane. You will find references to these points in Chapters 5, 9, 11 and 12.

Next, speed. Here again, the examiner will expect you to suit your speed to the road and traffic conditions. Crawling along unreasonably slowly on a clear road, perhaps holding up traffic behind you, would be regarded as a serious fault. You would be marked because you did not—**Make normal progress to suit varying road and traffic conditions.** Proper anticipation plays a large part in helping you to decide on the right speed, and it is just as important in avoiding the opposite fault of driving too fast. The examiner will expect you to obey the Highway Code rule about never driving so fast that you cannot stop well within the distance you can see to be clear; and to show him that you are ready to slow down (or keep your speed down) as necessary. If you don't, or if you break the speed limit, you will be marked because you did not—**Exercise proper care in the use of**

speed. You will find references to choosing the proper speed for general driving and when coming up to corners, bends, junctions and so on in Chapters 5, 6, 7, 8, 9, 11 and 12, together with another important point about speed—keeping a safe distance behind the vehicle in front.

The other two 'general behaviour' points also go together—mirror and signals. The mirror is so important that the whole of Chapter 3 is devoted to it. Almost everything that is said in that chapter can be summed up in the words used to describe faults under this heading—**Make proper use of the mirror well before/signalling/changing direction/overtaking/stopping.** The important words here are 'use', which means not just looking in the mirror but acting on what you see; and 'well before', which mean exactly what they say.

Signals need to be given in time for other road users to see what you are going to do before you do it and to react safely. The examiner will be looking to see that you not only give the correct signals but also give them in good time and, when you are using direction indicators, that you make sure they are cancelled when they have served their purpose. If you do not—**Give signals/ correctly/in good time/by direction indicators/by arm** you will be faulted.

A word here about giving signals by arm. Examiners do not expect, or want, hand flapping at every possible opportunity. But they do want to know that you know what arm signals mean and how they should be given. You may be asked to use arm signals for part of the test, but don't worry if you are not. The examiner will not make a special point of this if he has already seen you giving them. (Some disabled drivers may not be asked to give arm signals.) The thing to remember about arm signals is that only those shown in the Highway Code (and on pages 42 and 43 in this book) should be used, and that they should be given decisively and in good time.

All this is summed up in the safe routine, *mirror—signal— manœuvre.* You will find references to correct signalling in more detail in Chapters 5, 6 and 11.

The examiner will also be watching to see how you deal with other road users. Here again there is a group of five fault headings. All of them are related in one way or another to proper anticipation—that is, realising what other people are doing, are going to do or might do, and doing the right thing yourself to allow for them. Chapters 5 and 12 show the importance of thinking ahead and being prepared to deal with any situation smoothly and unhurriedly; the examiner will therefore be looking to see that you —**Show alertness and anticipation of the actions of/ cyclists/pedestrians/drivers.**

Having recognised a particular situation, you then have to show that you can deal with it properly—choosing the right time and place for overtaking; judging the right moment to complete a right turn across traffic coming the other way, and so on. The keynote is never to do anything which would hinder or balk other drivers; hold back if you are in doubt. Chapters 5, 7, 11 and 12 contain much advice on how to—**Overtake/meet/cross the path of/other vehicles safely.**

Crossroads and road junctions come under this heading too. The examiner will be watching to see that you apply the safe routine, *mirror—signal—manœuvre*, and the junction routine, *position—speed—look*; that you are in the correct position before and after the junction and that your speed is suitable. There will be many junctions on the test route; you will have to show the examiner that you can recognise the sort of junction, how important it is, and how to deal with it. If you follow all the advice in Chapters 5, 6 and 7 you will be able to—**Act properly at crossroads/road junctions.**

Dealing properly with other road users means that you must —**Allow adequate clearance to/cyclists/pedestrians/stationary vehicles.** In other words, give them plenty of room. Chapter 12 shows how important it is to be ready for pedestrians who suddenly step off the pavement or into the road from between parked vehicles, and for drivers or passengers getting out of parked cars. There is the story (true this time) of the examiner who had to mark his report sheet 'shaved elephant'. Clearly that driver was not allowing other road users enough room!

Almost every test route includes one or more pedestrian crossings. The fault marking on the Statement of Failure is rather long—**Pedestrian crossings/approach at a proper speed/stop when necessary/avoid overtaking at or approaching/avoid dangerous signals to pedestrians**— but it says all there is to say about things to avoid. Chapters 5, 8 and 12 show the proper way to use anticipation so that you approach these crossings safely.

At the beginning of the test the examiner will have asked you to follow the road ahead. In following 'the road ahead' you will be expected to notice and act on all traffic signs and signals, as well as signals given by other drivers. Ignoring a STOP sign, going through traffic lights at red or into a one-way street the wrong way—anything of this sort means failure. Signals by policemen, traffic wardens or school crossing patrols must be obeyed. Information signs such as hill signs, bend signs, lane arrows all come under this heading. You will find several references throughout Chapters 5–9 and in Chapter 12 to signs and signals of this sort, which add up to requiring you to—**Take correct and prompt action on all signals by/traffic signs/traffic controllers/take appropriate action on signals given by other road users.**

Now for the special exercises you will be asked to do during a driving test—not one after the other, but spaced out with normal driving in between. The first is the emergency stop.

Fairly early in the test, while you are pulled up at the kerb, the examiner will explain that he will give you a signal to stop the car as you would in an emergency such as a child running across the road. Then, when you are driving at a reasonable speed and he has made sure that an emergency stop would be safe, the examiner will give you the signal and expect to see you **—Stop vehicle in emergency/promptly and under control.** Notice the two parts; promptly, which means reacting quickly and stopping as soon as you can; and under control, which means keeping your car in a straight line. If you lock the wheels you may go out of control and skid. You will find this particular subject of stopping in an emergency dealt with in Chapter 4, and Chapters 2, 5 and 13 also have useful information about the way brakes operate and how to use them properly.

The second exercise that you will be required to do is— **Reverse into a limited opening either to the right or left/ under control/with reasonable accuracy/with proper observation.** If you are driving a car you will be asked to reverse into a side road or other opening on the left. The examiner will ask you to stop on the left before the opening and will then tell you just what you have to do—drive past the opening, stop again in a position from which you can back in, and then drive in reverse round the corner, straighten up and go back for a reasonable distance.

As you pass the corner, look into the road or opening and weigh it up; stop reasonably close to the kerb, but not so close as to make it unnecessarily difficult for you to reverse. When you reverse, keep your engine speed down so that the car moves slowly and your steering is fully effective. Remember which way your front wheels are pointing. Keep reasonably close to the kerb as you go round the corner and after you have straightened up to drive back for some distance. You should certainly keep on your own side of the road. The other thing to remember about reversing is that you must keep a proper look-out all the time for other vehicles and pedestrians. Remember that the front of your car will swing out towards the middle of the road as you turn.

If you are driving a small van or other vehicle without a clear view to the rear, you may be asked to reverse into an opening on the right. This involves different positioning, but it is explained in detail in Chapter 10 under the heading of 'Reversing'.

The last exercise is to turn round in the road. The idea is to show the examiner that you can manœuvre your vehicle in a restricted space smoothly and safely. The important thing is to take your time, letting the car move as slowly as possible but turning the steering wheel as briskly as you can. This exercise is sometimes called the 'three-point turn', but this is a bit misleading because the examiner will not necessarily expect you to complete the turn in three movements. The number of backward and forward movements you need to make certainly depends partly on how neatly you use the controls. But it also depends on the size and steering of your car, as well as the width of the road. The examiner will make allowance for these things. Finally, as with any other manœuvre, you must keep a good look-out all the time. If other traffic comes along while you are turning, be ready to stop and let it pass. Studying these points, and the section of Chapter 10 which deals with turning in the road, will help you to—**Turn round by means of forward and reverse gears/under control/with reasonable accuracy/ with proper observation.**

We have mentioned several times that the examiner will ask you to stop at various places during the driving test. And there will also be the most welcome stop of all—the one at the end of your test. Whenever you stop, the examiner will expect you to choose a safe place and to pull up as close to the side of the road as you reasonably can. He will not try to trap you by asking you to pull up where stopping is illegal. Sometimes he will be fairly exact about where he wants you to stop—for instance, before he gives you the instructions about reversing into an opening. But otherwise, you should choose a place where *you* think you can safely stop long enough for the examiner to give you further directions. If you don't pick a suitable spot you may find yourself with a fault marked because you did not—**Select safe position(s) for normal stop(s).**

The oral test

We have now been through the headings under which driving faults are marked on an unsuccessful candidate's Statement of Failure. But there is still one more part of the test. After getting back to the centre at the end of the driving part of the test, the examiner will ask questions to test your knowledge of the Highway Code and other motoring matters such as skidding, the importance of correct tyre pressures, and other similar general points. When the test is so near its end, and you are naturally keyed up about the result, the examiner will not expect a 100-percent answer to every question he asks, nor want you to recite the Highway Code parrot fashion. What he will expect are common-sense answers which show that you know the Code and have a reasonable knowledge of your responsibilities as a driver.

After the test

As soon as he has finished asking you these questions, the examiner will tell you whether you have passed or failed. If you have passed he will give you a Certificate of Competence (the much desired pink form) and ask you to sign it. You send this form to your local Licensing Authority to get a full driving licence.

If you have not passed, the examiner will mark your most serious driving faults on a Statement of Failure under the various headings we have talked about in this chapter. This form is almost as important as the Certificate of Competence—although a lot less welcome—because it shows both you and your instructor where you have gone wrong. At one time examiners used to explain verbally to unsuccessful candidates the reasons for their failure. But this just did not work. Sometimes candidates were so upset at not having passed that they could not take in what the examiner was saying; sometimes they misunderstood it; and sometimes they did not believe it. It is really much better in the long run, both for an unsuccessful candidate and for his instructor, to be able to sit down quietly afterwards, go through the various faults which have been marked and concentrate on putting them right.

But anyone who has really studied this book, paid attention to everything a good instructor has told him, and put it all into practice during the driving test should have no difficulty in qualifying for a 'pass'. The examiner will like it better too.

Conversion table of equivalent speeds

With metrication, distances will be shown in kilometres, and speed limit signs and speedometers will show kilometres per hour.

Kilometres per hour	Metres per second	Miles per hour	Feet per second
5	1·4	3·1	4·6
10	2·8	6·2	9·1
15	4·2	9·3	13·7
20	5·6	12·4	18·2
25	6·9	15·5	22·8
30	8·3	18·6	27·3
35	9·7	21·7	31·9
40	11·1	24·8	36·5
45	12·5	27·9	41·0
50	13·9	31·0	45·6
55	15·3	34·1	50·1
60	16·7	37·3	54·7
65	18·0	40·4	59·2
70	19·4	43·5	63·8
75	20·8	46·6	68·4
80	22·2	49·7	72·9
85	23·6	52·8	77·5
90	25·0	55·9	82·0
95	26·4	59·0	86·6
100	27·8	62·1	91·1
105	29·2	65·2	95·7
110	30·6	68·3	100·2
115	31·9	71·5	104·8
120	33·3	74·6	109·4
125	34·7	77·7	114·0
130	36·1	80·8	118·5

One kilometre is almost exactly five-eighths of one mile

Index

	Page
Acceleration	**58**
Accelerator	**6**
Acknowledging courtesies	**202**
Advance warning triangles	**201**
Animals	**156**
—in the car	**157**
Anticipation	**2, 38, 125**
Automatic transmission	**193**
—creep	**196**
—importance of accelerator	**196**
—importance of handbrake	**196**
—kick-down	**194**
—L (lock-up or hold)	**194**
—P (park)	**195**
—parking on hills	**109**
—right-foot-only	**196**
—selector settings	**193, 195**
Bends	**59**
—on snow and ice	**172**
—positioning for	**59**
Box junctions	**101**

Page

Brakes and braking **47, 49**
—and skidding **48, 162, 163**
—an important skill **50**
—downhill **107**
—engine braking **7, 28, 46, 107, 197**
—footbrake **7**
—handbrake **11, 49**
—on a curved course **48**
—on motorways **178**
—on snow and ice **172**
—on wet roads **167**
—progressively **48**
—weighing up conditions **48**

Buses and coaches **149**

Car doors **157**

Cars and lorries **145**

Checks **22**
—cockpit drill **22**
—every day **22**
—every week **22**

Children **155**

Choke **16**
—automatic **16, 195, 196**

Clear windows **201**
—in fog **170**
—in snow **172**
—on motorways **176**

Clothes **200**

Clutch **8**
—biting point **8**
—coasting **46**
—control **8**

Cockpit drill **22**

Concentration **2**

Confidence **2**

Corners **58**
—cutting right-hand **84**
—on snow and ice **172**

Cutting-in **141, 147**

Cyclists **149**

Daily checks **22**

215

Page

Dead ground **76**

Direction indicators **15, 40**

Disabled drivers **198**
—adapted cars **199**
—two-pedal cars **198**

Drinking and driving **201**

Driving position **6**
—do you fit your car? **199**
—when reversing **113**

Driving test **35, 204**
—alertness and anticipation **208**
—allowing adequate clearance **209**
—application and appointment **205**
—centres **204**
—Certificate of Competence **211**
—correct action on signs and signals **209**
—crossroads and road junctions **209**
—driving examiners **204–212**
—driving instructors **212**
—emergency stop **210**
—eyesight test **205**
—Highway Code **208**
—junction routine (PSL) **209**
—keeping well to the left **207**
—looking round **207**
—making normal progress **207**
—marking of faults **206**
—moving off **207**
—normal stop **211**
—oral test **211**
—overtaking, meeting, crossing **209**
—pedestrian crossings **209**
—pedestrians **208**
—practical test **206**
—precautions before starting up **206**
—proper care in use of speed **207–208**
—proper use of controls **207**
—proper use of mirror **208**
—requirements and routes **205**
—reversing **210**
—safe routine (MSM) **208, 209**
—signals by indicator and arm **208**
—Statement of Failure **206, 212**
—supervision **205**
—turning in the road **211**

Drugs and medicines **201**

Dual carriageways **131**

Page

Engine braking 7, 28, 46, 107
—with automatic transmission 197

Eyesight 52
—at night 187
—test 205

Floods 167

Fog 169, 171, 181

Fords 168

Gaps for turning vehicles 147

Gear changing 29
—changing down 31
—changing up 30
—double declutching 36
—to help acceleration 46
—using the gear lever 12
—when and how 46
—with automatic transmission 193

Gears 12
—correct use 46

Giving way 69, 94
—at roundabouts 86

Good driver 1

Good habits 199

Handbrake 11
—when stationary 49
—with automatic transmission 196

Headlamp flashing 45, 177

Headlights 16
—on motorways 185

Health and driving 200

Highway Code 27, 34, 41, 111, 119, 136, 154, 156, 207, 208, 211

Hills 104
—going down 104, 105
—going up 104, 105
—in town 107
—junctions on hills 107
—on snow and ice 173
—overtaking on 105, 106
—parking on 109

217

	Page
Horn	**16**
—how to use	**45**
—warning children	**156**
—when not to use	**45, 154, 192**
How far forward?	**71**
Ignition switch and starter	**16**
Joining a hill	**107**
Joining a motorway	**176**
Joining a new road	**77**
Junctions—approaching	**60**
—advance information	**60**
—assessment	**63**
—at night	**191**
—cyclists on left	**150**
—deceleration lanes	**56**
—downhill approach	**106**
—how far forward?	**71**
—junction routine (PSL)	**62, 66**
—lane discipline	**56**
—on hills	**106**
—roundabouts	**86–91**
—safe routine (MSM)	**60, 66**
—uphill	**106**
Junctions—emerging	**69**
—cutting corners	**84**
—cyclists on left	**82**
—new driver	**77**
—on the 'new' road	**77**
—other vehicles	**75**
—pedestrians	**84**
—road width	**73**
—roundabouts	**86–91**
—staggered junctions	**84**
—the vehicle ahead	**75**
—timing your approach	**77**
—turning	**81**
—wait or go on?	**76**
—Y junctions	**84**
—zones of vision	**70, 73, 75**
Lane arrows	**102**
Lane discipline	**54**
—approaching junctions	**56**
—on motorways	**177, 180**
Large vehicles	**137**
—overtaking	**137**
—turning left	**145**

	Page
Leaving a motorway	**179**
Level crossings	**142**
—automatic half-barriers	**142**
—open level crossings	**143**
Lights	**16**
—checking	**22**
—in fog	**170**
—when following other vehicles	**191**
—when meeting other vehicles	**189**
—when stationary	**191**
Litter	**202**
Looking round	**21**
Manœuvring	**111**
Mirror	**14**
—adjustment	**17**
—at night	**191**
—inside mirrors	**17**
—judging distance in	**18**
—MSM	**20**
—on motorways	**176, 178**
—outside mirrors	**17**
Motor-cyclists	**151**
Motorways	**175**
—at night	**185**
—braking	**178**
—cross-winds	**180**
—driver fitness	**175**
—emergencies and stops	**184, 185**
—fog	**181**
—headlamp flashing	**177**
—in poor weather	**180**
—joining	**176**
—lane discipline	**177, 180**
—leaving	**179**
—margins for error	**175, 185**
—mirror	**176, 178**
—overtaking	**178**
—safe routine (MSM)	**177, 180**
—seeing and being seen	**176, 177**
—separation distances	**177**
—service areas	**185**
—signals	**181**
—signs	**185**
—speed	**175, 180**
—vehicle condition	**175**
—ventilation	**177**

	Page
Moving off	**21, 25**
—at a junction	**76**
—at an angle	**32**
—downhill	**107**
—from rest	**21, 25**
—on snow	**173**
—uphill	**32, 107**
Necessary stops	**201**
Night driving	**187**
—avoiding noise	**192**
—following other vehicles	**191**
—junctions	**191**
—meeting other vehicles	**189**
—on motorways	**185**
—speed	**189**
—your eyes	**187**
—your vehicle lights	**189, 191**
One-way streets	**54**
Overdrive	**198**
Overtaking	**133**
—a routine for (PSL—MSM)	**140**
—at night	**191**
—large vehicles	**137**
—meeting speeds	**137**
—moving vehicles	**135**
—on hills	**105, 106, 139**
—on motorways	**178**
—on the left	**141**
—passing obstructions	**133**
—speed	**137**
Parking	**119**
—at night	**191**
—in a car park	**119**
—in fog	**171**
—on the road	**121**
—on hills	**109**
—parallel	**121–123**
Passing stationary vehicles	**133**
Patience	**2**
Pedestrian crossings	**154**
Pedestrians	**152–154**
—at junctions and corners	**84, 153**
Planning your journey	**200**
Pre-selectors	**198**

	Page
Radio	**201**
Reading the road	**53, 125**
Regular daily journeys	**200**
Responsibility	**2**
—for position of vehicle	**56**
Rest and refreshment	**200**
Reversing	**113**
—clear of children	**113**
—to the left	**114**
—to the right	**116**
Road markings	**100**
—in fog	**171**
Road positioning	**53**
—approaching a junction	**56**
—lane discipline	**54**
—one-way streets	**54**
Roundabouts	**86–91**
Safe routine (MSM)	**20**
—timing	**77**
Seat belts	**23, 156, 201**
Semi-automatics	**198**
Separation distances	**125–131**
—how big a gap?	**130**
—in good conditions	**125**
—in poor conditions	**128**
—on motorways	**177**
Signals	**40–45**
—at pedestrian crossings	**154, 155**
—by arm	**40**
—by direction indicators	**40, 149**
—by stop (brake) lights	**40**
—on motorways	**181**
Skids	**162**
—avoiding	**164**
—causes of	**162, 163**
—dealing with	**165**

		Page
Smoking		**201**
Snow and ice		**171**
—avoiding other vehicles		**173**
—black ice		**172**
—braking		**172**
—corners and bends		**172**
—moving off		**173**
—stopping distances		**164**
—wheelspin		**173**
Soft ground		**202**
Speed		**58**
—at corners		**58**
—at night		**189**
—feet per second		**128**
—going downhill		**106**
—in poor conditions		**166**
—leaving a motorway		**180**
—meeting other vehicles		**137, 189**
—near junctions		**62, 67**
—on bends		**60**
—on motorways		**175**
—on snow and ice		**172**
—table of metric equivalents		**213**
Starting the engine		**23**
—drill for		**23**
—using accelerator		**24**
—using choke		**16, 24**
Steering		**58**
—holding the wheel		**9**
—in reverse gear		**113**
—practice		**27**
—pull-push		**9**
—turning to left or right		**9**
Stopping		**28**
—braking distance		**33, 34, 125–131**
—in emergency		**35**
—judging distance		**34**
—on slippery surfaces		**164**
—road and weather conditions		**35**
—speed		**34**
—STOP sign		**63, 94**
—thinking distance		**34, 125–131**

	Page
Traffic signs	**93**
—directional	**98**
—GIVE WAY	**65, 94**
—information	**99**
—mandatory	**94**
—prohibitory	**97**
—road markings	**100, 171**
—STOP	**63, 94**
—traffic light signals	**102**
—warning	**97**
Tuition	**3, 4**
Turning by forward and reverse gears	**117**
Turning left	**81**
—cyclists and motor-cyclists on left	**82**
—into side roads	**81**
—position and speed	**82**
Turning right	**81**
—at a staggered junction	**84**
—cutting the corner	**84**
—incorrect positioning after turn	**79**
—offside to offside	**84**
—oncoming traffic	**82**
—position and speed	**77, 82**
Turning to go back	**116**
Tyres	**159**
—checking	**22, 160**
—cross-ply	**160**
—danger of mixing types	**160**
—pressures	**159**
—radial-ply	**160**
—wear and tear	**159**
Using a car park	**119**
U turns	**117**
Vehicle condition	**22**
—in bad weather	**166**
—its lights	**22, 189**
—on motorways	**175**

	Page
Ventilation	**166, 167**
—in bad weather	**166**
—on motorways	**177**
Wait or go on	**76**
Weather hazards	**166**
—floods	**167**
—fog	**169**
—fords	**168**
—loss of vision	**166**
—on motorways	**180**
—rain	**167**
—snow and ice	**171**
—surface water	**167**
Weekly checks	**22**
Wheelspin	**163, 173, 202**
White lines	**100**
Windscreen washers and wipers	**15, 167**
--in fog	**170**
—on motorways	**176**
Zones of vision	**70–76**

Printed in England for Her Majesty's Stationery Office by
W. S. Cowell Ltd, Ipswich.